Clive Oxenden
Christina Latham-Koenig

with **Brian Brennan**
Beatriz Martín

D1368300

New
ENGLISH FILE

Upper-intermediate
Teacher's Book

Paul Seligson and Clive Oxenden are the original co-authors of
English File 1 (pub. 1996) and *English File 2* (pub. 1997).

OXFORD
UNIVERSITY PRESS

Great Clarendon Street, Oxford OX2 6DP

Oxford University Press is a department of the University of Oxford.
It furthers the University's objective of excellence in research, scholarship,
and education by publishing worldwide in

Oxford New York

Auckland Cape Town Dar es Salaam Hong Kong Karachi
Kuala Lumpur Madrid Melbourne Mexico City Nairobi
New Delhi Shanghai Taipei Toronto

With offices in

Argentina Austria Brazil Chile Czech Republic France Greece
Guatemala Hungary Italy Japan Poland Portugal Singapore
South Korea Switzerland Thailand Turkey Ukraine Vietnam

OXFORD and OXFORD ENGLISH are registered trade marks of
Oxford University Press in the UK and in certain other countries

ISBN: 978 0 19 451844 4   Book
      978 0 19 451867 3   Pack

Printed in China

This book is printed on paper from certified and well-managed sources.

ACKNOWLEDGEMENTS

*The authors would like to thank all the teachers and students round the world whose
feedback has helped us to shape New English File and also all those at Oxford University
Press (both in Oxford and around the world) who have contributed their skills and ideas
to producing this course.*

*Finally very special thanks from Clive to Maria Angeles, Lucia, and Eric, and from
Christina to Cristina, for all their help and encouragement. Christina would also like to
thank her children Joaquin, Marco, and Krysia for their constant inspiration.*

*The authors and publisher are grateful to those who have given permission to reproduce
the following extracts and adaptations of copyright material:* p.233 *You Gotta Be.*
Lyrics by Des'ree Weekes. Music by Des'ree Weekes & Ashley Ingram © Sony/
ATV Music Publishing (60%) and © Copyright 1994 BMG Music Publishing
Limited (40%). All Rights Reserved. International Copyright Secured. Used by
Permission of Sony/ATV Music Publishing and Music Sales Limited. p.234
Englishman in New York. Words and Music by Sting © Copyright 1987 Magnetic
Publishing Limited/EMI Music Publishing Limited. Used by permission of
Music Sales Limited. All Rights Reserved. International Copyright Secured.
p.235 *It's Raining Men.* Words and Music by Paul Jabara and Paul Shaffer © 1982
Postvalda Music (50%) and EMI Sosaha Music Inc. USA (50%) EMI Music
Publishing Ltd, London WC2H 0QY. All rights on behalf of Postvalda Music
administered by Warner/Chappell Music Ltd, London W6 8BS. Reproduced by
permission of Faber Music Ltd and International Music Publications Ltd
(a trading name of Faber Music Ltd) and Warner/Chappell Music Ltd. All Rights
Reserved. p.236 *I Will Survive.* Words & Music by Dino Fekaris & Freddie Perren
© Copyright 1978 Perren-Vibes Music Company/PolyGram International
Publishing Incorporated, USA. Universal Music Publishing Limited. Used by
permission of Music Sales Limited. All Rights Reserved. International
Copyright Secured. p.237 *I don't want to miss a thing.* Words and Music by Diane
Warren © 1998, Realsongs, USA. Reproduced by permission of International
Music Publications Ltd (a trading name of Faber Music Ltd) and EMI Music
Publishing Co Ltd., London WC2H 0QY and All Rights Reserved. p.238
Space Oddity. Composed by David Bowie © Onward Music Limited. Reproduced
by permission. All Rights Reserved. p.239 *If I Could Turn Back Time.* Words and
Music by Diane Warren © 1988, Realsongs, USA. Reproduced by permission of
International Music Publications Ltd (a trading name of Faber Music Ltd) and
EMI Music Publishing Co Ltd., London WC2H 0QY and International Music
Publications Ltd (a trading name of Faber Music Ltd). All Rights Reserved.

*The authors and publisher would like to thank the following for their permission to
reproduce photographs:* Bridgman Art Library p.180 (Private Collection), Corbis
p.173 (Rick Gomez/Swedish man), Getty Images pp.173 (Randy Wells/
German woman, Blasius Erlinger/Queensland couple), 175 (Harald Sund/
Louvre, Walter Bibikow/Mont Blanc, Altrendo Nature/Lake Superior), 179
(Yellow Dog Productions/barbecue), 213 (James Emmerson/Lake Como),
213 (Paul Gilham/volleyball), 215 (Chris Mattison/toad, Frank Greenaway/bat,
Theo Allofs/alligator, Jane Burton/clam), 186 (Guillermo Hung/three children
playing/DK stock), NHPA/Photoshot p.215 (B Jones & M Shimlock/jellyfish),
Oxford University Press pp.181, 215 (bear), Pictures Colour Library p.175
(Edinburgh), Punchstock pp.159, 186 (Digital Vision/child with truck), Science
Photo Library pp.213 (astronaut), 238

Illustrations by: Cartoonstock/Ian Baker pp.170, 177, 211, Cartoonstock/
Clive Goddard pp.162, 164, 166, 189, 205, 219, Phil Disley pp.161, 169, 178,
183, 185, 206, 208, 235, Mark Draisey pp.176, 201, 202, Kath Hextall pp.160,
165b, 171, 188, 204, 225, Marie Helene Jeeves pp.163, 167, 187, 197, 234, 239,
Gavin Reece pp.184, 237, Colin Shelbourn pp.209, 229, Thorogood Illustration/
Kanaka and Yuzuru pp.174, 233

Photocopiables designed by: Bryony Newhouse

Picture research and illustrations commissioned by: Cathy Blackie

- **What do Upper-intermediate students need?**
- **Study Link**
- **Course components**
Student's Book Files 1–7
Back of the Student's Book
- **For students**
Workbook
MultiROM
Student's website
- **For teachers**
Teacher's Book
Video / DVD
Class audio CDs
Test and Assessment CD-ROM
Teacher's website

Contents
Grammar activity answers
Grammar activity masters
Mini grammar activity answers
Mini grammar activity masters
Communicative activity instructions
Communicative activity masters
Vocabulary activity instructions
Vocabulary activity masters
Song activity instructions
Song activity masters
Irregular verbs list

Syllabus checklist

Pronunciation	Speaking	Listening	Reading
intonation, stress, and rhythm in questions	guessing original questions from answers; getting to know each other	radio programme about speed dating	Three minutes to get to know the love of your life
using a dictionary to check word stress; intonation and sentence rhythm	describing personality	magazine writer talking about her visit to a psychic; song: *You gotta be*	What your signature says about you; Tricks of the trade?
consonant and vowel sounds	talking about first aid	the conclusions of two people talking about a life or death situation	Get stressed, stay young
vowel sounds	talking about how different nationalities dress	four people talk about the typical characteristics of people from their country; song: *Englishman in New York*	Watching the English: how the English dress
irregular past forms	telling an anecdote	an interview with two pilots about air safety	Air Babylon
word and sentence stress	talking about reading habits	the conclusion of a short story	Little Brother ™
the letter *u*	talking about creative punishments	radio interview about *Oliver Twist* and pickpockets	Making the punishment fit the crime
vowel sounds	telling anecdotes about the weather; talking about preventing climate change	an interview about flooding in Prague; song: *It's raining men*	Stormy weather
sentence stress and rhythm	talking about safety in the past	interview about the risks of driving in the USA; an interview about a special school	The Risk factor
sentence rhythm	talking about how you would react in a life or death situation	a disastrous adventure in the Amazon; song: *Survivor*	How to get out alive; Escape from the Amazon
weak form of *have*	roleplaying arguments	psychologist giving tips for people when they disagree	How I trained my husband
silent letters	describing a painting – describing a picture	a radio quiz about the senses	Let your body do the talking

Pronunciation	Speaking	Listening	Reading
ch and *y*	talking about music	music psychologist talks about why we listen to music and how it affects us	What's your soundtrack?
linking words	answering questions about sleep	a radio programme about sleepwalking; song: *I don't want to miss a thing*	Sleepy people – the dangers of sleep deprivation
word stress	having a debate	two journalists talk about the good side and bad side of their job	Irving Wardle, theatre critic and Pat Gibson, sports journalist
sentence stress	making a presentation	five people talk about disastrous presentations; song: *Space Oddity*	One small word, one big difference in meaning
word stress in multi-syllable words	talking about the Amish; telling a tourist about your town	a radio programme about London	Amish in the city
changing stress in word families	talking about science	a radio programme about creative thinking	Suffering for science
sentence rhythm	talking about annoying habits	five people talking about regrets; song: *If I could turn back time*	Regrets, I've had a few…
changing stress in nouns and verbs	talking about advertising	an interview with an American economist	Honest workers or thieves? Take the bagel test.
word stress	talking about words	a radio interview with a dictionary expert	The story behind the words

What do Upper-intermediate students need?

Upper-intermediate students rightly feel that they are now quite high-level learners of English and are ready to 'push on' to become very proficient users of the language. To achieve this they need motivating material and challenging tasks. They need to set clear course goals from day one in terms of both language knowledge and of fluency and accuracy in speaking. Finally, they need classes to be as fun and dynamic as they were at lower levels: there is no reason why higher-level teaching should become dry and over-serious. Students still want to enjoy their English classes – role plays, language games, challenges, quizzes and songs are still as valuable pedagogically as they were, and can often be exploited even better at this level.

Grammar, Vocabulary, and Pronunciation

At any level, the basic tools students need to speak English with confidence are Grammar, Vocabulary, and Pronunciation (G, V, P). In *New English File Upper-intermediate* all three elements are given equal importance.

Each lesson has clearly stated grammar, vocabulary, and pronunciation aims. This keeps lessons focused and gives students concrete learning objectives and a sense of progress.

Grammar

Upper-intermediate students need

- to revise their knowledge of the main structures.
- to learn more sophisticated grammar structures.
- opportunities to use their instinct.
- student-friendly reference material.

When extending students' knowledge of grammar, it is important to build on what they already know. Many Grammar presentations begin with **Check what you know**, short exercises which revise Intermediate Grammar points, and are cross referenced to the Workbook, where students who are having problems can find rules and further practice. **New grammar** signals the presentation of a grammar point not previously covered in *New English File*. The **Grammar Banks** give students a single, easy-to-access grammar reference section, with clear rules and example sentences. There are two practice exercises.

Mini grammar (one per File) focuses on smaller grammar, e.g. *so* and *such*, *would rather* and *had better*. There is a photocopiable activity to give more practice of each point.

The oral grammar practice exercise in the Student's Book (immediately after students have been to the Grammar Bank) and the photocopiable Communicative speaking activities in the Teacher's Book encourage students to use grammatical structures in controlled and freer contexts. The photocopiable Grammar activities in the Teacher's Book can be used for practice in class or for self-study.

Vocabulary

Upper-intermediate students need

- systematic expansion of their vocabulary in topic-based lexical areas.
- opportunities to put new vocabulary into practice.
- to further develop their ability to 'build' new words by adding affixes.
- practice in pronouncing new lexis correctly and confidently.
- reference material which aids memorization.

At this level, expanding students' vocabulary is the most visible and motivating measure of their progress. Every lesson has a clear lexical aim. Many lessons are linked to the **Vocabulary Banks** which help present and practise high-frequency, topic-based vocabulary in class and provide a clear reference bank designed to aid memorization. The stress in multi-syllable words is clearly marked and phonemic script is provided where necessary.

Students can practise using the vocabulary from all the **Vocabulary Banks** in context with the **MultiROM** and the *New English File* Student's website. There is also a photocopiable activity to revise the vocabulary from each File.

Pronunciation

Upper-intermediate students need

- 'fine-tuning' of pronunciation of difficult sounds.
- to be able to use appropriate rhythm and intonation.
- to continue to develop their instinct for spelling–pronunciation rules and patterns.
- to be able to use phonetic symbols in their dictionary to check pronunciation.

The objective is to make students totally *intelligible* to other speakers of English (native and non-native). However, it's also important to make clear that perfection is not the aim. Most non-native speakers will always retain an accent. Every lesson has a pronunciation focus which often prepares students for a speaking activity.

New English File has a unique system of sound pictures, which give clear example words to help students to identify and produce the sounds.

The pronunciation focus is linked to the **Sound Bank**, a reference section where students can see and practise common sound–spelling patterns.

Throughout the book there is also a regular focus on word and sentence stress where students are encouraged to copy the rhythm of English. This will help students to pronounce new language with greater confidence.

Speaking

Upper-intermediate students need

- up-to-date, stimulating topics to get them talking and exchanging opinions.
- the key words and phrases necessary to discuss a topic.
- practice in more extended speaking, e.g. role plays, debates.
- to improve accuracy as well as developing their fluency.

Every lesson gives students many opportunities to speak and put into practice grammar, vocabulary, and pronunciation that has been worked on earlier in the lesson. Every speaking activity has a **GET IT RIGHT** box which identifies an accuracy focus for that particular activity.

Photocopiable Communicative activities can be found in the

Teacher's Book. These include pairwork activities, mingles, and speaking games.

Listening

Upper-intermediate students need

- motivating, integrated listening material.
- achievable tasks but with an increasing level of challenge.
- exposure to longer listenings and a wide variety of accents.
- exposure to authentic and colloquial spoken language.

For most students listening is still the hardest skill and it is vital that listening material is both interesting and provides the right level of challenge. *New English File Upper-intermediate* has motivating listening texts and tasks which are challenging, but always achievable and which expose students to a wide variety of accents and speed of speech.

The Colloquial English lessons give students practice in listening to unscripted authentic speech when speakers are interviewed in a studio and in the street.

There are also seven songs which we hope students will find enjoyable and motivating. For copyright reasons, most of these are cover versions.

Reading

Upper-intermediate students need

- engaging topics and stimulating texts.
- exposure to a wide variety of authentic text types.
- challenging tasks which help them read better.

Many students need to read in English for their work or academic studies, or may want to read about their personal interests on English websites. Reading also plays an important in helping to extend students' vocabulary and to consolidate grammar. The key to encouraging students to read **outside** class is to give them motivating material and tasks **in** class which help them develop their reading skills. Reading texts have been taken from a variety of real sources (newspapers, magazines, the Internet) and chosen for their intrinsic interest, which we hope will stimulate students to want to read them and will help spark classroom discussion.

The **Revise & Check** sections include a more challenging text which helps students to measure their progress.

Writing

Upper-intermediate students need

- clear models.
- practice in planning, organising, writing and checking.
- an awareness of register, structure, and fixed phrases.
- a focus on 'micro' writing skills e.g. paragraphing.

The ever-growing amount of email communication and Internet-based writing (e.g. blogs, etc.) continues to raise the importance of writing skills. Students at this level may also be thinking about taking public exams where writing quickly and accurately is a vital skill. There is one Writing lesson per File, where students study a model before doing a guided writing task themselves. These writing tasks focus on both electronic and 'traditional' text types, and provide consolidation of grammar and lexis taught in the File.

There is also always a focus on a 'micro skill' in each Writing lesson, for example, writing headings, paragraphing and using connecting expressions.

Colloquial English

Upper-intermediate students need

- to get used to listening to authentic colloquial speech.
- to be able to deal with different speeds and accents.
- exposure to high frequency colloquial phrases and idioms.

Most listening material in the A–C lessons is controlled and graded in terms of language and level of difficulty. However, in these seven *Colloquial English* lessons students listen to completely unscripted and authentic English. The lessons consist firstly of an interview with a person who is an expert in his / her field (one of the File topics). In the second part of the lesson students hear street interviews where people answer questions related to the lesson topic. There is also a focus on 'Common phrases' where students listen again and complete high-frequency expressions used in spoken English.

The Colloquial English lessons are also on the *New English File Upper-intermediate* DVD which teachers can use instead of the class audio. Using the DVD will make the lessons more enjoyable and will help students to understand faster speech with the help of paralinguistic features. On the MultiROM students have the opportunity to watch and listen to more street interviews.

Revision

Upper-intermediate students need

- regular revision.
- motivating reference and practice material.
- a sense of progress.

The higher the level the harder it is to see your progress. Upper-intermediate students need to feel that they are increasing their knowledge, improving their skills, and using English more fluently and effectively. At the end of each File there is a Revise & Check section. **What do you remember?** revises the grammar, vocabulary and pronunciation of each File. **What can you do?** provides a series of skills-based challenges and helps students to measure their progress in terms of competence. These pages are designed to be used flexibly according to the needs of your students.

The photocopiable Grammar, Communicative, and Vocabulary activities also provide many opportunities for recycling.

Study Link

The Study Link feature in *New English File Upper-intermediate* is designed to help you and your students use the course more effectively. It shows **what** resources are available, **where** they can be found, and **when** to use them.

The Student's Book has these Study Link references:

- from the Colloquial English lessons ◯ MultiROM and website.
- from the Grammar Bank ◯ MultiROM and website.
- from the Vocabulary Bank ◯ MultiROM and website.
- from the Sound Bank ◯ MultiROM and website.

These references lead students to extra activities and exercises that link with what they have just studied.

The Workbook has these Study Link references:

- the Student's Book Grammar and Vocabulary Banks.
- the MultiROM.
- the student's website.

The Teacher's Book has Study Link references to remind you where there is extra material available to your students.

Student's Book organization

The Student's Book has seven Files. Each File is organized like this:

A, B, and C lessons Three four-page lessons which form the core material of the book. Each lesson presents and practises **Grammar** and **Vocabulary**, and has a **Pronunciation** focus. There is a balance of reading and listening activities, and lots of opportunities for spoken practice. These lessons have clear references ⊙ to the Grammar Bank, Vocabulary Bank, and Sound Bank at the back of the book.

Colloquial English One-page lessons where students develop their ability to listen to authentic English and learn common collocations, idioms, and colloquial vocabulary. The lessons link with the *New English File Upper-Intermediate* DVD.

Writing One-page focuses on different text types and writing 'micro' skills like punctuation and spelling.

Revise & Check A two-page section – the left- and right-hand pages have different functions. The **What do you remember?** page revises the **Grammar**, **Vocabulary**, and **Pronunciation** of each File. The **What can you do?** page provides **Reading**, **Listening**, and **Speaking** 'Can you…?' challenges to show students what they can achieve.

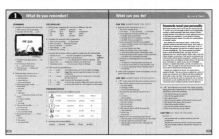

The back of the book

In the back of the Student's Book you'll find these three Banks of material:

Grammar Bank (*pp.132–145*)
Two pages for each File, divided into A–C to reflect the three main lessons. The left-hand page has the grammar rules and the right-hand page has two practice exercises for each lesson. Students are referred ⊙ to the Grammar Bank when they do the grammar in each main A, B, and C lesson.

Vocabulary Bank (*pp.146–156*)
An active vocabulary resource to help students learn, practise, and revise key words. Students are referred ⊙ to the Vocabulary Bank from the main lessons.

Sound Bank (*pp.158–160*) A three-page section with the *English File* sounds chart and typical spellings for all sounds. Students are referred ⊙ to the Sound Bank from the main lessons.

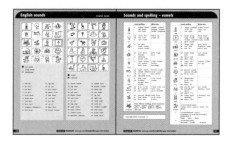

You'll also find:

- **Communication activities** (*pp.116–120*) Information gap activities and role-plays.
- **Listening scripts** (*pp.121–131*) Scripts of key listenings.
- **Phrasal verbs in context** (*p.157*)

More for students

Workbook Each A–C lesson in the Student's Book has a three-page section in the Workbook. This provides all the practice and revision students need. Each section ends with:

- **More Words to Learn**, which reminds students of new vocabulary from the lesson which is not in the Vocabulary Bank.
- **Listening**, which gives students extra listening practice based on the theme of the lesson. The material is on the audio section of the MultiROM.

Each Colloquial English lesson has a one-page section in the Workbook with practice of the Common phrases and a reading activity.

There is also a Key booklet.

MultiROM

The MultiROM has two functions:

- It's a CD-ROM, containing revision of **Grammar**, **Vocabulary**, **Pronunciation**, **Colloquial English** (with extracts from the DVD), **Dictation** activities and **Exam Practice**.
- It's an audio CD for students to use in a CD player. It has the audio material for the Workbook listening activities.

Student's website

www.oup.com/elt/englishfile/upper intermediate

Extra learning resources including

- grammar activities
- vocabulary puzzles
- pronunciation games
- Colloquial English activities
- Mini grammar activities
- learning records
- weblinks
- interactive games

More for teachers

Teacher's Book The Teacher's Book has detailed lesson plans for all the lessons. These include:

- an optional 'books-closed' lead-in for every lesson.
- **Extra idea** suggestions for optional extra activities.
- **Extra challenge** suggestions for ways of exploiting the Student's Book material in a more challenging way if you have a stronger class.
- **Extra support** suggestions for ways of adapting activities or exercises to make them more accessible for weaker students.

All lesson plans include keys and complete tapescripts. Extra activities are colour coded in orange so you can see where you are at a glance when you're planning and teaching your classes.

You'll also find over 85 pages of photocopiable materials in the Teacher's Book:

Photocopiable Grammar activities *see pp.159–181*

There is a photocopiable Grammar activity for each A, B, and C lesson.

Photocopiable Mini grammar activities *see pp.183–189*

There is a photocopiable Mini grammar activity for each File.

Photocopiable Communicative activities *see pp.197–220*

There is a photocopiable Communicative activity for each A, B, and C lesson.

Photocopiable Vocabulary activities *see pp.223–230*

There is a photocopiable Vocabulary activity for each File.

Photocopiable Song activities *see pp.233–239*

A photocopiable Irregular verbs list *see p.240*

All the photocopiable material is accompanied by clear instructions and keys.

DVD The DVD episodes link with the Colloquial English lessons in the Student's Book. There is an episode in each File and each episode is divided into two parts: the first is an extended interview with a person who has first-hand experience of one of the topics from the File, e.g. File 2 a flight attendant talking about air travel; the second part contains  shorter interviews with members of the public answering some general questions about the topic. All the interviews are unscripted and provide an opportunity for students to practise listening to English spoken at a natural speed and to learn some high-frequency vocabulary. Each episode can be used with the tasks in the Student's Book Colloquial English lessons as an alternative to the Class CD.

The *New English File Upper-intermediate* package also includes:

- **Four class / audio CDs**
  These contain all the listening materials for the Student's Book.
- **Teacher's website**
  www.oup.com/elt/teacher/englishfile/upperintermediate
  This gives you extra teaching resources, including
  – a guide to *New English File* and the Common European Framework
  – wordlists
  – mini web-projects
  – customizable cloze tests
  – student learning records

(**Teacher Link**)

You can subscribe to this free email service at www.oup.com/elt/teacherlink. You'll receive regular lesson ideas which will build up into a resource bank of extra material for every lesson and every level of *New English File*. You'll also receive updates and information about the course.

CEF mapping documents and Portfolios are available for download on the
English File Teacher's site, www.oup.com/elt/teacher/englishfile.

What is the CEF? What are its aims?

The CEF, developed by the Council of Europe, encourages us to learn languages and develop our ability to communicate with people from other countries and cultures. It consists of a carefully developed descriptive framework. It has educational and social aims – these are very often closely linked, and include the following:

- to encourage the development of language skills, so that we can work together more effectively.
- to encourage the development of inter-cultural awareness and 'plurilingualism'.
- to examine and define *what we can do* with a language.
- to help us compare the language levels of individuals in an accurate and impartial way, across different countries, education systems, ages, and cultures.
- to encourage learner autonomy and lifelong learning.
- to promote a coherent approach to language teaching – not by imposing a system, but by encouraging the sharing of ideas.

What are the CEF levels?

There are six global levels in the CEF. Behind these levels are a very large number of competences which make up a person's language ability – these are defined by 'descriptors'. The levels are intended to be common reference points. It's important to remember that they are *purely descriptive* – they don't necessarily correspond to a year of study, or to 100 hours of study. Everyone has different aims and learns at different speeds, in different environments, and in different ways. The CEF is careful to point out that the levels are not 'linear' – that is, the time needed to move from A1 to A2 may not be the same as that needed to move from B1 to B2 or C1 to C2, and progress from level to level slows down as we move up the levels.

A real strength of the CEF for students is that it focuses on the positive – on what students can do, not on what they can't do. All levels of performance from A1 upwards are valued, and students should feel positive about the growing list of things that they know they can do.

proficient	C2		This level doesn't equal 'native speaker' mastery – though a student at this level would be a very successful learner who can use a language with real precision and fluency.
	C1		At this level students command a wide range of language.
independent	B2	***New English File Upper-intermediate***	This level is where language use begins to become more 'abstract', for example giving opinions, summarizing a short story or plot, or giving detailed instructions.
	B1		At this level students can maintain a conversation and express ideas. They can also begin to deal with problems and situations where they meet unpredictable language.
basic	A2		This level has lots of descriptors for social functions, for example greeting people, asking about work and free time, and making invitations.
	A1		This is the lowest level of 'generative language use' – students can interact in a simple way and ask and answer simple questions.
The CEF recognizes a level of ability below **A1**, which includes descriptors like *'can say yes, no, please, thank you'*, 'can use some basic greetings', 'can fill in uncomplicated forms'.			For a breakdown of the six global levels above, see chapter 3 of the CEF.
The CEF also recognizes that there can be levels between these six global levels, like **A1+, A2+, B1+** and **B2+**.			For detailed scales for each area of competence, see chapter 4 of the CEF.

What is a Portfolio?

The European Language Portfolio is a document for learners. It has three parts:

- the Passport
- the Biography
- the Dossier

The main aim of the Portfolio is to facilitate mobility in Europe by presenting an individual's language qualifications in a clear and comparable way. It allows all language and language-learning experiences (whether in the classroom or not) to be recorded, and it should be regularly updated. In a teaching situation where a coursebook is used over a year of study, we'd recommend updating the Portfolio several times a year, perhaps at the end of each term.

■ The Passport

This is a summary of language-learning experience, including time spent abroad; courses attended; books used; an assessment grid for each language skill area (graded from **A1–C2**); and any certificates or diplomas. It also outlines future plans for language learning.

The Passport shows at a glance the user's current level of language proficiency in different languages.

■ The Biography

This summarizes the learner's language-learning history, including languages they've grown up with, their language-learning experience at school and university, and how they use their languages now. It helps learners plan their learning by asking them to reflect on how and where they learn languages, and how they can develop autonomous learning.

The Biography also contains the CEF checklists for self-assessment.

■ The Dossier

This is a collection of pieces of personal work of different kinds which illustrate what the learner has achieved in different languages. This work could include written work from a course (for example from the Writing lessons of *New English File Upper-intermediate*), self-assessment sheets, and audio and video recordings – anything that can 'prove' the learner's language history and level.

Is New English File CEF-compatible?

Yes, definitely. The CEF focuses on using language for a communicative purpose, and so does *New English File*. The CEF encourages the development of the ability to 'do things' in a foreign language, not just to 'know about' that language – though you also need to 'know about' a language in order to function successfully in that language. As the CEF says, '…a language learner has to acquire both form and meaning'. For example, take the B2 descriptor 'I can convey degrees of emotion and highlight the personal significance of events and experiences'. In order to do this, students need to have the necessary range of vocabulary to describe emotions (*scared stiff, absolutely furious*, etc.), confidence using a mixture of tenses, and appropriate use of intonation. *New English File* teaches the language and skills that students will need in order to develop their range of communicative competences.

Here are some examples of how *New English File* fits with the aims of the CEF:

- The Study Link feature, which helps students see where they can find extra help and extra practice. The CEF states that learners need to take responsibility for planning and carrying out their own learning, and that they need to 'learn to learn' and to be made aware of the ways they can do this. One of the main obstacles to autonomous learning is that students don't know what to do, and **Study Link** helps to make it clear. There are regular **Study Link** references to the Grammar Bank, the Vocabulary Bank, the MultiROM, and the student's website.

- A Grammar, Vocabulary, and Pronunciation syllabus that gives students the linguistic competences they need to be able to communicate successfully.

- Regular **receptive and productive work** in the four skills – every lesson has speaking activities, and every File has listening, reading, and writing – the emphasis is on what students *do* with English.

- Clear **lesson aims** for each lesson, so learners know what the lesson objectives are.

- The Colloquial English lessons, which are based on real factual interviews, help students identify both general messages and specific details – they help to develop both the receptive and productive competences of learners.

- The 'What can you do?' pages at the end of every File, which ask students to see what they can achieve with the language they've studied.

- The *English File* pronunciation pictures – these help students to work on pronunciation autonomously, and to use dictionaries more effectively.

- A Workbook, MultiROM, and student's website which all give students extra practice and learning resources.

- A Teacher's Book which gives you all the support you need, including extra photocopiable material and ideas so you can respond to your students' needs.

Remember – you can find full CEF mapping and Portfolio documents at www.oup.com/elt/teacher/englishfile.

G revision: question formation
V working out meaning from context
P intonation, stress and rhythm in questions

1A Q and A

File 1 overview

This first File (**1A–1C**) has a strong revision element and accuracy focus. The first lesson, **1A**, revises all aspects of question formation. The second, **1B**, revises and extends SS' knowledge of auxiliary verbs. Finally, the third lesson, **1C**, revises and extends uses of the present perfect simple and continuous.

Lesson plan

Even at upper-intermediate level many SS still have problems forming questions correctly. This lesson aims to revise all aspects of question formation including indirect questions, negative questions, and questions which end with a preposition. By the end of the lesson SS should be forming questions more accurately and more confidently, and we suggest that from then onwards you insist on questions always being formed correctly.

The lesson has two distinct parts. In the first half the context for question practice is two interviews from a regular feature in *The Guardian* newspaper. In the second half the topic is speed dating, where men and women have just three minutes to get to know each other by asking quick-fire questions. The vocabulary focus is on working out the meaning of new words (in a text) from context, and the pronunciation revises intonation, stress, and rhythm in questions.

If you would like to begin the first lesson without the book, there are two photocopiable 'first day' activities on *p.159* (key *p.157*) and *p.197* (instructions *p.190*).

Optional lead-in (books closed)

Write five pieces of information on the board which are answers to questions about you, e.g. **London, Iceland, 2001, Jazz,** etc. SS have to try to guess the questions to which these are your answers, e.g. *Where were you born? Where did you go last summer? When did you start teaching? What kind of music do you like?*, etc.

You can make your answers more or less cryptic according to the kind of class you have.

1 GRAMMAR revision: question formation

a • Books open. Focus on the task and on the two examples. Give SS a few minutes in pairs to complete the questions. Check answers.

   • Elicit / explain the difference between *Which…?* and *What…?* We tend to use *which* when there is a very limited choice, e.g. *There's tea or coffee – which would you like?* For a wider choice we generally use *what*, e.g. *What's your favourite song?*

   • You may also want to focus on the use of *How +* adjective, e.g. *How tall are you?* SS know *How old are you?* but may not realize that this pattern is used in many other similar questions, e.g. *How big is your flat? How heavy is your case? How high is it?*, etc.

3	How long	**8**	Do
4	Which	**9**	What kind (sort / type)
5	How often	**10**	Whose
6	How	**11**	Have
7	What	**12**	Who

b • Focus on the task and get SS, in pairs, to mark with a cross questions they wouldn't ask someone they didn't know well. Get feedback, and ask SS why they wouldn't ask them (e.g. too personal, rude, etc.).

> Answers will vary depending on the country and culture you are teaching in. In the UK questions 1, 2, 6, 7, 8, 11, and 12 would be considered inappropriate questions to ask someone you don't know well.

   • Now ask the class *Are there any questions which you would not even ask a good friend?* Answers will probably vary. Get SS to say why they wouldn't ask them.

   • Finally, ask *Which questions might you expect to find in a magazine interview with a famous person?* Again, answers will vary.

c • Focus on the photos with the two interviews in the article *Young star, old star*, and ask if SS know anything about either of the people.

   • Then tell SS to read the introduction to the article and the biographical information about each person. Then ask a student to tell you what they thought was the most significant piece of information about each person.

   • Now focus on the task. Set a time limit for SS to read both questionnaires. When time is up, get SS to work in pairs to decide which questions are the most personal, etc. Get feedback and see if SS agree.

d • Get SS to do this task individually and then compare their answers with a partner. Check answers.

1 L	**2** N	**3** N	**4** L	**5** N	**6** L	**7** L	**8** N

Extra challenge

Alternatively, you could get SS to close their books and then call out some of the answers from the two Q&A questionnaires to see if SS can remember the questions, e.g. **T**   *Onion, garlic, and butter cooking in a pan*
    SS *What's your favourite smell?*

e • Focus on the task and go through the five questions. Make sure SS remember what, for example, an auxiliary verb is (*do, have,* etc.). Get SS to do the task in pairs, or elicit the answers from the whole class. Check answers.

1	8 and 10	**3**	11	**5**	11 and 12
2	9	**4**	8		

f • Tell SS to go to **Grammar Bank 1A** on *p.132*. If your SS have not used the *New English File* series before, explain that all the grammar rules and exercises are in this part of the book.

   • Go through each example and its corresponding rule with the class.

Grammar notes

The Grammar notes in this Teacher's Book aim to add more information to the notes and rules on the **Grammar Bank** pages in the Student's Book. There is a direct link between the number of each rule in the Teacher's Book and the Student's Book. If there is no extra information about a rule in the Teacher's Book, this is either because we assume that SS at this level should already know it or because all the information needed is on the Student's Book page.

- **rules 1 and 2: basic word order in questions**

Although SS at this level will be familiar with basic rules regarding question formation, they will probably still make mistakes, especially when they speak.

- **rule 3: word order in negative questions**

When contracted forms are used the word order is the same as in normal questions, i.e. just add *n't* to the auxiliary verb, e.g. *Aren't you going to come? Why didn't you tell me?*

However, when full forms are used you have to put the **not** between the subject and verb, e.g. *Are you **not** going to come? Why did you **not** tell me?*

You should point out to SS that it is much more common to use the contracted negative, especially in spoken English.

- **rule 4: end preposition questions**

In your SS' L1 the preposition may come at the beginning of the question. Other examples of end preposition questions in English: *Who did you speak **to**? What does it depend **on**?*

- **rule 5: questions without auxiliaries**

SS should be familiar with this kind of question. If SS are not clear about this, you could give them these sentences to compare.

A Who does Bill love? **B** Mary. (Subject of question = **Bill**. You use an auxiliary to make the question.)
A Who loves Mary? **B** Bill. (Subject of question = **Who**. You don't use an auxiliary to make the question.)

- **rule 6: indirect questions**

An indirect question is a question (e.g. *What time does the bank open?*) which is introduced by another question, e.g. *Can you tell me...? / Do you know...? / Can you remember...?*, often to make the question less direct or more polite. In this kind of question the second question 'disappears', e.g. *Do you know **what time the bank opens**?* NOT ~~Do you know what time does the bank open?~~

- Focus on the exercises for **1A** on *p.133*. SS do the exercises individually or in pairs. Check answers after each exercise.

> **a** 1 Do you ever send text messages?
> 2 When was the last time you went to a party?
> 3 Could you tell me if there is a bank near here?
> 4 Who usually cooks the dinner?
> 5 Who do you like going shopping with?
> 6 What don't you like doing at the weekend?
> 7 What kind of car would you like to buy?
> 8 Do you know what time the concert finishes?

> **b** 1 do you do
> 2 wrote
> 3 this book costs (cost)
> 4 happens (happened)
> 5 Did you enjoy
> 6 does Tim usually listen to
> 7 stole (has stolen)
> 8 the swimming pool opens (opened)
> 9 are you meeting (are you going to meet)
> 10 she lives

- Tell SS to go back to the main lesson on *p.5*.

2 PRONUNCIATION intonation, stress, and rhythm in questions

Pronunciation notes

- Non-native speakers can unintentionally sound unfriendly or uninterested if they use very flat intonation. These exercises focus on encouraging SS to use a wide voice range when asking questions, and on stressing the right words.

- These exercises do not focus specifically on distinguishing between the different intonation patterns for yes / no questions and question-word questions (yes / no questions usually have a rising intonation and question-word questions a falling intonation). In practice we think it is very hard for SS to notice this distinction. However, when they are asked to copy the rhythm and intonation of a question, they can usually produce the correct pattern.

a • **1.1** Focus on the information box and read it aloud. Focus on the task and tell SS they are going to hear two speakers, a and b, asking the same question. SS must decide which one has the friendlier intonation.

- Play the CD once, pausing if necessary to give SS time to write. Play it again for them to check.

- Check answers.

> 1 b 2 a 3 a 4 b 5 b 6 a 7 b 8 a

> **1.1**   CD1 Track 2
> *There are two versions of each sentence.*
> 1 Where do you work?
> 2 Are you hungry?
> 3 How long have you been waiting?
> 4 Could you tell me the time, please?
> 5 Why didn't you like the film?
> 6 Excuse me. Is this the London train?
> 7 What do you think I should do?
> 8 Is this chair free?

b • **1.2** Focus on the task and elicit what kind of words are usually stressed in a sentence (information words, e.g. nouns, verbs, adjectives, etc.). You could also elicit what kind of words are <u>not</u> usually stressed (articles, prepositions, auxiliary verbs, pronouns, etc.).

- Play the CD once pausing after each sentence for SS to underline the stressed words. Get SS to compare with a partner and then play the CD again for SS to check. Check answers.

- Highlight that prepositions at the end of a question <u>are</u> stressed (e.g. *about* in 6).

1 <u>What's</u> your <u>favourite</u> <u>kind</u> of <u>music</u>?
2 Have you ever <u>been</u> to a <u>health</u> <u>club</u>?
3 <u>How</u> <u>often</u> do you <u>go</u> <u>away</u> at the <u>weekend</u>?
4 Do you <u>know</u> <u>what's</u> on <u>TV</u> <u>tonight</u>?
5 <u>How</u> <u>long</u> have you been <u>living</u> <u>here</u>?
6 <u>What</u> are you <u>thinking</u> <u>about</u>?
7 <u>Are</u> you a <u>vegetarian</u>?
8 <u>What</u> do you <u>do</u> to <u>relax</u>?

c ● Play the CD again and get SS to repeat the questions. Encourage them to use a wide voice range and to get the right rhythm.

3 SPEAKING

a ● Focus on the task and the photos. The aim here is to get SS to think of a possible question for each answer, even if it is not the question which was actually asked in *The Guardian*.

● Get feedback for each answer. Accept all correctly formed, possible questions which make sense and write them on the board. Then tell SS what the original question was.

The original questions were

1 What's your favourite building? Also possible *What was the last famous building you visited?*, etc.
2 When did you last cry? Also possible *When did you stop watching football?*, etc.
3 Who did you vote for in the last election? Also possible *What party do you usually vote for?*, etc.
4 If you could go back in time, where would you go? Also possible *What's your favourite period in history?*, etc.
5 What's your favourite journey? (Helena Christensen is Danish). Also possible *What makes you feel happy?*, etc.
6 What are you afraid of? Also possible *What makes you nervous?*, etc.

b ● Give SS time to choose their questions. Remind them that apart from the interviews they can also choose questions from exercises **1a, 2b**, and any that you may have written on the board from the previous stage.

Extra support

Demonstrate the activity by getting SS to choose questions to ask you. Give reasonably full answers and encourage SS to ask follow-up questions.

● Get SS to ask and answer their questions in pairs. Encourage 'questioners' to ask for more information where possible.
● Get feedback by asking SS for any interesting / funny answers.

4 READING & VOCABULARY

a ● Elicit from the class what they know about speed dating. Then set a time limit for SS to read the first half of the article once to check or find out how speed dating works. Check answers by getting SS to tell you how it works stage by stage, e.g. asking *Who is it for? When do they meet? Where do they sit?*, etc.

Single men and women meet for an evening. The women sit at tables and the men sit with each woman in turn. They have three minutes only to ask each other questions, and they then tick a scorecard if they would like to see the person again. If both a man and a woman choose each other, there is a 'match' and, in the next few days, they are given each other's email addresses.

Extra idea

It can be difficult to know how long to give when you set a time limit for reading, as some SS are slower readers than others. It is important for SS to realize that slower readers are not worse readers; in fact, they often retain what they have read better than fast readers. Talk about this with your SS and ask if they are fast or slow readers in their L1. Then set a time limit to suit the mid-pace readers. Tell the fast readers if they have finished already, to go back to the beginning, and encourage very slow readers to try to speed up a little.

b ● Now focus on the **Working out meaning from context** box and go through it with the class. Many of the texts in *New English File Upper-intermediate* have glossaries, but obviously there will sometimes be other words whose meaning SS can't guess, so encourage them to bring dictionaries to use as a last resort.

● Focus on the task. Get SS to cover **Glossary 1** with a piece of paper. Then tell them to read the text again, trying to guess what the highlighted words or phrases mean. In pairs, they compare guesses and then check with **Glossary 1**.

● Get feedback to find out how many of the words SS could guess, and deal with any other vocabulary problems.

⚠ Make sure SS are aware of the two meanings of *partner*, a person you work with in class / share a business with, or as here in the text, a person you are married to or having a relationship with.

c ● Focus on questions 1–4 and give SS, in pairs, a minute or two to answer them. Encourage them to try to use their own words rather than just quoting directly from the article. Check answers.

1 In the Stone Age a man used to bring food to a woman he was interested in; in Victorian times (the 19th century) a man and woman would meet for tea but always with someone else watching.
2 For people who are single and too busy to spend a long time getting to know other people.
3 Because she thinks you can get an idea of what someone is like in three minutes.
4 Because she didn't want people to know she was a journalist, so they would behave naturally with her.

d ● Now give SS a time limit to read the second half of the article. Check answers to the two gist questions. Ask SS if they can think of any other advantages, e.g. if you don't like someone at all, you don't have to spend much time with them as you only have three minutes.

1 They got twice the number of dates that they normally had in a year from just one night of speed dating. Going speed dating means they don't have to try to talk to people they don't know in bars. You meet 20 or 30 single people in one night. It's safe, and like being at a party.

2 She seems to think it is a good idea as she got four new dates in 66 minutes.

e ● Focus on the task. Give SS a time limit to read the second half of the text again trying to guess the meaning of the highlighted words from the context. They then compare guesses with a partner.

f ● SS complete **Glossary 2** with the highlighted words and phrases. Tell them to write nouns in the singular and verbs in the infinitive even if they don't appear in the singular or the infinitive in the text.

1	a badge	4	raise (your) eyebrows
2	a grimace	5	chat up
3	giggle	6	chat

g ● Focus on the questions and give SS, in pairs, a minute or two to answer them. Check answers.

1 Because she was wearing jeans and other women were wearing fashionable dresses and smart suits.

2 Mostly professional men with good jobs.

3 She raised an eyebrow if she thought the man she was talking to was a possibility, and made a grimace if she thought he was awful.

4 More interesting and imaginative questions like *If you could be an animal, what would you be and why?*

Extra support

At this point you could go through the article with the class, one by one highlighting useful expressions and eliciting / explaining the meaning of new words and phrases.

h ● Ask these questions to the whole class and elicit responses.

5 LISTENING

a ● (1.3) Tell SS they're going to listen to a radio programme where a man and a woman, Alex and Emily, who tried speed dating, will talk about their experiences. Emphasize to SS that the information in the listening is 100% real.

● Tell SS that the first time they listen all they have to do is find out whether their speed dating experiences were successful or not.

It was successful for Alex – he married his second date, but Emily didn't have any successful dates.

1.3   CD1 Track 4

(tapescript in Student's Book on *p.121*)

I = interviewer, E = Emily, A = Alex

I … and with me I've got Emily and Alex. Emily, what kind of questions did you ask?

E Well, the organizers of the event suggested a list of topics, you know, sort of pre-prepared questions but I thought that they were very er artificial, you know,

strange. So I asked quite normal questions like 'Why did you come tonight?' or er 'Have you been speed dating before?' or er 'What do you like doing in your free time?' I found that the conversation ran more smoothly when I asked people these kinds of normal questions.

I How about you Alex?

A Yes, same as Emily, really. I also asked quite normal things like, 'What do you do? Have you done this before? Do you enjoy living in Oxford?' Things like that.

I Did other people ask *you* interesting questions?

A Yes, some were quite interesting. Ones I can remember are, 'If you were an animal, what would you be?' Or 'If you had to choose a different career from your current one, what would it be?' One woman even said 'I've heard that you were in prison once – is that true?' I don't know where she got that from!

I And you, Emily, were you asked anything unusual?

E Not really! The most common questions were 'Are you American?' or 'Where are you from?' The second most common question was 'Why do you live in England?' Although one person did ask me 'If you could be invisible for a day, what would you do?'

I How did you answer that?

E I said I would go to work and play tricks on my colleagues in the office like hiding things!

I How many matches did you get?

E I chose six men that I would be happy to see again and, of those six, four of them had chosen me too, so I got four matches.

A I got three.

I Did you go out with any of the people?

E Yes, I went on one date with a guy who teaches biochemistry at university. It was a bit of a disaster though, because earlier that morning I'd been to the dentist, and I'd had an injection, so by the time that we met for coffee I had terrible toothache and I was in agony. I had to go home after half an hour. We've exchanged a few emails since then, but we haven't managed to meet. We're both very busy.
Also, to be honest, I don't think he's really my type. He seems to be really keen to get married and have children straight away and I'm not.

I What about the other three matches?

E The second man contacted me directly after the event and invited me to dinner. But then he sent me a text message the next day and cancelled. He said that he had met someone else. The other two have been in touch, but we haven't been able to meet yet. But in fact, I've decided that for the moment, I'm actually happy being single so I don't think I'll be speed dating again anytime soon.

I How about you Alex?

A I emailed one of the matches, a woman I quite liked and we met at a bar in Oxford. At the speed dating event she seemed really bubbly and good fun, but after spending a few minutes with her it was very clear that we had *nothing* in common. The atmosphere was awful and it was all very awkward, and I think she felt the same so we just finished our drinks and left. We didn't contact each other again. Then I arranged to meet another of my matches. We'd really got on well at the speed dating so I was quite excited about meeting her. Unfortunately, on that morning, I'd found out that I'd lost my job and I was really worried that I would not give the right impression because I was feeling so unhappy about my work situation. But actually, Susanna quickly made me forget everything and we had a great evening. We then met up the next day and went for a long walk. And well, to cut a long story short, six months later I took her to Paris and proposed, and two months ago we got married!

E Aaaah!

I So a real success story for you then?

A Absolutely!

b ● Focus on the task and go through the questions. You may want to warn SS that some of the answers from the tapescript are given in a different order to the order of the questions. Then play the CD again. Get SS to compare answers with a partner, and then play the CD another time if necessary. Check answers.

> 1 B 2 B 3 E 4 A 5 E 6 E 7 A
> 8 A 9 E

Extra support

If there's time, get SS to listen to the CD with the tapescript on *p.121* so they can see exactly what they understood / didn't understand. Translate / explain any new words or phrases.

c ● Do this as an open class question.

6 SPEAKING

a ● Tell the class that they are now going to do a 'speed getting to know you' activity. Focus on the task and give SS a few minutes to think of five questions. Emphasize that the aim is to get to know the other SS better. If SS don't know each other at all, they will probably want to ask factual questions, e.g. *What do you do?* If SS already know each other quite well, encourage them to write more imaginative / unusual questions.

● Go through the **GET IT RIGHT** box and give SS some intonation practice with the words and phrases. Remind them to use friendly, interested intonation.

b ● Explain the task and make sure SS know what they have to do before calling out 'Start'. After three minutes call out 'Change' and, if possible, carry on until SS have spoken to at least three or four other people. If you have an odd number of SS, either get two SS to work together or take part yourself.

● Monitor and correct any mistakes in question formation.

Extra idea

You could recreate the dynamics of a speed dating event by getting SS to sit opposite each other. After three minutes shout 'change' as above.

c ● Do this as an open class question and elicit ideas.

Extra photocopiable activities

Grammar
question formation *p.160*
Communicative
Q and A *p.198* (instructions *p.190*)

HOMEWORK

Study Link **Workbook** *pp.4–6*

G auxiliary verbs; *the...the...*+ comparatives
V personality
P using a dictionary to check word stress; intonation and sentence rhythm

1 B Do you believe it?

Lesson plan

In this lesson SS revise the use of auxiliary (and modal) verbs in short answers, question tags and *So do I / Neither do I*, and learn to use them for emphasis (I *do* like coffee!) and in echo questions. The first context is an extract from a book on graphology and SS find out how to interpret personality from signatures. In the second part of the lesson, SS listen to the real experience of a journalist who visited a psychic, which raises the issue of whether psychics really can see the future. They also learn, in mini grammar, how to use the structure *the... the...*+ comparatives, e.g. *the sooner the better*. SS expand their vocabulary of adjectives and phrases to describe personality, and the pronunciation focus is on improving SS' intonation and rhythm when they use auxiliaries.

Optional lead-in (books closed)

- Copy the following on the board:
  their star sign (e.g. Leo)   **their position in the family** (e.g. first born, only child)
  the lines on the palm of their hands   **their handwriting**
  and ask SS *Do you think any of these things can tell you anything about a person's personality?*

- Put SS in pairs and give them a few minutes to discuss the question. Get feedback, and ask them if they know any other ways of finding out about people's personality.

1 READING & SPEAKING

a ● Books open. Focus on the signatures and get SS to try to decipher them. Check answers and write them on the board.

A Mahatma Gandhi	**D** Jack Nicholson
B Orlando Bloom	**E** Tom Hanks
C Albert Einstein	**F** Victoria Beckham

b ● Get SS to read the first paragraph of the book extract (or read it aloud with SS). Then tell SS to imagine they had just written a formal letter, e.g. applying for a job. Get them to write on a piece of paper *I look forward to hearing from you* and then their normal formal signature underneath. Tell SS they will need this piece of paper later in the lesson.

c ● Focus on the task. Pre-teach *prominent* (= easily seen), *imply* (= to suggest sth is true without saying so directly), *rise* (= to go in an upward movement), and *descend* (= to go downwards). Set a time limit for SS to read the rest of the extract. You may want to point out that SS first need to focus on 'Your formal signature' and then on the other three sections of the text. Now focus on question 1, and elicit what kind of signature shows that someone isn't very assertive (one where the signature is illegible). Then ask them to look at the signatures and see which one has this feature (B).

- Then tell SS to continue in pairs with 2–6. Check answers.

1	B	**4**	D
2	A	**5**	E
3	F	**6**	C

d ● Focus on the task. Give SS a few minutes in pairs to discuss what the words mean. Then get SS to explain what kind of person the adjectives / phrases describe.

assertive = expressing his / her opinion with confidence
optimistic = having a positive attitude to life
ambitious = wanting to be successful
lack self-confidence = not believing in his / her ability to be successful
stable = calm and reasonable
well-balanced = being emotionally in control of his / her own life, not moody
self-confident = believing in his / her ability to be successful
arrogant = believing that he / she is better than other people
insecure = unsure of himself / herself
have low self-esteem = not feel happy with his / her own character and abilities

e ● Now get SS in pairs to exchange their pieces of paper with their signature. Tell them to check their partner's signature against the information in the text, and then explain to each other what their signatures mean.

Extra idea

Before SS interpret each other's signatures you could sign your name on the board and get SS to tell you what they can find out about you from it, according to the information in the text.

f ● Do this as an open class question. Get feedback.

Extra support

At this point you could go through the extract with the class, highlighting useful expressions and eliciting / explaining the meaning of new words and phrases.

2 VOCABULARY personality

a ● Tell SS to cover the text and try to remember the ten adjectives / phrases which were highlighted in the text.

b ● Tell SS to go to **Vocabulary Bank *Personality*** on *p.146*. Focus on section **1 Adjectives and phrases to describe personality** and get SS to do it individually or in pairs. Check answers and drill pronunciation where necessary. Draw SS' attention to the fact that the phonetic transcription is given for words where the spelling / pronunciation relationship is unusual, and that the stressed syllables are underlined.

1	vain	13	ambitious
2	conscientious	14	loyal
3	open-minded	15	wise
4	insincere	16	calm
5	eccentric	17	possessive
6	easy-going	18	reserved
7	well-balanced	19	immature
8	stubborn	20	impulsive
9	assertive	21	bad-tempered
10	cheerful	22	arrogant
11	self-confident	23	optimistic
12	insecure	24	funny

- Highlight that the phrases used in the chart (*She's the kind of person who… He's good at… He tends to…*, etc.) are often used to describe someone's personality instead of using specific adjectives. They are also useful for paraphrasing if SS don't know or can't remember a specific adjective.

- You may also want to tell SS that the opposite of *open-minded* is *narrow-minded*, and that a common synonym for *stubborn* is *obstinate*.

- Focus on section **2 Adjective suffixes** and the chart, and go through the different adjective endings. Highlight to SS that knowing typical endings will help them to recognize which words are adjectives when they are guessing words from context, and also to have a go at forming an adjective from verbs or nouns they already know.

- Give SS a few minutes in pairs to do **2b** and **c**. Check answers, and model and drill pronunciation. Make sure SS know the difference between *sensible* and *sensitive*.

b	-ible	-able	-ful	-y
	sensible	reliable	forgetful	moody
	-ive	**-ous**	**-al**	**-ic**
	sensitive	adventurous	critical	pessimistic

c **sensible** = able to make good judgements
   reliable = that can be trusted to do sth well
   forgetful = often forgetting things
   moody = having moods that change quickly and often
   sensitive = able to understand other people's feelings
   adventurous = willing to take risks and try new ideas
   critical = expressing disapproval
   pessimistic = expecting bad things to happen

Extra challenge

Alternatively, quickly elicit a phrase to describe each of the adjectives, e.g. *a person who has a lot of common sense*, etc.

- Now focus on section **3 Idioms**. Several of the **Vocabulary Banks** include a short **Idioms** section. We have tried to choose idioms that we think native speakers really use rather than including some of the more obscure / old-fashioned idioms. Give SS a few moments to match the idioms and definitions. Check answers, and ask SS if they have a similar idiom in their language for the different personality types.

1 C **2** B **3** D **4** A

- Finally, focus on the final instruction 'Can you remember the words on this page? Test yourself or a partner'.

Testing yourself

For **Adjectives and phrases to describe personality** SS can cover the column on the right and try to remember the adjectives by reading the definitions. For **Adjective suffixes** they can cover the adjectives in the chart and look at the endings, and try to remember two adjectives for each ending. For **Idioms** they can cover the idioms and look at the definitions in **b** and try to remember them.

Testing a partner

Alternatively, SS can take it in turns to test each other. **B** closes the book and **A** defines or explains a word for **B** to try and remember, e.g. *What do you call a person who's good at keeping his head in a crisis?* After a few minutes, SS can change roles.

In a monolingual class, SS could also test each other by saying the word in their L1 for their partner to say in English.

Study Link SS can find more practice of these words and phrases on the MultiROM and on the *New English File Upper-intermediate* website.

- Tell SS to go back to the main lesson on *p.9*.

c - Focus on the task, and remind SS that if the sentence requires a negative adjective, they will have to add a negative prefix, e.g. *un-*, *in-*, or *dis-*. Give SS a few minutes to complete the task. Check answers.

2	talkative	6	imaginative
3	unreliable	7	dishonest
4	cheerful	8	unhelpful
5	insincere		

3 PRONUNCIATION using a dictionary to check word stress

Pronunciation notes

SS at this level will already be familiar with the fact that multi-syllable words are stressed more strongly on one of the syllables. Here SS are introduced to the idea that some words have secondary stress, i.e. have another syllable which is also stressed but less strongly. This is frequent in very long or compound nouns / adjectives, e.g. *communication* /kəˌmjuːnɪˈkeɪʃn/ and *well-balanced* /ˌwelˈbælənst/. It is worth pointing this out to SS as they sometimes get confused by the secondary stress symbol in the dictionary, but emphasize that when they look up a word the most important thing is to check where the main stress is.

a - Focus on the information box and go through it with SS. Then focus on the task and give SS a few minutes to underline the syllable with the main stress.

b - **1.4** Play the CD once or twice for SS to check. Then check answers. The negative prefixes or suffixes are not stressed. You may want to highlight that *bad-tempered*, *conscientious*, and *immature* also have secondary stress.

<table>
<tr><td>

1.4   CD1 Track 5

1 <u>arr</u>ogant
2 a<u>sser</u>tive
3 bad-<u>tem</u>pered
4 cre<u>a</u>tive
5 con<u>si</u>derate
6 consci<u>en</u>tious
7 po<u>sse</u>ssive
8 <u>loy</u>al
9 <u>stu</u>bborn
10 im<u>pa</u>tient
11 un<u>so</u>ciable
12 imma<u>ture</u>
</td></tr>
</table>

c ● Get SS in pairs to read the sentences alternately, focusing on stressing the adjectives correctly. Check by getting individual SS to read the five sentences.

4 SPEAKING

● Focus on the **GET IT RIGHT** box and on the task. Then put SS into groups of three or four. Give them time to discuss each type of person and exchange ideas. Get each group to appoint a secretary to make notes after they have discussed each type of person, so that he / she can then feed back to the class.

● Monitor and help with any words they need while they are talking.

● Get feedback asking one group what they think makes *a bad flatmate*, another group *a bad travelling companion*, etc., and then asking the other groups if they agree.

Extra support

You could start by eliciting ideas from the whole class, e.g. about what makes a bad flatmate and writing their ideas on the board.

Extra challenge

Alternatively, you could also get SS to describe the opposite type of person for each case, e.g. a good flatmate.

MINI GRAMMAR   *the…the…* + comparatives

● This regular feature focuses on extra, smaller grammar points that come out of a reading or listening. Go through the examples and then the rules.

● Highlight that:
– *the* + comparatives (+ pronoun or noun) come at the beginning of a phrase.
– occasionally we just use the two comparatives, especially when one of them is *better*, e.g. *the sooner the better* or *the bigger the better*.
– You mustn't separate *the more*, etc. from the adjective / adverb it goes with, e.g. *The more interesting the book is, the more slowly I read* NOT ~~The more the book is interesting~~…

● Elicit sentence 1 from the whole class and write the answer on the board (*The more you study, the more you learn*). Then get SS to do the other three. Check answers.

1 The more you study, the more you learn.
2 The sooner we leave, the earlier we'll get there.
3 The more sociable you are, the more friends you have.
4 The happier you are, the nicer you are to other people.

Extra support

If you think your class need more practice, use the extra photocopiable exercises on *p.183*.

5   **1.5**   SONG ♫   *You gotta be*

● This song was originally made famous by Des'ree in 1994. If you want to do this song in class, use the photocopiable activity on *p.233*.

<table>
<tr><td>

1.5   CD1 Track 6

You gotta be

Listen as your day unfolds,
Challenge what the future holds
Try and keep your head up to the sky

Lovers they may cause you tears
Go ahead release your fears
Stand up and be counted
Don't be ashamed to cry

You gotta be…

Chorus
You gotta be bad
You gotta be bold
You gotta be wiser
You gotta be hard
You gotta be tough
You gotta be stronger
You gotta be cool
You gotta be calm

you gotta stay together
All I know, all I know
Love will save the day

Herald what your mother said
Read the books your father read
Try to solve the puzzles in your own sweet time
Some may have more cash than you
Others take a different view
My oh my

Chorus

Time asks no questions, it goes on without you
Leaving you behind if you can't stand the pace
The world keeps on spinning, can't stop it if you tried to
The best part is danger staring you in the face

Remember, listen as your day unfolds, etc.
</td></tr>
</table>

6 LISTENING & READING

a ● Focus on the task, and model and drill the pronunciation of *psychic* /ˈsaɪkɪk/. Ask the questions to the whole class. Focus on the photos and ask SS what they can see (a psychic with a crystal ball, a palm, and a woman with Tarot cards.) and if they believe any of these things can really help predict someone's future.

- You could ask for a show of hands to find out what proportion of the class believes in psychics and what proportion is sceptical /ˈskeptɪkl/ (i.e. find it difficult to believe).

b ● **1.6** Tell SS that they are going to listen to a journalist talking about her visit to a psychic and emphasize that this is a true story.

- Focus on the instructions. Get SS to read the three questions for **Part 1**. Play the CD once and get SS to answer the questions in pairs orally. Play the CD again and then check answers.

> 1 Positive – Sally's office was more normal than she expected and Sally looked kind and sincere.
> 2 *Are you married?* and *Do you have any children?*
> 3 Because she mentions two things which don't mean anything to Jane, i.e. the name Caroline and Australia.

> **1.6**   CD1 Track 7
>
> (tapescript in Student's Book on *p.121*)
> **J = Jane, S = Sally**
> J   When I arrived I was shown into Sally's office – which was much more normal than I'd expected. Sally looks like a kind and sincere woman. She says that she inherited from her grandmother the ability to 'see' the past and future of other people. First she asked me a few basic questions – was I married, did I have children and so on. However, her next questions rather surprised me …
> S   Who's Caroline?
> J   I'm afraid I don't know. I don't know anybody called Caroline.
> S   Well, somebody called Caroline is going to have a powerful and positive effect on your finances. Australia is very important in your life.
> J   Is it? I've never been to Australia.
> S   Well, you'll be going there very soon.

- **1.7** Focus on sentences 1–5 in **Part 2**, and give SS time to read them. Play the CD once and get SS to answer true or false together orally. Play the CD again and check answers. Get SS to say why the F sentences are false.

> 1 T (She grew up there.)
> 2 F (He is someone she already knows.)
> 3 T (She's 1m 90.)
> 4 F (It is his brain that will attract her.)
> 5 F (She can't think of anyone who fits the description.)

> **1.7**   CD1 Track 8
>
> (tapescript in Student's Book on *p.121*)
> S   Another place which is very important in your life is Ireland.
> J   Yes, that's true. Ireland *does* play a big role in my life. In fact, I grew up there.
> S   Ireland is a place where you will find answers to a lot of your problems. Look for the Irish connection. I am very very optimistic that an Irish man is going to be 'the one for you'.
> J   Ah, very interesting! What does he look like?
> S   He's very tall.
> J   That's good – I'm 1 metre 90 myself.
> S   And he's highly intelligent; in fact it's his brain that will really attract you to him. He is a distinguished public figure – perhaps a professor?

> J   So when am I going to meet him?
> S   Actually, you already know him. It's just you don't think of him in that way.
> J   I immediately started thinking about all the people I know, but, to be honest, I couldn't think of anyone who fitted the description.

- **1.8** Focus on sentences 1–3 in **Part 3**, and give SS time to read them. Play the CD once and get SS to choose the best option together orally. Play the CD again and check answers.
- Ask SS what they think Jane probably feels at this point (sceptical but perhaps interested in 'the Irish man').

> 1 a   2 b   3 b

> **1.8**   CD1 Track 9
>
> (tapescript in Student's Book on *p.121*)
> J   I decided to ask Sally some questions myself. What about my health?
> S   Let's see, your mother suffer from headaches, doesn't she?
> J   Yes she does, actually. She gets bad headaches.
> S   Well, you'll need to watch out for headaches, and so will your mother, because hers are going to get worse. But in general, you're a healthy woman, and you'll have a long life without any major illnesses, but you must *never* be tempted to have plastic surgery – if you do, it will go horribly wrong.
> J   So far it had all been quite positive, but I wasn't really convinced. It was only when she started talking about my children that I really started listening.
> S   Your son Conor is very like you. He's good with language and he may end up working with words, maybe a poet or a songwriter.
> J   In fact he *does* like words and writing, and last week he won a poetry prize at school.
> S   But your daughter Clara is more like your ex-husband. She's not good with words at all.
> J   It's true! They're both dyslexic. This was beginning to make me wonder…

c ● Now focus on the text 'Tricks of the trade?' and elicit that the title means *tricks or irregular practices associated with certain jobs*. Focus on the task and check SS understand *flatter* (= to say something very positive about sb which may not necessarily be true). Set a time limit for SS to match the titles to the paragraphs. Check answers and elicit / explain / translate the meaning of any problematic vocabulary.

> 1 C   2 D   3 A   4 B

d ● Now play the three parts (1.6, 1.7 and 1.8) of the tapescript again. Pause after each section and ask SS if Sally uses any of these 'tricks'.

> In part 1 she gets information from the client (*Are you married?*, etc.) and uses a name. In part 3 she identifies a common medical problem (headaches).

e ● **1.9** Focus on the task. Then play the CD once. Get SS to check with a partner, and then play the CD again. Check answers.

> She thinks Sally is good at judging people's character but doesn't have any special abilities. However, since she saw Sally, she has met a professor who has invited her to go to Australia – two things which Sally predicted.

1.9   CD1 Track 10

(tapescript in Student's Book on *p.121*)

J I left Sally's office feeling very positive. She gave me a recording of our conversation on a CD, because she said I needed to listen to everything she had told me a few times. When I got home I put on the CD. When I listened again, I realized that for every thing that Sally got right, she got several things wrong. I came to the conclusion then that Sally *doesn't* have any paranormal abilities. She is just very good at judging people's character and makes good guesses about their lives from the information she gets from you. But strangely enough, recently I've been seeing a lot more of an old friend of mine who is a professor. He's not Irish, but he has just invited me to join him on a lecture tour ... of Australia.

- Finally, remind SS that this is a true story and ask them if it has changed their attitude to psychics at all.

Extra support

If there's time, you could get SS to listen again to 1.6 – 1.9 with the tapescripts on *p.121*. Translate / explain any new words or phrases.

f • Do this as an open class question and see if SS have any anecdotes.

7 GRAMMAR auxiliary verbs

a • Focus on the task and give SS a few moments to circle the correct auxiliary verbs. Let them compare with a partner.

b • **1.10** Now play the CD for them to check. Check answers.

1 Is		4 does	
2 does		5 will	
3 doesn't			

1.10   CD1 Track 11

1 Australia is very important in your life.
   <u>Is</u> it? I've never been to Australia.
2 Yes, Ireland <u>does</u> play a big role in my life.
3 Let's see, your mother suffers from headaches, <u>doesn't</u> she?
4 Yes, she <u>does</u>, actually.
5 Well, you'll need to watch out for headaches, and so <u>will</u> your mother.

c • Focus on the task and get SS to do it in pairs. Check answers.

A 4 **B** 2 **C** 3 **D** 1 **E** 5

d • Tell SS to go to **Grammar Bank 1B** on *p.132*. Go through each example and its corresponding rule with the class.

Grammar notes

Auxiliary verbs (*are, is, do, did, will*, etc.) and modal verbs (*can, must*, etc.) have a variety of uses in English and a good command of these will help SS become more proficient speakers. Most of these language rules should be familiar to SS but here they are pulled together.

- **rule 4: echo questions**
Highlight that these are used especially to show interest in what someone is saying. They have a rising intonation (the voice goes up).

- **rule 5: using auxiliaries to show emphasis**
This will probably be new for many SS who may find it strange to see an auxiliary verb used in a positive sentence. This use of auxiliaries is common when we contradict or deny what someone has said or when we want to give extra emphasis, e.g.

A Are you a vegetarian?
B No, I <u>do</u> eat meat but I prefer fish.
A You can't swim, can you?
B I <u>can</u> swim but not very well.

Highlight that SS must stress the auxiliary verb in these sentences.

- **rule 6: question tags**
These probably won't be new to most SS but they are not easy to use with fluency because they require quick manipulation of auxiliaries. In many languages this kind of question is covered by the simpler '..., no?'
When we expect someone to agree with us (*It's hot today, isn't it?*) we use the same falling intonation as in a statement (because it isn't really a question).
When we use a question tag to check information (*The capital of Kenya is Nairobi, isn't it?*) we use the rising intonation of a yes / no question (because it is a real question).

- Focus on the exercises for **1B** on *p.133* and get SS to do them individually or in pairs. Check answers after each exercise.

a	1	isn't	3	didn't	5	does	7	won't
	2	did	4	would	6	Has	8	Can't
b	1	am	4	Don't	7	have	10	don't
	2	isn't	5	Have	8	don't	11	do
	3	is	6	haven't	9	do	12	would

- Tell SS to go back to the main lesson on *p.11*.

8 PRONUNCIATION intonation and sentence rhythm

Pronunciation notes

- **Short answers** [+] and [–] are normally stressed, e.g. *Do you like it? Yes, I <u>do</u>.*

- **Echo questions** are used to show interest in what someone is saying. The auxiliary is stressed and the intonation rises as in a normal question, e.g.
A *I'm a vegetarian.* B <u>*Are you?*</u> The important thing is to encourage SS to use a friendly, interested intonation.

- **Emphatic use of an auxiliary** This is used to contradict what someone has said or emphasize a point, e.g.
A *You didn't lock the door.* B *I <u>did</u> lock the door.* In these sentences the auxiliary is stressed strongly.

- *So (do) I / Neither (do) I.* In these responses the auxiliary is normally <u>unstressed</u> with the strong stress falling on the other two words.

- **Question tags** The intonation native speakers give to a question tag depends on whether we are asking a real question or not. If we genuinely don't know the answer, we tend to use the rising intonation of a question, e.g.

You haven't seen my car keys, have you? (= I don't know if you have seen my car keys). However, if we are not asking a real question but are just making conversation or asking for confirmation of something we already know to be true, our intonation falls and the question tag sounds like a statement, not a question, e.g. *It's a beautiful day, isn't it? (= I know you will agree with me).*

a • **1.11** Focus on the dialogue and the task. Play the CD once. Get SS to compare answers and then play the CD again for SS to check. Check answers.

1.11   CD1 Track 12

A What's your sister like?
B Well, she's rather shy and quiet.
A <u>Is</u> she? So is my brother.
B <u>Isn't</u> your brother a doctor?
A That's right. And your sister works in a bank, <u>doesn't</u> she?
B No, she <u>doesn't</u>. She's a journalist.
A Oh yes, you <u>did</u> tell me, but I forgot. I think they'd probably get on well.
B <u>Do</u> you? But if my sister doesn't talk much and neither does your brother …
A Yes, you're probably right. We <u>won't</u> introduce them then.

---

b • Play the CD again pausing after each line and get SS to copy the rhythm and intonation. You may want to highlight:
  – the interested intonation in the echo question '*Is she?*'
  – the falling intonation in the question tag '*doesn't she?*', where **A** is simply checking information.
 • Give SS a few minutes to practise the dialogues, swapping roles when they get to the end. Monitor and help them with their intonation.

c • **1.12** Focus on the task. Demonstrate first by saying a sentence, preferably with some quite surprising information, for SS to respond with an echo question, e.g. *I don't drink coffee* (to elicit *Don't you?*).
 • Then play the CD pausing after each sentence to elicit the echo question. Encourage SS to use interested intonation. Repeat, this time getting individual SS to respond.

1.12   CD1 Track 13

1 I saw your brother last night. (beep) Did you?
2 I don't like seafood. (beep) Don't you?
3 I'd like to live in Australia. (beep) Would you?
4 I haven't been sleeping well recently. (beep) Haven't you?
5 I'm not very good at cooking. (beep) Aren't you?
6 My father's a doctor. (beep) Is he?
7 I was born in India. (beep) Were you?
8 My mother can't drive. (beep) Can't she?

Extra idea

Get SS to think of three quite surprising / unusual facts about themselves and write them down. They then tell a partner to get them to respond with an echo question.

d • Focus on the task and give SS time to complete the sentences about themselves. Then focus on the first sentence and the response column. Make sure SS are clear that they should first respond with an echo question, and then say if they are the same (*Neither am I.*) or different (*I am.*).
 • Demonstrate the activity first by completing the first two sentences for yourself and getting SS to respond. Then put them in pairs and get them to respond to each other.

Extra support

If you think your SS are going to find the responses difficult, elicit what the alternatives are for the last three sentences and write them on the board, i.e.
Don't you? Neither do I / I do.
Have you? Neither have I / I have.
Is it? So is mine. / Mine isn't.

e • Sit SS in pairs, **A** and **B**, preferably face to face. Tell them to go to **Communication** *You're psychic, aren't you?* **A** on *p.116*, **B** on *p.119*.
 • Go through the instructions and make sure SS know what they have to do. Elicit that when they check their guesses they should be using rising intonation on the question tags unless they are 100% sure of the information.
 • Get feedback to find out who was the most psychic in each pair.

Extra photocopiable activities

Grammar
auxiliary verbs *p.161*
Communicative
A walk through the forest *p.199* (instructions *p.190*)
Song
You gotta be p.233 (instructions *p.231*)

HOMEWORK

Study Link Workbook *pp.7–9*

G present perfect (simple and continuous)
V illness and treatment
P consonant and vowel sounds

You're the doctor!

Lesson plan

In this lesson SS revise and extend their knowledge of the present perfect simple and continuous. These verb forms are problematic for most SS as their use with *for* and *since* is normally expressed with a different form in many other languages. The lesson topic is illness and treatment. In the first half of the lesson the angle is first aid, and SS own knowledge is tested and discussed. In the second half the angle is a controversial article, which argues that certain sorts of stress can actually be good for you. SS expand their vocabulary of medical words to describe symptoms, illnesses and treatment. The pronunciation focus is on consonant and vowel sounds, and how phonetics in a dictionary can help you to pronounce words correctly.

Optional lead-in (books closed)

- Mime that you have a headache, and elicit and write on the board
  I have a headache.

- Then ask SS what other parts of the body can be used as a noun with *ache*, and elicit the following sentences:
  I have a stomach-ache.
  I have backache.
  I have toothache.
  I have earache.

- Highlight that *a* is used only with *headache* and *stomach-ache.*

1 SPEAKING & VOCABULARY illness and treatment

a • Books open. Focus on the quiz *You're the doc!* and the task. Give SS, in pairs, a minute to read about the two situations and choose a, b, or c.

- Ask SS what they think the highlighted words mean, and explain / translate / mime, or show from the illustrations.

  nosebleed = blood is coming out of your nose
  blood pressure = the pressure of blood as it travels round your body; it can be high or low
  pinch = take sth between your thumb and first finger and squeeze hard
  burns = injures by fire
  hurts = causes physical pain
  blisters = swellings on the surface of the skin that are filled with liquid, e.g. which you often get on your feet if your shoes are too tight
  antiseptic cream = cream that helps to prevent infection

- Then get feedback to see which answers SS chose, but don't tell them yet if they are right or wrong.

b • Tell SS to go to **Communication** *You're the doc!* on *p.116* and check their answers. Get feedback to see how many SS got the right answers.

c • Tell SS to go to **Vocabulary Bank** *Illness and treatment* on *p.147*. Get them to do section **1 Symptoms** individually or in pairs. Check answers and drill pronunciation where necessary. Some of the words may be similar in SS' L1, e.g. *diarrhoea*, but the pronunciation is likely to be quite different.

a	**1**	a blister.	**7**	Her back hurts / aches.
	2	a rash.	**8**	She's sneezing.
	3	a cough.	**9**	His ankle is swollen.
	4	a pain (in his chest).	**10**	He's being sick.
	5	a headache.	**11**	Her finger is bleeding.
	6	a temperature.		

- Highlight that *cough* is both a noun and a verb.

b 1 B **2** F **3** A **4** C **5** D **6** E

- Highlight that *ache, hurt* and *pain* can all be used to describe the same thing, e.g. *I have a pain in my back.* / *My back hurts.* / *My back aches.* There is a slight difference between *ache* and *hurt* – *ache* = a continuous, dull pain; *hurts* = often stronger (especially sudden) pain, e.g. *Ouch! That hurts! ache* is used both as a noun and a verb whereas *hurt* is generally used as a verb.

- Highlight that *be sick* = vomit. *Sick* is also sometimes used as a synonym for *ill*. Also highlight that *swallow* means to make food, drink, etc. go down your throat into your stomach.

Extra challenge

If you didn't do the optional lead-in, tell SS which other words can be combined with *ache* and elicit *earache, toothache, stomach-ache* and *backache*, and drill the pronunciation.

- Focus on section **2 Illnesses and injuries** and give SS time to do the exercises. Check answers and drill pronunciation where necessary.

1 I **2** E **3** H **4** G **5** A **6** B **7** C **8** D
9 K **10** J **11** F

- Now focus on section **3 Treatment**. Give SS a few moments to write the words in the **treatment** column. Check answers and drill pronunciation where necessary. Check also that SS understand, and can pronounce, the words in bold in each sentence.

- Elicit / point out that *medicine* is usually uncountable, *rest* = to relax and not do anything, *a specialist* is a doctor who is an expert in a particular area, *a scan* = a medical test where an image of the inside of the body is produced on a computer screen, *stitches* = pieces of thread used to close a cut, *a needle* is a thin piece of metal on the end of a syringe, *a wound* is a general word for an injury on the body, especially when there is a cut or hole.

1 medicine
2 rest
3 specialist
4 X-ray (**scan** = a medical test where an image of the inside of the body is produced on a computer screen)
5 stitches
6 injection
7 bandage (**wound** = a general word for an injury on the body, especially when there is a cut or hole)
8 operation

- Finally, focus on the instruction 'Can you remember the words on this page? Test yourself or a partner'.

Testing yourself

For **Symptoms a)**, SS can cover the words and look at the pictures, and for **Symptoms b)** they can cover sentences 1–6, look at A–F and try to remember 1–6. In **Illnesses and injuries** they can do the same thing with A–K, and in **Treatment** they can cover the **treatment** column and try to remember the words.

Testing a partner

See **Testing a partner** *p.20*.

Study Link SS can find more practice of these words and phrases on the MultiROM and on the *New English File Upper-intermediate* website.

- Tell SS to go back to the main lesson on *p.12*.

2 PRONUNCIATION consonant and vowel sounds

Pronunciation notes

At this level you should be encouraging SS to check the pronunciation of new words in their dictionary. SS who have used previous levels of *New English File* should be fairly confident with phonetic symbols. If your SS are new to the series, you will need to explain to them that the sound pictures show the phonetic symbols, and give a clear example of a word with the target sound to help them to remember the pronunciation of the symbol. There is one for each of the 44 sounds of English. SS will find the chart and more example words in the **Sound Bank** *p.158*.

a • **1.13** Focus on the information box and go through it with SS. Then focus on words 1–6 and give SS, in pairs, a few moments to practise saying them. Then elicit the words from individual SS, and finally play the CD for them to check. If SS are having problems with the pronunciation, play the CD again, and pause after each word for SS to repeat.

1.13		CD1 Track 14
1 cough	4	bruise
2 heart	5	blood
3 asthma	6	diarrhoea

b • Now focus on the four sound pictures and elicit the words and consonant sounds (shower /ʃ/; jazz /dʒ/; chess /tʃ/; keys /k/). Then give SS time to put the words in the right columns. Get them to compare with a partner. Check that SS know the meaning of *choking* (= unable to breathe because the passage to your lungs is blocked and you cannot get enough air).

c • **1.14** Play the CD for SS to check their answers. Then play it again pausing after each word for SS to repeat.

1.14			CD1 Track 15
/ʃ/	infection	pressure	rash
	specialist	unconscious	
/dʒ/	allergy	bandage	GP
/tʃ/	check-up	choking	temperature
/k/	ache	ankle	chemist	stomach

d • Now tell SS to go to the **Sound Bank** on *p.160*. Explain that here they can find all the sounds of English and their phonetic symbols and also the typical spellings for these sounds plus some more irregular ones.

- Focus on the four sounds that SS have just been working on and the typical spellings. Highlight that they have to be careful with *ch* because although it is usually pronounced /tʃ/, it can also be /k/ as in *chemist*, or occasionally /ʃ/ as in *machine*.

Study Link SS can find more practice of English sounds on the MultiROM and also on the *New English File Upper-intermediate* website.

e • Focus on the task and give SS a few moments to ask and answer in pairs. The focus here is on recycling the vocabulary rather than getting involved in a conversation about illnesses.

See **Vocabulary Bank** *p.147*

Extra idea

If you have a doctor in the class, you could get him / her to be the authority for the answers to 2.

3 READING & LISTENING

a • Focus on the texts and photos and divide SS into pairs, **A** and **B**. Set a time limit for them each to read their article. Monitor and help with any vocabulary they are having problems with while they read, and encourage them to use the photos to help.

b • Focus on the task and elicit the meaning of *first aid* (= simple medical treatment that is given to sb before a doctor comes). Encourage SS to communicate their story using their own words, and not just read it aloud. Monitor and help.

c • When both SS are clear about the two stories, tell them to decide who they think did the right thing and why. Elicit ideas but don't tell them the answer yet.

Extra support

Elicit the two stories from the class, and mime the actions that Trisha and Peter's mother did. Then do the discussion as an open class question.

d • **1.15** Now tell SS they are going to find out what happened. Focus on question 1. Play the CD once. Get SS to check answers and then play it again. Check answers.

1 When Trisha put her arms around Mrs Johnson's waist and pulled hard inwards and upwards the piece of steak came out. Trisha did exactly the right thing.

- Ask SS if anybody heard the name of the technique Trisha used (the Heimlich manoeuvre – you may need to write it on the board), and also where Trisha learnt first aid from and what she thinks about learning first aid.

1.15 CD1 Track 16

(tapescript in Student's Book on *p.121*)
When I saw the lady's face, I knew it was really serious. Her face was starting to turn blue. I put my arms around her waist and I pulled hard in and up three times, and the piece of steak came out. Then I just put my arm round the lady and gave her a hug.
I knew exactly what to do because before I started to work as a television presenter, I used to be a flight attendant. We were taught a lot about first aid. The technique I used is called the Heimlich manoeuvre and it's what you should do when someone is choking. I must admit I was a bit embarrassed by all the attention I got in the restaurant and then the next day the story was in all the newspapers. But I'm very glad I was there to help. And maybe this story will make people think about learning first aid. I really think it's something which should be taught at school. It's so important!

- **1.16** Now focus on question 2. Play the CD once. Get SS to check answers and then play it again. Check answers.

2 Peter started coughing after his mother managed to touch the tomato with her fingers, and the tomato came out. His mother did the right thing hitting him on the back, but should not have put her fingers down his throat.

- Ask SS why she shouldn't have put her fingers down his throat (she could have pushed the tomato further down), and what she should have done (called an ambulance).

1.16 CD1 Track 17

(tapescript in Student's Book on *p.121*)
I knew I was hurting Peter, but I carried on pushing my fingers down his throat. I managed to touch the tomato with two of my fingers and I was able to move it a little. That was enough – Peter started coughing and the tomato came out.
But I was very lucky. Afterwards, I found out that my ignorance of first aid had nearly killed my son. Hitting Peter on the back was OK, but putting my fingers down his throat was a big mistake. I could have pushed the tomato even further down his throat and he could have died. I'd made every mistake possible and I nearly killed him because of my ignorance. I should have called an ambulance immediately, because I don't know first aid, and the ambulance staff would have told me exactly what to do … and what not to do.

- Finally, ask SS what they would have done if they had been with someone who was choking.

Extra support

If there's time, you could go through the text with the class, highlighting useful expressions and eliciting / explaining the meaning of new words and phrases. You could also look at the tapescripts on *p.121* so that the SS can see exactly what they understood / didn't understand.

4 SPEAKING

- Focus on the **GET IT RIGHT** box and remind SS that when they don't know a word there are strategies they can use to carry on, e.g. paraphrasing or even miming.
- Then focus on the flow chart. Give SS time to interview each other. Monitor and help, encouraging SS to paraphrase if they are stuck for a word.
- Get feedback about SS' experiences of first aid, and check answers to the last three questions.

a If the sting is on the body, put ice on it for about ten minutes. If the person has been stung on the mouth or throat, give him / her an ice cube to suck. If the person starts to show an allergic reaction, call an ambulance or go to A & E.
b Call an ambulance or go to A & E. While you are waiting for help, cover the person with a coat or blanket. Open the person's mouth and check breathing.
c If the person is conscious, help them into a comfortable position and ask what he / she has taken. Call an ambulance or go to A & E. Do not try to make the person vomit. Look for any empty containers and give them to the doctors or ambulance crew.

5 GRAMMAR present perfect (simple and continuous)

a ● Exercises highlighted as **Check what you know** provide some useful revision of what SS should know before dealing with the new grammar point. If the majority of the class have problems with this exercise, we suggest you get them to look at the corresponding Workbook exercise and go through the basic rules before starting the new grammar.
- Focus on the highlighted phrases and give SS time to correct the mistakes in pairs. Check answers.

1 A ✓ B ✗ I broke my leg …
2 ✗ … has your uncle been …
3 ✓
4 ✗ Have you been …
5 ✗ I've cut …
6 ✗ I've known …

- If SS are having problems, go to the Workbook *p.11*. Go through the rules and do the exercise.

b ● **1.17** **New grammar** indicates that SS are about to move onto something new for their level. Focus on the jokes and the instructions. Highlight that often the best way to choose between two words or verb forms is to use your instinct, and go for what sounds / feels right. SS at this level have been exposed passively to a lot more grammar than they have actively studied, and will often have a feel for what is right without being able to explain why.
- Give SS time to choose the right form. Then play the CD once for SS to check. Check the correct answers.

See **bold** verbs in tapescript

1.17 CD1 Track 18

Patient Doctor, my son **has swallowed** my pen, what should I do?
Doctor Use a pencil until I get there.

Doctor You look exhausted!
Patient Yes. **I've been running** after a cat.
Doctor After a cat?
Patient Yes, I think I'm a dog, doctor.
Doctor I see. How long **has this been going on** for?
Patient Since I was a little puppy.
Doctor OK. Just lie down here on the couch and we'll talk about it.
Patient I can't!
Doctor Why not?
Patient I'm not allowed on the furniture.

Patient **Have they sent** you the results of my tests yet?
Doctor Yes. The news isn't good, I'm afraid.
Patient How long have I got to live, doctor?
Doctor Ten…
Patient Ten WHAT? Months? Weeks?
Doctor Nine, eight, seven, six…

c ● Tell SS to go to **Grammar Bank 1C** on *p.132*. Go through each example and its corresponding rule with the class.

Grammar notes

● **present perfect simple (rules 1–6) and continuous (rules 1–3)**
SS at this level should already have a reasonable grasp of the uses referenced here for the two tenses.

● **present perfect simple or continuous? (rules 1 and 2)**
SS may not be clear about when both tenses are possible, e.g. *How long have you lived / have you been living here?* (i.e. **action verbs** with How long? + *for* and *since*). Highlight that the present perfect continuous emphasizes both the continuity and / or temporary nature of an action, e.g. *I've been waiting for you for two hours!* (= more common than *I've waited…*)

● *for* and *since*. SS should be very familiar with how these words are used (*for* = period of time, *since* = point of time) but you may want to highlight that *for* is omitted with *all day / morning / night*, etc., e.g. *I've been working all morning* NOT *… ~~for all morning~~*.

● Focus on the exercises for **1C** on *p.133* and get SS to do them individually or in pairs. Check answers after each exercise.

a	1 ✓	b	1 've known
	2 has phoned		2 Have you been
	3 they've been playing		running?
	4 He hasn't seen		3 hasn't done
	5 I've never met		4 they've moved
	6 ✓		5 have Daisy and Adam
	7 I've been tidying		been going out
	8 He's just left		6 haven't had
	9 have you had		7 've been walking
	10 has broken		8 Have you been eating

● Tell SS to go back to the main lesson on *p.14*.

d ● This is an oral grammar practice activity. Focus on the task and questions. Elicit that the first question will be in the present simple or continuous, but the second one will be either the present perfect simple or continuous. Point out that in question 4 they should choose between *school, work*, or *university* as appropriate.
● Check that SS know what verb forms to use but encourage them not to write down the questions but just use the prompts.

Extra support

Give SS time to think what the questions are. Then demonstrate the activity by eliciting the questions from SS and answering them yourself. You could then write the questions on the board.

1 Do you drink much water? How many glasses have you drunk today?
2 Do you do any physical exercise? What? How long have you been doing it (playing tennis, going to a gym, etc.)?
3 Do you eat a lot of fruit and vegetables? How many portions have you had today?
4 Do you walk to school, etc.? How far have you walked today?
5 Do you smoke? How long have you been smoking? How many cigarettes have you had today?
6 Are you taking any vitamins at the moment? How long have you been taking them?
7 How many hours do you sleep a night? Have you been sleeping well recently?
8 Are you allergic to anything? Have you ever had a serious allergic reaction?

● Give SS time to ask and answer the questions in pairs. Monitor and correct any mistakes with the present perfect.

6 READING

a ● Do this as an open class question and elicit ideas. Accept all reasonable possibilities, e.g. sleeping problems, headaches, stomach problems, high blood pressure, etc.

Extra support

You may want to pre-teach the word *cell* (= the smallest unit of living matter that can exist on its own) to help SS to understand the text.

b ● Focus on the instructions and give SS time to read the situations and choose the three they think are most stressful. Get them to compare with a partner. Get feedback.
c ● Now set a time limit for SS to read the article once and tick the activities which are bad for you. Check answers and find out if they were in the SS' top three.

SS should have ticked *Being stuck in a traffic jam …,* and *Looking after a family member who has a chronic illness.*

● Then ask SS what the article says about the others.

They are examples of 'good stress'.

d ● Focus on the task. Get SS to do it individually and then compare with a partner, and justify their choices. Highlight that two of the options are true but SS must decide which one is the main idea of the paragraph. Check answers.

> 1 b 2 c 3 b 4 a

e ● SS now focus on some more medical words and phrases which appear in the article. Explain that the number in brackets after the definitions refers to which paragraph the word is in. Elicit the first one from the class and write it on the board (*cut down*). Then give SS time to find the others.

f ● Check answers and elicit the correct pronunciation from the SS.

Extra idea

You could give a dictionary to a student and ask him / her to look up the trickier words (e.g. disease, muscles) to check the pronunciation by looking at the phonetics and then trying to say it correctly.

> 1 cut down
> 2 chronic /krɒnɪk/
> 3 beneficial /benɪfɪʃl/
> 4 strengthen /streŋθn/
> 5 cells /selz/
> 6 damage /dæmɪdʒ/
> 7 disease /dɪziːz/
> 8 harmful
> 9 muscles /mʌslz/

● You may want to explain the difference between *illness* and *disease*.
illness (n) = the general term for the state of being unwell, e.g. *My uncle has a serious illness.*
disease (n) = is used for infectious illnesses, e.g. *malaria*, and for illnesses affecting the organs, e.g. *She has heart disease.*

g ● Either get SS to discuss the questions in pairs, or elicit answers from the whole class.

● Finally, tell SS to go to *Phrasal verbs in context File 1* on *p.157* and complete the phrasal verbs which have come up in this File. (Answers *p.155*)

Extra photocopiable activities

Grammar
present perfect simple and continuous *p.162*
Communicative
Doctor, doctor *p.200* (instructions *p.191*)
Vocabulary
Split crossword *p.223* (instructions *p.221*)

HOMEWORK

Study Link Workbook *pp.10–12*

Lesson plan

This is the first in a series of seven Colloquial English lessons where SS practise listening to completely unscripted authentic spoken English. Each of these lessons picks up on one of the topics of the preceding File, and consists of a studio interview with a person who has some expertise related to the topic, and then some short street interviews where members of the public give their opinions on an aspect of the same topic. These lessons give SS opportunity to practise listening to the sort of English they will hear if they go to an English-speaking country. The level of challenge in these listening exercises is higher than in the listening exercises in the A–C lessons, something which should be pointed out to SS. Encourage them to feel pleased with themselves if they can get the 'gist' of these interviews, rather than a detailed understanding. We suggest that teachers let SS have a final listen while reading the tapescripts. This will let them see what they did or didn't understand, and help to develop their awareness of features of spoken English, e.g. running words together, leaving out pronouns, etc. In both parts of the lesson there is a focus on colloquial expressions used by the speakers.

In the first part of this lesson the person interviewed is Frank Clifford, an astrologist and palmist, who teaches at the London School of Astrology (www.astrolodge.co.uk) and is the author of several books on astrology and palmistry. In the second part, people are asked what their star signs are, if they read horoscopes, and if they think their star sign has an influence on their personality.

Study Link These lessons are on the *New English File Upper-intermediate* DVD / Video which can be used instead of the class CD (See Introduction *p.9*). SS can get more practice on the MultiROM, which contains more of the short street interviews with a listening task and tapescripts.

Optional lead-in (books closed)

● Ask SS if they can remember who Sally was in lesson **1B**, and elicit that she was a psychic. Then ask SS what other kinds of fortune-tellers there are, e.g. clairvoyant, palmist, astrologer. Now tell SS that they are going to hear a real interview with Frank Clifford, who is a well-known astrologer and palmist.

THE INTERVIEW

a ● Books open. Focus on the photos and get SS to tell you what they can see.

> A man (Frank Clifford), a (birth) chart and a palm.

● Now focus on the task and on the glossary. Go through it with the class eliciting from them how to pronounce the words and phrases. Highlight that *scared the life out of me* is an idiomatic expression, and that we say *to **put** a curse **on** someone.*

b ● **1.18** Focus on the task. Put SS in pairs and give them time to read the questions. Encourage SS not to write anything down when they listen the first time. They should listen and try to get the gist of what he is saying, and then discuss the questions with their partner.

● Play the CD once (**Part 1**). Give SS time to discuss the questions and tell each other what they understood. Then play the CD once or twice more. This time SS might want to jot down things they heard to help them remember the answers to the questions. Check answers.

> 1 Their temperament, character, and emotional needs.
> 2 Their character, their past, and possible future events.
> 3 They can help people to influence their own future, and not feel that it is an unalterable destiny.
> 4 No, he wouldn't because he isn't a doctor. (However, if someone is already ill, he might discuss this.)

1.18   CD1 Track 19

(tapescript in Student's Book on *p.121*)
I = interviewer, F = Frank Clifford
I Frank Clifford is an astrologer and palmist. What does an astrologer do?
F An astrologer will take your date, place, and time of birth, construct a map of the heavens, a horoscope, that will look at temperament, character, emotional needs and a number of other different factors.
I What does being a palmist mean?
F Well, as a palmist is quite different from being an astrologer, a palmist will look at your hands as they are now of course, or he may do a print and have a look at what is being shown in the hands now, but whereas astrology is a birth chart set up, a horoscope set up for somebody's birth moment, the hands are your living hands so they've developed and grown with you of course, so they reflect where you are today and what you do and palmists will read, again, character, perhaps past events, possible future events from the hand.
I So can astrologers and palmists predict people's future?
F A lot of astrologers and palmists would say that it's not really about reading somebody's future, it's about understanding where they are today and being able to understand who they are, where they are today, and future possibilities and I think people should come to a palmist or astrologer not to be told about an unalterable destiny or future, but to be told or given tools enough to make it themselves, and be very proactive in that area themselves. So it's our job really to encourage people to live their own lives and decide their own future, not feel as though it's written anywhere and that they have nothing to do or say about the outcome.
I If you saw on someone's hand that they were going to have a serious illness, would you tell them?
F I'm not a doctor so I wouldn't go there. I certainly wouldn't talk about anything medical. But if somebody comes and they've had cancer or they're in the process of being treated for an illness, that's something we might discuss, but it's certainly something I wouldn't predict, because I don't necessarily believe in making predictions.

Extra challenge

You could use the tapescript above to elicit more detailed answers from SS.

c ● **1.19** Focus on the task and play the CD once (**Part 2**). Give SS time to discuss the questions and what they understood. Then play the CD once or twice more. Check answers.

> 1 He suggests choosing one who has been recommended.
> 2 The palmist told him that he would be married at 21 and that his partner would die. (This didn't happen but it made him want to learn more about palmistry.)
> 3 All kinds of people, e.g. sportspeople, politicians, people in the media. More women than men.
> 4 Men are more interested in palmistry because it's more physical and open and they think horoscopes are more for women.
> 5 He doesn't do this. He prefers to just live his life and experience his future.

1.19   CD1 Track 20

(tapescript in Student's Book on *p.122*)
I How should people choose which astrologer or which palm reader to see?
F Well, I would recommend going to somebody who has been recommended to you, there are a lot of people out there who, a lot of people doing a genuine job, but will talk about things that no palmist really should talk about, like health matters, as I've spoken about, death, other illnesses, things that take away somebody's ability or right to choose. The reason that I got into palmistry was at the age of seventeen, I was told by a palmist that I would be married at 21 and then my partner would die, which scared the life out of me at the time, and I felt I had this curse on my back, and so I thought I'd learn this subject and understand what on earth she was talking about and I realized that what she was looking at was a very big 'if', a very big possibility rather than a probability and it never happened.
I What kind of people come to see you?
F A lot of people would expect bored housewives and people with nothing better to do, or too much money, more money than sense, to come, but in fact the truth is you tend to get all sorts of people from every type or walk of life. I've had sportspeople, politicians, people in the media, in every type of profession you can think of, male, female. Usually it tends to be more women, you tend to get more men looking at palmistry because it's perhaps more physical and open and they feel that … some men tell me they believe more in the hand rather than a horoscope, because a horoscope is something that women read in their magazines or newspapers.
I Do you ever look at your own future?
F Well, rather than try to look at my own future or predict it I try and have it, I try and experience it. I don't think most astrologers or palmists actually do predict or try to predict what's going on in their life. They just live it from day to day as anyone else would, but they try to live it with some understanding and some knowledge or at least some meaning of why we're here and what's happening at this time.

d • **1.20** This exercise gives SS intensive listening practice in deciphering phrases where words are often run together, and introduces them to some common expressions often used in spoken English. Focus on the phrases and give SS time to read them. Play the CD, pausing after the first phrase and replaying it as necessary. Elicit the missing words, and then the meaning of the whole phrase. Repeat for the other five phrases.

> 1 **have a look** at (= another way of saying *look at*)
> 2 **live their own lives** (= make their own decisions about their lives)
> 3 **wouldn't go there** (= informal way of saying *wouldn't do it*)
> 4 **what on earth** (= informal and stronger way of saying *what*)
> 5 **nothing better to do** (= people who don't have anything interesting to do)
> 6 **all sorts of people** (= many different kinds of people)

1.20   CD1 Track 21

1 …or he may do a print and have a look at what is being shown in the hands now…
2 So it's our job really to encourage people to live their own lives
3 I'm not a doctor so I wouldn't go there.
4 …so I thought I'd learn this subject and understand what on earth she was talking about.
5 A lot of people would expect bored housewives, and people with nothing better to do.
6 …but in fact the truth is you tend to get all sorts of people.

---

e • Tell SS to go to *p.121* and to look at the tapescript for the interview. Play the CD (**Part 1** and **Part 2**) again, and tell SS to read and listen at the same time. Deal with any vocabulary problems and get feedback from SS on what parts they found hard to understand and why, e.g. speed of speech, elision, pronunciation, etc.

• Finally, focus on the question. You could also ask SS *Did anything he said make you change your opinion of astrologers and palmists?* Get SS to answer in pairs or as a whole class. Then get feedback from the whole class.

IN THE STREET

a • **1.21** Focus on the photos of the people and elicit impressions (e.g. *How old do they look? What job do you think they do?*, etc.) Tell SS that they were all interviewed in Covent Garden, a busy shopping area in Central London.

• Focus on the task. First elicit the pronunciation of the different star signs. Then remind SS that for each speaker they need to write their number next to a star sign, and tick it if they believe strongly that star signs have an influence on people's personality.

• Play the CD once. Then play it again pausing after each speaker to check answers.

> 1 (Cherry)   Capricorn
> 2 (Miles)   Scorpio
> 3 (Mike)   Aries ✓
> 4 (Theresa)   Capricorn ✓
> 5 (Kurt)   Aries

1.21   CD1 Track 22

(tapescript in Student's Book on *p.122*)
I = interviewer, C = Cherry, M = Miles, Mk = Mike, T = Theresa, K = Kurt

Cherry
I What's your star sign?
C Capricorn.
I Do you ever read your horoscope?
C Occasionally, but not because I particularly believe in them, but just because they're there. And it's quite fun.
I Do you think someone's star sign has an influence on their personality?
C Not particularly, no. I don't really think so.

Miles
I What's your star sign?
M Scorpio, I had to think about that one.
I Do you ever read your horoscope?
M No, never.
I Do you think someone's star sign has an influence on their personality?
M Well, possibly. I'm not a great believer I have to say, although perhaps the time of year someone is born may vaguely reflect on their characteristics. But I think it's pretty minimal the effect, to be perfectly honest.

Mike
I What's your star sign?
MK Aries
I Do you ever read your horoscope?
MK Oh, I'm a big believer in horoscopes. Some people say it's quite sad, but I tend to live every day on a horoscope. See if it ever comes true. It doesn't really, but it's just nice to know.
I Do you think someone's star sign has an influence on their personality?
MK Yes, I think it does. You can definitely tell with some star signs. You can definitely tell their, sort of personality straight away. It does play a big role, I think.

Theresa
I What's your star sign?
T I was born under the star sign of Capricorn, so I'm an old goat, basically.
I Do you ever read your horoscope?
T I do occasionally, yes.
I Do you think someone's star sign has an influence on their personality?
T Well, I think it has an influence on mine because Capricorn is the goat and goats are always climbing onwards and upwards and that really is very much me.

Kurt
I What's your star sign?
K Aries, Aries.
I Do you ever read your horoscope?
K No.
I Do you think someone's star sign has an influence on their personality?
K None, whatsoever, not unless they read it first and then change their personality to match.

b ● Focus on the task and give SS time to go through the sentences. Check SS understand *sceptical* in question 4 (= doubting that something is true). Play the CD once. Get SS to compare what they think. Play it again if necessary and check answers.

1	Theresa	4	Kurt
2	Mike	5	Cherry
3	Miles		

c ● **1.22** Focus on the phrases and give SS time to read them. Play the CD, pausing after the first phrase and replaying it as necessary. Elicit the missing word, and then the meaning of the whole phrase. Repeat for the other three phrases.

1 **Not particularly.** (= not especially)
2 I think it's **pretty minimal.** (= quite minimal; *pretty* = informal way of saying *quite*)
3 You can **definitely tell** (their personality straight away) (= you can know what their personality is immediately. *Tell* is often used colloquially meaning *know*, e.g. *It's often difficult to tell if someone is asleep or not. Straightaway* means *immediately.*)
4 **None whatsoever.** (= none at all)

1.22   CD1 Track 23
1 Not particularly, no.
2 I think it's pretty minimal.
3 You can definitely tell their, sort of, personality straight away.
4 None whatsoever.

---

d ● Tell SS to go to *p.122* and to look at the tapescript for **IN THE STREET.** Play the CD again and tell SS to read and listen at the same time. Deal with any vocabulary problems and get feedback from SS on what parts they found hard to understand and why, e.g. speed of speech, pronunciation, etc.
● Finally, focus on the three questions that the interviewer asked the people, and get SS to interview each other in pairs. Then get feedback from the whole class.

HOMEWORK

Study Link **Workbook** *p.13*

1 **WRITING: AN INFORMAL EMAIL / LETTER**

Lesson plan

This is the first of seven Writing lessons; there is one at the end of each File. In today's world of email communication, being able to write in English is an important skill for many SS. We suggest that you go through the exercises in class but set the actual writing (the last activity) for homework, although you may want SS to do the planning in class.

In this lesson SS consolidate the language they have learnt in **File 1** by writing an informal email.

a ● Focus on the information box and highlight that this is the main difference between writing an email and an informal letter.
● Now focus on the email and the task. First ask SS to read it quickly, ignoring the mistakes for the moment, and check comprehension by asking a few questions, e.g. *Why was Chris late replying?* (He was ill) *What does he do?* (He's a student), etc.
● Give SS time to correct the mistakes and then check answers, asking SS what kind of mistake each is.

havent (punctuation) **haven't**
temprature (spelling) **temperature**
since (grammar) **for**
Luckly (spelling) **Luckily**
Anything exciting (punctuation) **Anything exciting?**
are (grammar) **is**
record-company (punctuation) **record company**
a good news (grammar) **some good news**
may (punctuation) **May**
recomend (spelling) **recommend**
siteseeing (spelling) **sightseeing**
you'll can show (grammar) **you'll be able to show**

b ● Focus on the instructions and get SS to underline or highlight the phrases.

I haven't been in touch.
I've been catching up on my emails.
Please give my regards to your family.

c ● Now focus on the **Useful language** box and give SS time to complete it. Point out that many of the expressions are in Chris's email. Check answers.

1	for	5	to	9	for	12	care
2	to	6	to	10	forward	13	Best
3	not	7	with	11	Give / Send	14	PS
4	hope	8	are / get				

WRITE an email

Go through the instructions and get SS to do the first two parts of **PLAN** the content. Check answers.

They need to answer the following questions:

How are you?
What have you been doing? Anything exciting?
How are your family?
Could you recommend a hotel?
Do you think you'll be able to show me around?

They should probably respond to the following:

> I've been ill.
> My brother Ian has just started his new job…
> I have some good news.

Either get SS to complete the planning and write the email in class (set a time limit of about 20 minutes) or get them to complete the planning and write the email for homework.

If SS do the writing in class, get them to swap their emails with another student to read and check for mistakes before you collect them all in.

Test and Assessment CD-ROM

CEF Assessment materials
File 1 Writing task assessment guidelines

The File finishes with two pages of revision. The first page, **What do you remember?**, revises the grammar, vocabulary, and pronunciation. These exercises can be done individually or in pairs, in class or at home, depending on the needs of your SS and the class time available. If SS do them in class, check which SS are still having problems, or any areas which need further revision. The second page, **What can you do?**, presents SS with a series of skills-based challenges. First, there is a reading text (which is of a slightly higher level than those in the File) and two listening exercises. Finally, there is a speaking activity which measures SS' ability to use the language of the File orally. We suggest that you use some or all of these activities according to the needs of your class.

GRAMMAR

a	1 about	4 Have
	2 did	5 been
	3 does	
b	1 a 2 b 3 c 4 a 5 b	

VOCABULARY

a 1 wise – the others describe negative characteristics
2 insincere – the others describe positive characteristics
3 blister – it's a symptom but the others are illnesses
4 A & E – it's part of a hospital but the others are people

b	1 to	3 in	5 for
	2 at	4 to	
c	1 forgetful	3 reliable	5 sensitive
	2 ambitious	4 moody	
d	1 bleed	4 bad-tempered	
	2 swollen	5 bossy	
	3 bandage	6 arrogant	

PRONUNCIATION

a 1 headache (it's /k/) 3 flu (it's /uː/)   5 earache (it's /ɪə/)
2 bossy (it's /s/)   4 cough (it's /ɒ/)
b <u>a</u>rrogant, imma<u>ture</u>, in<u>jec</u>tion, a<u>ll</u>ergic, <u>spe</u>cialist

CAN YOU **UNDERSTAND THIS TEXT?**

a 1 c 2 b 3 a 4 a 5 c
b **correspondence** = the letters / emails you send and receive
genres = particular styles or types of something
family ties = strong connections between members of a family
random = chosen without deciding in advance, or without any regular pattern
on the spot = at that exact moment, immediately

CAN YOU **UNDERSTAND THESE PEOPLE?**

a 1 b 2 a 3 c 4 b 5 a
b 1 Because she was having a lot of problems with her fiancé.
2 That the problems would be resolved.
3 No, it wasn't.
4 That the psychic wasn't very professional.
5 Because Alice believes that psychics can really see into the future.
6 She told Alice she would have a new job.
7 She didn't get depressed when she lost her job.
8 Not to depend too much on psychics.

1.23   CD1 Track 24

1 A So how did you meet Tony?
  B Well, I'd tried lots of things, I mean I'd been on my own for two years – since the divorce – and I felt it was time to start dating again so I used an Internet site and I even tried speed dating, but the men I met weren't really my type, though I quite liked one or two of them. Then I went to a dinner given by a friend of mine and she'd invited Tony as a 'spare man', you know, as a sort of blind date for me and we really hit it off right from the start.

2 A So what was she like?
  B Well, she wasn't at all what I'd expected from what she'd written on her web page – I mean, I'm not saying she was lying exactly, but she made out that she was really bubbly and lively – you know a real extrovert, but in fact I had to do all the talking and it was quite hard work. She hardly opened her mouth all evening.

3 A So what time will you be coming?
  B Well, I think I'll have finished work by around 6.00, so I should be able to get the 6.42 train, which gets me in at about 7.15. So if I take a taxi from the station, I should be there about 7.30.
  A Actually, there's a good bus service now so you don't need to get a taxi if you don't want to. It goes every 15 minutes and it stops really near our house.
  B Oh right. Well, I'll do that then. So expect me between half past and quarter to.
  A Perfect.

4 A Right Mr Strong, I think you've probably got the flu virus that's going around at the moment.
  B Flu? But I haven't had a temperature. I've just had this awful headache.
  A Yes, but not everybody gets a temperature. In fact, a headache's the most common symptom. So just carry on with the painkillers and you should feel better in a day or two.
  B So I don't need any antibiotics?
  A No, this is a virus, so antibiotics wouldn't do any good. Drink lots of fluids and take the painkillers up to three times a day. If you haven't started feeling better by Monday, then come back and see me.
  B Well, I hope I won't have to. Thank you very much doctor.

5 A So it's Gibson moving into space and it's a superb pass to Lambert who's on his own and he's past the Chelsea defence and…oh no, he's been brought down by Marsh, and that was a really hard tackle. In fact, it looks as if he's badly hurt. Yes, they're coming on with the stretcher. I think it's his knee.

  B No, I don't think it was his knee. If you look at the replay – there, look how he falls – it looks like the ankle to me, I think it's a ligament that's gone. If it's an ankle ligament, he could be out for six months.
  A That's a bit pessimistic, don't you think? I'd say more like three, if it is his ankle that is.
  B They're taking him off now, and I imagine we'll hear something as soon as the doctor's seen him. But he won't be playing in the return match on Wednesday night that's for sure.
  A Not unless we've both got it wrong and it's not a serious injury. But that looks like really bad news for United not to have him for the return match.

1.24   CD1 Track 25

A I went to see a psychic about ten years ago because I was having a lot of problems with my boyfriend, my fiancé in fact. I was supposed to be getting married the following year and I wanted to know what kind of future I was going to have with this man. I had serious doubts about him as a person and in fact I was thinking of leaving him. The psychic read my future in Tarot cards and she told me that the problems I was having with this man would be resolved. She told me to stay with him and that we would be very happy together. So, I got married – and it was a disaster. My new husband ran off with my best friend after six months. I am divorced now. Of course, I wish that I hadn't gone to see this woman who obviously had no special powers whatsoever. I should have trusted my own instincts, which were not to marry my fiancé. In my experience, clairvoyants just tell you what they think you want to hear. They aren't seeing it at all. It's just a way of getting your money.
B Well, I don't think the psychic you saw was very professional. A good psychic will never tell you what to *do*. A good psychic will identify what's happening in your life and offer guidance, but it's up to you to decide what to do.
C I must say I don't agree with Lorenna at all. I think clairvoyants *can* see into the future. Maybe not all of them, but a lot of them can. I went to a clairvoyant last year and she said several things about my future and they have come true and they weren't all good things. For example, she told me that I would soon have a new job. In fact I was very happy in the job I had at that time, but two months later the company was taken over by another company and I lost my job. But because the psychic had told me about the new job, I didn't get depressed. I felt optimistic. And in fact I was only unemployed for a couple of months and then I did get another job. Now I go and see my psychic every time I have any kind of problem.
B OK, but I think it's important that people do not come to depend too much on a psychic. I know people who won't do anything without consulting their psychic first and this isn't very healthy. Psychics can help you understand your own thoughts and feelings better, but they can't live your lives for you.

Test and Assessment CD-ROM

File 1 Quicktest
File 1 Test

2 A

G adjectives as nouns, adjective order
V clothes and fashion
P vowel sounds

National stereotypes: truth or myth?

File 2 overview

Lesson **2A** looks at national stereotypes and clothes vocabulary; it focuses on how adjectives can be used as nouns (e.g. *the French, the rich*) and the word order of multiple adjectives (e.g. *a lovely old house*). **2B** revises narrative tenses and introduces the past perfect continuous through the context of air travel. Finally, **2C** focuses on adverb position and adverbs which are often confused (e.g. *hard* and *hardly*). The context is reading (and writing) 'mini sagas' – 50-word short stories.

Lesson plan

In this first lesson SS extend their knowledge of how to use adjectives. In the first part they learn to use nationality adjectives as nouns when they talk about the people from a particular country (e.g. *The British, the Americans*) or a particular group of people (e.g. *the rich, the unemployed*), and in the second part they focus on adjective order. The lesson begins with some new research about national stereotypes, which provides the context for SS to talk about their own national characteristics. In the second half of the lesson, an extract from the book *Watching the English* shifts the focus to how different nationalities dress. The lexical focus in the lesson is on clothes and fashion, and pronunciation looks at short and long vowel sounds and diphthongs.

Optional lead-in (books closed)

- Write the following in columns on the board:
  NATIONAL CHARACTERISTICS
  The English, the Scottish, the Irish, the Americans

- Put SS in pairs and give them a few minutes to brainstorm what they think are the national characteristics (positive and negative) of these four nationalities (from their own experience, heard from other people or seen in films, etc.)

- When the time limit is up, get feedback from the class. You could leave it on the board for the next exercise.

1 LISTENING & SPEAKING

a • Books open. Focus on the task and give SS, in pairs, a few minutes to brainstorm their predictions. Get some feedback and write some of the SS' ideas on the board. (N.B. Leave out this stage if you did the optional lead-in.)

b • **2.1** Focus on the task. Play the CD once the whole way through and SS try to match the speakers to their nationality group. Play the recording again if necessary.

Extra support

You may want to pre-teach *melancholy* (= deep feeling of sadness) and *nostalgic* (= feeling sad and happy when you think of happy times in the past) to help SS to understand the listening.

English	3	Scottish	4
Irish	2	American	1

2.1   CD1 Track 26

(tapescript in Student's Book on *p.122*)

1   I think above all we are strong individualists. We want as few rules as possible governing our lives. We are also very hard-working. People here live to work and don't work to live. We are also very optimistic, and we think that if we work hard, we can achieve anything. On the negative side, I think we are extremely materialistic. The measure of success for most people here is money. We are extremely concerned with 'things' – possessions and the bigger the better. Personally, I think I have inherited the typical optimism and drive, and I'm also an individualist, so I think I'm probably quite typical, but I hope I'm less materialistic than many of my countrymen seem to be.

2   Generally speaking, I think we are very sociable and easy-going, and we're great storytellers. People are also quite religious and family oriented, we're also very patriotic. Maybe this is because we are a small country and so many of us live abroad. Historically there has always been a lot of emigration. Weaknesses? I think we can be very melancholic and nostalgic, you only have to listen to our music to hear this – it's often quite sad and slow. It's probably because of our climate and our history. The stereotypical image is that one minute we are laughing and telling you a funny story and the next minute we are crying into our beer. Which reminds me that we also drink quite a lot. I think I'm quite typical in many respects, although I'm not particularly melancholic.

3   It's difficult to generalize about us as a people, especially as our big cities now have such a multi-ethnic population, but I would say that we're basically very tolerant and open-minded. We're not nearly as insular as we used to be. We defend the things that we believe in – when we have to – and we avoid taking extreme positions, which I think is another strength. One of our main weaknesses, though, is that we can be quite self-satisfied and arrogant towards foreigners. Just think of our inability, or our unwillingness, to learn foreign languages! I'd also say that we can be lazy, and we're a bit careless about the way we dress, and also we drink too much. I don't think I'm very typical, though I do definitely have one of the weaknesses – but I'm not going to say which!

4 As a nation we're very proud of our identity and our cultural heritage. We're an inventive people, but we often feel marginalized and forgotten by our bigger neighbour, England that is. We're very sociable and like to have a good time. We're also great travellers and people often compliment us on the good behaviour of our sports fans abroad.
On the other hand, we do have a tendency to melancholy – maybe it's something to do with the weather, you know we tend to think that life is hard. There's also a negative attitude towards our neighbour – and this can range from humorous comments to actual violence. And although we are keen travellers, we can be quite negative towards foreigners. Some people would like to see the country kept only for us, without apparently understanding how negative that could be.
I don't think of myself as a typical example. I love the country, and think it has some of the most beautiful scenery in the world, but I feel that we tend to focus too much on the wrongs done to us in the distant past, rather than trying to move on.

c • Focus on the task and then play the CD again until the end of the first speaker (The American). Give SS time to write down the adjectives and whether the speaker is typical or not (and why). Then get SS to compare what they understood with their partner before playing the recording again. Check answers, writing SS' ideas on the board and then repeat the process for the other three speakers.

> **Speaker 1 (American)**
> (+) individualistic, hard-working, optimistic
> (–) materialistic, very interested in money
> He is quite typical (optimistic and individualistic and has drive = energy and ambition), but is not materialistic.
> **Speaker 2 (Irish)**
> (+) sociable, easy-going, religious, family oriented, good storytellers
> (–) melancholic, nostalgic, drink a lot
> She is quite typical but not melancholic.
> **Speaker 3 (English)**
> (+) tolerant, open to new ideas
> (–) self-satisfied, arrogant towards foreigners, lazy, careless in the way they dress, drink too much
> He is not very typical but admits to having one of the weaknesses.
> **Speaker 4 (Scottish)**
> (+) proud of their identity, inventive, sociable, like to have a good time, great travellers, well behaved abroad
> (–) melancholic, negative attitude towards their neighbours (the English), quite negative towards foreigners
> She is not typical but is patriotic.

d • **2.2** Focus on the task and play the CD pausing briefly after each sentence to give SS time to write in the missing words. Play the recording again if necessary. Then check answers before eliciting the meaning of each word either through paraphrase or translation.

> **1 a** achieve (manage to do, succeed in reaching a goal)
> **b** inherited (to receive qualities or characteristics – or possessions – from previous generations of your family)
> **2 a** emigration (leaving your own country to live permanently in another)
> **b** climate (the weather in a particular place)
> **3 a** multi-ethnic (including people of many different races, religions and languages)
> **b** unwillingness (not wanting to)
> **4 a** attitude (the way you feel about and behave towards sb / sth)
> **b** wrongs (bad things)

> **2.2**   CD1 Track 27
> **1 a** We think that if we work hard, we can achieve anything.
> **b** I think I have inherited the typical optimism and drive.
> **2 a** Historically there has always been a lot of emigration.
> **b** It's probably because of our climate and our history.
> **3 a** It's difficult to generalize about us as a people, especially as our big cities now have such a multi-ethnic population.
> **b** Just think of our inability, or our unwillingness, to learn foreign languages!
> **4 a** There's also a negative attitude towards our neighbour.
> **b** I feel that we tend to focus too much on the wrongs done to us in the distant past.

Extra support

If there's time, get SS to listen to the CD with the tapescript on *p.122* so they can see exactly what they understood / didn't understand. Translate / explain any new words or phrases.

e • Put SS into pairs or small groups and set them a time limit to answer the same questions that the four speakers answered in exercise **1**. Highlight that for questions 1 and 2 they should talk generally, but for question 3 they should talk personally. You could appoint a secretary for each pair or group to report back afterwards. Get feedback from some or all of the pairs / groups.

2 GRAMMAR adjectives as nouns

a • Focus attention on the joke and read it through with the class. Make sure SS know what they have to do and emphasize that they should try and write the 'perfect' nationality for each job in **HEAVEN**, using five different nationalities. Then they do the same for **HELL**, repeating, if they want, some or all of the previous nationalities. Put SS in pairs and give them a couple of minutes to complete the task. Then ask each pair of SS to compare their version of the joke to the pair nearest them.

• Now ask the whole class if they think there is any truth in nationality stereotypes (fixed ideas or images we have about people from another country), e.g. English people are cold and reserved. Get some feedback.

- Focus attention on the photos that go with the article and ask SS to identify the three nationalities shown (English, Japanese, and Brazilians). Then ask SS if they think the photos show real aspects of how these nationalities are / behave, or if they are just stereotypes.

- Then focus attention on the title and subtitle of the article and elicit what it means (= some research has been done around the world which suggests that national stereotypes may not be reliable.)

b • Set SS a time limit for them to read the article once quite quickly to find out the answers to the two questions. Check answers.

> 1 They used personality tests to get shared characteristics of a particular nationality group (the reality). Then they interviewed people from the same nationality groups and asked them to describe the typical characteristics of people from their country (the stereotypical image). They then compared the two pieces of research.
> 2 The research showed that there was often a big difference between the reality and the stereotype. This shows us that national stereotypes are inaccurate and unhelpful.

c • Focus on the task and set SS another time limit to read the article again and answer questions 1–6. Get SS to compare their answers with their partner before checking answers.

> 1 The Czechs and the Argentinians
> 2 The Italians, the Russians, and the Spanish
> 3 The Spanish
> 4 The Poles
> 5 The English
> 6 The Brazilians

d • Ask this question to the whole class and elicit ideas.

e • Focus on the sentences and give SS time to correct the wrong sentences, either individually or in pairs. Check answers.

> 2 ✓
> 3 ✗ The Spanish
> 4 ✗ Chinese and Japanese people
> 5 ✓
> 6 ✗ a Polish man / a Pole

f • Tell SS to go to **Grammar Bank 2A** on *p.134*. Go through each example and its corresponding rule for adjectives as nouns with the class.

Grammar notes

- **nationalities**

  SS should already have a good knowledge of nationality adjectives in English, especially for the countries in their part of the world.

  Highlight that for most nationalities you can use either *the* + **adjective** (*The French*) or **adjective** + *people* (*French people*) to talk about people from a particular country. The exception is where the nationality word is an adjective *and* a noun (see **rule 2**), e.g. *The Italians* or *Italian people*.

- **rules 1–3**
  1 You may want to give some more examples here, e.g. *the Swedish, the French, the Swiss, the Japanese*.
  2 You may want to give some more examples here, e.g. *the Brazilians, the Hungarians, the Russians,* etc.
  3 Other examples of specific words for people from a country: *Sweden – the Swedes, Scotland – the Scots, Spain – the Spaniards, Denmark – The Danes, Finland – the Finns*.

  Highlight that to talk about one person from a particular country you can use *a / an* + noun, e.g. *an Italian, a Pole,* but if there is no noun, or you want to specify gender, you must use the adjective + *man / woman / boy / girl,* e.g. *A Spanish man, a Chinese woman* NOT ~~a Spanish, a Chinese~~. These are usually written as two words but occasionally as one (with *man*), e.g. *an Englishman, a Frenchman*.

- **specific groups of people**

  Other common group words you could teach your SS are: *the sick* (= ill people), *the old, the injured / the wounded, the deaf* (= people who can't hear).

  Point out that you can also express the same idea using people (e.g. *old people, unemployed people*). If you want to talk about one person use, e.g. *an old person* NOT ~~an old~~.

- **one, ones**

  This structure is very common in spoken English. Highlight that you can't use *the* + adjective without using *one / ones,* e.g. *Do you prefer the big one or the small one?* NOT ~~Do you prefer the big or the small?~~

- Get SS to do exercise **a** only on *p.135* in pairs or individually. Check answers.

> **a** 1 The Dutch
> 2 The injured
> 3 the blind
> 4 The French
> 5 the ill / the sick
> 6 the Swiss
> 7 the homeless
> 8 the unemployed

- Tell SS to go back to the main lesson on *p.21*.

g • This is an oral grammar practice exercise. Put SS in pairs and tell them to discuss the seven statements, saying whether they agree or disagree, and why. Get some feedback from the class.

3 READING

a • Focus attention on the photos and elicit answers from the class.

b • Explain to the class that the text they are going to read is an extract from a book by Kate Fox who is an anthropologist. Elicit what anthropologists do (they study the behaviour and customs, etc. of human beings.) Explain that Kate Fox (who is herself English) spent many years observing the habits and behaviour of other English people and her book *Watching the English* looks at all aspects of life, e.g. social life, attitudes to food, sense of humour, etc. The extract SS are going to read is about how the English dress.

- Focus on the pre-reading task and give SS, in pairs, a few moments to discuss the statements and mark them true or false. If SS have little knowledge or experience in this area, they can guess. Get quick feedback but don't say if the SS' answers are right or wrong.

c ● Set a time limit for SS to read the first part of the text once to check whether, according to Kate Fox, sentences 1–7 are true or false.

1 T	2 T	3 T	4 T	5 F	6 T	7 F

d ● Focus attention on the photo and elicit answers to the question (He belongs to the Goths). Set a time limit for SS to read the second part of the text and to answer the two questions. Check answers.

> Kate Fox spoke to a Goth because she wanted to find out if the Goths could laugh at themselves. She discovered that they had a sense of humour and didn't take their way of dressing too seriously.

e ● Tell SS to look at the highlighted adjectives and to try to guess what the words could mean. Tell them to look carefully at each word. Is it similar to another word they know or to a word in their language? Do the other words in the sentence help? Does their knowledge of the subject (the way English people dress) help them?

● Give SS, in pairs, a few minutes to try to guess the meaning of the adjectives. If they have dictionaries, they can then check their guesses. Finally, check answers using the definitions below or translation. Elicit / help with the pronunciation. Highlight that *large* is a slightly more formal way of saying *big*, e.g. a large town. *Large* is also used instead of *big* in clothes sizing (often abbreviated to L).

> **dysfunctional** /dɪsfʌŋkʃənl/ = not working properly
> **innovative** /ɪnəveɪtɪv/ = introducing new ideas or ways of doing something
> **outrageous** /aʊtreɪdʒəs/ = shocking
> **macabre** /məkɑːbrə/ = unpleasant and strange, connected with death
> **conspicuous** /kənspɪkjuəs/ = easy to see or notice

f ● Now give SS a few minutes to read the whole text again and choose the best summary of the article.

> A

● Now ask SS whether they think this is true from their own knowledge and experience of English people.

Extra support

At this point you could go through the text with the class, highlighting useful expressions and eliciting / explaining the meaning of new words and phrases.

4 **VOCABULARY** clothes and fashion

a ● Get SS to look at the photos with the article again and get individual SS to describe in detail what people are wearing. Help with any vocabulary problems.

> The Queen is wearing a matching green hat and top; she is wearing a necklace and earrings. The woman is wearing a black top, red shorts, and long black and white striped socks. The man is wearing a blue suit, a green shirt and a purple tie. The two judges are wearing wigs and robes with a purple hoods. The couple are wearing plastic ponchos.

b ● Tell SS to go to **Vocabulary Bank** *Clothes and fashion* on *p.148*.

● Focus on section **1 Describing clothes a** and get SS to do it in pairs or individually. Check answers and elicit and drill pronunciation. Repeat the process for **1b** and **1c**. Make sure SS know what all the words mean. Highlight that all the adjectives in **1c** are used to express an opinion about clothes or how someone is dressed.

a	**1** loose	**7** striped
	2 tight	**8** spotted
	3 long-sleeved	**9** checked
	4 sleeveless	**10** plain
	5 V-neck	**11** patterned
	6 hooded	
b	**1** a velvet bow	**7** a fur collar
	2 nylon stockings	**8** suede slippers
	3 a silk scarf	**9** a Lycra swimsuit
	4 a linen suit	**10** a cotton vest
	5 leather sandals	**11** a denim backpack
	6 a woollen cardigan	
c	**1** trendy	**4** smart
	2 stylish	**5** old-fashioned
	3 scruffy	

● Now get SS to do section **2 Verb phrases**. Check answers and drill pronunciation. Make sure SS are aware of the difference in meaning between *match, suit, fit* and *get changed / dressed / undressed*. Highlight that the phrasal verb *dress up* means *to wear smart clothes*. Elicit / point out that *dress up, match, fit,* and *suit* are regular verbs and that *hang up* is irregular (past *hung up*).

2 a 1 C	2 A	3 F	4 H	5 G	6 B	7 E	8 D

● Finally, get SS to do section **3 Idioms**. Check answers and ask them if they have a similar idiom in their own language for each situation.

3 b 1 C	2 D	3 A	4 B

● Finally, focus on the instruction 'Can you remember the words on this page? Test yourself or a partner'.

Testing yourself

For **Describing clothes a** and **b** SS can cover the words and look at the pictures and try to remember the words. For **Describing clothes c** they can cover the opinion column and try to remember the adjectives. In **Verb phrases** they can cover the left-hand column and try to remember the verbs phrases. In **Idioms** they can cover the idioms and remember them by looking at the definitions A–D.

Testing a partner
See **Testing a partner** *p.20*.

Study Link SS can find more practice of these words and phrases on the MultiROM and on the *New English File Upper-intermediate* website.

● Tell SS to go back to the main lesson on *p.22*.

c • This exercise recycles the vocabulary SS have just learnt. Sit SS in pairs, **A** and **B**, preferably face to face. Tell them to go to **Communication** *Clothes quiz*, **A** on *p.116*, **B** on *p.119*.

• Go through the instructions and make sure SS know what they have to do. When the activity finishes you could ask who got the most right answers in each pair.

5 PRONUNCIATION vowel sounds

Pronunciation notes

SS can improve their pronunciation by making an effort to distinguish between long and short sounds and diphthongs (a combination of two vowel sounds, e.g. the sound in *hair* /eə/). When upper-intermediate SS come across new words they will instinctively pronounce them correctly especially if there is a regular sound-spelling relationship. If they are unsure, they should use their dictionaries to check the phonetic transcription. Remind SS that /ː/ = a long sound.

a • Focus on the task and elicit answers.

/buːt/, /triː/ and /bɜːd/ are long sounds.
/bʊl/, /fɪʃ/ and /kəmpjuːtə/ are short sounds.
/baɪk/ and /treɪn/ are diphthongs.

b • **2.3** Focus on the task and give SS a few minutes, in pairs, to complete it. Then play the CD for SS to listen and check their answers.

2.3		CD1 Track 28
/uː/	loose	suit
/ʊ/	put on	woollen
/ɪ/	linen	slippers
/iː/	high-heeled	sleeveless
/ə/	collar	sandals
/ɜː/	fur	shirt
/aɪ/	Lycra™	striped
/eɪ/	plain	suede

Extra support

You could play the CD again for SS to repeat the words.

c • Get SS to practise saying the phrases to each other in pairs, before choosing individual SS to say them.

d • Now tell SS to go to the **Sound Bank** on *p.159*. Focus on the eight sounds that SS have just been working on.

6 SPEAKING

• Focus on the **GET IT RIGHT** box and give SS a moment to choose the right option.

1 dress	2 wear

• Elicit / point out that *wear* always needs an object (e.g. *I'm going to wear a jacket tonight*) and *dress* doesn't (e.g. *She dresses well*).

• Put SS in small groups and set a time limit. You could appoint a secretary to ask the questions and organize the discussion. Get feedback from the whole class afterwards.

7 GRAMMAR adjective order

a • Focus on the task and give SS a few moments to try and order the adjectives. Get them to compare with their partner. Check answers.

1	spiky black hair	3	big black leather bag
2	beige linen suit	4	white nylon running vest

b • Tell SS to go to **Grammar Bank 2A** on *p.134*. Go through each example and its corresponding rule for adjective order with the class.

Grammar notes

adjective order

It's important to point out that in practice people rarely use more than two adjectives (occasionally three) together so SS should not be put off by the chart showing adjective order. Encourage SS to use their instinct as to what sounds right rather than try to memorize the chart, and to remember that opinion adjectives always come first. Learning common combinations will also help them to remember the rule, e.g. *long fair hair, a big old house*, etc.

• Get SS to do exercise **b** only on *p.135* in pairs or individually. Check answers.

b 1	an attractive young man
2	dirty old shoes
3	a stylish purple leather jacket
4	a tall thin woman
5	a long sandy beach
6	a lovely new wooden floor
7	a smart Italian suit
8	beautiful big dark eyes
9	a friendly old black dog

• Tell SS to go back to the main lesson on *p.23*.

c • Focus on the instructions and ask SS if they have ever bought or sold anything on eBay. Then give SS time to write their descriptions. Go round helping with vocabulary.

Extra support

You could write a description on the board of an item of clothing you want to sell to give SS ideas, e.g. *For sale! White linen jacket – hardly worn. Size 40. Perfect for the summer.*

d • Get SS to move around the class trying to interest other SS in the clothes they want to sell. If they find someone who is interested, they should agree a price. Stop the activity when you think most SS have found a buyer.

• Get feedback to find out who bought / sold what.

8 **2.4** **SONG** 🎵 *Englishman in New York*

- This song was written and recorded by the British singer Sting in 1987. For copyright reasons this is a cover version. If you want to do this song in class, use the photocopiable activity on *p.234*.

2.4   CD1 Track 29

Englishman in New York

I don't take coffee, I take tea my dear
I like my toast done on one side
And you can hear it in my accent when I talk
I'm an Englishman in New York

See me walking down Fifth Avenue
A walking cane here at my side
I take it everywhere I walk
I'm an Englishman in New York

Chorus
I'm an alien I'm a legal alien
I'm an Englishman in New York
I'm an alien I'm a legal alien
I'm an Englishman in New York

If 'Manners maketh man' as someone said
He's our hero of the day
It takes a man to suffer ignorance and smile
Be yourself, no matter what they say

Chorus

Modesty, propriety can lead to notoriety
You could end up as the only one
Gentleness, sobriety are rare in this society
At night a candle's brighter than the sun

Takes more than combat gear to make a man
Takes more than a licence for a gun
Confront your enemies, avoid them when you can
A gentleman will walk but never run

If 'Manners maketh man' as someone said
He's our hero of the day
It takes a man to suffer ignorance and smile
Be yourself, no matter what they say

Chorus

Extra photocopiable activities

Grammar
adjectives *p.163*
Communicative
Spot the difference *p.201* (instructions *p.191*)
Song
Englishman in New York p.234 (instructions *p.231*)

HOMEWORK

Study Link **Workbook** *pp.14–16*

G narrative tenses, past perfect continuous; *so / such…that*
V air travel
P irregular past forms

Air travel: the inside story

Lesson plan

In this lesson SS revise the three narrative tenses they already know (past simple, past continuous, and past perfect) and learn a new one, the past perfect continuous. The topic is air travel, and in the first half of the lesson SS read an extract from a best-selling book called *Air Babylon*, which claims to give the inside story about what really happens at airports and on flights. They also learn, in mini grammar, how to use *so / such…that*. In the second half they listen to an interview with two pilots who answer a lot of the questions air travellers ask themselves when they board a plane. The vocabulary focuses on words related to air and long-distance travel, and in pronunciation SS look at the pronunciation of tricky irregular past verb forms.

Optional lead-in (books closed)

- Write on the board
  How often do you travel by plane?
  Do you enjoy flying? Why (not)?
- Get SS to ask and answer with a partner.
- Get feedback and find out how many people have never travelled by plane, how many people are afraid of flying and how many people enjoy it and why. (NB If you have a class where you think not many people will have been on a plane, you could change the questions to *Have you ever flown? Did you enjoy it?*)

1 READING

a • Books open. Focus on the task. Read the back cover aloud, and ask SS why they think the identities of the airline staff 'must remain anonymous' (because if their bosses found out, they might lose their jobs). Give SS a few minutes in pairs to discuss the questions. Get feedback but don't tell them yet if they are right or not.

Extra support

Ask the questions to the whole class and elicit ideas.

b • Set a time limit for SS to read the extract and check the answers to the questions in **a**. Get feedback by reading out the questions again one by one and eliciting answers.

> They are sending messages to each other about passengers.
> The flight crew like to turn the heating up to get the passengers to go to sleep. (That way they have less work to do and everything is very quiet.)
> At Heathrow 80 per 1,000 bags or cases are lost.
> Because people who don't really need them ask for them.
> Because a bird has crashed into the plane and been burnt in the engine.

- Finally, ask SS if they guessed correctly. Elicit some answers.

c • Focus on the task and encourage SS to read sentences A–F first, and elicit / explain / translate any vocabulary they don't know. SS then read the article again and put the sentences in. Highlight that there is <u>one</u> sentence they don't need. Check answers.

> **1** D   **2** F   **3** E   **4** A   **5** B

Extra support

At this point you could go through the five paragraphs with the class, highlighting useful expressions and eliciting / explaining the meaning of new words and phrases.

d • Do this as an open class question.

2 VOCABULARY   air travel

a • Focus on the instructions. Tell SS if they are not sure of a word, they should look for it in the text. (The words are not in the same order as in the text.)

Extra support

Get SS to underline all the words in the text related to air travel <u>before</u> doing exercise **a**.

- Check answers and model and drill pronunciation where necessary. Highlight that:
  – *baggage* is more formal than *luggage* and used in the expression *excess baggage* and in the sign *baggage reclaim*. In conversation we would normally use *luggage*.
  – *crew* has a plural meaning and is used with a plural verb (*The crew are …*NOT *The crew is…*)
  – *aisle* /aɪl/ (seat) = the seat next to the passage between seats on a plane

> | **2** Arrivals | **10** crew |
> |------------------------|-------------------------|
> | **3** luggage and baggage | **11** passengers |
> | **4** check-in | **12** flight attendant |
> | **5** passport control | **13** seat |
> | **6** pick up (or get) | **14** flight |
> | **7** customs | **15** taking off |
> | **8** porter | **16** landing |
> | **9** airlines | |

b • Elicit the answers from the class. You could get them to write b/t next to words that can also be used for other types of transport.

> 1, 3, 5, 7, 8, 11, 13

c • Get SS to test themselves by covering the words and looking at the definitions and remembering the words.

Extra idea

Get SS to test each other. **A** (book open) reads out definitions 1–9. **B** (book closed) says the words. Then they swap roles for words 10–16.

MINI GRAMMAR *so / such…that*

- Go through the examples and then the rules. Highlight that *that* is optional after *so / such*.
- You may want to point out that we often use *so / such* simply for emphasis, e.g. *That steak was so good. / We had such a nice day!*
- Elicit sentence 1 from the whole class and write the answer on the board. Then get SS to do the rest of the exercise. Check answers.

1	so	5	so
2	such a	6	such
3	such a	7	so
4	so	8	such

Extra support

If you think SS need more practice, use the extra photocopiable exercises on *p.184*.

3 GRAMMAR narrative tenses, past perfect continuous

- **a** ● Focus on the newspaper article, and tell SS that this is a true story from a British newspaper. Set a time limit for SS to read it. Remind them that there is a glossary to help them. Then ask the questions to the class and get feedback.

> One of the flight attendants panicked and started screaming when the plane hit some turbulence.

Extra support

You could go through the text with the class checking SS understand everything.

- **b** ● Focus on the highlighted verbs and get SS to write them in the chart. Check answers, and elicit that the past perfect continuous = *had been* + verb + *-ing*

past simple regular	screamed
past simple irregular	hit
past continuous	was going
past perfect	had been
past perfect continuous	'd been reading

Extra idea

At this point you may want to revise other common irregular verbs. You could photocopy the irregular verb list on *p.240* and test the class, or get SS to test each other.

- **c** ● Now get SS in pairs to look at the sentences and circle the right form. Check answers.

> 1 screamed (because <u>first</u> the plane hit turbulence and <u>then</u> the passengers screamed)
> 2 were relaxing (because the passengers were in the middle of relaxing)
> 3 had finished lunch (because they had their lunch <u>before</u> the plane hit turbulence)
> 4 had been flying for two hours (because the flight started two hours previously and had continued up to that moment)

- **d** ● Tell SS to go to **Grammar Bank 2B** on *p.134*. Go through each example and its corresponding rule with the class.

Grammar notes

- **rules 1–3: narrative tenses**
  This should all be revision for SS at this level.
- **rule 4: past perfect continuous**
  This will probably be a new tense for most SS. It has the same form as the present perfect continuous except that *had* is used instead of *have / has*. As with the present perfect continuous it is not usually used with non-action verbs, e.g. *be, like, have, know*, etc.
- **past perfect simple or continuous?**
  As with the present perfect simple and continuous you often have to use one or the other. However, again, there are some instances where either can be used but with a difference in meaning.
  In the examples given in the box, highlight that *she'd been reading a book* = she may have just finished or still be reading the book. *She'd read the book* = she has definitely finished the book.

- Get SS to do the exercises for **2B** on *p.135* in pairs or individually. Check answers.

> **a** 1 we'd been queuing
> 2 had stolen
> 3 had been raining (had rained)
> 4 'd had
> 5 'd changed
> 6 'd been sunbathing; ('d sunbathed); hadn't put on
> 7 had been arguing (had argued)
> 8 'd fallen
> **b** 1 were checking in
> 2 had won
> 3 had been looking forward
> 4 had forgotten
> 5 had arrived
> 6 ran
> 7 went
> 8 was filling
> 9 hurried
> 10 caught

- Tell SS to go back to the main lesson on *p.26*.
- **e** ● Focus on the task and get SS to work either in pairs or groups of three. Set a time limit and remind SS that they have to try to use the four different tenses in the endings.
- Get feedback and accept all correct meaningful sentences.

> **Possible answers**
> 1 … wasn't wearing a seat belt.
> … was driving too fast.
> … had been using his mobile phone.
> … had jumped a red traffic light.
> 2 … I was feeling stressed.
> … it was very hot.
> … I had been watching scary films.
> … I had drunk too much coffee after dinner.

4 PRONUNCIATION irregular past forms

Pronunciation notes

This exercise focuses on commonly mispronounced irregular past verb forms. Sometimes SS at this level still have some ingrained pronunciation problems with some of the trickier irregular past and past participle forms, e.g. the *-ought* / *-aught* endings.

a • Focus on the picture words and elicit the eight sounds (/uː/, /ɪ/, /ɔː/, /ɜː/, /ʌ/, /əʊ/, /e/, /eɪ/)
 • Then get SS in pairs to look at the sentences, focusing on the irregular verbs, and match them to the sound pictures.

b • **2.5** Play the CD for SS to check. Check answers.

1 C	2 B	3 E	4 A	5 G	6 F	7 D	8 H

 • Give SS time to practise saying the sentences correctly.
 • Remind SS that:
  – verbs ending in *-aught* are pronounced exactly the same as ones which end in *-ought*, e.g. *thought, bought, brought, fought*.
  – the *u* in *built* is silent.
  – the *ea* in *read* and *dreamt* is irregular and pronounced /e/
  – although *paid* is pronounced /peɪd/, *said* is pronounced /sed/.

> **2.5**   CD1 Track 30
>
> 1 I **though**t he'd **caugh**t that flight. I **saw** him checking in.
> 2 The hotel was b**uil**t in 1950. The date was wr**i**tten above the door.
> 3 The company had bec**o**me successful since it w**o**n the prize for Best Airline.
> 4 I fl**ew** to Mexico City. I kn**ew** the city very well.
> 5 She r**ea**d for a while before she f**e**ll asleep. Then she dr**ea**mt about her childhood.
> 6 We'd fl**ow**n from New York that day. We'd ch**o**sen a bad day to travel.
> 7 I h**ea**rd that they'd been h**ur**t in the accident, but they w**e**ren't.
> 8 She said she'd p**ai**d for the train with money she'd t**a**ken from my wallet.

Extra idea

If you think your SS still have problems with regular *-ed* endings, you could revise these. Get SS to draw three columns, /t/, /d/, and /ɪd/. Dictate these sentences and get SS to write the verb in the correct column:

We **arrived** at the airport.
We **needed** a cup of coffee.
We **checked** in late.
We nearly **missed** our flight.
The plane **landed** on time.

The train **started** to move.
We **travelled** all night.
The train **crashed** into a cow.
We **stayed** at an awful hotel.

/t/	/d/	/ɪd/
checked	arrived	needed
missed	travelled	landed
crashed	stayed	started

Remind SS that:
 – verbs which end in an unvoiced sound (made without using the voice box), e.g. which end in /k/, /f/, /p/, /t/, /tʃ/, and /ʃ/ are pronounced /t/ when you add *-ed* / *-d*.
 – verbs which end in a voiced sound (sounds which are made using the voice box – you can feel the sound vibrate if you touch your throat) are pronounced /d/ when you add *-ed* / *-d*.
 – verbs which end in the sound /t/ or /d/, e.g. *mend, need, invite,* and *want,* are pronounced /ɪd/ when you add *-ed* / *-d*.

5 LISTENING

a • Focus on the task and the six questions. Then give SS time to discuss them in pairs.

b • **2.6** Play the CD once. Ask SS how many they guessed right.

> **2.6**   CD1 Track 31
>
> (tapescript in Student's Book on *p.122*)
> **I = interviewer, S = Steven, R = Richard**
> I With me in the studio today I have two pilots, Richard and Steven, who are going to answer some of the most frequently asked questions about flying and air travel. Hello to both of you.
> S & R Hello.
> I Right, the first question is what weather conditions are the most dangerous when flying a plane?
> S Probably the most dangerous weather conditions are when the wind changes direction very suddenly. This tends to happen during thunderstorms and typhoons, and it's especially dangerous during take-off and landing. But it's quite unusual – I've been flying for 37 years now and I've only experienced this three or four times.
> I Is all turbulence dangerous?
> S No, in fact it's not normally dangerous. Pilots know when to expect turbulence and we try to avoid it by changing routes or flight levels.
> I Which is more dangerous, take-off or landing?
> R Both take-off and landing can be dangerous. They're the most critical moments of a flight. Pilots talk about the 'critical eight minutes' – the three minutes after take-off and the five minutes before landing. Most accidents happen in this period.
> S I would say take-off is probably slightly more dangerous than landing. There is a critical moment just before take-off when the plane is accelerating, but it hasn't yet reached the speed to be able to fly. If the pilot has a problem with the plane at this point, he has very little time – maybe only a second – to abort the take-off.
> I Passengers often think that putting on seat belts in a plane is really a waste of time. Is that true?
> S Not at all. When the plane is moving on the ground and the pilot suddenly puts the brakes on, passengers can be thrown out of their seats, just like in a car. But more importantly, during the flight if there is sudden and severe turbulence, you could be thrown all over the cabin if you aren't wearing your seat belt. That's why airlines usually recommend you wear your belt even when the seat belt light is off.

I Should we really listen to the safety information?

S It's definitely worth listening to the information about emergency exits. If there's a fire on a plane, it may be dark and the plane will be full of smoke and fumes. So listening to where the exits are, and working out which one is the nearest exit to you, might save your life. Most aircrew can even tell you where the emergency exits are in the hotels where they stay.

I What about life jackets?

R Fortunately, planes very rarely have to land in the sea, but to be honest the chances of surviving if your plane did crash into the sea are not high.

I Are some airports more dangerous than others?

S Yes, some are – particularly airports with high mountains around them and airports in countries with older or more basic navigation equipment.

R For some difficult airports like, let's say Kathmandu, they only allow very experienced pilots to land there. And for some of these airports pilots have to practise on a simulator first before they are given permission to land a plane there.

I How important is it for pilots and controllers to have good clear English?

S It's the official language of the air, so obviously it's vital for pilots and controllers to have good English. To be honest, it doesn't always happen.

R And apart from people's English not being good, some countries don't respect the convention and don't force their pilots to speak in English. But most of them do, luckily.

c ● Play the CD again for SS to listen for more detail. Check answers.

> 1 Sudden changes of wind direction, especially during thunderstorms and typhoons. But most turbulence isn't dangerous as pilots are prepared.
>
> 2 Both are dangerous, but take-off is a bit more dangerous than landing, especially if there is a problem just before the plane goes into the air.
>
> 3 Yes, because if the plane moves suddenly, e.g. in turbulence or when the plane brakes on the ground, you can be thrown out of your seat.
>
> 4 Yes, because if there's a fire, it might be dark and knowing where the nearest exit is could save you.
>
> 5 Yes, especially ones with mountains or in countries with older more basic equipment. Only very experienced pilots are allowed to land at these airports.
>
> 6 Very important as it's the official language of the air. Most pilots and controllers speak good English, but not all.

d ● **2.7** Focus on the task and play the CD. Elicit the three questions.

> 1 Have you ever had a problem with a famous person as a passenger?
>
> 2 What's your most frightening experience as a pilot?
>
> 3 Have you ever been taken ill during a flight?

2.7 CD1 Track 32

(tapescript in Student's Book on *p.123*)

I Have you ever had a problem with a famous person as a passenger?

R I've carried a lot of famous people and they are usually very well behaved. But I remember once I had the actor Steven Seagal as a passenger – and the cabin crew told me that he had just got on board and he was carrying an enormous samurai sword. Weapons aren't allowed on board, of course, so I had to go and speak to him. He looked very imposing standing in the cabin. He was nearly 2 metres tall, dressed completely in black, carrying a sword and he is – as you probably know – a martial arts expert. But in fact, he was very happy to give us the sword, which was gold and which had been given to him as a present in Bali.

I What's your most frightening experience as a pilot?

S Crossing the road outside the airport terminal! That's certainly the most dangerous thing I do. Probably in connection with flying, my most frightening experience would have to be a near miss I had when I was flying a Boeing 747 at night. A small aeroplane passed in the opposite direction just 15 metres below my plane… Just after this happened, a flight attendant brought us some hot snacks and I distinctly remember how good they tasted!

I Have you ever been taken ill during a flight?

R Once I was flying from Hong Kong to London, that's a 13-hour flight, and I got food poisoning after six hours. I felt terrible – incapable of doing anything at all for the rest of the flight. Luckily though, the rest of the crew were fine, because on all flights the crew are given different meals, just in case. So as my co-pilots had eaten a different meal and felt fine, the flight was able to continue safely.

Extra support

If there's time, get SS to listen to the CD with the tapescript on *p.122* and *p.123* so they can see exactly what they understood / didn't understand. Translate / explain any new words or phrases.

e ● Now play the CD again and give SS, in pairs, time to remember the stories. Then elicit the stories from SS.

f ● Do this as an open class question.

6 SPEAKING

a ● Focus on the **GET IT RIGHT** box and go through it with SS. Remind SS to use interested / surprised intonation as appropriate.

● Put SS in pairs, **A** and **B**, and tell them to go to **Communication** *Flight stories*, **A** on *p.116* and **B** on *p.119*. Go through the instructions and make sure SS know what they have to do.

● Give SS time to read and retell their stories. Then find out which story SS thought was the most incredible and why (in fact they are both true stories).

b • Focus on the task, and on the **Story plan**. Give SS plenty of time to plan their stories and go round checking whether they need any help with vocabulary.

c • Focus on the instructions. Monitor and help while SS tell each other their stories, correcting any misuse of narrative tenses and encouraging the listener to listen actively.

Extra support

Tell one of the stories yourself first, and elicit responses and questions from the class. Then ask SS if they think the story is true or invented.

When SS have finished telling their own anecdotes, you could get them to swap partners and retell it.

Extra photocopiable activities

Grammar
narrative tenses *p.164*
Communicative
Did it really happen to you? *p.202* (instructions *p.192*)

HOMEWORK

Study Link **Workbook** *pp.17–19*

G adverbs and adverbial phrases
V confusing adverbs and adverbial phrases
P word and sentence stress

2C Incredibly short stories

Lesson plan

In this lesson the grammar focus is on adverbs and adverbial phrases, and their position in sentences. The topic is stories and reading. In the first half of the lesson SS read, and later write, mini-sagas, 50-word stories with a twist. In the second half they read and listen to an American short story. The ending of the story is on the CD in order to create more suspense. The vocabulary focus is on certain pairs of adverbs which are often confused, and the pronunciation is on word and sentence stress.

Optional lead-in (books closed)

● Revise adverb formation. Write the following adjectives on the board:

unfortunate careful angry fast slow good bad

● Give SS a moment to write the adverb for each adjective. Check answers.

unfortunately, carefully, angrily, fast, slowly, well, badly

● Remind SS that adverbs are often formed from adjectives by adding -ly, but that there are also many other adverbs which are not formed from adjectives and which don't end in -ly (e.g. *always, never, just,* etc.). They can also be phrases, e.g. *twice a week*.

● Point out that there are also some words which end in -ly which aren't adverbs, e.g. *friendly, likely* (they are adjectives).

● Elicit / remind SS that adverbs are used either to describe an action (*he walked slowly*) or to modify an adjective or other adverbs (*it's extremely expensive*).

1 GRAMMAR adverbs and adverbial phrases

a ● Books open. Focus on the task. Set a time limit the first time SS read the mini-sagas, and tell SS to use the pictures and the glossary to help them. Check answers.

A Written in the cards	**C** Meeting the boss
B Generation gap	**D** Good intentions

b ● Focus on the instructions and elicit the meaning of *cryptic* (= the meaning is not immediately understood). Get SS to talk about what they think each story is about. Then get feedback from different pairs.

A A woman has a relationship with a man. She goes to see a Gypsy who says the relationship has no future. The man goes to the USA and she doesn't see him for five years and is very lonely. Suddenly she gets a letter from him inviting her to come and join him. The 'twist' is that she gets a ticket to go to New York on the *Titanic* (which sinks). So the Gypsy was right.

B A man, whose wife has died, lives with his teenage daughter. He thinks she is being difficult because he likes going out at night but she gets worried when he comes back late. This time he stayed out really late and when he got home his daughter was very angry. The 'twist' is that the reader imagines that the situation is the other way round, i.e. that the man is waiting for his daughter to come home.

C A new maid, who knows nothing about the master of the house, has been employed. She is given instructions about what she will have to do for her master, and then asks who the master is. She discovers that she will be looking after the dog that she has just tripped over and not a person.

D A woman who is disorganized and untidy decides to become more organized and buys a book to help her. She starts cleaning and tidying up her house. The 'twist' is that when she is cleaning the bookcase she finds exactly the same book, which she had bought last year but which has obviously had no effect!

Extra support

Do story 1 with the whole class. Elicit the story from SS by asking, e.g. *Who had the woman originally gone to see?* (a Gypsy), *What did the Gypsy tell her?* (that she had no future with the man she loved), *How long had it been since she last saw him?* (five years), *What had she just received from him?* (a letter asking her to go to New York and join him), *Why is it probable that the Gypsy was right?* (Because she's about to go on the *Titanic* and so will most probably die when the ship sinks).

Then get SS to explain the other three stories in pairs.

c ● Focus on the instructions and go through the five categories of adverbs. Make sure SS understand the categories by giving more examples if necessary. Focus on the example. Then get SS to continue in pairs. Check answers.

Types of adverbs
Time: *immediately, early, five minutes later, last year*
Manner: *angrily*
Frequency: *always*
Degree: *unbelievably, increasingly, so*
Comment: *unfortunately*

d ● Explain that one of the problems with adverbs is where to put them in a sentence, and elicit that there are three possible positions: at the beginning or end of the phrase / sentence, or in the middle (usually before the main verb). Tell SS that although the rules may seem a bit complicated, they will probably have a good instinct for where adverbs should go, and to try saying them a few times to see which position sounds best.

● Get SS in pairs to put the adverbs in the sentences. Check answers.

> 1 He speaks three languages fluently.
> 2 I hardly ever have breakfast during the week.
> 3 My brother was in a car crash, but fortunately he wasn't hurt.
> 4 It's often extremely hot in Greece in July and August.
> 5 When I know the date I'll call you straight away.

e ● Tell SS to go to **Grammar Bank 2C** on *p.134*. Go through each example and its corresponding rule with the class.

Grammar notes

This is an area of grammar where practice and SS' own instinct as to what sounds right will probably be more useful in the long run than memorizing rules. A useful tip to tell SS is that with adverbs that don't end in *-ly* (e.g. *even*, *just*, etc.), if in doubt, to put them in mid-position, e.g. before the main verb.

● **rule 1: adverbs of manner**

In spoken English adverbs of manner usually go after the verb or verb phrase, e.g. *He opened the door quietly.* However, in written English, e.g. a novel, they are sometimes used before the verb for dramatic effect, e.g. *He quietly opened the door and came in. Jane quickly explained why she was leaving.*

Give SS some more examples of adverbs of manner in passive sentences: *Their house is beautifully designed. It's a well written story.*

● **rule 5: comment adverbs**

Other common ones are *surprisingly, ideally, in fact, basically.*

● Get SS to do the exercises for on *p.135* in pairs or individually. Check answers after each exercise.

> **a** 1 very much ✗ | She likes the theatre very much.
> 2 late, yesterday ✓
> 3 Immediately ✗ | The ambulance arrived immediately.
> 4 usually, after work ✗ | They usually go jogging after work.
> 5 extremely ✓
> 6 easily, brilliantly ✗ | They won the match easily because they played brilliantly.
> 7 almost ✗ | I almost forgot your birthday.
> 8 luckily ✗ | Luckily we had taken an umbrella.
> 9 always, healthily ✓
> 10 apparently ✗ | Apparently he's been sacked.

> **b** 1 The building was badly damaged in the fire last week.
> 2 Obviously we need to do something quickly.
> 3 Ben is often at his friend's house in the evening.
> 4 She just walked out and she didn't even say goodbye.
> 5 He always drives extremely fast.
> 6 She danced beautifully at the ballet last night.
> 7 Luckily she wasn't seriously injured when she fell.
> 8 Apparently he nearly broke his leg when he was skiing.
> 9 My father usually sleeps a bit in the afternoon.

● Tell SS to go back to the main lesson on *p.29*.

f ● **2.8** This is an oral grammar practice activity. Focus on the instructions and tell SS the sound effects will tell them what is happening in each situation and they then need to complete each sentence using the adverb in bold. Demonstrate by playing the CD and pausing after 1. Then continue, pausing the CD each time for SS, in pairs, to write the sentences. Play each sound effect again if necessary. Check answers.

> **Possible answers**
> 2 … the electricity suddenly went off / there was suddenly a power cut / the lights suddenly went out / suddenly the lights went out, etc.
> 3 … luckily he found it in his pocket.
> 4 … they hardly know / knew each other.
> 5 … it was raining (so) hard, etc.
> 6 … he spoke / was speaking incredibly fast / quickly.

> **2.8** CD1 Track 33
> 1 *sound effects of man running*
> 2 *sound effects of power cut at party*
> 3 A Can I see your boarding pass?
>   B Oh my God! I've lost it! Where is it? Where is it?
>   A I'm afraid you can't fly if you haven't got your boarding pass.
>   B Oh thank God, it's in my pocket.
> 4 A Tom, this is Andrea – but of course you two know each, don't you?
>   B Actually, we've only met once, so not really. Hi Andrea.
> 5 I can't see a thing. I think we'd better stop for a bit.
> 6 **Frenchman** Excuse me. Please could you tell me how to get to the train station?
>   **London cabbie** Yeah mate. Straight down the High Street, left at the lights, straight through the underpass, then it's right in front of you.

2 VOCABULARY confusing adverbs and adverbial phrases

a ● Focus on the pairs of adverbs and tell SS that first they just have to match each pair to a pair of sentences, but not to worry yet about which adverb goes where. Check answers.

especially / specially	4
ever / even	8
hard / hardly	1
in the end / at the end	3
late / lately	2
near / nearly	6
still / yet	7

b ● Focus on the instructions and stress that SS should think about the two sentences, and then write the missing adverb in the **Adverb** column. Give SS time to do this in pairs and discuss each pair of sentences. Check answers.

1	**a** hardly, **b** hard
2	**a** late, **b** lately
3	**a** At the end, **b** in the end
4	**a** especially, **b** specially
5	**a** actually, **b** at the moment
6	**a** nearly, **b** near
7	**a** yet, **b** still
8	**a** ever, **b** even

● Highlight that:
  – *hard* = not easy, *hardly* = almost nothing
  – *late* = not early, *lately* = recently
  – *at the end* must be used with a noun, e.g. road, film; *in the end* is used on its own
  – *specially* goes with adjectives, e.g. *specially designed*, *especially* = in particular
  – *actually* never means at the moment, it means the same as *in fact* or *to tell the truth*
  – *nearly* and *almost* mean the same
  – Sentences like: *I haven't found a job yet* and *I **still** haven't found a job* mean more or less the same but the use of *still* is more emphatic than *not yet*.

c ● Give SS time to test themselves on the adverbs.

3 PRONUNCIATION word and sentence stress

Pronunciation notes

Remind SS that if they aren't sure where the main stress is in a word to first try it out with the stress in different places and see which 'sounds best', and if they are still unsure, to check with a dictionary.

a ● Focus on the adverbs and give SS time to underline the main stressed syllable.

b ● 2.9 ▸ Play the CD and then check answers.

2.9	CD1 Track 34
abso<u>lu</u>tely	<u>e</u>ven
<u>ac</u>tually	<u>for</u>tunately
<u>al</u>most	i<u>de</u>ally
ap<u>pa</u>rently	in<u>cre</u>dibly
<u>de</u>finitely	<u>lu</u>ckily
es<u>pe</u>cially	un<u>for</u>tunately

c ● 2.10 ▸ Focus on the information box and remind SS that adverbs, like adjectives, are always stressed in a sentence. Then give SS time to underline the stressed words. Play the CD. Check answers, and get SS to practise saying the sentences.

2.10	CD1 Track 35

1 There was a <u>lot</u> of <u>traffic</u>, and <u>unfortunately</u> we <u>arrived</u> <u>extremely</u> <u>late</u>.
2 We <u>definitely</u> <u>want</u> to go <u>abroad</u> <u>this</u> <u>summer</u>, <u>ideally</u> somewhere <u>hot</u>.
3 It's <u>incredibly</u> <u>easy</u> – <u>even</u> a <u>child</u> could <u>do</u> it!
4 I <u>thought</u> he was <u>Portuguese</u>, but <u>actually</u> he's <u>Brazilian</u>.
5 You <u>said</u> they'd <u>already</u> <u>gone</u>, but <u>apparently</u> they're <u>still</u> <u>here</u>.
6 I <u>absolutely</u> <u>love</u> <u>Italian</u> <u>food</u>, <u>especially</u> <u>pizza</u>.

4 WRITING

a ● Focus on the instructions and the rules. Then put SS in pairs and get them to choose a title.

b ● Get SS to write their plot together. Encourage them to make it as short as possible but not to count the words yet.

c ● Now give SS time to edit their story to get the right number of words. Remind them that they have to include two adverbs. Monitor and help as they write, suggest ways they could cut down or expand their stories.

d ● When SS have finished get them to swap stories with other pairs, or get the pairs to read their stories aloud for the class to vote for their favourite.

Extra support

Tell SS you're going to dictate a plot for the story 'A holiday romance'. Then dictate the following story:

They met on the beach and immediately they fell in love. They spent every day together. When she left he promised faithfully to write. At home she sat by the computer but her inbox was always empty.

Now tell SS that the story is 37 words long. They need to add 13 more words to improve the story and make it into a mini-saga. Give SS time to do this in pairs, and then get them to read out their stories.

5 SPEAKING

Put SS in pairs and tell them to go to **Communication** *Reading habits* on *p.117*. Go through the instructions and the questionnaire, and check SS understand all the text types. **A** then interviews **B** with the questionnaire. Monitor, and encourage **A** to ask for more information where appropriate. They then swap roles.

6 READING & LISTENING

a ● **2.11** Focus on the **Reading for pleasure** box and go through it with SS. Then focus on the instructions. Tell SS that this story recently won an Internet short-story competition. It is unadapted, so should be challenging but not too difficult; remind SS to use the illustrations and glossaries to help them.

● Tell SS they are going to read and listen to a story in chunks, and then answer a few questions. Now play the CD. Get SS to discuss the questions. Check answers.

> **1** Little Brother™ is a robot doll. TM stands for trademark, which means a name or a symbol which a company uses for its products, e.g. Kleenex™, Lycra™.
> **2** Talking like a baby, before he / she can say actual words.
> **3** He pressed a button which switched Little Brother™ off.

● You could ask a few more comprehension questions, e.g. *Why did Peter want a Little Brother? Why did Peter's mother make him wait for so long?*

2.11   CD1 Track 36

Little Brother™
by Bruce Holland Rodgers
Peter had wanted a Little Brother™ for three Christmases in a row. His favourite TV commercials were the ones that showed just how much fun he would have teaching Little Brother™ to do all the things that he could already do himself. But every year, Mommy had said that Peter wasn't ready for a Little Brother™. Until this year.
This year when Peter ran into the living room, there sat Little Brother™ among all the wrapped presents, babbling baby talk, smiling his happy smile, and patting one of the packages with his fat little hand. Peter was so excited that he ran up and gave Little Brother™ a big hug around the neck. That was how he found out about the button. Peter's hand pushed against something cold on Little Brother™'s neck, and suddenly Little Brother™ wasn't babbling any more, or even sitting up. Suddenly, Little Brother™ was limp on the floor, as lifeless as any ordinary doll.

● **2.12** Play the CD. Get SS to discuss the questions. Check answers.

> **4** She bounced him on her knee and told him what a good boy he was.
> **5** With the skin of the face in lines / folds, e.g. when you are going to cry.
> **6** It makes you think that later Peter will change his mind and decide Little Brother™ was not such a good present.

● You could ask a few more comprehension questions, e.g. *Why did Peter like the fire engine? Why didn't Peter get as many presents as last year?*

2.12   CD1 Track 37

'Peter!' Mommy said.
'I didn't mean to!'
Mommy picked up Little Brother™, sat him in her lap, and pressed the black button at the back of his neck.

Little Brother™'s face came alive, and it wrinkled up as if he were about to cry, but Mommy bounced him on her knee and told him what a good boy he was. He didn't cry after all.
'Little Brother™ isn't like your other toys, Peter,' Mommy said. 'You have to be extra careful with him, as if he were a real baby.'
She put Little Brother™ down on the floor, and he took tottering baby steps toward Peter. 'Why don't you let him help open your other presents?'
So that's what Peter did. He showed Little Brother™ how to tear the paper and open the boxes. The other toys were a fire engine, some talking books, a wagon, and lots and lots of wooden blocks. The fire engine was the second-best present. It had lights, a siren, and hoses just like the real thing. There weren't as many presents as last year, Mommy explained, because Little Brother™ was expensive. That was okay. Little Brother™ was the best present ever! Well, that's what Peter thought at first.

● **2.13** Play the CD. Get SS to discuss the questions. Check answers.

> **7** He took the torn wrapping paper out of the wagon and threw it on the floor; he turned the pages of Peter's book too fast.
> **8** Suddenly took and held hard.
> **9** Accept all possible answers here but don't tell them what is going to happen.

● You could ask a few more comprehension questions, e.g. *What happened when Peter tried to build a tower? Why do you think Peter didn't want Little Brother to cry?*

2.13   CD1 Track 38

At first, everything that Little Brother™ did was funny and wonderful. Peter put all the torn wrapping paper in the wagon, and Little Brother™ took it out again and threw it on the floor. Peter started to read a talking book, and Little Brother™ came and turned the pages too fast for the book to keep up.
But then, while Mommy went to the kitchen to cook breakfast, Peter tried to show Little Brother™ how to build a very tall tower out of blocks. Little Brother™ wasn't interested in seeing a really tall tower. Every time Peter had a few blocks stacked up, Little Brother™ swatted the tower with his hand and laughed. Peter laughed, too, for the first time, and the second. But then he said, 'Now watch this time. I'm going to make it really big.'
But Little Brother™ didn't watch. The tower was only a few blocks tall when he knocked it down.
'No!' Peter said. He grabbed hold of Little Brother™'s arm. 'Don't!'
Little Brother™'s face wrinkled. He was getting ready to cry.
Peter looked toward the kitchen and let go. 'Don't cry,' he said. 'Look, I'm building another one! Watch me build it!'
Little Brother™ watched. Then he knocked the tower down.
Peter had an idea.

● **2.14** Play the CD. Get SS to discuss the questions. Check answers.

> **10** Because she saw that Little Brother™ was on the floor and had been switched off.
> **11** Because even when he is switched off, he can still see, hear and feel.
> **12** Because she hadn't noticed his tower and hadn't noticed that he had already picked up the wrapping paper once.
> **13** Accept all possible answers here but don't tell them what is going to happen.

> **2.14** CD1 Track 39
>
> When Mommy came into the living room again, Peter had built a tower that was taller than he was, the best tower he had ever made. 'Look!' he said.
> But Mommy didn't even look at the tower. 'Peter!' She picked up Little Brother™, put him on her lap, and pressed the button to turn him back on. As soon as he was on, Little Brother™ started to scream. His face turned red.
> 'I didn't mean to!'
> 'Peter, I told you! He's not like your other toys. When you turn him off, he can't move but he can still see and hear. He can still feel. And it scares him.'
> 'He was knocking down my blocks.'
> 'Babies do things like that,' Mommy said. 'That's what it's like to have a baby brother.'
> Little Brother™ howled.
> 'He's mine,' Peter said too quietly for Mommy to hear. But when Little Brother™ had calmed down, Mommy put him back on the floor and Peter let him toddle over and knock down the tower.
> Mommy told Peter to clean up the wrapping paper, and she went back into the kitchen. Peter had already picked up the wrapping paper once, and she hadn't said thank you. She hadn't even noticed.
> Peter wadded the paper into angry balls and threw them one at a time into the wagon until it was almost full. That's when Little Brother™ broke the fire engine. Peter turned just in time to see him lift the engine up over his head and let it drop.

b ● **2.15** Tell SS that they are now going to hear the end of the story. Focus on the questions. Then play the CD once. Get SS to discuss the questions. Then play the CD again. Elicit answers from SS but don't tell them exactly what the answers are.

> **2.15** CD1 Track 40
>
> (tapescript in Student's Book on *p.123*)
> 'No!' Peter shouted.
> The windshield cracked and popped out as the fire engine hit the floor. Broken. Peter hadn't even played with it once, and his second best Christmas present was broken.
> Later, when Mommy came into the living room, she didn't thank Peter for picking up all the wrapping paper. Instead, she scooped up Little Brother™ and turned him on again.
> He trembled and screeched louder than ever.
> 'My God! How long has he been off?' Peter's mother demanded.

'I don't like him!'
'Peter, it scares him! Listen to him!'
'I hate him! Take him back!'
'You are not to turn him off again. Ever!'
'He's mine!' Peter shouted. 'He's mine and I can do what I want with him! He broke my fire engine!'
'He's a baby!'
'He's stupid! I hate him! Take him back!'
'You are going to learn to be nice with him.'
'I'll turn him off if you don't take him back. I'll turn him off and hide him someplace where you can't find him!'
'Peter!' Mommy said, and she was angry. She was angrier than he'd ever seen her before. She put Little Brother™ down and took a step toward Peter. She would punish him. Peter didn't care. He was angry, too.
'I'll do it!' he yelled. 'I'll turn him off and hide him someplace dark!'
'You'll do no such thing!' Mommy said. She grabbed his arm and spun him around. The spanking would come next.
But it didn't. Instead he felt her fingers searching for something at the back of his neck.

c ● Now get SS to go to the tapescript on *p.123*, and play the CD again for them to listen and read, and check their answers to **b** 1–4. Explain / translate any vocabulary problems.

> **1** He switched him off.
> **2** She was very angry with Peter.
> **3** He threatened to turn Little Brother™ off and hide him somewhere where his mother can't find him.
> **4** She switched Peter off!

d ● Do this as an open class question.
● Finally, tell SS to go to **Phrasal verbs in context File 2** on *p.157* and complete the phrasal verbs which have come up in this File. (Answers *p.155*)

Extra photocopiable activities

Grammar
adverbs *p.165*
Communicative
Guess my adverb *p.203* (instructions *p.192*)
Vocabulary
Revision race *p.224* (instructions *p.221*)

HOMEWORK

Study Link Workbook *pp.20–22*

Lesson plan

In the first part of this lesson the person interviewed is Hayley Levine, who has been working for several years as a flight attendant with *First Choice Airways*. In the second part of the lesson, people in the street are asked how they feel when they fly, what they like least about flying, and if they have ever had any frustrating experiences when travelling by air.

Study Link These lessons are on the *New English File Upper-intermediate* DVD / Video which can be used instead of the class CD (See Introduction *p.9*). SS can get more practice on the MultiROM, which contains more of the short street interviews with a listening task and tapescripts.

Optional lead-in (books closed)

- Tell SS to go to *p.25* and revise the vocabulary they learnt for Air Travel. They can either test themselves by covering the column on the right and trying to remember the words, or they can test each other: **A** (book open) reads the sentences in **At the airport** and **B** (book closed) says the missing words. They then swap roles for **On the plane**.

THE INTERVIEW

a ● Books open. Focus on the photos and get SS to tell you what they can see.

> A flight attendant, a plane safety card, and an emergency exit in a plane.

- Now focus on the task and on the glossary. Go through it with the class eliciting from them how to pronounce the words and phrases.

b ● **2.16** Focus on the task. Put SS in pairs and give them time to read the questions. Encourage SS not to write anything down when they listen the first time. They should listen and try to get the gist of what she is saying, and then discuss the questions with their partner.

- Play the CD once (**Part 1**). Give SS time to discuss the questions and tell each other what they understood. Then play the CD once or twice more. This time SS might want to jot down things they heard to help them remember the answers to the questions. Check answers.

> 1 Because she always wanted to travel, and saw an advert in the newspaper.
> 2 customer service (= how to look after passengers), relations (= public relations)
> 3 safety training (e.g. how to deal with fires, evacuations, water landing, passengers) and immediate care
> 4 someone outgoing (= extrovert), who can work well in a team, someone who is competent and confident in what they do
> 5 Good side: you see the world. Bad side: sick bags (i.e. passengers being sick), gruelling on your social life (= it's hard to have a normal social life)
> 6 Don't wear a watch; if you're going east, try to stay up and fight the jetlag.

(tapescript in Student's Book on *p.123*)

I = interviewer, H = Hayley Levine

I Hayley Levine is a flight attendant for *First Choice Airways*. What made you want to be a flight attendant?

H I never really wanted to be a flight attendant, I just kind of knew that I always wanted to travel, always had this idea that I wanted to see the world, saw an advert in a newspaper, went for the interview, got the job and loved it. So, and it's definitely for me, definitely.

I What kind of training did you have?

H In order to become a flight attendant, you have your group interview first, you're singled out, you have a one-on-one interview, and then if you pass that stage, you go on to your training which is five weeks: first week's all about customer service, relations, things like that, and then you go on to all your safety training which is four weeks' intensive training, you know, how to deal with fires, evacuations, water landing, passengers and then you're also, you're quite well trained on immediate care, so you know, that's quite an important part of our job, if something happens up in the air, something medical, you know, you need to be trained to deal with it quickly, efficiently.

I What kind of person do you think the airlines are looking for? I mean what kind of person makes a good flight attendant?

H I don't know exactly what they're looking for but I can only think they look for someone who's quite outgoing, someone who can work quite well in a team, you have to be a certain kind of character to do what we do, I mean you fly with different people every day, you know, you go into work, anything could happen, there's thousands and thousands of crew, you don't work with the same people, you need to be able to just get on with people that you've never met before, work under pressure sometimes, so I think they're looking for someone who is, you know, quite competent in what they do, quite confident, just someone who's a team player really.

I Tell me, what do you think are good and bad sides of the job?

H Good sides, obviously I get to see the world pretty much for free. I mean it's amazing, you couldn't ask for anything more really.
Bad sides, would be sick bags, probably, and obviously it's really gruelling on your social life, it's more like a way of living than a job. You know, you have to work around it. So…, but yeah, it's good. I wouldn't change it for the world.

I Are there any other downsides?

H Probably the jet lag, that's quite bad. Definitely, you do suffer a lot, but you know, it's part of the job. You just sort of get on with it.

I Have you got any tips for dealing with jet lag?

H Tips? I don't wear a watch, sometimes that helps. And if you're going sort of east, just try and stay up, just try and fight the jet lag, that's the best way. I definitely find it easier going east than I do west. I don't know why that is.

Extra challenge

You could use the tapescript above to elicit more detailed answers from SS.

c ● **2.17** Focus on the task and play the CD once (**Part 2**). Give SS time to discuss the questions and what they understood. Then play the CD once or twice more. Check answers.

> 1 Try to talk to them and calm them down.
> 2 They usually let you know, they walk on shaking, or ask for vodka.
> 3 There was one man who was very scared of flying. She tried to calm him down but just before take-off he had a panic attack, and tried to open the emergency exit door. They had to take him off the plane.
> 4 She has never had to do it and hopes she never will.
> 5 She never feels nervous or afraid. She feels really safe.

2.17 CD1 Track 42

(tapescript in Student's Book on *p.123*)

I You must come into contact with a lot of passengers who are afraid of flying. How do you deal with this?

H A lot of passengers are afraid of flying. There's not really a lot you can do. Just try and sit and talk to them, calm them down. I think your confidence is sort of always a good booster, as well if they know that you're competent in what you do, I think that helps. Most of them are OK after take-off, it's just that initial getting into the air, and then they're all right.

I How can you tell if someone's scared?

H If they're a scared flyer, they do usually let you know, or they walk on shaking so much that it's pretty obvious that they're scared of flying. You do feel sorry for them. Everyone's scared of something. But, yeah, they usually make themselves known. Or come straight up and ask for vodka. That's when you usually know someone's scared of flying. I did have a guy once, though, just before take-off and he was really really scared of flying and I'd spent a good half an hour with him before the flight trying to calm him down and we just got towards take-off and he tried to open the emergency exit door. He was having a panic attack. So, yeah, that was probably the worst thing. He didn't want to fly, we got him off. Poor guy, I felt really sorry for him.

I Have you ever been in a dangerous situation, for example, have you had to evacuate a plane?

H I've never had to evacuate an aircraft, never, and hopefully never will. But we're trained to do that, so, you know, really well trained to do that, but hopefully nothing like that will ever happen. Never even remotely come close to it. So, that's good.

I Have you ever felt nervous or frightened on a flight?

H No, not really. Never, actually. I think the worst thing is probably a bit of turbulence, but to be honest, that's an excuse to sit down and have a cup of tea. So, you know, no, I've never really felt frightened in the air. I feel really safe up there, really safe, otherwise I wouldn't do it.

---

d ● **2.18** This exercise gives SS intensive listening practice in deciphering phrases where words are often run together, and introduces them to some common expressions often used in spoken English. Focus on the phrases and give SS time to read them. Play the CD, pausing after the first phrase and replaying it as necessary. Elicit the missing words, and then the meaning of the whole phrase. Repeat for the other five phrases.

> 1 **deal with it** (= solve the problem)
> 2 **team player** (= idiomatic way of saying a person who works well in a team)
> 3 I wouldn't **change it for the world** (= idiomatic way of saying *I wouldn't change it for anything*)
> 4 **get on with it** (= phrasal verb meaning *carry on and do what you have to do*)
> 5 I felt really **sorry for him** (= feel pity or sympathy for someone)
> 6 **otherwise** (= if not), e.g. *Go to bed otherwise you'll feel tired tomorrow.*

2.18 CD2 Track 2

> 1 (if something happens) … you need to be trained to deal with it quickly, efficiently.
> 2 …just someone who's a team player really.
> 3 Yeah, it's good. I wouldn't change it for the world.
> 4 You do suffer a lot, but, you know, it's part of the job. You just sort of get on with it.
> 5 Poor guy, I felt really sorry for him.
> 6 I feel really safe up there, really safe, otherwise I wouldn't do it.

---

e ● Tell SS to go to *p.123* and to look at the tapescript for the interview. Play the CD (**Part 1** and **Part 2**) again and tell SS to read and listen at the same time. Deal with any vocabulary problems and get feedback from SS on what parts they found hard to understand and why, e.g. speed of speech, pronunciation, etc.

● Finally, focus on the question. You could also ask SS *Do you know anyone who is afraid of flying? What effect does it have on their lives?* Get SS to answer in pairs or as a whole class. Then get feedback from the whole class.

IN THE STREET

a ● **2.19** Focus on the photos of the people and elicit impressions (possible age, occupation, etc.). Tell SS that they were all interviewed in Covent Garden, a busy shopping area in Central London.

● Focus on the task. Play the CD once, and get SS to compare ideas. Then play it again pausing after each speaker to check answers. Elicit that none of the speakers is afraid of flying.

> not enough space… 4 (Ben)
> bad weather conditions 2 (Jordan)
> what you are given to eat 1 (Anne)
> not being able to control… 3 (Jeff)

2.19 CD2 Track 3

(tapescript in Student's Book on *p.123*)

I = interviewer, A = Anne, Jo = Jordan, J = Jeff, B = Ben

Anne

I How do you feel when you fly?

A I love it. I really love flying. I like going to different places, it doesn't matter how long it takes. I just love flying.

I What do you least like about flying?

A The meals on the plane, that's what I don't like about flying.

I Have you ever had a frustrating experience when you were flying?

A Yes, I did actually. Last year, but it wasn't actually on the plane, it was beforehand. I had too much luggage at Delhi airport and they wouldn't let me on the plane and they were trying to say that I'd have to pay a lot of money. But eventually I bribed somebody!

Jordan
I   How do you feel when you fly?
JO I love flying. I do.
I   What do you least like about flying?
JO I don't like turbulence a lot because when it shakes it makes me a little nervous. But I like flying because you're isolated and you can't use your cell phone or anything. I like that.
I   Have you ever had a frustrating experience when you were flying?
JO Yeah, one time they lost my baggage, so I had to spend my holiday without my luggage.

Jeff
I   How do you feel when you fly?
J   Predominantly comfortable, I think it's a state of mind.
I   What do you least like about flying?
J   That I'm not in control of the situation that I'm in, that I'm putting my safety in someone else's hands.
I   Have you ever had a frustrating experience when you were flying?
J   Air travel, security-wise is very frustrating – not being able to take things on a plane and the huge queues at the airports.

Ben
I   How do you feel when you fly?
B   Safe, I mean I have no problems with travelling at all. Security checks are a bit annoying, but it's a kind of necessary evil, I suppose.
I   What do you least like about flying?
B   Probably either the leg room or the food. They're probably the two worst.
I   Have you ever had a frustrating experience when you were flying?
B   A stopover in Chicago for quite a while, a few years ago but nothing major, no.

b ● Focus on the task and give SS time to go through the sentences. Check SS understand *excess baggage* in question 4 (= luggage which is heavier than the limit permitted by the airline. You often have to pay extra for the extra weight.) Play the CD once. Get SS to compare what they think. Play it again if necessary and check answers.

> 1 Jordan
> 2 Ben
> 3 Jeff
> 4 Anne

c ● **2.20** Focus on the phrases and give SS time to read them. Play the CD, pausing after the first phrase and replaying it as necessary. Elicit the missing word, and then the meaning of the whole phrase. Repeat for the other three phrases.

> 1 But it wasn't **actually** on the plane (= informal way of saying *in fact, really*)
> 2 Yeah, **one time** they lost my baggage (= informal way of saying *on one occasion*, especially in American English)
> 3 Air travel **security-wise** is very frustrating. (= informal way of saying *as regards / concerning* security. In spoken English we sometimes add *-wise* to a noun, e.g. *Moneywise my new job is better.*)
> 4 **Nothing major** (= informal way of saying *important*)

2.20   CD2 Track 4
1 But it wasn't actually on the plane.
2 Yeah, one time they lost my baggage.
3 Air travel security-wise is very frustrating.
4 Nothing major, no.

---

d ● Tell SS to go to *p.123* and to look at the tapescript for **IN THE STREET**. Play the CD again and tell SS to read and listen at the same time. Deal with any vocabulary problems and get feedback from SS on what parts they found hard to understand and why, e.g. speed of speech, elision, pronunciation, etc.

● Finally, focus on the three questions that the interviewer asked the people, and get SS to interview each other in pairs. Then get feedback from the whole class.

HOMEWORK

Study Link **Workbook** *p.23*

Lesson plan

This second writing lesson focuses on using the narrative tenses practised in **File 2**, and also on using adjectives and adverbs to make a story more vivid.

a ● Focus on the instructions and give SS a few minutes to read the story. Elicit the answers to the questions.

> He wrote an email, which had a negative comment about his boss's wife in it, and accidentally sent it to his boss. He was sacked.

Extra idea

Ask more questions about the story, e.g. *What company did he work for? Why didn't he like his boss's wife?*, etc.

b ● Now focus on the task and on the adverbs and adjectives in the list. Remind SS to think about both the meaning and the position when they are choosing which word to put in the gap. Check answers.

1 family-run	6 new
2 reasonably	7 extremely
3 well	8 quick
4 aggressive	9 immediately
5 frequently	10 An hour later

c ● Focus on the instructions. Remind SS that in a story they can either use reported speech or direct speech, i.e. dialogue, but that if they use dialogue, they must punctuate it properly. Give SS time to write out the sentences with the correct punctuation. Remind them to look at the dialogue in the story to help them. Check answers either by getting a student to write the text with punctuation on the board or by writing it yourself.

> 'Sit down,' Mr Simpson said coldly. 'I want to talk to you about an email you sent.'

● Highlight that inverted commas go outside any other punctuation, e.g. full stops, commas, and question marks. Inverted commas can be single or double (").

d ● Focus on the task and the **Useful language** box, and give SS a few moments to correct the mistakes. Check answers.

1 At that moment	4 One morning in
2 As soon as	September
3 Ten minutes later	5 just in time

WRITE a short story

Go through the instructions. Then either get SS to plan and write the story in class (set a time limit of about 20 minutes) or get them just to plan in class and write at home, or set both planning and writing for homework.

If SS do the writing in class, get them to swap their stories with another student to read and check for mistakes before you collect them all in.

Test and Assessment CD-ROM

CEF Assessment materials

File 2 Writing task assessment guidelines

For instructions on how to use these pages, see *p.33*.

GRAMMAR

1 a	2 c	3 c	4 b	5 a	6 c	7 b	8 a		
9 c	10 b								

VOCABULARY

a
1 hooded – the others describe the design of a material
2 smart – the others are materials
3 station – the others are to do with air travel
4 backpack – the others are clothes
5 hang up – the others describe how clothes look on a person
6 friendly – the others are adverbs

b
1 off	5 in
2 out	6 like
3 behind	7 at
4 up	

c
1 lately	5 luggage
2 fit	6 especially
3 even	7 getting changed
4 hard	

PRONUNCIATION

a
1 linen (it's /ɪ/)	4 took (it's /ʊ/)
2 nearly (it's /ɪə/)	5 changed (it's /d/)
3 weren't (it's /ɜː/)	

b <u>sty</u>lish, un<u>dressed</u>, <u>a</u>rrivals, <u>pa</u>ssenger, <u>ac</u>tually

CAN YOU UNDERSTAND THIS TEXT?

a 1 E 2 A 3 B 4 D 5 C

b **bullets** = small metal objects that are fired from a gun
allayed my fears = calmed me down, stopped me being afraid
rotten = that has gone bad and can't be eaten
overhead locker = small cupboard above your head on a plane where you can leave your clothes, bags, etc.
flipped the plane over = turned the plane upside down
fellow = used to describe sb who is the same as you in some way

CAN YOU UNDERSTAND THESE PEOPLE?

a 1 b 2 c 3 c 4 a 5 b

b 1 Cold, reserved, often depressed, and maybe suicidal.
2 Quite a lot, except for the suicide rate.
3 Because it hasn't fought in a war for 200 years.
4 They are very patriotic, passionate about protecting the environment, and very good at recycling.
5 They are very good in the house.

1 A So what did you get in the end?

B Well, I tried on loads of things but they were either the wrong size or the wrong colour. There was this divine bright blue leather jacket and it was really reduced, but I could only find a small and I very nearly got a black cashmere sweater, but then I thought, actually I've got one just like it already, so I left it and in the end I went back to where the jackets were and I found the blue one in a medium so I got it. But now I'm not sure if I'll ever wear it.

2 Well, I've been here for about six months and I can tell you that the English are a lot stricter about being punctual than we are in Australia. Some English friends of mine asked me to dinner and I said what time and they said about eight o'clock. Well, I didn't want to come too early because in Australia that's not good manners. So I arrived at about eight twenty-five and when my friend opened the door she said 'At last! Here you are! We thought you'd got lost.' I mean she made it pretty clear that I was late! Apparently it's OK to come about 15 minutes later than the time people say but not more…strange huh? Back home people wouldn't mind at all, would they?

3 A So, what did you think, John?

B Well, I have to say that I didn't really enjoy it – in fact, I didn't like it at all. Of course I know some people love her style. And I quite enjoyed the last one – what was it? – *The Station master's daughter* but that had a good plot and this one was just all over the place. And it's not that the characters weren't interesting – they were, but as soon as I started to get interested in one of them they would suddenly disappear and new ones would appear. In the end, I just couldn't work out what was happening.

4 Air Brittania announces a change of gate for Flight AB 578 flight to Budapest. This flight will now be departing from gate B 50.

5 A Excuse me?

B Yes?

A Do you know if the flight from Santiago has arrived yet?

B Er yes, it arrived about half an hour ago.

A The Iberia one that came via Madrid?

B That's right. But it arrived in Terminal 2. This is Terminal 3.

A Oh no. Then I've been waiting in the wrong place. Do you think all the passengers will have come out by now?

B It's hard to say. It all depends how long it takes for them to get their luggage and come through customs.

A Is there any way you could put a message out in Terminal 2 so that I can let them know I'm coming? Otherwise they might think I'm not here to meet them.

B Yes, I can. What are their names?

A lot of people think of us as cold and reserved, and often depressed, maybe even suicidal, but I don't think this is a good description of us. I suppose it's true that we have a tendency to be rather melancholic, maybe because of our long dark winters, but I don't think our suicide rate is especially high at all.

I think the Swedes do take life very seriously. And we are very self-conscious, especially in social situations, so maybe we do sometimes appear to be quite shy and cold when you first meet us. But, when you get to know a Swede, I think you will find us to be very friendly and hospitable. Even, may I say, warm.

I think another very common characteristic of Swedish people is a wish to avoid conflict. It's not a coincidence that the Swedish army has not fought in a war for 200 years. But even in our day-to-day life we always try to reach agreement with each other, we don't like fighting or arguing. Personally, I think that's a very positive feature of the Swedish personality.

I think as a nation we are very patriotic – maybe because we are such a small country. If you go to Sweden, you will see the Swedish flag everywhere you go: on houses, on the tables in restaurants, even on birthday cakes. We are great nature lovers – we love being in the countryside. In the winter we ski and in the summer we walk and have picnics. We are also very ecologically minded. We also believe very passionately in protecting the environment – we are very good at recycling and at using cleaner and greener technologies.

Oh, and Swedish men are very good in the house – that's something people always think of us and it's true. It is not uncommon in Sweden for the woman to go out to work and for the man to stay at home looking after the house and after a young baby. I think I can say that Swedish men are very good at changing nappies.

Test and Assessment CD-ROM

File 2 Quicktest

File 2 Test

G passive (all forms), *it is said that…, he is thought to…,* etc.
V crime and punishment
P the letter *u*

The one place a burglar won't look

File 3 overview

Lesson **3A** revises all forms of the passives, and introduces the structure *it is said that… / he is thought to…,* etc. **3B** introduces two new tenses, the future perfect and the future continuous. Finally, in **3C**, SS consolidate and expand their knowledge of future time clauses, and first and zero conditionals. The vocabulary areas of the File are crime, weather and common expressions with *take*.

Lesson plan

In this lesson the general topic is crime. In the first part, there is a speaking and listening which give practical tips on how to protect your house from being burgled, and how to avoid being pickpocketed. In the second half of the lesson SS read about an American judge who gives unusual and creative sentences. Crime provides a natural context for the revision of passive forms and SS also learn how to use the structure *it is said that… / he is said to…* The vocabulary focus in on words related to crime and punishment, and the pronunciation focuses on the different sound-spelling relationship of the letter *u*.

Optional lead-in (books closed)

- Elicit / explain the meaning of the verb 'burgle'.
- If you think SS won't mind, ask them to discuss the following:
  – Has your home (or your friend's or family's) ever been burgled? What was stolen? Which room was it in?
  – Were the burglars ever caught?
  – Was any of the stolen property ever recovered?

1 SPEAKING & LISTENING

a • Books open. Focus on the quiz and elicit / explain what burglars are if you didn't do the optional lead-in above. Then focus on the **GET IT RIGHT** box and go through the expressions with SS.

- As an example discuss the first question with the whole class. Ask them what they think and get individual SS to explain why. Then give SS, in pairs, time to discuss each question explaining the reasons for their answers. Point out that they don't have to agree, they may well have different opinions, and should mark their own answers in their books.

- Get quick feedback from the class as to what they answered for each question, but don't tell them if they are right yet.

b • Tell SS to go to **Communication** *There's only one place burglars won't look…* on *p.117*. Highlight that the information was provided by 50 ex-burglars who were visited in prison by researchers.

- Give SS time to read the answers, and then get feedback on how well they did on the quiz. Ask them if there was any information which surprised them.

c • Focus on the photos and do the questions with the whole class.

> The old man (Fagin) is teaching the boys to become pickpockets (steal money / wallets from people in the street).

d • **3.1** Focus on the instructions. Play the CD once, and then get SS to discuss the questions. Check answers.

> 1 They get people to look at something else, so that they are concentrating on that and not on their money, watch, etc.
> 2 Because pickpockets know that they are going to look at monuments, sights, etc. and will be easy to steal from at that moment.

Extra idea

Get SS in pairs to try to predict the answers to the questions before they listen.

3.1   CD2 Track 7

(tapescript in Student's Book on *p.124*)

I = interviewer, JF = John Freedman

I How did you become the pickpocket consultant for *Oliver Twist*?

JF Well, I'm the director of a company which supplies magicians for live events, and for TV and films. Roman Polanski, the director of the film, he was looking for someone to train the actors – the young boys – to teach them to be pickpockets. He wanted them to be able to pick pockets so fast and so skilfully that it would look like they'd been doing it for years, so that they would look like professional pickpockets. So anyway, the film company got in touch with my company, and then I flew to Prague, where they were shooting the film, to meet Polanski.

I What happened when you met him?

JF Well, he didn't give me a normal interview. He just asked me to steal his watch, without him noticing.

I And did you?

JF Yes, I did. So he gave me the job!

I How long did it take the boys to learn to pick pockets?

JF Not very long. They learned really quickly. To be a good pickpocket you need confidence and children have that confidence. In the end, they got so good that they were stealing from everybody on the film set, even from me. I started to feel a bit like Fagin myself.

I So what's the trick of being a pickpocket?

JF The real trick is to make people notice some things but not others. Some magicians call it 'misdirection', but I call it 'direction' – you have to direct people *towards* what you *want* them to see, and of course *away* from what you *don't want* them to see. Let me show you. What do you have in your jeans pockets?

I Er, just keys.

JF Can you show me them?

I Wow! That's amazing! You've stolen my wallet… and my pen. I really didn't notice a thing…

JF That's the trick you see. All I had to do was to direct your attention to your jeans pocket and your keys, and you forgot about your jacket pocket and your wallet.

I That's incredible. I mean I was prepared – I knew you were going to try to steal from me. And I still didn't see you. So if someone wasn't prepared, it would be even easier?

JF That's right. If you know where people are looking, you also know where they're *not* looking. So for example if someone comes up to you in the street with a map and asks you where something is, they make you look at the map, and perhaps while you're doing that they are stealing your wallet or your phone from your back pocket.

I Tourists are especially at risk from pickpockets, aren't they?

JF Yes, and that's because pickpockets know exactly what they're going to look at, which is usually a building or a monument. For example, take tourists in London. When they come out of Westminster tube station, the first thing people do is look up at Big Ben. And when they look up, it's easy for pickpockets to do their work. And, of course, thieves *love* the posters in the Tube that warn people to be careful with their belongings – you know the ones that say 'Watch out! pickpockets about!'. As soon as men read that, they immediately put their hand on the pocket that their wallet is in, to make sure it's still there. The pickpockets see that and so they know exactly where it is.

I Well, I'm sure that information will be very helpful to everyone and especially to tourists. James Freedman, thank you very much for talking to us this afternoon.

JF You're welcome.

e ● Focus on the questions. Then play the CD once. Get SS to discuss the questions with a partner, and then play the CD again. Check answers.

> 1 Polanski needed someone to train the boy actors so that they would look like professional pickpockets.
> 2 Polanski asked James to come to Prague, where they were shooting the film, for an interview.
> 3 Instead of asking James questions, Polanski asked him to steal his watch without him noticing, which James did successfully.
> 4 He was such a good teacher that soon the boys were successfully stealing from everybody on the film set without them noticing, and this made him feel like the character Fagin.
> 5 'Misdirection' is what some magicians call directing people to what you want them to see, and away from what you don't want them to see.
> 6 James asked what the journalist had in his jeans pocket and he said some keys.
> 7 James managed to steal the journalist's wallet and pen, which were in his jacket pocket, because he had directed his attention to his keys, which were in his jeans pocket.
> 8 If someone comes to you with a map and asks for help, you will look at the map, and then they might steal from you.
> 9 When tourists come out of Westminster tube station they immediately look up at Big Ben and pickpockets often steal from them then.
> 10 When men see this sign they immediately put their hand on the pocket where their wallet is, which tells the pickpockets where it is.

Extra support

If there's time, get SS to listen to the CD with the tapescript on *p.124* so they can see exactly what they understood / didn't understand. Translate / explain any new words or phrases.

f ● Elicit this information from the whole class.

> **a** Hide your valuables in a child's bedroom. Have a dog if possible. Have strong doors and windows. Don't have bushes or trees in front of your house which burglars could hide behind, etc.
> **b** Be careful if someone comes up to you in the street (e.g. with a map) and asks for help. If you see a notice saying beware of pickpockets, don't immediately touch your purse / wallet. Be especially careful with your bag, wallet, etc. when you are looking at, or taking photos of, a famous monument or sight.

2 VOCABULARY crime and punishment

a ● Focus on the instructions. Get SS to compare with a partner.

b ● **3.2** Play the CD for SS to check answers and underline the stressed syllable. Check answers and drill pronunciation.

> See tapescript below

> **3.2**   CD2 Track 8
> 1 <u>bur</u>glar   4 <u>pick</u>pocket
> 2 <u>ro</u>bber   5 <u>mug</u>ger
> 3 <u>shop</u>lifter   6 thief

Extra support

Help SS to remember the words by getting them to close their books and ask *What's a thief? What's a shoplifter?* or *What do you call a person who…?*, etc.

c ● Tell SS to go to **Vocabulary Bank** *Crime and punishment* on *p.149*. Focus on section **1 Crimes and criminals** and get SS to do it individually or in pairs. Check answers and drill pronunciation where necessary.

> **1** I **2** L **3** E **4** F **5** K **6** C **7** A **8** O
> **9** B **10** D **11** J **12** G **13** M **14** N **15** H

● Focus on the box about the difference between *murder, manslaughter* and *assassination* and make sure the difference is clear to SS.

● Point out that:
 – the words for the criminal and the verb are usually another form of the crime word. The exceptions are *drug dealing* where we tend to say *sell* drugs rather than *deal in, terrorism* where there is no general verb, and *theft* where the verb is *steal*.
 – all new verbs are regular except for *set (set – set)*, and *steal* and *sell* which SS should already know.

- Now focus on section **2 What happens to a criminal** and give SS a few minutes to do it. Remind them to write the words in the column at the end, <u>not</u> in the sentences. Check answers and drill pronunciation where necessary.

1	committed	9	jury / evidence
2	investigated	10	verdict
3	caught	11	guilty
4	arrested	12	judge, punishment
5	questioned	13	sentenced
6	charged	14	not guilty
7	court	15	proof
8	Witnesses	16	acquitted

- Highlight that:
  – *charged* = formally accused
  – *court* can refer to the building, or to the institution, e.g. judge and jury. Common expressions with *court* are *to go to court* or *take sb to court*
  – the use of the verb *find* in the expression *found guilty / innocent*. Here *found* = declared
  – the difference between *evidence* (= things which indicate that sb might be guilty) and *proof* (= things that show that sb is definitely guilty)
- Now focus on **Punishments**. You could ask SS if these are also typical punishments in their country.
- Finally, focus on the instruction 'Can you remember the words on this page? Test yourself or a partner'.

Testing yourself

For **Crimes and criminals** SS can cover the chart on the right and try to remember the words for the crimes by reading the example cases. They could then cover the right hand part of the chart to test themselves on the criminals and verbs. For **What happens to a criminal** they can cover the column on the right and read the sentences, and try to remember the missing words.

Testing a partner

See **Testing a partner** *p.20*.

> **Study Link** SS can find more practice of these words and phrases on the MultiROM and on the *New English File Upper-intermediate* website.

- Tell SS to go back to the main lesson on *p.37*.

3 PRONUNCIATION the letter *u*

Pronunciation notes

Like all vowels in English, the letter *u* can be pronounced in different ways and crime vocabulary has several examples of the different pronunciations. Highlight to SS that *ur*, unless followed by an *e*, is normally pronounced /ɜː/, and to watch out for the 'hidden' /j/ in words like *accuse*, *music*, etc.

a • Focus on the task, and get SS to do it individually or in pairs. Encourage them to say the words out loud before deciding which column they go into.

b • **3.3** Play the CD for SS to check. Then check answers and elicit the answers to the two questions.
- Play the CD again pausing after each group of words for SS to listen and repeat.

> See tapescript.
> *caught* and *court* are pronounced exactly the same, and the *u* in *guilty* is silent (as in, e.g. *build*).

3.3	CD2 Track 9
/ʌ/	
drugs	
judge	
mugger	
punishment	
smuggling	
/ɜː/	
burglar	
murderer	
/ɔː/	
caught	
court	
fraud	
manslaughter	
/juː/	
accuse	
community	
/ʊə/	
jury	
/ɪ/	
guilty	

c • Focus on the sentences and get SS to read them alternately in pairs. You could read them first to give SS a model.

d • Focus on the task and give SS time to ask and answer in pairs. Monitor and correct pronunciation where necessary.
- Finally, get feedback from individual SS, and contribute opinions / experiences of your own if appropriate.

Extra support

You could do this as an open class activity eliciting answers from different SS, and contributing yourself.

4 GRAMMAR passive (all forms), *it is said that…, he is thought to…*, etc.

a • **Check what you know.** This exercise revises formation of the present and past passive, and SS' ability to choose between the active and passive forms.
- Focus on the first two stories and the different tasks. Tell SS they are all true stories. Give SS time to do the exercises and then correct answers.

World Cup thief's own goal
1 stole
2 was caught
3 was mugged
4 discovered
5 took
6 was met
7 found
8 were informed
9 was arrested

Parrot held in prison
1 being interrogated
2 ordered
3 is called
4 to be held
5 belonged
6 be sent
7 support

Extra challenge

Alternatively, get SS in pairs to retell one story each from memory.

- If SS are having problems, go to the Workbook *p.25*. Go through the rules and do the exercise.
b • **New grammar**. Get SS to read the third story. Elicit the answer to the question from the class.

He hypnotizes cashiers and gets them to hand over money.

c • Get SS to focus on the highlighted phrases, and then ask the class the questions.

They only suspect it.
After *it is said* (*thought / believed*), etc. you use *that* + a clause
After *he is said* (*thought / believed*), etc. you use *to* + infinitive
NOTE: After *I / you / we / they*, you also use *to* + infinitive

d • Tell SS to go to **Grammar Bank 3A** on *p.136*. Go though the examples and rules with the class.

Grammar notes

- **passive (all forms)**
  SS at this level should be familiar with all the different forms of the passive but it is likely that they will be more confident with the present and past forms that they have been using since Pre-intermediate level than with the more complex forms (e.g. past continuous, past perfect, gerund and infinitive).
- Some SS may tend to overuse *by* and want to include it every time they use the passive. One of the exercises given here is to try to correct this tendency.
- *It is said... He is thought to...*
  These 'advanced' passive structures are included more for recognition than production as they are low frequency in spoken English. However, SS will certainly come across them if they read news websites or watch TV in English.

- Focus on the exercises for **3A** on *p.137* and get SS to do them individually or in pairs. Check answers after each exercise.

a 1 The road was closed after the accident.
2 My handbag has been stolen.
3 My house is being painted.
4 A meeting will be held tomorrow.
5 They were fined (for travelling without a ticket).
6 You can be arrested for drink-driving.
7 Miranda thinks she was being followed last night.
8 The house had been sold five years earlier.

b 1 It is believed that the burglar is a local man. The burglar is believed to be a local man.
2 It is said that the muggers are very dangerous. The muggers are said to be very dangerous.
3 It is thought that the robber entered through an open window. The robber is thought to have entered through an open window.
4 It is said that the murderer has disappeared. The murderer is said to have disappeared.
5 It is expected that the trial will last three weeks. The trial is expected to last three weeks.

- Tell SS to go back to the main lesson on *p.38*.
e • Focus on the fourth story and get SS to use the prompts to write the missing phrases / sentences. Check answers.

1 is believed to be
2 is said to be
3 is thought that he has robbed
4 is reported to be

- Finally, ask SS which of the four stories they thought was the most incredible.

5 READING

a • Focus on the task and questions and make sure SS understand all the vocabulary, e.g. *kittens* = baby cats, *residential area* = area where lots of people live, *loaded* = with bullets in it. Then get SS to discuss the questions in pairs.
- Get feedback and elicit ideas. Get SS to justify their punishments.
b • Now focus on the article and the task. You might want to pre-teach *to offend* (= to commit a crime) and *an offender* (= a person who commits a crime). Tell SS to read the first four paragraphs of the article to find the answers to the questions.
- Get SS to compare with a partner and then check answers. Ask the class what they think of his punishments.

1 She had to spend the night in the same forest.
2 They have to choose between having their licence suspended for 90 days or for less time and working for a day as a school crossing guard.
3 He had to go to a mortuary to view dead bodies.
4 They had to organize a picnic for primary school children.
5 They had to spend a day of silence in the woods or listen to classical music instead of rock.

c • Focus on the information box and go through it with the class. Then read the questions and set a time limit for SS to read the whole article to find the information. Then get SS to answer the questions orally in pairs.

Extra idea

You could get SS to underline the parts of the text that give them the answers.
- Check answers.

1   Hard. He was from a poor family, the oldest of nine children. He has been very successful (president of the American Judges Association).
2   Michelle Murray, the man with the loaded gun, and the noisy neighbours learn from personal experiences. The drivers and the teenage vandals have to do something for other people.
3   His background. He thinks he understands why some people commit crimes. He thinks they are better than conventional punishments because people don't reoffend, and the evidence that he is right is that only two people have.

Extra support

Help SS by explaining / translating any new vocabulary which they couldn't guess from context.

d • Ask the question to the whole class and elicit opinions. Give your opinion too.

6 SPEAKING

a • Go through the **GET IT RIGHT** box with SS. Point out that in the passive *make* is followed by *to* + infinitive, e.g. *I was made to tidy my room*. SS have previously learnt that in the active *make* is followed by the infinitive <u>without</u> *to*, e.g. *My parents made me tidy my room*.

   • Go through the six crimes and elicit the meaning of any words you think your SS don't know, e.g. *an arsonist, to set fire to sth*, etc.

   • Put SS in groups of three or four. They should choose a secretary who will make notes of their decisions. You may want to set a time limit, e.g. five minutes, for SS to discuss the creative punishments, but extend it if they need more time. Monitor and encourage SS to use the structures from **GET IT RIGHT**.

b • Get feedback. Start with the first crime and ask each secretary what their group suggest. Then get the class to vote to see which group's punishment they think is best. Do the same with the other five crimes.

Extra photocopiable activities

Grammar
passive *p.166*
Communicative
Crime and punishment *p.204* (instructions *p.192*)

HOMEWORK

Study Link Workbook *pp.24–26*

G future perfect and future continuous
V weather
P vowel sounds

3

B Stormy weather

Lesson plan

This lesson begins with extracts from three Internet blogs about extreme weather, and SS go on to expand their weather vocabulary. After listening to an eyewitness account of the floods in Prague, the topic moves to climate change and what we can do to halt it. The grammar focus is on two tenses, which will be new for most SS, the future continuous and future perfect. The pronunciation focus is on combinations of vowels which can be pronounced in different ways, e.g. *ea* and *oo*.

Optional lead-in (books closed)

- Write on the board
  a boiling hot day   a freezing cold day   a very wet day
- Get SS in pairs to say which kind of day they would find the most unpleasant and why. Encourage them to give examples.
- Monitor and input any vocabulary they need.
- Get some feedback from the class and also tell SS your opinion.

1 READING

a • Books open. Focus on the three blogs and the photos, and ask SS if any of them write their own blogs. Then focus on the task, and give SS a few minutes to read the blogs and try to guess the country / city. Tell them that there are clues in the blogs. Check answers, asking SS which words helped them to guess the places

> 1 Amsterdam, Holland (bikes, canals)
> 2 London, UK (underground, pub)
> 3 The State of California, USA (yard, truck, Interstate 5, awesome)

b • Now get SS to read the blogs again and answer the questions. Encourage them to try to guess new vocabulary from context, and to underline any words they couldn't guess to check later with their partner.
- Check answers.

> 1 1✓ 3✓
> 2 2✓
> 3 3✓
> 4 2✓
> 5 3✓
> 6 1✓ 3✓
> 7 1✓
> 8 1✓ 3✓
> 9 2✓

c • Tell SS to focus on the highlighted words which are all weather related, and to say with a partner what they think they mean. Encourage them to try to give definitions, rather than just translating. Check answers.

storm = very bad weather with strong winds and rain
hurricane-force winds = very strong winds
blown = past participle of *blow* (*blow, blew, blown*) = what the wind does
scorching = very hot
heat = the noun of *hot*
melting = becoming liquid because of the heat
sweat = to lose water through your skin when you are hot, ill or afraid
fan = a machine with blades that go round to create a current of air, or a thing you move in your hand to create air
frozen = past participle of *freeze* = to become hard and often turn to ice
thaws = (of snow) to become water again

- You could point out that *melt* and *thaw* are synonymous when talking about ice and snow only. Ice cream melts; it doesn't thaw.
- Now get SS to compare with their partner any other words they have underlined and help each other to work out the meaning. Explain / translate any they can't work out.

Extra support

At this point you could go through the three blogs with the class, highlighting useful expressions and eliciting / explaining the meaning of new words and phrases.

d • Do these as open class questions. Don't encourage long anecdotes as SS will have the opportunity to describe their own experiences later.

2 VOCABULARY weather

a • Tell SS to go to **Vocabulary Bank *Weather*** on *p.150*. Focus on section **1 What's the weather like?** and point out that the phrases above the weather icons refer to not very cold / hot / rainy / windy weather, and the phrases below the icons refer to very cold / hot / rainy / windy weather. Get SS to do the exercise individually or in pairs. Check answers and drill pronunciation where necessary.

> a 1 cool   8 damp
>   2 chilly   9 drizzling
>   3 freezing   10 showers
>   4 below zero   11 pouring (with rain)
>   5 mild   12 breeze
>   6 warm   13 gale-force
>   7 scorching
> b 1 Mist
>   2 Fog
>   3 Smog

- Highlight that with the weather it's important to be sure whether the word you are using is an adjective or a noun:
  – compare *It's windy* (adj) with *There's a breeze* (n)
  – the difference between *chilly* and *cool* is a question of how pleasant / unpleasant it is. 12° may be cool for one person and chilly for another. This may also vary depending on the part of the world where SS are.
- Now focus on section **2 Extreme weather** and give SS a few minutes to do it. Check answers and drill pronunciation where necessary.

1	heatwave	6	blizzard
2	drought	7	flood
3	hailstorm	8	hurricane
4	lightning	9	tornado
5	thunder	10	monsoon

- Now focus on section **3 Adjectives to describe weather** and give SS a few minutes to do it. Check answers and drill pronunciation where necessary.

1	strong	6	bright
2	heavy	7	changeable
3	thick	8	sunny
4	icy	9	settled
5	clear		

- Point out that:
  – despite having similar meanings, certain adjectives are only used with certain nouns, e.g. you can say *strong winds* but <u>not</u> *strong rain* (you have to say *heavy rain*), and we say *bright sunshine* (<u>not</u> *strong sunshine*)
  – *settled* is the opposite of *changeable*
- Now focus on section **4 Adjectives and verbs connected with weather** and give SS a few minutes to do it. Check answers and drill pronunciation where necessary.

1 C	2 F	3 E	4 G	5 D	6 B	7 A

- Check SS have guessed the meaning of the **bold** words.

slippery = difficult to stand or walk on because it is wet or icy
shivering = shaking a little because you are cold
sweating = losing water through your skin when you are hot, ill or afraid
got soaked = got very very wet
humid = warm and damp
melt = (of snow) become water
get sunburnt = have red skin because of having spent too long in the sun

- Highlight that all the new verbs in this **Vocabulary Bank** (*pour, drizzle, shiver, slip* and *melt*) are regular.
- Finally, focus on the instruction 'Can you remember the words on this page? Test yourself or a partner'.

Testing yourself

For **sections 1–3** tell SS to look at the words in the lists only and try to remember what sort of weather they are associated with. For **section 4** tell SS to cover 1–7, look at A–G and try to remember the sentence that came before.

Testing a partner

See **Testing a partner** *p.20*.

Study Link SS can find more practice of these words and phrases on the MultiROM and on the *New English File Upper-intermediate* website.

- Tell SS to go back to the main lesson on *p.41*.

b ● Focus on the task and give SS a few minutes to talk in pairs and recycle the vocabulary they have just learnt.

Possible answers
1 **a** good: sunny, warm but not scorching; bad: wet, cold, windy
 b good: cool and bright but not too hot; bad: mist or fog, heavy rain, strong winds, etc.
 c good: dry, cool not windy; bad: hot, wet or windy
 d good: a strong breeze; bad: no wind or gale-force winds
 e good: bright, cool and dry; bad: heavy rain, scorching heat, fog / mist
2 (answers will depend on where SS are from)
 a e.g. Milan, London, etc. (SS often have this image of London because of old films and it is true that the city had terrible fog and smog in the first half 20th century but since the Clean Air Act of 1968, which reduced smoke pollution, there has been no more smog and fog is not very common.)
 b e.g. Santiago (Chile), Beijing, etc.
 c e.g. Moscow, New York, etc.
 d e.g. Bangladesh, China, etc.
 e e.g. the Caribbean islands, the USA, etc.

3 PRONUNCIATION vowel sounds

a ● Go through the information in the box about vowels. Then focus on the instructions. Encourage SS to say the words out loud to help them to identify the one that is different.

b ● **3.4** Play the CD once. Check answers.

1	showers	5	flood
2	heat	6	drought
3	mild	7	humid
4	warm	8	world

3.4			CD2 Track 10
1 blow	snow	showers	below
2 weather	sweat	heavy	heat
3 drizzle	blizzard	chilly	mild
4 hard	warm	yard	farm
5 flood	cool	monsoon	loose
6 fought	ought	drought	brought
7 muggy	sunny	hurricane	humid
8 scorching	tornado	world	storm

Extra support

Play the CD again, pausing after each group of words for SS to listen and repeat.

c ● **3.5** Books closed. Tell SS to first listen to the five sentences. Play the CD once without pausing. Then play it again, pausing after each sentence for SS to write. Finally, play it again without pausing.

- Check answers by writing the sentences on the board.

3.5   CD2 Track 11

1 It'll be below zero tomorrow with some snow showers.
2 He was sweating heavily because of the heat.
3 It's windy, chilly, and starting to drizzle.
4 The river is going to flood soon.
5 The day before the hurricane was sunny and muggy.

- Give SS a few minutes to practise saying the sentences.

4 LISTENING

a • **3.6** Focus on the photos, and ask SS to describe what they can see. Then focus on the task and give SS a few moments to read the sentences.

- Play the CD once. Get SS to compare answers and then play it again. Check answers.

Extra support

To help SS understand the listening you could pre-teach *river bank* (= the side of a river and the land near it) and *a looter* (= someone who steals from places after a fire, riot, etc.).

1 F	2 F	3 T	4 F	5 F	6 T	7 T	8 T
9 F	10 F						

3.6   CD2 Track 12

(tapescript in Student's Book on *p.124*)
I was at work when I heard the news on TV. It had been pouring with rain for several days and I could see that the River Vltava was swollen. Now it appeared that there was a real danger that the river would overflow. All of us who lived or worked near the river were being advised to get out and move to a place of safety. My office is in the centre of Prague only a hundred metres from the river bank and I live in a flat in a small town just a few kilometres north of Prague, right on the banks of the River Vltava, so I was in danger both at work and at home.
My wife and baby were at my flat, so I did the sensible thing and went home immediately. I packed my wife and my child into the car and I drove them to her parents' house. They would be completely safe there. So far, so good! But then I stopped being sensible, and I jumped back into the car and went back to our flat. Why did I do that? I told myself that it was because I was afraid of looters breaking into our flat and stealing things, but the truth was that I felt that I wanted to be in the middle of things, to be involved in what was happening.
I stayed up all night watching the TV bulletins. They were giving regular reports on how fast the water level was rising at various places throughout the Czech Republic. There was a journalist reporting from just down the road from where I was, north of Prague, so I could sit in my sitting room and watch the danger increase as the minutes passed, but I still didn't move. I suppose I had a kind of perverse desire to be the last person to leave our block of flats. I could hear cars starting up and setting off all evening, and from time to time I looked out at our car park and I could see that it was almost empty. At about three in the

morning, my car was the only one left in the car park and my nerves gave out – or maybe I just came to my senses, because I finally decided to get into the car and escape. The roads towards Prague were flooded, so I decided to try to get to a relative's house, which was a few kilometres away in the opposite direction, away from the river. I tried various escape routes but even these roads were impassable now. I was about to give up – I thought I'd left it too late. On my last attempt, I drove until I met another car which was blocking the road. The road ahead was flooded, but the driver of the other car was wading into the water to see how deep it was. He said he thought he could make it, so I decided to follow him. The water was rising quickly now, but he drove really really slowly through the water and I felt a bit impatient. Anyway, he managed to get through the water safely. I followed him, but I went much more quickly. Water was coming into the car under the door, and the engine made a funny noise like a cough a couple of times, but I got through and finally arrived safely at my relative's house.
I was one of the lucky ones. My office escaped the flood and my flat wasn't damaged at all as it's on the third floor. But the poor people who lived on the ground floor – their flats were very badly damaged. They had been completely under water.

b • Play the CD again for SS to correct the false sentences. Pause halfway through (after …*I could see that it was almost empty*) for SS to correct 1–5 in pairs. Then play till the end and give them time to correct 6–10. Check answers.

1	He was in danger both at work and at home.
2	He took them to <u>her</u> parents' house.
4	He watched from inside his flat.
5	He saw that it was almost empty.
9	The engine made a funny noise but it didn't break down.
10	Only the ground floor flats were badly damaged.

c • Do this as an open class question, and say what you would have done.

Extra support

If there's time, get SS to listen to the CD with the tapescript on *p.124* so they can see exactly what they understood / didn't understand. Translate / explain any new words or phrases.

5 SPEAKING & WRITING

a • Focus on the **GET IT RIGHT** box and tell SS to think carefully about the modifiers (*very, really,* etc.) and if they are being used correctly. Check answers.

1	It's very cold! ✓ / ~~It's very freezing!~~
2	✓
3	It's really boiling today. ✓ / ~~It's incredibly boiling today.~~
4	~~I was absolutely frightened.~~ / I was absolutely terrified! ✓

- Remind SS that with normal adjectives, e.g. *cold*, you can use *very, really, incredibly* but NOT *absolutely*. With strong adjectives, e.g. *freezing*, you can use *really* and *absolutely* but NOT *very* or *incredibly*.

- Focus on the task. Tell SS to try to choose two kinds of extreme weather that they could talk about, and to think about how they are going to answer the questions.

Extra support

Demonstrate first by telling SS about an experience of your own.

- Put SS in groups of three. One student starts by saying 'I'm going to tell you about at time when…' (you could write this on the board as a prompt).
- Monitor groups and correct any misuse of modifiers. When SS have finished, get feedback by eliciting one experience for each type of weather.

b • Either do this in class, setting a time limit of about 15 minutes, or set it for homework.

6 **3.7** **SONG** ♫ *It's raining men*

- This song was first recorded by the Weather Girls in 1982, but has been re-recorded by various artists including ex-Spice Girl Geri Halliwell, whose version was used on the soundtrack of the film Bridget Jones's Diary. For copyright reasons this is a cover version. If you want to do this song in class, use the photocopiable activity on *p.235*.

3.7   CD2 Track 13

It's raining men

Humidity is rising – barometer's getting low
According to all sources, the street's the place to go
'Cause tonight for the first time
At just about half past ten
For the first time in history
It's gonna start raining men.

It's raining men! Hallelujah! – It's raining men! Amen!

I'm gonna go out, I'm gonna let myself get
Absolutely soaking wet!
It's raining men! Hallelujah!
It's raining men! Every specimen!
Tall, blond, dark and lean
Rough and tough and strong and mean

God bless Mother Nature, she's a single woman too
She took on the heavens and she did what she had to do
She taught every angel to rearrange the sky
So that each and every woman could find her perfect guy

It's raining men! Hallelujah! – It's raining men! Amen!
It's raining men! Hallelujah! – It's raining men! Amen!
(Go get yourselves wet girls, I know you want to)

I feel stormy weather
Moving in, about to begin
Hear the thunder
Don't you lose your head
Rip off the roof and stay in bed

It's raining men! Hallelujah! – It's raining men! Amen!
It's raining men! Hallelujah! – It's raining men! Amen!
It's raining men! Hallelujah! – It's raining men! Amen!

---

7 GRAMMAR future perfect and future continuous

a • **Check what you know**. This exercise revises the three basic future forms, i.e. *will* / *shall*, *going to* and the present continuous. SS should be familiar with the three different forms and their use.

- Focus on the instructions and give SS a few minutes to do the exercise. Get them to compare with a partner and then check answers.

---

1 Shall I close
2 's going to be **or** 'll be
3 **A** it'll rain
   B 'm taking **or** 'm going to take
4 **A** Shall we have
   A 'll lay
5 **A** are you leaving **or** are you going to leave
   B 'll drive, won't be

- If SS are having problems, go to the Workbook *p.28*. Go through the rules and do the exercise.

b • **New grammar**. Focus on the photo and ask SS what they can see (a polar bear on ice), and why they may not be able to see this in the future (because the ice in the North Pole is melting and polar bears will probably become extinct). Ask SS why this is (because of global warming, i.e. the increase in temperature of the world's atmosphere).

- Focus on the article and tell SS they have to complete it with verbs from the list. Elicit that some of them are past participles and some are *-ing* forms, and make sure SS know the meaning of *closed down* (= closed for ever), *doubled* (= increased by 100%) and *risen* (= gone up). Deal with any other vocabulary problems.
- Tell SS to read through the article quickly first, and then try to complete it with the verbs. Get them to compare with a partner. Then check answers. Elicit / explain that *will have* + past participle is the future perfect, and *will be* + verb + *-ing* is the future continuous.

---

1 become	**6** having
2 melted	**7** risen
3 closed down	**8** risen
4 risen	**9** suffering
5 doubled	**10** having

---

c • Now get SS to quickly read the predictions again. Then ask the questions to the whole class and elicit reactions and SS' own experience of climate change.

Extra challenge

Alternatively, get SS to answer the two questions in pairs.

d • Focus on the three sentences and pictures, and get SS to match them. Check answers.

A 2 **B** 3 **C** 1

- Elicit / explain the basic difference between the future, the future continuous and the future perfect:
  – the future simple + time expression = an action will start at that future time
  – the future continuous + time expression = an action will be in progress at that future time
  – the future perfect + time expression = an action will be finished at the latest by that time
- Highlight that *by* + time expression = by that time at the latest

e ● Tell SS to go to **Grammar Bank 3B** on *p.136*. Go though the examples and rules with the class.

Grammar notes

● **the future perfect and continuous**

Although SS will have seen these two tenses passively in reading, this is new grammar and TT's aim should be to make these tenses part of SS' active knowledge.

If SS have the same or similar tense in their L1, it will be worth drawing comparisons. If not, then you will need to make sure the concept is clear. Both tenses are projections in the speaker's mind into the future.

● If we use **the future perfect** instead of the simple future, we are **emphasizing the certain completion of the action**. However, the difference between the two tenses is often quite small.

● The future continuous is essentially the present continuous projected into the future. The speaker imagines himself / herself doing a certain action in the future. You could not use the simple future instead of the future continuous in these situations. Typical mistakes: ~~This time next week I'll lie on the beach / I'm lying on the beach.~~

● Focus on the exercises for **3B** on *p.137* and get SS to do them individually or in pairs. Check answers after each exercise.

a 1 'll / will be flying
2 'll / will have saved
3 'll / will be driving
4 'll / will be having
5 'll / will have paid
6 'll / will have finished
b 1 won't be lying
2 'll / will be working
3 will have disappeared
4 will have doubled
5 will be moving / will have moved
6 will have grown
7 will have run out
8 will have invented
9 'll / will be driving

● Tell SS to go back to the main lesson on *p.43*.

f ● This is an oral practice activity. Focus on the first prediction and the speech bubbles. Then ask the class what they think and elicit ideas. Then get SS to continue in pairs.

Extra idea

You could elicit some more oral practice with these tenses by asking individual SS:
What will you be doing a) in two hours time? b) this time tomorrow?
When do you think you will have finished your studies?, etc.

8 LISTENING & SPEAKING

a ● 3.8 Focus on the photo of Barbara and get SS to say what kind of person they think she is (She looks quite sporty and easy-going).

● Play the CD once. Get SS to compare with a partner what they understood and then elicit answers to the questions from the class.

> She travelled to Australia overland because she didn't want to fly and produce a lot of carbon emissions.

3.8   CD2 Track 14

(tapescript in Student's Book on *p.124*)
More and more of us are trying to do our bit for the environment. But would you go as far as Barbara Haddrill? Six years ago, Barbara, from Powys in Wales, decided to make big changes to her lifestyle because she was worried about climate change, especially about the amount of carbon dioxide emissions that she herself was producing. So she stopped driving, and she started buying organic food from local shops and using a wood fire to heat her home.
But then Barbara was invited to be a bridesmaid at her best friend's wedding in Australia. The flight to Australia takes 24 hours and produces a huge amount of carbon dioxide emissions. But she really wanted to go to the wedding. So now she had a terrible dilemma. To fly or not to fly?
Instead of flying, Barbara decided to travel to Australia over land! She travelled by train and bus through Russia, China, Vietnam, Thailand, then by boat to Singapore, and finally to Australia. The epic journey took her nearly two months. Fortunately, Barbara works part-time at the Centre for Alternative Technology and they were happy to give her such a long holiday.

---

b ● Before playing the CD again, make sure SS understand what *carbon dioxide emissions* are (= the carbon dioxide that is produced and escapes in the atmosphere, e.g. as smoke, fumes, etc.) Get SS to answer the questions with a partner. Check answers.

> 1 To fly or not to fly. She wanted to go to Australia, but on the other hand she didn't want to cause a lot of CO_2 emissions.
> 2 She has stopped driving, has started buying organic food from local shops, and uses a wood fire to heat her house.
> 3 She travelled overland through Russia, China, Vietnam, Thailand and Singapore.
> 4 Because she works for the Centre for Alternative Technology and they allowed her to take a long holiday.

c ● **3.9** Now focus on the chart, and then play the CD twice. Pause if necessary to give SS time to note down the information. Check answers.

cost	distance	time	CO$_2$
£2,000	14,004 miles	51 days	1.65 tonnes
£450	10,273 miles	25 hours	2.7 tonnes

3.9 CD2 Track 15

(tapescript in Student's Book on *p.124*)
But… how much has Barbara *really* done to help the planet? Let's compare the two journeys. Barbara's trip cost her £2,000. She travelled 14,004 miles, and it took her 51 days. The total amount of CO$_2$ emissions her trip produced was 1.65 tonnes. If she had travelled by plane, it would have cost her a quarter of the price, only £450, she would have travelled 10,273 miles, and it would have taken her just 25 hours. But the CO$_2$ emissions would have been 2.7 tonnes.
So yes, Barbara's overland journey did produce less carbon dioxide. On the other hand, of course, if she hadn't gone at all, she wouldn't have produced *any* emissions. So, what do you think of Barbara's trip? We would be very interested in hearing your comments. You can email us at newsday@radio24.co.uk

---

Extra support

If there's time, get SS to listen to the CD with the tapescripts on *p.124* so they can see exactly what they understood / didn't understand. Translate / explain any new words or phrases.

d ● Ask the class what they think, and if they think it was really worth travelling overland.

e ● Focus on the tips and give SS a few minutes to read them. Explain / translate any expressions which SS can't guess – use the photo to explain *energy-saving lightbulbs*.

● Put SS into pairs or small groups. Focus on the task and give them time to talk about each tip. Monitor and help where appropriate.

● Get feedback and find out how ecologically-minded your SS are.

Extra support

Demonstrate the activity first by saying what you do for each thing.

Extra photocopiable activities

Grammar
future perfect and future continuous *p.167*
Communicative
In twenty years' time *p.205* (instructions *p.193*)
Song
It's raining men p.235 (instructions *p.231*)

HOMEWORK

Study Link Workbook *pp.27–29*

3 C

G conditionals and future time clauses; *likely* and *probably*
V expressions with *take*
P sentence stress and rhythm

Taking a risk

Lesson plan

In this lesson SS expand their knowledge of future time clauses and real conditionals, and see the variety of tenses that can be used apart from the present simple and future simple. The topic is risk and the lesson begins with an article which explains how bad we are at assessing risk. In the second half of the lesson SS read and listen to two contrasting attitudes towards exposing young children to risk. The vocabulary focus is on common collocations with *take* (e.g. *take a risk, take seriously*), and pronunciation gives more practice with sentence stress and rhythm. Finally, there is a mini grammar focus on the use of the adverbs *likely* and *probably*.

Optional lead-in (books closed)

- Choose sth you are afraid of (e.g. flying) and ask your SS *How do you think I feel about flying?* Elicit these three ways of talking about what we are afraid of and write them on the board:
  I'm **frightened** of flying.   Flying is **frightening**.
  Flying **frightens** me.
- Elicit / point out that a synonym of *frightened* is *scared* and get SS to give you the three forms, i.e.
  I'm **scared** of flying.   Flying is **scary**.   Flying **scares** me.
- Finally, remind SS that *afraid* is a synonym of *frightened* / *scared* and that it doesn't exist in the other two forms.

1 READING

a • Books open. Focus on the pairs of alternatives. If you didn't do the optional lead-in, make sure SS understand *scares* (= frightens). To help SS you could pre-teach *horrify* (= to make sb feel extremely frightened), *to assess risk* (= to make a judgement about how dangerous sth is), and *probability* (= how likely sth is to happen).

- Get SS to talk to a partner. For each pair, they have to say which alternative scares or worries them more.
- Get feedback. Ask for a show of hands to see which alternative in each pair scares the class more.

b • Focus on the article. Set a time limit for SS to read the article fairly fast and find out which of the two alternatives is actually more dangerous. Check answers.

> drowning for children
> bacteria in the kitchen
> flying and driving carry a very similar risk
> heart disease

c • Now get SS to read the article again carefully. Then get them to discuss the multiple choice questions with a partner, explaining why they think one is right. Remind SS that the best way to be sure they have chosen the right alternative is by eliminating the others.

- Check answers.

> **1** b **2** b **3** a **4** a **5** b

- Deal with any vocabulary problems by explaining / translating any words SS couldn't guess.

d • This exercise revises common adverbs and adverbial phrases used for linking sentences or introducing new ideas. Get SS to look carefully at the highlighted words and phrases to remember how they are used.

> | | | | |
> |---|---|---|---|
> | **1** | However | **5** | whereas |
> | **2** | According to | **6** | Since |
> | **3** | although | **7** | instead |
> | **4** | in fact | | |

- Elicit / explain that:
  - *according to* is used to introduce an idea which is supported by a person / people or research / statistics, e.g. *According to doctors, stress is very bad for our health. According to* is always followed by a noun / name and a comma.
  - *instead (of)* = in place of somebody / something, e.g. *It was too cold to go the park so we went to the cinema instead. / Instead of going to the park we went to the cinema.*
  - *however* is used to add a comment to a previous sentence (often introducing a contrast), e.g. *It poured with rain all day yesterday. However, the forecast for tomorrow is good. However* comes at the beginning of a sentence and is followed by a comma.
  - *In fact* is used to emphasize that something is true or to introduce more detailed information, e.g. *Heart disease is a serious health problem. In fact it is the most common cause of death in many countries.*
  - *whereas* is used to compare and contrast two facts or opinions, e.g. *I love meat whereas my husband is a complete vegetarian.* It is used to join two clauses and is not normally used at the beginning of the sentence.
  - *although* is used to contrast two clauses, e.g. *Although she was ill, she went to work. / She went to work, although she was ill.* Put a comma between the two clauses.
  - *Since* (in this context) = because, as, e.g. *Since John can't come to the meeting on Tuesday, we'll have to have it on Wednesday.*
- Then get SS to use each word or phrase once in the sentences. Check answers.

Extra support

At this point you could go through the article with the class, highlighting useful expressions and eliciting / explaining the meaning of new words and phrases.

e • Do this as an open class question, and tell SS (if you feel you want to share this information) if you have any irrational fears.

2 LISTENING

a • Focus on the task and instructions. Go through the sentences. Elicit *fatal accident* = where sb is killed.

   • Give SS a few minutes to discuss the sentences and choose which they think is the right option.

b • **3.10** Play the CD once for SS to check. Check answers.

1 a	2 c	3 b	4 b	5 c	6 a	7 c

3.10 CD2 Track 16

(tapescript in Student's Book on *p.124*)

We spend an awful long time in our cars. The average driver spends nearly an hour and a half a day in the car, so obviously the risks involved in driving are something we should take very seriously.

Driving gets a lot of bad publicity and there are a lot of myths about how dangerous it is – but the fact is that, kilometre for kilometre, it is riskier to be a pedestrian or a jogger than to drive a car, or ride a motorbike for that matter. We are also more likely to be injured at work or at home than we are driving a car.

But accidents *do* happen and the reason why a lot of them happen is because people break the rules. In fact 50% of all fatal accidents occur because someone has broken the law. The most frequent reason is breaking the speed limit and the second most frequent is drunk driving. The third cause of fatal accidents is when a driver falls asleep, a surprising 10%.

When we drive is also a significant factor in assessing our risk of having an accident. Driving at night, for example, is four times as dangerous as during the day. This is mainly because visibility is so much worse at night. By day a driver's visibility is roughly 500 metres, but at night driving with headlights it is much worse, maybe as little as 120 metres.

What are the most dangerous times and days to be on the road? Well, between 2.00 and 3.00 a.m. on a Saturday morning is the most dangerous time of the week, when you are most likely to have a *fatal* accident. So if possible, try to stay off the road then. The time of day when you are most likely to have a *non-fatal* accident is Friday afternoon between 4.00 and 6.00 p.m. This is when people are finishing work for the week and it is a time when drivers need to concentrate especially hard. Curiously, Tuesday is the safest day of the week to be on the road.

Which brings us onto *where* accidents happen. Most fatal accidents happen on country roads, so highways or freeways (what you call A-roads or motorways) are much safer. Also 70% of fatal accidents happen within 30 or 40 kilometres of where we live. Why should that be? The answer seems to be that we concentrate less when we are in familiar territory.

And finally let's look at *who* has accidents. Another myth about driving is that women are worse drivers than men. While it's true that kilometre for kilometre women have more *minor* accidents than men, a man is *twice* as likely to be killed in a car accident as a woman. Men take too many unnecessary risks when they're driving. Women are more careful and cautious drivers. But the most important factor of all is age. A driver aged between 17 and 24 has double the risk of an older driver. Which is why a lot of people would like to see the age limit for having a driving licence raised to 21.

---

c • Play the CD again. Pause after each paragraph (see tapescript), and elicit as much of the information as possible from SS.

Extra support

If there's time, get SS to listen to the CD with the tapescript on *p.124* so they can see exactly what they understood / didn't understand. Translate / explain any new words or phrases.

d • Put SS in pairs to discuss the questions. Get feedback.

Extra support

Do these as open class questions.

3 VOCABULARY expressions with *take*

a • Focus on the questionnaire, and quickly go through the questions making sure SS understand any new vocabulary, e.g. *a cautious person* = someone who avoids danger, *demonstration* = a meeting where people protest about sth.

   • Now focus on the first question and elicit the missing word (*risks*). Then get SS to complete the gaps in the other questions. Check answers.

1	risks	5	easy	9	advantage
2	decisions	6	notice	10	part
3	seriously	7	care	11	up
4	after	8	time	12	place

   • Highlight:
     – the prepositions SS need after some of the expressions, e.g. *take advantage **of**, take care **of**, take part **in***, etc.
     – that with the expression *take…easy* you must have an object or *it* in the middle, e.g. *take things easy, take it easy,* etc.

b • Get SS to choose a few questions to ask you. Then give them time to interview each other in pairs. First **A** interviews **B** with all the questions, and then they swap roles.

MINI GRAMMAR *likely* and *probably*

   • Go through examples and then the rules with SS. Point out that the opposite of *likely* is *unlikely*, which is often used instead of *not likely*, e.g. *He's unlikely to come now. / He isn't likely to come now.* However, we don't use *improbably*. Instead we say *probably not*, e.g. *he probably won't come now.*

   • Give SS a few minutes to complete the exercise and check answers.

1	likely	3	likely
2	probably	4	probably

Extra support

If you think your class need more practice, use the extra photocopiable exercises on *p.185.*

4 GRAMMAR conditionals and future time clauses

a • **Check what you know**. This exercise revises the basic tense usage in first conditional and future time clauses, i.e. the present simple after *if, unless, until*, etc. and *will* + infinitive in the main clause.

• Focus on the exercise and give SS a few minutes to circle the right forms. Get them to compare with a partner and then check answers.

1	I like	4	won't have to
2	I won't go	5	I have
3	gets	6	I hear

• If SS are having problems, go to the Workbook *p.31*. Go through the rules and do the exercise.

b • **New grammar**. Now focus on the sentence halves and give SS time to match them. Check answers.

1	F	2	J	3	I	4	B	5	G	6	C	7	A	8	D
9	E	10	H												

c • Give SS in pairs time to answer the questions. Check answers.

1 2
2 In the main clause: any future form, e.g. *will, going to*, present continuous (with future meaning), future perfect, future continuous, or an imperative. In the other clause after *if, in case, when*, etc. any present tense, i.e. present simple, present continuous, or present perfect.
3 *in case* = it's possible that this will happen

Extra support

Do these as open class questions.

d • Tell SS to go to **Grammar Bank 3C** on *p.136*. Go through the examples and rules with SS.

Grammar notes

SS have previously been taught that in first conditional sentences and future time clauses we use the present simple after *if, when*, etc. and *will* + infinitive in the other clause. This is a simplification, and here SS learn that in fact you can use any present tense after *if, when*, etc., e.g. the present continuous or perfect, and any future form in the other clause. SS are also introduced to the zero conditional.

Remind SS that although a present tense is used after *if, when*, etc., the meaning is future.

• **zero conditional**
  This has not previously been focused on. Emphasize here that a zero conditional is used to generalize or give facts (*If you heat water, it boils.*) Although zero conditionals are usually based on present tenses, they can also be used in the past, e.g. *If people didn't have money, they didn't eat that day.*

• **first conditional**
  Up to now SS have probably been given a simplified version of the first conditional (i.e. that we always use *if* + present simple, future). In this lesson they learn that a wider variety of tenses is possible (including the two new tenses they have just studied in 3B – the future perfect and continuous).
  Remind SS that although a present tense is used after *if*, the meaning is future.

• **future time clauses**
  Perhaps the most important point to emphasize is that a future tense can never be used after *if* or after *when, as soon as, until, unless, before, after, in case*. Typical mistakes are:
  – ~~I'll be ready as soon as I'll have had a shower.~~
  – ~~We'll probably be watching the cup final when you'll arrive.~~

• The *in case* expression may be new to SS. Be careful that they do not confuse it with *in case of* which is sometimes seen in notices, e.g. *In case of fire, break glass.* You may want to point out that *in case* can also be used in the past tense, e.g. *I took a jacket in case it was cold.*

• Focus on the exercises for **3C** on *p.137* and get SS to do them individually or in pairs. Check answers after each exercise.

a		b	
1	I'm not feeling	1	before
2	won't be going	2	in case
3	will be bathing	3	unless
4	aren't wearing	4	when
5	we'll have sold	5	after
6	die	6	If
		7	in case
		8	until

• Tell SS to go back to the main lesson on *p.46*.

e • Focus on the sentence stems and get SS to complete them in pairs. Elicit ideas for sentence 1 from the whole class to demonstrate the activity.

• Get feedback. You could write the continuations on the board and get the class to vote for the best tips.

Possible answers
1 …they can swim / …there is an adult watching them
2 …it's a hot day / …you are going to be away for a long time
3 …someone has an accident / …someone cuts himself/herself
4 …they are at least 12 years old / …they are old enough
5 …you have finished using them
6 …a child or baby tries to eat or drink them
7 …they show you identification / …you are sure who they are
8 …don't throw water on it / …cover it with a towel

5 PRONUNCIATION sentence stress and rhythm

a ● **3.11** Tell SS that the six sentences that they are going to hear are the missing bits of the six dialogues, so they should write them after **B**.

● First, play the CD the whole way through for SS just to listen. Then play it again pausing after each sentence to give SS time to write.

● Check answers.

> See tapescript

3.11   CD2 Track 17

1 I'll <u>tell</u> you as <u>soon</u> as I <u>know</u> my <u>plans</u>.
2 If you <u>come</u> back <u>tomorrow</u>, I'll have <u>finished</u> them.
3 I'll be <u>waiting</u> by the <u>ticket</u> <u>office</u> when you <u>get</u> <u>there</u>.
4 If she <u>doesn't</u> <u>hurry</u> up, we'll have <u>eaten</u> all the <u>food</u>.
5 I'm <u>taking</u> my <u>laptop</u> in <u>case</u> I <u>need</u> it for <u>work</u>.
6 There <u>won't</u> be <u>enough</u> <u>steak</u> <u>unless</u> you <u>go</u> and <u>get</u> some <u>more</u>.

---

b ● Play the CD again and get SS to underline the stressed words. Check answers.

c ● Give SS time to practise saying the dialogues.

6 LISTENING

a ● Focus on the photos and title of the article *Japan's children play safe*. Elicit what SS think it means. They will probably answer, e.g. 'play safely / don't do dangerous things', etc. You could point out that the title is in fact a play on words. The idiom *play safe* = be careful, not take any chances, e.g. *We'd better play safe and get to the airport very early tomorrow in case there are big queues at security*.

● Set a time limit for SS to read it. Get them to underline the safety measures and discuss them with a partner. Get feedback, and encourage SS to say whether they think the measures are normal / necessary or extreme.

> The main safety measures are providing proof of identification, making people take their shoes off and disinfecting wheels of baby buggies, security cameras, pets are not allowed, sterilized sand, and inflatable toys to avoid injury.

b ● **3.12** Before doing the listening, elicit two reasons why the Japanese school is the way it is (to protect the children and because parents of an injured child might sue the school). Check SS know the meaning of the verb *sue* (= to formally ask for sth, especially in court)

● Now focus on the other photo and headline, and elicit the meaning of a *breath of fresh air* which means *sth new and stimulating*.

● Explain that they are going to listen to part of an interview with a head teacher, who has a very different philosophy to that of the Japanese school.

● Play the CD once. Get SS to discuss with a partner the main difference between her attitude and that of the Japanese nursery.

> She thinks that children today are overprotected, and that they need to be allowed to take risks.

3.12   CD2 Track 18

(tapescript in Student's Book on *p.124*)
I = interviewer, S = Sue Palmer

I And this afternoon on *Around Britain* we are visiting an unusual little nursery school in a village in southern England. What makes this school different is that whatever the weather's like, the 20 children spend most of their day not in a classroom, but playing outside. Sue Palmer is the head of the nursery. Hello Sue.

S Hello.

I Sue, do the children *really* spend all day outside?

S Yes, even in the winter, and even if it's raining. They only come inside for breaks so they probably spend about 90% of their day outside. We think this is a much better way of teaching children than by shutting them up in classrooms all day.

I What kind of things do children learn from being outside?

S They can learn about the world by doing things. We have a large field next to the nursery so they are in the field all day – playing, exploring, experimenting. They learn about how plants and trees grow, they can learn about insects. They can learn about the danger of fire by sitting around a real fire. They can climb trees and walk on logs...

I And don't you think that this is a bit dangerous for young children? They might easily fall over, have accidents.

S No, no, not at all. I think that today's children are totally overprotected, they don't have enough freedom. People have forgotten just how important it is to give our children some freedom. They need to be allowed to take risks during play. My children know which plants can hurt them. They know that fire is dangerous. But nowadays schools do all they can to avoid adventure and risk.

I Why do you think schools have become so obsessed with eliminating risk?

S I think it is because schools and teachers are so worried nowadays that if a child has an accident of any kind, however small, that the child's parents will sue the school for thousands of pounds, and maybe put them out of business.

I Have you ever had any problem with parents?

S On the contrary, they are very positive indeed about the school and our teaching methods and philosophy. I've heard parents say that children who come to our school are healthier and stronger than other children – and that's in spite of being out in the rain – or maybe it's because of that. I think, and the parents agree with me, that the way we are teaching is the way that childhood should be.

I Well, thanks very much Sue, that's all we've got time for. Coming up on...

---

c ● Now focus on the sentences and give SS time to read them and think about what the missing word or phrase is. Point out that the sentences are not taken word for word from the listening, but sum up what it says. Then play the CD again. Pause after each part to give SS time to write. Get them to compare with a partner and play it again if necessary. Check answers.

> | | |
> |---|---|
> | 1 village | 5 take risks |
> | 2 outside, winter | 6 have an accident |
> | 3 doing things | 7 very positive |
> | 4 freedom | |

d ● Do this as an open class question and say what you thin

7 SPEAKING

- Tell SS that they are going to talk about things they did as children, and whether they think it is safe to do them today.
- Focus on the **GET IT RIGHT** box, and tell SS that the sentences are examples of the sort of language they will need to do the speaking. Give them a few minutes in pairs to cross out the wrong forms. Check answers.

1 ~~must~~ / had to
2 ✓
3 used to / ~~use to~~; ✓
4 ✓
5 go / ~~to go~~

- Focus on the questions. You could demonstrate for one of the prompts by talking a bit about what you used to do, and whether you think it is safe for children today.
- Put SS in groups of three or four. Encourage them to compare experiences for each point.
- Get some feedback from the whole class.
- Finally, tell SS to go to *Phrasal verbs in context File 3* on *p.157* and complete the phrasal verbs which have come up in this File. (Answers *p.155*)

Extra photocopiable activities

Grammar
conditionals and future time clauses *p.168*
Communicative
Are you a risk-taker? *p.206* (instructions *p.193*)
Vocabulary
Describing game *p.225* (instructions *p.221*)

HOMEWORK

Study Link **Workbook** *pp.30–32*

COLLOQUIAL ENGLISH
HIGH RISK?

Lesson plan

In the first part of this lesson the person interviewed is EZ (real name Paul Corkery), an expert in 'free running' (also called *parkour*), who set up a very successful organization called Urban Freeflow (www.urbanfreeflow.com), which amongst other things provides people to do stunts for films and advertisements. If SS are not aware of what free running is, they should understand once they see the photos on the page, and read the explanation. In the second part of the lesson, people in the street are asked if they have ever done a risk sport, what it was like, and if there is any kind of risk sport they would like to do.

Study Link These lessons are on the *New English File Upper-intermediate* DVD / Video which can be used instead of the class CD (See Introduction *p.9*). SS can get more practice on the MultiROM, which contains more of the short street interviews with a listening task and tapescripts.

Optional lead-in (books closed)

- Put SS in pairs to brainstorm risk sports. Elicit their ideas onto the board.

Possible answers	
White-water rafting	Potholing / caving
Bungee jumping	Skateboarding
Rock climbing	Surfing
Abseiling (US rappelling)	Skiing
Horse riding	Gliding / paragliding /
Snowboarding	hang-gliding
Parachuting	

- Ask SS if anyone knows what 'free running' is. If nobody knows anything, tell them they will find out in this lesson.

THE INTERVIEW

a
- Books open. If you didn't do the optional lead-in, ask SS if they know what the people in the photos are doing (free running) and get SS to read the description.
- Now focus on the glossary. Go through it with the class eliciting how to pronounce the words and phrases.

b
- **3.13** Focus on the task. Put SS in pairs and give them time to read the questions. Encourage SS not to write anything down when they listen the first time. They should listen and try to get the gist of what he is saying, and then discuss the questions with their partner.
- Play the CD once (**Part 1**). Give SS time to discuss the questions and tell each other what they understood. Then play the CD once or twice more. This time SS might want to jot down things they heard to help them remember the answers to the questions. Check answers.

1 Yes, but people usually do it in one particular place.
2 He usually does it in a group of about ten people.
3 He was a boxer.
4 Because his life changed (he got married and had a child). He tried martial arts but didn't like it, and then found out about free running.
5 There are 20 athletes. They work in commercials (= advertisements) and movies, teach in schools, and teach the army and police.
6 It helps youth offenders stop doing 'bad things'. They think it's a 'cool' thing to do. In schools, where a lot of kids don't do any PE and maybe have an obesity problem, they also like free running because it's cool and, as a result, they do exercise.

3.13   CD2 Track 19

(tapescript in Student's Book on p.125)

I = interviewer, E = EZ

I EZ is a free runner who started the organization Urban Freeflow. Free runners use obstacles in a town or city to create movement, by running, jumping, and climbing. Can you do free running anywhere, I mean, for example, if you're on your way somewhere?

E Yeah, I mean if you wanted to, you could kind of you know do it anywhere, you know if you're on your way to work you could do it, but generally the people who practise would go to a particular spot and practise there and then and then move on elsewhere.

I Where do you most enjoy doing it?

E The most rewarding for me would be running in London, here, around the South Bank, and we'd do it in a team of maybe ten of us, and just like someone leading the way and the rest following, and just using basic obstacles, like lamp posts and walls and just moving.

I How did you first get into free running?

E My background is in boxing, which I did for about 20 years and I boxed at international level. And I got married and had a kid and had to just change my life around and become sensible all of a sudden. I gave up the boxing and there was a huge void in my life, so I drifted into martial arts, which didn't really do it for me. And I was looking for the next thing to do and I saw this on TV one day, and I remember sitting in bed watching it and said 'That's what I'm looking for'.

I Tell us about the organization Urban Freeflow.

E Well, Urban Freeflow started out as a website, but then we devised a performance team, we have 20 athletes in the team now, eight who are very very high-profile now we're sponsored by Adidas now. We take care of all sorts of commercials and movies in that sense. We teach as well, we teach in schools, we've taught the army and police.

I What do you do with the police?

E The police run these schemes for youth offenders, and they're trying to get them out of, you know, doing bad things. It's seen as a very positive thing to do, it's seen as a very cool thing to do and for the youths it's very engaging, so that's what we do for them.

I What about in schools?

E In terms of schools, same again, there's a big problem in the UK with obesity and kids just aren't practising anything. They're not doing any PE, they're not doing any kind of sport, whereas what we do is perceived as being very cool, and unwittingly they're taking part and exercising so that seems to be a very positive thing.

Extra challenge

You could use the tapescript to elicit more detailed answers from SS.

c ● **3.14** Focus on the task and play the CD once (**Part 2**). Give SS time to discuss the questions and what they understood. Then play the CD once or twice more. Check answers.

1 They are very safety conscious when they work in movies or commercials. They don't take risks. They practise and do things again and again.
2 The sense of freedom is what attracted EZ to free running. You don't need anything to be able to do it, just a pair of trainers.
3 These are the normal kinds of injuries that people get doing free running.
4 He once fell out of a tree and had to go to hospital.
5 They are sports which can help you with free running.

3.14   CD2 Track 20

(tapescript in Student's Book on p.125)

I How dangerous is free running?

E On the face of it, what we do seems to be quite dangerous, but it doesn't touch on what we do, we're very very safety conscious, we work in movies and commercials where safety is paramount, I mean, everything we do is calculated, there's no risk-taking. If you see a big jump being done, we'd have practised that at ground level thousands of times, over and over and over. I think if anything, the key word for what we do is repetition.

I What attracted you especially about free running? Was it the risk element?

E To a degree, the risk element played a part, but it was more about the sense of freedom, the way to be able move within your environment with no limitations, you know, you don't need any equipment to take part, no skateboard, or no BMX, you can just, a pair of trainers and I'm ready to go, that was the real draw for me, just the freedom aspect.

I Have you had many accidents since you've been doing it?

E If you're practising this sport, you will pick up the odd scrapes here and there, you'll get blisters on your hands, and calluses, which is normal. You might get the odd sprained ankle. Personally, I fell out of a tree once, and fell on my head, which wasn't very nice and I had to go to hospital here.

I Is free running really something that anyone can do?

E It helps if you have a background in some kind of sport, but it isn't essential, you can start from being a complete beginner. Gymnastics would help, but you could be you know, just someone who plays football, or does a bit of running and pick it up straight away. As long as you start out very small-scale, take your time, there's no problem.

d ● **3.15** This exercise gives SS intensive listening practice in deciphering phrases where words are often run together, and introduces them to some common English expressions. Focus on the phrases and give SS time to read them. Play the CD, pausing after the first phrase and replaying it as necessary. Elicit the missing words, and then the meaning of the whole phrase. Repeat for the other five phrases.

> 1 **a particular spot** (= informal way of saying *place*)
> 2 **leading the way** (= going in front and showing the others where to go)
> 3 **all of a sudden** (= idiomatic way of saying *suddenly*)
> 4 **On the face of it** (= By looking at it)
> 5 **To a degree** (= to a certain extent)
> 6 **As long as** (= *on the condition that*, e.g. *You can go out as long as you are home by 10.00.*)

> **3.15**   CD2 Track 21
> 1 …but generally the people who practise would go to a particular spot…
> 2 …someone leading the way and the rest following.
> 3 I had to just change my life around and become sensible all of a sudden.
> 4 On the face of it what we do seems to be quite dangerous.
> 5 To a degree, the risk element played a part.
> 6 As long as you start out very small-scale, …

e ● Tell SS to go to *p.125* and to look at the tapescript for the interview. Play the CD (**Part 1** and **Part 2**) again and tell SS to read and listen at the same time. Deal with any vocabulary problems and get feedback from SS on what parts they found hard to understand and why, e.g. speed of speech, elision, pronunciation, etc.

● Finally, focus on the question. You could also ask SS *Do you think it would be a good Olympic sport?* Get SS to answer in pairs or as a whole class. Then get feedback from the whole class.

IN THE STREET

a ● Focus on the photos of the people and elicit impressions (possible age, occupation, etc.). Tell SS that they were all interviewed in Covent Garden, a busy shopping area in Central London.

● Focus on the task. (If you did the optional lead-in, you can leave out this stage). You might need to explain *bungee* /ˈbʌndʒi/ *jumping* (= jumping off a high place, e.g. a bridge, with an elastic rope attached to your ankles), *potholing* or *caving* (= going into underground caves), *white-water rafting* (= going in dangerous water or rapids in an inflatable boat).

⚠ Don't ask SS if they have done any of these sports at this stage as they will be talking about this later.

b ● **3.16** Focus on the task. Tell SS they will not need to use all the sports. Play the CD once. Then play it again pausing after each speaker to check answers.

> climbing 4 (Ray)
> parachuting 3 (Mark)
> potholing / caving 2 (Anne), 4 (Ray)
> skiing 1 (Agne)
> white-water rafting 4 (Ray)

> **3.16**   CD2 Track 22
> (tapescript in Student's Book on *p.125*)
> **I = interviewer, Ag = Agne, A = Anne, M = Mark, R = Ray**
> **Agne**
> I Have you ever done any high-risk sports or activities?
> AG Yeah, I've done skiing.
> I What was it like?
> AG It was pretty difficult because it's difficult to coordinate. So it was scary and it was funny, and it was just making a fool of myself.
> **Anne**
> I Have you ever done any high-risk sports or activities?
> A Not really, no, except for potholing, but that was in my younger days.
> I What was it like?
> A I wouldn't say it was particularly high-risk, but it was a very enjoyable experience.
> I Is there anything you'd like to try?
> A I've always wanted to try skiing but I've never done it, but I think that would be really exciting – to go skiing and to go down the mountains free and what have you, but I think I'm a bit old now.
> **Mark**
> I Have you ever done any high-risk sports or activities?
> M Yeah, I've jumped out of a plane.
> I What was it like?
> M Oh, it was awesome! You see the ground below you and the plane door opens and you're suddenly… the distance goes like from there to there as soon as the door opens you're suddenly, you know, you're hurtling towards the ground, you know, at a couple of hundred miles an hour or whatever. And your chute opens and you get sucked back up into the sky. It's kinda cool.
> **Ray**
> I Have you ever done any high-risk sports or activities?
> R I've climbed, I've caved, I've white-water rafted down the Zambezi. Do they count?

c ● Focus on the task and give SS time to go through the sentences. Play the CD once. Get SS to compare what they think. Play it again if necessary and check answers.

> 1 Ray   2 Agne   3 Anne (skiing)   4 Mark

d ● **3.17** Focus on the phrases and give SS time to read them. Play the CD, pausing after the first phrase and replaying it as necessary. Elicit the missing word, and then the meaning of the whole phrase. Repeat for the other three phrases.

> 1 **making a fool of myself** (= do sth stupid in front of other people which makes them think you are an idiot)
> 2 **in my younger days** (= when I was younger)
> 3 **it was awesome** (= wonderful, fantastic, especially in North American English)
> 4 **Do they count?** (= is that included? Here = is that included in risk sports?)

> **3.17**   CD2 Track 23
> 1 It was just making a fool of myself.
> 2 That was in my younger days.
> 3 Oh, it was awesome!
> 4 Do they count?

e ● Tell SS to go to *p.125* and to look at the tapescript for **IN THE STREET**. Play the CD again and tell SS to read and listen at the same time. Deal with any vocabulary problems and get feedback from SS on what parts they found hard to understand and why, e.g. speed of speech, elision, pronunciation, etc.

● Finally, focus on the three questions that the interviewer asked the people (i.e. including *Is there anything you'd like to try?*), and get SS to interview each other in pairs. Then get feedback from the whole class.

HOMEWORK

Study Link Workbook *p.33*

Lesson plan

This writing lesson gives SS practice in writing a composition expressing their opinion. There is a focus on linking expressions, e.g. *firstly, in addition*.

a ● Focus on the composition title and elicit opinions from the class to see whether the majority agree or disagree. Then give SS a few minutes to read the composition. Elicit that the writer agrees with the title.

Extra idea

You could elicit the author's reasons for agreeing with community service for young people.

b ● Now focus on the task and on the linking expressions in the list. Give SS a few minutes to fill the gaps. Get them to compare with a partner and then check answers.

2 in most cases	6 In addition
3 Firstly	7 Finally
4 whereas	8 so
5 Secondly	9 In conclusion

● Highlight that:
  – *Firstly / secondly* are used to introduce main arguments. *Finally* is used to introduce the final main argument.
  – *In addition* (or *Also*) can be used to add an extra point to an argument.
  – *whereas* is used to contrast two ideas.
  – *so* is used to introduce a consequence or result, e.g. *I was tired so I went to bed.*
  – *In conclusion* (or *To sum up*) is used to introduce your final paragraph where you summarize your opinion.

c ● Focus on the instructions and the **Useful language** box. Go through them with SS, and highlight that:
  – *Personally…* and *In my opinion…* are both used to emphasize what you think.
  – *For example / for instance* can be used at the beginning of a sentence or in the middle.
  – *Such as* can only be used in the middle of a sentence.

WRITE a composition

Go through the instructions. Then either get SS to plan and write the composition in class (set a time limit of about 20 minutes) or get them just to plan in class and write the composition at home, or set both planning and writing for homework.

If SS do the writing in class, get them to swap their composition with another student to read and check for mistakes before you collect them all in.

Test and Assessment CD-ROM

CEF Assessment materials
File 3 Writing task assessment guidelines

For instructions on how to use these pages, see *p.33*.

GRAMMAR

a 1 was being
  2 probably never be
  3 to be a
  4 said that
  5 won't come
b 1 'll be lying
  2 will…have started / will have…started
  3 has landed
  4 drink / have drunk / have been drinking
  5 finish / have finished

VOCABULARY

a 1 kidnapper – the others all steal
  2 smuggler – the others are crimes
  3 evidence – the others are people
  4 scorching – the others refer to cold weather
  5 mist – the others are extreme weather

b 1 committed   6 blew
  2 caught   7 sweated
  3 sentenced   8 poured
  4 kidnapped   9 melted
  5 murdered   10 took
c 1 with   4 out
  2 up   5 in
  3 after

PRONUNCIATION

a 1 weather (it's /ð/)   4 slip (it's /ɪ/)
  2 jury (it's /ʊə/)   5 sweat (it's /e/)
  3 guilty (it's /g/)
b accuse, blackmail, community, blizzard, seriously,

CAN YOU UNDERSTAND THIS TEXT?

1 b 2 c 3 a 4 a 5 b 6 a

CAN YOU UNDERSTAND THESE PEOPLE?

a A 5 B – C 2 D 1 E 4 F 3
b 1 N 2 D 3 N 4 M 5 D 6 M 7 N 8 M

3.18 CD2 Track 24

1 Young offenders are getting younger all the time. In the past the average age was probably seventeen or eighteen but nowadays we find ourselves dealing with kids of thirteen and fourteen, and even younger. The other week we were called to a house where the burglar alarm had gone off and we found these kids hiding in the garden with the things they'd just stolen from the house and one was fourteen and the other was only twelve.

2 So really what they need is sort of stricter control and er rules and I know that lots of people think we're too tolerant and that it's our fault and I suppose it's partly true that we find it difficult to say no to them sometimes. It's not easy I mean you want your kids to have the same as everyone else. I think the problem is nowadays that children get bored and that's why they do these things to get a bit of excitement.

3 So then I looked at her and said, *aren't you ashamed of yourself trying to rob an old lady pensioner? I could be your grandmother.* And you know what she did? She spat at me and then she laughed and then she just ran off with my handbag. I was so angry.

4 The trouble is that most of us just feel helpless – we can't do anything. They're just not interested and what's worse – they distract and disrupt the other kids who do want to learn, and sometimes they insult us or even get violent. The problem is that they don't have enough discipline at home.

5 When I was doing my research I talked to a lot of young people in schools and I asked them if they thought a fine would stop them committing a crime and they said no it wouldn't. They said that the only thing they were frightened of was getting sent to prison. I've also spoken to the police, social workers, lawyers, and they all agree that fines and community service just aren't working.

3.19 CD2 Track 25

I = interviewer, D = Dan, M = Marion

I Marion and Dan, you are both mountain climbers and you regularly attempt some very difficult and dangerous climbs. Some people might say that you're taking an unnecessary risk.

D Many things we do in life have an element of risk. You drove here today on a motorway in the rain. That was a risky thing to do. People try to minimize risks – when they drive, they wear a seat belt for example – and I do the same when I go climbing. Before I go, I do my research so that I can avoid avalanche areas, I check the weather forecast, and I make sure my equipment is all working properly. And when I'm on the mountain I use my common sense and I don't take unnecessary risks.

M Also life isn't just about protecting ourselves from risks. We can't live in a bubble. We have to live life and do things which make us feel alive. Mountain climbing gives me energy to do other things in my life. I'm a secondary school teacher and climbing at the weekend gives me the extra energy I need to be a good teacher.

D Exactly. I spend most of my time sitting down in an office. It's not the most exciting of jobs and I would go mad if I didn't have the chance to feel the adrenaline pumping through my body when I'm climbing a vertical rock face 3,000 metres up in the air.

I Now you are both married and you, Dan, have young children. How do your partners feel about you climbing?

M I was already a mountain climber when I met my partner, but I won't pretend that he's exactly over the moon when I walk out of the door with my climbing gear on a Friday evening. I don't enjoy making him feel worried, but on the other hand, he does know and believe that I would never do anything that would put my life at risk.

D I used to have a lot of arguments with my partner about whether I was being selfish and irresponsible, especially when our first child was born. But now she's fine with it.

I But bad things can happen in climbing. Climbers do get killed, don't they?

M Yes, but this is usually because a climber gets over-confident or too careless, or because they don't do the necessary preparation before the climb.

D Or just bad luck.

M Yes, sometimes.

Test and Assessment CD-ROM

File 3 Quicktest
File 3 Test
Progress test 1–3

4
A

G unreal conditionals
V feelings
P sentence rhythm

Would <u>you</u> get out alive?

File 4 overview

This File begins, in **4A**, with a review of second and third conditionals. In **4B** the grammar focus is on past modals, *must / might / can't have (been) / should have*, etc. Finally, lesson **4C** presents the verbs of the senses *look / feel / taste / smell / sound* + adjective / *like / as if*. The vocabulary areas in this File are feelings, verbs sometimes confused, and the body.

Lesson plan

In this lesson the topic is survival. In the first part SS read part of an article from *Time* magazine about surviving disasters. The grammar focus is on unreal conditionals, i.e. second and third conditionals. SS should have seen both these structures before, but will still need practice in using them, especially third conditionals. The vocabulary focus is on feelings, e.g. *devastated*, *stunned*, etc. and pronunciation looks at sentence rhythm. The second part of the lesson is based on the true story, later made into a documentary for Discovery TV, about three young backpackers and their guide who got lost in the Amazon jungle.

Optional lead-in (books closed)

- Write on the board
  <u>Life or death disaster situations</u>
  Natural   Man-made
- Elicit from the class one for each column, e.g. flood (natural), fire (man-made)
- Then get SS in pairs to try to add some more to each column.
- Get feedback and write them on the board. Model and drill pronunciation.

Possible answers	
Natural	**Man-made**
earthquake	fire
flood	terrorist attack
volcanic eruption	major accident, e.g. plane crash,
tsunami (tidal wave)	train crash, etc.
hurricane	

- Then ask the class *Have you (or anyone you know) ever experienced any of these things? How did you / they react?* and elicit information.

1 SPEAKING & READING

a ● Books open. Focus on the questionnaire and give SS a few moments to read and discuss answers with a partner. Get some feedback but <u>don't</u> tell them yet what the right answer / best thing to do is.

b ● Now focus on the photo with the article and ask SS what disaster it shows (people escaping from the World Trade Centre in New York 11th September 2001).

Then set a time limit for SS to read the introduction to the article (the part on *p.52*).

- Then, in pairs, SS check their answer to **number 1 only** in the questionnaire, and answer the three questions in **b**. Emphasize that the first two questions are on the text, and in the third question they give their own opinion.
- Check answers and elicit from different SS how they think <u>they</u> would react in a crisis.

Answer to question 1 in questionnaire
1 c (They 'freeze' and can't do anything)
Answers to 1b
1 Because in a crisis our minds take longer to process information, people can't take a decision about what to do. People also often refuse to believe that the disaster is happening to them.
2 No, because people's normal personality is not a good guide to how they will react in a crisis.

c ● Divide SS into pairs, **A** and **B**. Now focus on the task and make sure SS are clear which part of the text they have to read. Focus on the sets of questions and tell SS to use these as a memory aid to tell their partner in their own words what they have read about.
- Set a time limit for SS to read their half of the text and then tell SS **A** to tell SS **B** what they have read. When you think they have done this, tell SS **B** to tell SS **A** what they have read. Monitor and help SS, and encourage them to use their own words.

d ● Now focus on the eight true / false sentences. Tell SS to read the whole article, focussing more on the part they hadn't read previously, and then together mark the sentences T or F. Check answers, and get SS to explain why the F ones are false.

1 F (She didn't run. She waited for someone to tell her everything was all right.)
2 T
3 F (She was looking for things to take with her.)
4 T
5 T
6 F (They had very little time. The plane caught fire after 60 seconds.)
7 T
8 F (Because they think it's not 'cool' to do so.)

e ● Finally, focus on the highlighted words and phrases. Give SS time to look at them in context and guess their meaning. Check answers, and model pronunciation. Elicit / explain any other vocabulary that SS have problems with.

evacuation = moving people from a place of danger to a safer place
explosion = the noun of *explode*, the action caused by sth such as a bomb

in a trance = a state in which you are thinking so much about something that you are doing that you don't notice what is happening around you, like a hypnotized person
shook = past tense of *shake* = to move from side to side or up and down
made it = succeeded in doing sth, such as reaching a place in time, e.g. *We made it to the station just in time to catch the train.*
collided with = crashed into
survivors = people who survive, do not die in an accident or terrorist attack
caught fire = started burning
paralysed = unable to move at all

Extra support

At this point you could go through the article with the class, highlighting useful expressions and eliciting / explaining the meaning of new words and phrases.

f • Do this with the whole class, and elicit responses.
   • Probably the most important tip is to always know where emergency exits are both in planes and in buildings. Also to act immediately and not try to take possessions with you. The right options in the questionnaire in **a** are 2c and 3b.

2 VOCABULARY feelings

a • Focus on the instructions and give SS a few moments to find the adjectives. Check answers.

1	confused	3	shocked
2	calm	4	stunned

b • Tell to go to **Vocabulary Bank** *Feelings* on p.151. Focus on section **1 Adjectives**. Give SS time to do exercise **a** individually or in pairs. Check answers and go through the information in the box about *fed up* and *upset*. Point out that *fed up* is usually followed by *with*, e.g. *I am fed up with this awful weather.* Model and drill pronunciation.

a	3	grateful	7	lonely
	4	relieved	8	nervous
	5	disappointed	9	glad
	6	homesick	10	offended

   • Now focus on **1b** and point out that these are strong adjectives. Give an example of a strong adjective, e.g. *enormous* = very big (but you can't say *very enormous*). When SS have finished, check answers and go through the information in the ⚠ box below. Model and drill pronunciation.

b	2	devastated	7	furious
	3	delighted	8	astonished
	4	exhausted	9	desperate
	5	thrilled	10	miserable
	6	terrified		

   • Now focus on section **2 Idioms** and give SS time to match them to their meanings. Check answers.

1 C	**2** D	**3** F	**4** E	**5** A	**6** B

   • Finally, focus on the final instruction 'Can you remember the words on this page? Test yourself or a partner'.

Testing yourself

For **Adjectives** SS can cover the column on the right, look at situations and definitions, and try to remember the adjectives. For **Idioms** they can first cover the feelings A–F and try to remember what each idiom means. They could then cover them, look at A–F, and try to remember the idiom.

Testing a partner

See **Testing a partner** *p.20*.

Study Link SS can find more practice of these words and phrases on the MultiROM and on the *New English File Upper-intermediate* website.

   • Tell SS to go back to the main lesson on *p.53*.

c • Focus on the pictures. SS, in pairs, first try to remember an adjective and an idiom for each. Check answers.

1	fed up, sick and tired
2	astonished, couldn't believe her eyes
3	delighted, over the moon
4	miserable, down in the dumps
5	exhausted, worn out
6	terrified, scared stiff

d • Focus on the instructions. Tell SS to choose their two adjectives and think about what they are going to say. Help them with vocabulary if necessary.

Extra support

You could demonstrate first by choosing one of the feelings and telling SS about an experience of your own.

   • Give SS time to exchange experiences with a partner.

Extra challenge

If SS are enjoying the activity, you may want to get them to choose more adjectives from the **Vocabulary Bank** *Feelings*.

   • Get feedback, trying to elicit an experience for each adjective.

3 GRAMMAR unreal conditionals

a • Focus on the task, and elicit answers from the class.

1 refers to a hypothetical situation in the present or future
2 refers to a hypothetical situation in the past

b • Again, elicit answers from the class.

1 *would* + infinitive in the main clause, past simple in the *if*-clause
2 *would have* + past participle in the main clause, past perfect in the *if*-clause

c • Focus on the task and give SS a few minutes to complete the sentences. Check answers.

1	were	3	had got off
2	would have got out	4	wouldn't pay

d • Tell SS to go to **Grammar Bank 4A** on *p.138*. Read the examples and go through rules with the class.

Grammar notes

SS will have studied both the second and third conditionals separately but here they are contrasted. SS should be fairly confident with the concept of both, although they will probably still have problems using them orally with fluency, especially the third conditional.

second conditional

- **rule 2:** SS also widen their knowledge of these two conditionals by seeing how other tenses can be used in either clause.

second or third conditional?

The point to emphasize here is that the second conditional refers to a hypothetical situation in **the present or future** which can sometimes be changed and sometimes not, e.g. *If she were taller, she could get a job as a model* (situation can't be changed). *If you studied more, you would pass the exam* (situation could be changed). The third conditional refers to hypothetical situations in the past, **which didn't happen**, e.g. *If we had known you were in hospital, we would have visited you* (we didn't know so we didn't visit you).

⚠ **mixed conditionals**

Sometimes the second and third conditionals are mixed. We suggest that you draw SS' attention to this for passive recognition but this is not practised in the exercises.

- Focus on the exercises for **4A** on *p.139* and get SS to do them individually or in pairs. Check answers after each exercise.

a
1 would have bought
2 had gone
3 would lend
4 found
5 hadn't been driving (hadn't driven)
6 lived
7 wouldn't have died
8 would have heard
9 had known
10 were (was)

b
1 …he wouldn't have been late for the interview.
2 …she wouldn't sleep badly at night.
3 …we would have reached the top of the mountain.
4 …she had had enough money.
5 …there wasn't so much traffic.
6 …he would get the job.

- Tell SS to go back to the main lesson on *p.54*.

4 PRONUNCIATION sentence rhythm

Pronunciation notes

The focus here is on getting SS to say second and third conditional sentences with good rhythm by stressing the important words (i.e. the ones that carry information). You may want to encourage your SS to produce the weak forms of *would* and *have* in these sentences, i.e. /wəd/ and /əv/.

a ● **4.1** Focus on the task. Then play the CD once the whole way through for SS to listen. Then play it again, pausing after each sentence for SS to write. Then play it again the whole way through for SS to check.

> **4.1**   CD2 Track 26
> 1 I would have <u>been</u> <u>terrified</u> …
> 2 If I <u>told</u> you what <u>happened</u>, …
> 3 If I <u>hadn't</u> <u>read</u> the <u>safety</u> <u>information</u>, …
> 4 I <u>wouldn't</u> <u>fly</u> with <u>that</u> <u>airline</u>…
> 5 If I'd <u>stayed</u> in the <u>building</u> <u>longer</u>, …
> 6 I'd <u>travel</u> <u>more</u>…

- Then get SS to match the endings A–F.

b ● **4.2** Play the CD for SS to check their answers. Finally, check they have written / spelt the first parts correctly by eliciting them onto the board.

1 E	2 F	3 D	4 C	5 A	6 B

> **4.2**   CD2 Track 27
> 1 I would have been terrified if I'd been in that situation.
> 2 If I told you what happened, you wouldn't believe me.
> 3 If I hadn't read the safety information, I wouldn't have acted so quickly.
> 4 I wouldn't fly with that airline if I were you.
> 5 If I'd stayed in the building longer, I would have died.
> 6 I'd travel more if my husband wasn't afraid of flying.

c ● Play the CD again for SS to underline the stressed words. Check answers (see tapescript 4.1) and then get SS to practise saying the sentences with the right rhythm.

d ● Focus on the instructions and example with SS.

> **Possible answers**
> 1 …, I wouldn't have gone to the party. If I hadn't gone to the party, I wouldn't have met the man of my life.
> 2 …, I wouldn't have missed the train. If I hadn't missed the train, I wouldn't have been late for work.
> 3 …, I would have got the message. If I'd got the message, I would have known the dinner was cancelled.
> 4 …, I would have revised. If I'd revised, I would have passed.

- Get SS to practise reading their 'chains' aloud, focusing on getting the right rhythm.

5 READING & LISTENING

a ● Do this as an open class question. Elicit ideas and write them on the board.

b ● Focus on the article and photo, and stress that this is a true story which happened a few years ago. Set a time limit for SS to read the beginning of the story and answer the questions in pairs. Check answers to 1–3, and then elicit from SS their own answers to 4 and 5.

1 To go into the rainforest and visit an undiscovered indigenous (= native) village, then raft (= travel on pieces of wood tied together and used as a boat) down the river, then fly to La Paz.
2 **a** Karl (the guide) didn't seem to know where the village was.
   b Marcus was complaining about everything, especially his feet.
3 Because Kevin wanted to raft, as they had originally planned, but didn't want Marcus to come.

- Now check whether there is any vocabulary SS couldn't guess and elicit / explain the meaning.

Extra support

If you want to check that SS have really understood the first part, you could ask them the following comprehension questions before moving on to the listening:
What did Karl promise the three friends? What promise did they make to each other? How do you think the three friends felt before going into the jungle? What made Kevin angry? What decision did he take?...

c - Now focus on the instructions and photos. Get SS to look at the photos first, and use them to pre-teach some of the vocabulary that comes up in the listening, e.g. *rapids, jaguar, footprint, hiking boot, log*, etc.
   - **4.3** Stress that SS shouldn't write anything while they listen. Then play the CD for SS to listen to the first part. Play it again, and then get SS to answer the questions orally in pairs. Check answers and elicit ideas in answer to the question in bold. Make sure SS use the right verb form *'I would have…'*.
   - You may want to ask a few more questions (e.g. *Can you remember what was in the backpack?*) to make sure SS got all the details.

1 The river went faster and faster, they got into rapids and then hit a rock. Kevin swam to land but Yossi was swept away.
2 He found their backpack with a lot of important and useful things in it, especially the map.

4.3   CD2 Track 28

(tapescript in Student's Book on *p.125*)
Yossi and Kevin soon realized that going by river was a big mistake. The river got faster and faster, and soon they were in rapids. The raft was swept down the river at an incredible speed until it hit a rock. Kevin managed to swim to land, but Yossi was swept away by the rapids. But Yossi didn't drown. He came up to the surface several kilometres downriver. By an incredible piece of luck he found their backpack floating in the river. The backpack contained a little food, insect repellent, a lighter, and most important of all… the map. The two friends were now separated by a canyon and six or seven kilometres of jungle.

- **4.4** Repeat the process for part 2.

3 Kevin – desperate, responsible for what had happened to Yossi. Yossi – optimistic, sure he would find Kevin.
4 Yossi woke up and found a jaguar looking at him, but he managed to scare it away (by setting fire to insect repellent with a cigarette lighter).

4.4   CD2 Track 29

(tapescript in Student's Book on *p.125*)
Kevin was feeling desperate. He didn't know if Yossi was alive or dead, but he started walking downriver to look for him. He felt responsible for what had happened to his friend. Yossi, however, was feeling very optimistic. He was sure that Kevin would look for him so he started walking upriver calling his friend's name. But nobody answered. At night Yossi tried to sleep but he felt terrified. The jungle was full of noises. Suddenly he woke up because he heard a branch breaking. He turned on his flash light. There was a jaguar staring at him… Yossi was trembling with fear but then he remembered something that he once saw in a film. He used the cigarette lighter to set fire to the insect repellent spray and he managed to scare the jaguar away.

- **4.5** Repeat the process for part 3.

5 Because he found a footprint which he thought was Kevin's, but eventually he realized it was his own. He had been walking around in a circle.

4.5   CD2 Track 30

(tapescript in Student's Book on *p.125*)
After five days alone, Yossi was exhausted and starving. Suddenly, as he was walking, he saw a footprint on the trail – it was a hiking boot. It had to be Kevin's footprint! He followed the trail until he discovered another footprint. But then he realized, to his horror, that it was the same footprint and that it wasn't Kevin's. It was his own. He had been walking around in a circle. Suddenly Yossi realized that he would never find Kevin. He felt sure that Kevin must be dead. Yossi felt depressed and on the point of giving up.

- **4.6** Repeat the process for part 4.

6 He had been looking for Yossi. He had floated down the river on a log, and had been rescued by two Bolivian hunters.
7 Because the hunters only went to that part of the rainforest once a year.

4.6   CD2 Track 31

(tapescript in Student's Book on *p.125*)
But Kevin wasn't dead. He was still looking for Yossi. But after nearly a week he was weak and exhausted from lack of food and lack of sleep. He decided that it was time to forget Yossi and try to save himself. He had just enough strength left to hold onto a log and let himself float down the river. Kevin was incredibly lucky – he was rescued by two Bolivian hunters in a canoe. The men only hunted in that part of the rainforest once a year, so if they had been there a short time earlier or later, they would never have seen Kevin. They took him back to the town of San José and he spent two days recovering.

- **4.7** Repeat the process for part 5.

8 He asked the Bolivian Army to look for Yossi.
9 Because although they flew over the rainforest, they couldn't see anything.
10 He paid a local man to take him up the river.

4.7 CD2 Track 32

(tapescript in Student's Book on *p.125*)

As soon as Kevin felt well enough, he went to a Bolivian Army base and asked them to look for Yossi. The army were sure that Yossi must be dead, but in the end Kevin persuaded them to take him up in a plane and fly over the part of the rainforest where Yossi could be. It was a hopeless search. The plane had to fly too high and the forest was too dense. They couldn't see anything at all. Kevin felt terribly guilty. He was convinced that it was all his fault that Yossi was going to die in the jungle. Kevin's last hope was to pay a local man with a boat to take him up the river to look for his friend.

- **4.8** Repeat the process for part 6. Encourage SS to use *must have, might have*, etc. when they speculate about what happened to Karl and Marcus.

11 For nearly three weeks.
12 He thought it was a bee, but in fact it was the engine of the boat Kevin was in.

4.8 CD2 Track 33

(tapescript in Student's Book on *p.126*)

By now, Yossi had been on his own in the jungle for nearly three weeks. He hadn't eaten for days. He was starving, exhausted and slowly losing his mind. It was evening. He lay down by the side of the river ready for another night alone in the jungle. Suddenly he heard the sound of a bee buzzing in his ear. He thought a bee had got inside his mosquito net. When he opened his eyes he saw that the buzzing noise wasn't a bee…
It was a boat. Yossi was too weak to shout, but Kevin had already seen him.
It was a one in a million chance but Yossi was saved. When Yossi had recovered, he and Kevin flew to the city of La Paz, and they went directly to the hotel where they had agreed to meet Marcus and Karl. But Marcus and Karl were not there. The two men had never arrived back in the town of Apolo. The Bolivian army organized a search of the rainforest, but Marcus and Karl were never seen again.

d • Focus on the instructions. Then tell SS to go to *p.125*. Play the CD again the whole way through. SS listen and underline any words they didn't know or didn't recognize. Then get SS to compare with a partner, and get feedback to find out which words or phrases caused problems.

e • Do this as an open class question.
- You might like to tell SS that Yossi Ghinsberg now works giving talks at conferences about motivation based on his experience. He has also devoted a lot of time and raised money to help protect the rainforest where he got lost. He now lives in the Australian rainforest. Kevin Gale works as a manager of a gym. The documentary made about their experience is based on Yossi's book *Jungle* and can be seen on the Discovery Channel as part of the series called *I shouldn't be alive*.

6 **4.9** **SONG** ♫ I will survive

- *I will survive* was originally recorded by Gloria Gaynor in 1978. For copyright reasons this is a cover version. If you want to do this song in class, use the photocopiable activity on *p.236*.

4.9 CD2 Track 34

I will survive

At first I was afraid, I was petrified
Kept thinking I could never live without you by my side.
But then I spent so many nights
Thinking how you did me wrong.
And I grew strong, and I learned how to get along

So you're back from outer space
I just walked in to find you here
with that sad look upon your face.
I should have changed that stupid lock
I should have made you leave your key
If I'd known for just one second
You'd be back to bother me.

Chorus
Go on now go, walk out the door.
Just turn around now, 'cos you're not welcome anymore.
Weren't you the one who tried to hurt me with goodbye?
Did you think I'd crumble? Did you think I'd lay down and die?
Oh no, not I, I will survive.
For as long as I know how to love I know I'll feel alive
I've got all my life to live and I've got all my love to give.
And I'll survive, I will survive, hey, hey.

It took all the strength I had not to fall apart,
Though I tried hard to mend the pieces of my broken heart.
And I spent oh so many nights
Just feeling sorry for myself
I used to cry. But now I hold my head up high.

And you see me, somebody new
I'm not that chained up little person still in love with you.
And so you felt like dropping in
And just expect me to be free
Well now I'm saving all my loving for someone who's loving me.

Chorus

Extra photocopiable activities

Grammar
unreal conditionals *p.169*
Communicative
Snakes and ladders *p.207* (instructions *p.193*)
Song
I will survive p.236 (instructions *p.231*)

HOMEWORK

Study Link Workbook *pp.34–36*

G past modals; *would rather, had better*
V verbs often confused
P weak form of *have*

How I trained my husband

Lesson plan

Your SS should have learned to use modals of deduction (*must / might / can't* + infinitive) and *should* (+ *infinitive*) for advice at intermediate level. In this lesson they learn how to use these same modals to make deductions about the past (e.g. *He must have forgotten*) and to make criticisms (e.g. *You shouldn't have said that*). The topic is arguments, a context in which these modals naturally occur. In the first part of the lesson SS read how a woman used animal training techniques to 'train' her husband out of some annoying habits. In the second part of the lesson SS listen to a psychologist giving advice on how to argue successfully. The vocabulary focus is on verbs which are sometimes confused (e.g. *argue* and *discuss*) and the pronunciation focus is on the weak form of *have* in past modals. Finally, there is a mini grammar focus on *had better* and *would rather*.

Optional lead-in (books closed)

- Ask SS *What do you think men and women often argue about?* Write on the board:
  in the car   in the kitchen   on holiday
  when they're shopping together
- Get SS to talk to a partner and then elicit some ideas.

1 GRAMMAR past modals

a ● Books open. **Check what you know**. This exercise provides quick revision of using modals of deduction in the present, which SS should already know.

- Focus on the photo and the questions. Stress that SS should use a modal verb to talk about each of the three possibilities. Encourage them to eliminate one (*It can't be…*), and then from the two possibilities left (*It might be ... or ...*) decide which one they think is the right answer (*It must be …*), and give a reason to justify their final answer.
- Elicit ideas for each one.

> **Possible answers**
> 1 It can't be 2.00 p.m. because they're having breakfast. It might be 8.00 a.m. or 6.00 a.m. but I think it must be 8.00 a.m. because that's when people usually go to work.
> 2 It can't be Sunday because people don't usually go to work then. It might be Friday or Saturday, but I think it must be Friday because he looks like a businessman and they don't usually work on Saturdays.
> 3 It can't be Brazil because the newspaper is in English. It might be the UK or the United States.
> 4 He can't be looking for his glasses because he's wearing them. I think he must be looking for his keys because his briefcase is on the chair.

- Elicit / remind SS that an alternative to *might* is *may*.
- If SS are having problems, go to the Workbook *p.37*. Go through the rules and do the exercise.

Extra support

You could start by writing on the board:
1 a You must go to the doctor's.
   b He must be the doctor – he's wearing a white coat.
2 a You can't park there.
   b She can't be his wife, she's too young.
3 a I might see a film tonight.
   b He's not in class today – he might be ill.
4 a You should drink less coffee.
   b I don't think people should drive 4x4s.

- Put SS in pairs and ask them to decide what the modal verbs are being used for in each pair of sentences.
- Check answers.
1 a *must* = obligation (You have to…),
   b *must* = deduction (I'm sure it's true)
2 a *can't* = permission (You're not allowed to…)
   b *can't* = deduction (I'm sure it's not true)
3 a *might* = possible intention (Perhaps I'll go…)
   b *might* = deduction (I think it's a possibility)
4 a *should* = advice (It's would be a good idea)
   b *should* = opinion (I (don't) think it's right)

b ● **4.10** Tell SS that they are now going to hear a conversation between the people in the picture in **a** to see if they made the correct deductions. Play the CD once. Check answers.

> **1 b** 8.00 a.m.   **3 b** the UK
> **2 b** Saturday   **4 b** his car keys
> The man had lost his car keys.

> **4.10**   CD2 Track 35
> **Conversation 1**
> **MAN**   Have you seen my car keys? I can't find them.
> **WOMAN** No, I haven't.
> **M** I don't believe it. They disappeared.
> **W** When did you have them last?
> **M** When I came in last night. I'm sure I left them on the table in the hall, but they're not there now.
> **W** You may have left them in your jacket pocket. Have you looked?
> **M** I can't have left them there – I wasn't wearing a jacket. You must have moved them.
> **W** I haven't touched them. What's the first thing you did when you came in last night?
> **M** I turned the television on to watch the news.
> **W** They must be in the living room, then. Have a look. Have you found them?
> **M** Yes, they were on the top of the TV. But I definitely didn't leave them there. Someone must have moved them. You're so lucky you don't have to work on Saturdays.

c ● **4.11** Focus on the instructions. Play the CD once, then get SS to discuss what they heard in pairs, then play the recording again. Check answers, eliciting as much information as possible.

The man and woman are trying to find the way to a club but they keep getting lost. The woman is driving and she blames the man for giving her wrong directions (saying right instead of left). The man thinks the woman should know the way as she has been to the club before.

The man has cooked sweet and sour pork, following a recipe and the woman says he has used too much sugar. The man takes offence and says that next time they will get a takeaway from the Chinese restaurant.

4.11   CD2 Track 36
Conversation 2
WOMAN So where are we now?
MAN Well, I think we must be in Park Street. Look, what does that sign say?
W Merton Avenue.
M Oh no. We must have taken the wrong turning again. We should have turned left at the last traffic lights.
W Left! You said 'right'!
M OK, I might have said 'right'. It's difficult to read the map in the dark. Anyway, I thought you'd been to this club before and knew where you were going.

Conversation 3
M So, what do you think?
W Mmm. Nice.
M Only nice?
W It's a bit…er sweet.
M Sweet? It's supposed to be sweet. It's sweet and sour pork.
W Yeah, but I think you should have used less sugar.
M I used exactly what the recipe said.
W Well, you can't have read it properly. It's definitely too sweet.
M OK. Next time we'll get a takeaway from the Chinese restaurant.
W Oh, don't be so sensitive. I'm only making a constructive criticism.

d • **New grammar.** Focus on the instructions. Point out that apart from *must, may* and *might* (+ *have*) SS can also use *should have*. Give SS a few moments to read the sentences and guess which expression goes where. Play 4.10 and 4.11 again, pausing after each conversation for SS to complete the sentences. Check answers.

Conversation 1	Conversation 2	Conversation 3
1 may have	4 must have	7 should have
2 can't have	5 should have	8 can't have
3 must have	6 might have	

e • Focus on the task and give SS time to do it in pairs. Check answers, and elicit that A = *must have*, B = *might* (or *may*) *have*, C = *can't have* and D = *should have*.

Conversation 1	Conversation 2	Conversation 3
1 B	4 A	7 D
2 C	5 D	8 C
3 A	6 B	

f • Tell SS to go to **Grammar Bank 4B** on *p.138*. Go through the examples and rules with SS.

Grammar notes

- *must / might / may / can't* + *have* + **past participle**
  SS have previously seen these modal verbs to make deductions about the present, e.g. *John must be ill. She might be French.* Here they learn to use the same modals to make deductions about the past.
- **rule 1:** SS may sometimes try to use *mustn't have* (which doesn't exist) instead of *can't have*, e.g. *You can't have seen me yesterday. I was in bed all day.* NOT ~~you mustn't have…~~
- **rule 2:** Remind SS that *may* and *might* in these sentences are interchangeable (although *might have* must be used in reported speech). Highlight that *could / couldn't have…* can also be used.
- *should* + *have* + **past participle**
  SS have previously seen *should* + infinitive to express opinion and advice (e.g. *You should drink less coffee*). Here they learn to use *should have* + participle to criticize or admit blame for a past action.

- Focus on the exercises for **4B** on *p.139* and get SS to do them individually or in pairs. Check answers.

a 1	Ben must have read my email.
2	She might have had an argument with her boyfriend.
3	Sam and Ginny can't have got lost.
4	You can't have seen Elli.
5	John might not have heard you.
6	Lucy must have bought a new car.
7	Alex can't have been very ill.
8	They might not have received the invitation.
b 1	should have learnt
2	should have saved
3	shouldn't have gone
4	shouldn't have invited
5	shouldn't have bought
6	should have gone

- Tell SS to go back to the main lesson on *p.56*.

2 PRONUNCIATION weak form of *have*

Pronunciation notes

- When *have* is an auxiliary verb, not a main verb, it usually has a weak pronunciation, e.g. *I might have lost it* = /əv/. SS may mishear this as the weak form of *of*.
- The dictation below will help SS recognize the weak form of *have*.
- To encourage SS to use the weak form of *have*, tell them the most important thing is for SS to stress the modal and the participle strongly and not to stress *have* at all.

a • **4.12** Focus on the instructions and the extracts from the dialogues. Play the CD pausing after each sentence for SS to underline the stressed words. Elicit that the modal verbs and the main verbs are stressed but that *have* is not stressed and is pronounced /əv/.

See tapescript

4.12   CD2 Track 37

1 You <u>may</u> have <u>left</u> them in your <u>jacket</u> pocket.
2 I <u>can't</u> have <u>left</u> them <u>there</u> – I wasn't wearing a jacket.
3 <u>Someone</u> <u>must</u> have <u>moved</u> them.
4 We <u>must</u> have <u>taken</u> the <u>wrong</u> <u>turning</u> <u>again</u>.
5 We <u>should</u> have <u>turned</u> <u>left</u> at the <u>last</u> <u>traffic</u> <u>lights</u>.
6 OK, I <u>might</u> have <u>said</u> 'right'.
7 <u>Yes</u>, but I <u>think</u> you <u>should</u> have <u>used</u> <u>less</u> sugar.
8 You <u>can't</u> have <u>read</u> it <u>properly</u>.

b • **4.13** Focus on the task. Then play the CD once the whole way through for SS to listen. Then play it again, pausing after each sentence for SS to write. Then play it again the whole way through for SS to check.

4.13   CD2 Track 38

1 You shouldn't have told her.
2 He might have got lost.
3 She can't have forgotten!
4 You must have felt stupid.
5 He may have made a mistake.
6 You should have known the answer.

• Check answers by eliciting the sentences onto the board.

c • Focus on the task. Highlight that in 1–4 they are given the modal verb, but in 5–9 they have to choose an appropriate one. Give SS a few minutes to complete **B**'s responses. Elicit ideas from different pairs, accept responses which are grammatically correct and make sense in the context.

Possible answers
2 You can't have looked properly.
3 He may have got lost.
4 You shouldn't have eaten so much.
5 You must have made a mistake. / The meeting can't have been today.
6 You can't have worked very hard. / You should have studied more.
7 You must have said something horrible to her. / She might have seen someone she wanted to avoid.
8 She might have been ill. / She should have come – it was fantastic.
9 We should have left earlier. / We shouldn't have driven.

• Then get SS to read their dialogues in pairs practising stressing the right words. Finally, check pronunciation by getting a different pair to read each dialogue.

3 READING

a • Focus on the title of the article and the photos. Then ask the whole class the question and elicit some ideas, but don't tell them if they are right or not.

b • Tell SS that you are going to read the text together. (For copyright reasons this text is unsimplified, so there are a higher proportion of new words compared to other texts in the book.)

• Focus on the glossary, and give SS time to read the definitions. Check that they understand all the words.

• Focus on the first paragraph and either give SS time to read it themselves or read it aloud with your SS. Encourage SS to guess the meaning of other new words or phrases from context, but if any words are causing

problems, e.g. *stomp* (= walk around angrily) or *full-blown* (= fully developed), elicit, explain or demonstrate the meaning.

• Then give SS a moment to answer the questions in pairs and then elicit answers.

Extra support

You could get SS to re-read the paragraph first.

1 She used to stop what she was doing and help him. Now she doesn't pay him any attention.

• Repeat the process with paragraph 2. Words that may need explaining: *rapt* (= very interested in what you are watching / listening to), *flip* (= turn over with a sudden quick movement).

2 Because she was writing a book about exotic animal trainers, she spent a lot of time watching them training animals.
It occurred to her that she could use the same techniques to 'train' her husband.
That you reward good behaviour and ignore bad behaviour.

• Repeat the process with paragraph 3. Words that may need explaining: *toss* (= throw lightly) and *a hop* (= a jump).

3 Teaching someone new behaviour by rewarding each small step they take. She began to praise him every time he did something she wanted him to do, like put dirty washing in the hamper, etc.

• Repeat the process with paragraph 4. Words that may need explaining: *crested* (= with a group of feathers standing on their heads) and *hover* (= wait somewhere especially near sb).

4 He wanted to stop the birds landing on his head and shoulders. He trained them to land somewhere else (on mats). She stopped him from getting in her way in the kitchen when she was cooking by giving him a job to do, e.g. grating cheese, at the other end of the kitchen island.

• Repeat the process with paragraph 5. Words or phrases that may need explaining: *for a few beats* (= for a short time) and *die away* (= disappear little by little).

5 She learned a technique called L. R. S. which means not responding at all when someone does something wrong. The idea is that if you don't respond to it, the bad behaviour will disappear. When her husband was looking for his keys she just said nothing and carried on with what she was doing.

• Repeat the process with paragraph 6. A phrase that may need explaining is *launched into* (= started energetically).

6 They start to use the same technique on their trainer. He used the L. R. S. technique – he ignored her when she was complaining about her braces.

c Do these as open class questions and elicit opinions.

Extra support

At this point you could go through the article with the class, highlighting useful expressions and eliciting / explaining the meaning of new words and phrases.

4 LISTENING

a ● **4.14** Focus on the question and elicit responses from the class (*a discussion* = people having a conversation about a particular topic, *an argument* = people talking, often angrily, because they disagree about sth).

● Focus on the task and give SS a few moments to read the ten sentences. Play the CD once. Check answers.

| 1 ✓ | 3 ✓ | 5 ✓ | 6 ✓ | 7 ✓ | 9 ✓ |

4.14 CD2 Track 39

(tapescript in Student's Book on *p.126*)

In life we sometimes have disagreements with people. It could be with your partner, with your boss, with your parents, or with a friend. When this happens, the important thing is to try not to let a calm discussion turn into a heated argument. But of course this is easier said than done.

The first thing I would say is that the way you begin the conversation is very important. Imagine you are a student and you share a flat with another student, who you think isn't doing her share of the housework. If you say, 'Look, you never do your share of the housework. What are we going to do about it?', the discussion will very soon turn into an argument. It's much more constructive to say something like, 'I think we'd better have another look about how we divide up the housework. Maybe there's a better way of doing it.' My second piece of advice is simple. If you're the person who is in the wrong, just admit it! This is the easiest and best way to avoid an argument. Just apologize to your flatmate, your parents or your husband, and move on. The other person will have much more respect for you in the future if you do that. The next tip is don't exaggerate. Try not to say things like 'You *always* come home late when my mother comes to dinner' when perhaps this has only happened twice, or 'You never remember to buy the toothpaste.' This will just make the other person think you're being unreasonable, and will probably make him or her stop listening to your arguments.

Sometimes we just can't avoid a discussion turning into an argument. But if you do start arguing with someone, it is important to keep things under control and there are ways to do this.

The most important thing is don't raise your voice. Raising your voice will just make the other person lose their temper too. If you find yourself raising your voice, stop for a moment and take a deep breath. Say 'I'm sorry I shouted, but this is very important to me', and continue calmly. If you can talk calmly and quietly, you'll find your partner will be more ready to think about what you are saying.

It is also very important to stick to the point. Try to keep to the topic you are talking about. Don't bring up old arguments, or try to bring in other issues.

Just concentrate on solving the one problem you are having, and leave the other things for another time. So, for example, if you're arguing about the housework, don't start talking about mobile phone bills as well. And my final tip is that if necessary call 'Time out', like in a sports match. If you think that an argument is getting out of control, then you can say to the other person, 'Listen, I'd rather talk about this tomorrow

when we've both calmed down'. You can then continue the discussion the next day when perhaps both of you are feeling less tense and angry. That way there is much more chance that you will be able to reach an agreement. You'll also probably find that the problem is much easier to solve when you've both had a good night's sleep. Well, those are my tips.

But I want to say one last important thing. Some people think that arguing is always bad. This is not true. Conflict is a normal part of life, and dealing with conflict is an important part of any relationship, whether it's three people sharing a flat, a married couple, or just two good friends. If you don't learn to argue properly, then when a real problem comes along, you won't be prepared to face it together. Think of the smaller arguments as training sessions. Learn how to argue cleanly and fairly. It will help your relationship become stronger and last longer.

b ● Get SS to focus on the six sentences they have ticked. Play the CD again. Pause after each tip is mentioned, and then give SS a minute or two to discuss <u>briefly</u> with a partner what else the psychologist said. Then try to elicit all the extra information from SS.

● Repeat for the next five tips. Finally, play the last part (from '*I want to say one last important thing…*') Pause at this point and ask SS if they can remember what the last important thing was. Elicit ideas and then play the CD to the end. Elicit the reasons why the psychologist says that arguing can be a good thing.

c ● Either get SS to discuss this in pairs, or elicit opinions from the whole class.

d ● Now focus on some extracts from the listening. Give SS a few moments in pairs to read the sentences and try to guess / remember any of the missing phrases, or at least some of the words. Tell them to write their suggestions in pencil at the end of each sentence.

e ● **4.15** Play the CD pausing after each sentence to give SS time to write the missing words. Finally, check answers making sure SS understand what the phrases mean.

1	easier said **than done**
2	**in the** wrong
3	**keep** things **under** control
4	**lose** their temper
5	**take** a deep breath
6	**stick to** the point
7	**reach** an agreement
8	**Dealing with** conflict

4.15 CD2 Track 40

1 But of course this is easier said than done.
2 If you're the person who is in the wrong, just admit it!
3 It is important to keep things under control.
4 Raising your voice will just make the other person lose their temper too.
5 Stop for a moment and take a deep breath.
6 It is also very important to stick to the point.
7 There is much more chance that you will be able to reach an agreement.
8 Dealing with conflict is an important part of any relationship.

Extra support

If there's time, you could get SS to listen again with the tapescript on *p.126* so that they can see exactly what they understood / didn't understand. Explain / translate any words or phrases that SS aren't sure about.

5 SPEAKING

a • Sit SS in pairs, **A** and **B**. Tell them to go to **Communication** *Argument!* **A** on *p.117*, **B** on *p.120*. If you have a mixed-sex pair, get the male to be **B**. Explain that they are going to 'act out' two arguments, and have to read their roles carefully before they start. A male student may have to play a female role and vice versa.

• Get them to read their role in roleplay 1. Then tell the **B**s to start. Monitor to see if SS are doing any of the things the psychologist said they shouldn't.

• Stop the roleplay when you think it has gone on long enough. Then tell SS to read their roles for roleplay 2, and then tell **A**s to start. Monitor as before.

⚠ If you have a young class which might not enjoy or be able to do the husband / wife roleplay successfully, just get them to do roleplay 2.

• Tell SS to go back to the main lesson on *p.58*.

b • Do this as an open class question. Tell SS about any things you noticed they were doing that, according to the psychologist, they shouldn't have done.

6 VOCABULARY   verbs often confused

a • Focus on the task. Give SS a few minutes to individually circle the right verb.

b • Get SS to compare answers with a partner, explaining what the difference is. Check answers.

1 a realized, b notices   realize = to understand or become aware of a particular fact or situation; notice = to see, hear, or become aware of sth, e.g. *After a week in my new job I realized I had made a mistake in accepting it; I noticed that she had changed her hairstyle.*

2 a rising, b raise   rise = to go up (can't have an object); raise = to make sth go up (needs an object), e.g. *the sun rises, a company raises salaries.*

3 a discuss, b argue   discuss = have a conversation about sth; argue = talk often angrily to sb because you disagree about sth

4 a prevent, b avoid   prevent = stop sth from happening; avoid = stop yourself from being in a situation, e.g. *Jane's parents prevented her from seeing David; John avoids seeing his ex-girlfriend.*

5 a remember, b Remind   remind = make sb remember, e.g. *This song reminds me of last summer.*

6 a hope, b expecting   hope = want sth to happen; expect = think sth is going to happen, e.g. *I hope it doesn't rain tomorrow – we're having a barbecue. I expect Sarah will be late – she always is.*

7 a mind, b matter   mind = be annoyed or worried by sth (so always needs a person as subject); matter = be important, often used with 'it', e.g. *Does your teacher mind if you don't go to all the classes? Does it matter if you don't go to all the classes?*

8 a stolen, b robbing   steal = take sth that is not yours. The object of *steal* must be a thing; rob = to take sth that is not yours from a person or place. The object must be a person or a place, not a thing, e.g. *He stole money from the bank. He robbed the bank.*

9 a heard, b listened to   hear = receive sounds with your ears; listen to = pay special attention to hear sth, e.g. *I heard what you were saying – I was outside the door. You never listen to what I tell you.*

10 a looks, b seemed   look = give an impression from what you can see; seem = give a general impression, e.g. *Mario looks ill – he's very pale. Maria seems unhappy but I don't know why.*

c • Focus on the task and give SS a few minutes, in pairs or individually, to fill the gaps. Remind SS that they may need to change the form of the verb. Check answers.

1	notice	5	remembering	9 listening
2	raise	6	expecting	10 look
3	argue	7	matters	
4	avoid	8	stolen	

• Now get SS to ask each other the questions. Encourage them to ask for more information where appropriate.

• Get feedback from different pairs.

MINI GRAMMAR   *would rather, had better*

a • Focus on the examples and questions. Elicit answers.

'd rather = would prefer to (*'d* = would)
'd better = should (*'d* = had)

b • Go through the rules with SS. Highlight that we almost always contract *had* and *would* after pronouns. Highlight that *had better* is often used as a warning, i.e. it gives the idea that if you don't do something, there will be a negative consequence, e.g. *You'd better not tell mum you failed your exam* (= mum won't be very pleased).

c • Give SS a few minutes to do the exercise. Check answers.

1 … I'd better go now…
2 I'd rather go out…
3 You'd better not walk home…
4 … she'd rather meet…
5 … had better be careful…
6 Would you rather not go to the party…?
7 You'd better not leave your bag there…
8 My wife would rather not fly…

• If you think your class need more practice, use the extra photocopiable exercises on *p.186*.

Extra photocopiable activities

Grammar
past modals *p.170*
Communicative
Communication breakdown! *p.208* (instructions *p.193*)

HOMEWORK

Study Link Workbook *pp.37–39*

4

C

G verbs of the senses
V the body
P silent letters

Let your body do the talking

Lesson plan

The general topic of this lesson is body language. The grammar focus is on verbs of the senses and how they are used grammatically, e.g. *he looks tired, he looks like his father, he looks as if he has seen a ghost*. SS extend their vocabulary related to the body, learning, in addition to new body parts, verbs and idioms connected to the body (e.g. *nod your head, put your foot in it*). The first part of the lesson is based on a book of photography where a photographer asked actors to imagine they were a person in a particular situation and then he took their photo. In the second half of the lesson SS read an article about body language and how certain postures and movements can betray our emotions. The pronunciation focus is on silent letters.

Optional lead-in (books closed)

- For a fun lead-in to the lesson ask for some volunteers to mime a particular feeling to the class.
- Either whisper to each person which feeling they have to mime or write it on a piece of paper. Choose from the following:
  exhausted   shocked   astonished   disappointed
  offended   furious   terrified   delighted
  fed up   confused
- Tell the rest of the class that the SS are going to mime some feelings. All the adjectives are in **Vocabulary Bank Feelings** on *p.151*.
- The volunteers take turns to do their mimes and the rest of the class have to try to guess the adjectives.

1 GRAMMAR   verbs of the senses

a • Books open. Focus on the photo and three sentence stems. Get SS to choose what they think is the best continuation for each sentence. Elicit ideas and get SS to say why. Don't tell them if they are right.

b • Get SS to read the introduction to the book 'Actors acting'. Elicit answers to the questions from the class.

> 1 The man is the actor Christopher Lloyd.
> 2 He is pretending to be a violin teacher listening to a pupil massacre a Mozart piece, i.e. playing it very badly.

- Then ask SS how many of them chose 1b, 2a and 3c in exercise **a**. If most of them did, then the actor was clearly playing his role well!
- Finally, ask SS what kind of words / phrases come after *looks* (+ adjectives), *looks like* (+ nouns) and *looks as if* (+ subject and verb).

c • Tell SS to go to **Grammar Bank 4C** on *p.138*. Go through the examples and rules with SS.

Grammar notes

- **look / feel / smell / sound / taste**
  SS have previously studied *look* + adjective and *look like* + noun. Here SS learn the other verbs of the senses and also the construction *as if* (e.g. *He looks as if he needs a holiday*).

- **rule 3**: The use of *like* instead of *as if* (e.g. *He looks like he needs a holiday*) is quite colloquial. In written English *as if* or *as though* are usually preferred.

  You may want to point out that *smell* and *taste* are also often used with *of* when we think something really is what it smells / tastes of, e.g. *Open the window – it smells of gas in here. The strawberry ice cream really tastes of strawberries.* When we use these verbs with *like* we are saying that something smells or tastes <u>similar</u> to something else, e.g. *This meat tastes like chicken.*

- Focus on the exercises for **4C** on *p.139* and get SS to do them individually or in pairs. Check answers after each exercise.

a	1	look as if	b	2	G
	2	smells		3	A
	3	sounds like		4	B
	4	taste like		5	K
	5	sound as if		6	J
	6	feels		7	C
	7	look		8	E
	8	feels like		9	D
	9	tastes		10	I
	10	smells as if		11	H

- Tell SS to go back to the main lesson on *p.60*.

d • Tell SS to cover **e** with a piece of paper and just look at the photos. The two actors are acting a different role in each photo. SS should try to make three sentences, one with each *look* structure, for each photo. Elicit ideas and make sure SS are using the structures correctly.

e • Now get SS to uncover **e** and read the instructions the actors were given. In pairs, they match them to the photos. Check answers.

1	D	3	C	5	H	7	F
2	A	4	B	6	G	8	E

f • **4.16** Focus on the instructions. Tell SS they are going to hear some sounds which they have to identify. You could do this as a whole class activity and get SS to call out answers as you play each recording, or get SS in pairs to silently write down their answers and check answers at the end.

- Point out that SS may feel they are missing some of the vocabulary they need to describe the sounds accurately (*saw, drill,* etc.). Encourage them to think laterally and use the words that they know to describe what they think is happening, e.g. *It sounds as if someone is cutting down a tree. It sounds like a dentist,* etc. with each one.

> **4.16** CD2 Track 41
>
> [sound effects]
> 1 *football crowd shouting after a near miss*
> 2 *hair being cut*
> 3 *plane taking off*
> 4 *a cat howling*
> 5 *someone sawing*
> 6 *a school bell ringing*
> 7 *people screaming on a roller coaster*
> 8 *dentist's drill*
> 9 *mobile phone vibrating on a table*
> 10 *gentle waves lapping against the beach*

g ● Focus on the instructions and give SS a moment to put the adjectives in pairs. Check answers, encouraging SS to use the phonetics to get the right pronunciation for *rough* and *smooth*. For each pair ask SS if they usually describe how something feels or how something tastes / smells.

> hard – soft   how sth feels (e.g. a table – a pillow)
> loose – tight   how sth feels (e.g. pyjamas – cycling shorts)
> rough – smooth   how sth feels (e.g. the skin on your elbow / heel – glass)
> sour / bitter – sweet   how sth smells / tastes (e.g. lemon / dark chocolate – sugar)
> strong – weak   how sth tastes (e.g. tea depending on how long you leave the tea bag in for)

Extra idea

Ask SS for an example for each adjective.

h ● Focus on the instructions. Demonstrate by describing one of the objects yourself, e.g. *It smells disgusting and often it makes the whole room smell for days* (a full ashtray). Point out that they need to make a sentence with *smells / tastes / feels* and then give another clue.
● SS then continue in pairs. Finally, quickly elicit a sentence for each object.

> **Possible answers**
> It smells disgusting.
> It feels smooth and silky.
> It smells wonderful.
> It tastes sour / like vinegar.
> It smells very strong.
> It feels smooth and cold.
> It feels soft and cold.
> It tastes sour.
> He / She smells lovely and clean / feels soft and smooth.
> It feels rough.
> It tastes bitter.
> It feels rough.
> It tastes hot / spicy.
> They feel tight.

2 LISTENING

a ● **4.17** Focus on the instructions. To help set the scene, you could pre-teach *a blindfold* (= sth that is put over sb's eyes so they cannot see). Play the CD once, pausing after the 'mystery drink' for SS to write down what they think it is. Then repeat the process for the food, object and sound.

> **4.17** CD2 Track 42
>
> (tapescript in Student's Book on *p.126*)
> **P = presenter, J = Joanna, S = Steve**
> **P** And welcome to tonight's edition of *Use your senses*. First with us we have Joanna and Steve from Stepney.
> **J & S** Hi / hello.
> **P** Now, the blindfold's on – you can't see anything, can you?
> **J & S** No, nothing at all.
> **P** Right so first the mystery drink. Remember you can smell it but you can't taste it… starting… now!
> **J** It doesn't really smell of anything.
> **S** It smells fruity to me, not very strong but definitely fruity.
> **J** Yeah, it smells a bit like orange juice but sweeter.
> **S** It could be (beep) then.
> **P** OK so now the food. This you can taste, but you can't see of course… ready… now!
> **J** Well, it's meat, isn't it? It tastes a bit like chicken but I don't think it is chicken.
> **S** I don't think I've had it before – the texture isn't quite like chicken – it tastes quite light, I don't think it's duck…
> **P** You've got ten more seconds…
> **J** It must be (beep).
> **S** OK.
> **P** Now the object.
> **S** It feels like a coin.
> **J** Can I feel it? Yes, it definitely feels metallic, but it's completely smooth – it doesn't seem to have any markings – oh, it's got two tiny little holes in the middle. I know, it's a (beep).
> **S** That's it.
> **P** So now we're going to take off the blindfolds – there we are.
> **J & S** Thanks / That's better.
> **P** And now to the sound effect. I'm going to play you a sound and you've got to decide what it is you're hearing. Remember you can hear it twice only. Ready? Now…
> **S** It sounds like thunder to me.
> **J** Well, maybe, but it sounds very distant. Could it be a train?
> **S** No, I think it's something natural, you know not a machine. Can we hear it again, please?
> **P** Of course.
> **S** Yes, I think it's (beep). What do you think?
> **J** Could be. I'll go with that.
> **P** Right. Time's up. So now, the moment of truth. Did Steve and Joanna get it right? Remember you need all the answers right to win today's prize. Our assistant Vanessa will give us the answers, a round of applause for Vanessa.

b ● Focus on the task. Now play the CD again, pausing after pairs of sentences for SS to write. Check answers.

> **Mystery drink**
> It smells **fruity**.
> It smells a bit **like orange juice**.
> **Mystery food**
> It tastes a bit **like chicken**.
> It tastes quite **light**.
> **Mystery object**
> It feels like **a coin**.
> It definitely feels **metallic**.
> **Mystery sound**
> It sounds like **thunder**.
> It sounds **very distant**.

c ● Now get SS to compare their answers to **a** with a partner. Tell them to check that the phrases in **b** work for the things they have chosen.

● Elicit their ideas onto the board but don't tell them who is right.

d ● **4.18** Finally, play the end of the competition. Pause after each thing to see how many SS guessed correctly.

> **4.18**   CD2 Track 43
>
> Well, we'll start with the sound effect, and Steve and Joanna said they thought it was horses galloping… and that was right. Our mystery object today – well, Steve and Joanna said… a button… and that was the right answer, so congratulations again. The mystery drink. What did they think it was?… Yes, it was pineapple juice. And finally the mystery food. Steven and Joanna said turkey. So was it turkey? No, it was… rabbit. So I'm afraid it's goodbye to Steve and Joanna. Give them a big round of applause.

Extra support

If there's time, you could get SS to listen to the recording again with the tapescript on *p.126* so that they can see exactly what they understood / didn't understand. Explain / translate any words or phrases that SS aren't sure about.

3 VOCABULARY the body

a ● Focus on the photo and the words in the list and get SS in pairs to label the picture. Check answers and drill pronunciation.

Extra support

Before you start the exercise, you could revise the basic vocabulary of the face. Quickly sketch a face on the board with eyes, nose, ears, head, hair and mouth, and check SS remember and can pronounce these words.

1	forehead	5	eyelashes
2	eyebrow	6	wrinkles
3	cheek	7	chin
4	lips	8	neck

b ● Tell SS to go to **Vocabulary Bank** *The body* on *p.152*. Focus on section **1 Parts of the body and organs** and give SS time to match the words and pictures individually or in pairs. Check answers and drill pronunciation where necessary.

1	brain	9	lungs
2	heart	10	kidneys
3	liver	11	wrist
4	nails	12	palm
5	chest	13	elbow
6	waist	14	calf
7	hip	15	ankle
8	thigh	16	heel

● Now focus on section **2 Verbs and verb phrases a** and give SS time do the exercise. Check answers, and get SS to mime the actions to show that they have understood.

2	nose	8	head
3	hair / teeth	9	head
4	hands	10	eyebrows
5	hair	11	hands
6	arms	12	shoulders
7	hand		

● Now focus on **b**. Explain that these verbs are not used with a part of the body as in **a**, but describe the movement of a part of the body, e.g. *wink* (demonstrate it). Then get SS in pairs to do the exercise. Check answers and again get SS to mime the action.

2	teeth	7	forehead
3	arms	8	eyes
4	nails	9	mouth / arms (and / or legs)
5	hand	10	finger
6	knees		

● Focus on the **Idioms** section. Tell SS that there are many English idioms which include a part of the body. Again, get them to do this exercise in pairs. Check answers and then ask SS from the context what they think the phrases mean.

> 1 give me a **hand** = help
> 2 put your **foot** in it = said or did sth stupid that upset, offended or embarrassed
> 3 pulling my **leg** = joking
> 4 on the tip of my **tongue** = I can almost remember it but not quite
> 5 get cold **feet** = become worried about sth and think you might change your mind
> 6 have (got) butterflies in my **stomach** = feel nervous, usually before an important event, e.g. an exam, giving a speech in public
> 7 broke his **heart** = made him feel very unhappy
> 8 can't get…out of my **head** = can't stop thinking about it
> 9 learn…by **heart** = memorize
> 10 get…off my **chest** = talk about sth that has been worrying you so that you feel less anxious

● Finally, focus on the instruction 'Can you remember the words on this page? Test yourself or a partner'.

Testing yourself

For **1 Parts of the body and organs** SS can cover the words, look at the pictures and try to remember the words. For **2 Verbs and verb phrases** they can cover the parts of the body and try to remember them. With **3 Idioms** they can cover the column on the right and remember the missing parts of the body.

Testing a partner

See **Testing a partner** *p.20*.

> **Study Link** SS can find more practice of these words and phrases on the MultiROM and on the *New English File Upper-intermediate* website.

- Tell SS to go back to the main lesson on *p.62*.

c ● SS now recycle the words they have just learnt to help fix them in their memory. Get them to do the quiz in pairs and set a time limit. Check answers.

> **A** 1 wrist   4 cheeks
>   2 waist, hips   5 lungs
>   3 ankle   6 chest
> **B** 1 I have (got) butterflies in my stomach.
>   2 It's on the tip of my tongue.
>   3 I can't get it out of my head.
>   4 You're pulling my leg.
>   5 I've learned it by heart.
>   6 I've put my foot in it.

d ● **4.19** Tell SS they are going to hear instructions and they have to mime the action. Demonstrate by saying 'Shake hands with the person next to you' and check SS are all doing the right thing.

- Play the CD pausing after each imperative and checking that SS are doing it correctly.

Extra idea

You could repeat the activity by reading out the instructions yourself in a different order.

> **4.19**   CD2 Track 44
> Shake your head.
> Fold your arms.
> Raise your eyebrows.
> Scratch your head.
> Clap your hands.
> Comb your hair.
> Bite your nails.
> Shake hands with the person next to you.
> Nod your head.
> Touch your chin.
> Snap your fingers.
> Wink.
> Stare at the person next to you.
> Point at the board.
> Stretch your arms.
> Shrug your shoulders.
> Wave goodbye.

4 PRONUNCIATION silent letters

Pronunciation notes

SS by now will be familiar with the concept of silent consonants, i.e. consonants which are not pronounced (e.g. the silent **b** in *thumb*). Encourage SS to use their instinct (from their knowledge of similar looking words) to detect silent consonants in new vocabulary. Emphasize that when they check the pronunciation of a new word in a dictionary, the phonetic transcript will help them to see when a letter (or syllable) is not pronounced. They should cross these letters through when they note down a new word. You may want to give your SS more examples:

silent **t** (**after** *s*): listen, whistle, etc.

silent **k** (**before** *n*): know, knowledge, knife, etc.

silent **w** (**before** *r*): write, wrong, wrap, etc.

silent **w** (**before** *h*): who, whose (! *wh* is normally pronounced /w/, e.g. *when*)

silent **b** (**after** *m*): lamb, bomb, etc.

silent **g** (**after** *i* and **before** *n*, when *i* = /aɪ/): resign, design
⚠ But the *g* is not silent in, e.g. *signature, resignation*.

silent **h**: hour, exhausted, etc. (This is a <u>very</u> unusual. /h/ is normally pronounced.)

silent **l**: calm, could, would, etc.

silent **p** (**before** *s*): psychic, psychoanalysis, etc.

a ● Focus on the task. Remind SS to say the words aloud to help them.

b ● **4.20** Play the CD and check answers.

> ca[ł]f [w]rist pa[ł]ms [w]rinkles com[b]
> [k]neel thum[b]

> **4.20**   CD2 Track 45
> calf   comb
> wrist   kneel
> palms   thumb
> wrinkles

c ● Focus on the task and give SS time to do it in pairs. You could do the first two with the class.

d ● **4.21** Play the CD and check answers.

> as[th]ma cas[t]le cu[p]board si[g]n dou[b]t
> ha[ł]f [h]onest i[s]land [k]nock [p]syc[h]ologist
> recei[p]t [w]hole

> **4.21**   CD2 Track 46
> asthma   doubt   knock
> castle   half   psychologist
> cupboard   honest   receipt
> sign   island   whole

e ● **4.22** Tell SS to close their books. Play the CD once the whole way through. Then play it again pausing after each sentence to give SS time to write.

- Check answers by writing them on the board.

4.22   CD2 Track 47

1 I doubt if you'll have wrinkles before you're forty.
2 The psychologist told me to sign my name.
3 He broke his wrist and thumb.
4 I honestly believe the whole thing is wrong.
5 Would you like a receipt?
6 Let's climb to the castle on the island.

Extra idea

Get SS to practise saying the sentences in pairs.

5 READING

a ● Get SS to look at the title *Let your body do the talking* and ask them what they think it means. Elicit / explain the term *body language* and elicit that body language is the way we use our bodies, not just our voices, to communicate things to other people, e.g. we raise our eyebrows to show we are surprised.

b ● Focus on the drawings and give SS time in pairs to match them to the feelings. Don't check answers yet.

c ● Read the introduction with SS; explain / elicit the meaning of *convey* (= to make ideas, feelings, etc. known) and *deliberate* (= done on purpose). Check SS know how to pronounce *gesture* /dʒestʃə/. Now focus on the article and get SS to read it fairly quickly to check their answers. Check answers.

| A 8 | B 7 | C 6 | D 3 | E 4 | F 2 | G 1 | H 5 |

d ● Now tell SS to focus on the highlighted words and phrases and try to guess what they mean. Check answers getting SS to either demonstrate or point to the part of the body.

fidgeting = keep moving, e.g. your hands and feet, because you are nervous or bored
tapping = hitting sb / sth quickly and lightly
clasped = hold sth tightly in your hand
index finger = the finger next to your thumb
strokes = moves hand gently over a surface, usually several times
ear lobes = the soft parts at the bottom of your ears
a lock = a few hairs that hang or lie together on your head
tuck their hair behind their ears = to push their hair so that it is held in place
rubbing (your eyes) = moving your hand backwards and forwards over sth while pressing firmly

e ● Focus on the instructions. Then get SS to re-read paragraph 1. When they have finished, get them to demonstrate the gestures. Elicit / explain the meaning of any words or phrases which are causing problems.

● Repeat for the rest of the paragraphs.

● Now ask the class which of the gestures they use a lot, and tell them (or ask them) about any you use.

6 SPEAKING

a ● Go through the **GET IT RIGHT** box, and check SS understand *in the background* and *in the foreground* when talking about a painting or photo.

● Focus on the painting and the body language of the woman. Put SS in pairs and get them to discuss where she is, how she is feeling, etc.

● Get feedback from different pairs and see if the class agrees.

b ● Put SS in pairs, **A** and **B**, and tell them to go to **Communication** *Two paintings* **A** on *p.118*, **B** on *p.120*.

● Go through the instructions. Monitor and encourage SS to use *It looks as if…, they look as if…,* etc.

● Get feedback to find out who did / didn't create an image that their partner then recognized.

● Finally, tell SS to go to *Phrasal verbs in context File 4* on *p.157* and complete the phrasal verbs which have come up in this File. (Answers *p.155*)

Extra photocopiable activities

Grammar
verbs of the senses *p.171*
Communicative
What is it? *p.209* (instructions *p.194*)
Vocabulary
Split crossword *p.226* (instructions *p.221*)

HOMEWORK

Study Link **Workbook** *pp.40–42*

Lesson plan

In the first part of this lesson the person interviewed is the Canadian actor Trevor White, who has appeared in theatre, film and TV (www.imdb.com/name/nm0925544/). In the second part of the lesson people in the street are asked if they have ever acted, and how they felt.

Study Link These lessons are on the *New English File Upper-intermediate* DVD / Video which can be used instead of the class CD (See Introduction *p.9*). SS can get more practice on the MultiROM, which contains more of the short street interviews with a listening task and tapescripts.

Optional lead-in (books closed)

- Write on the board **Advantages and disadvantages of being an actor**. Either put SS in pairs to brainstorm ideas, or elicit ideas from the class. Write their ideas onto the board.

THE INTERVIEW

a • Books open. Focus on the photos and ask SS what they can see.

> Some men acting.

- Now focus on the task and on the glossary. Go through it with the class eliciting from them how to pronounce the words and phrases.

b • **4.23** Focus on the task. Put SS in pairs and give them time to read the questions. Encourage SS not to write anything down when they listen the first time. They should listen and try to get the gist of what he is saying, and then discuss the questions with their partner.

- Play the CD once (**Part 1**). Give SS time to discuss the questions and tell each other what they understood. Then play the CD once or twice more. This time SS might want to jot down things they heard to help them remember the answers to the questions. Check answers.

> 1 theatre, film work, radio work, commercials, voice-over work.
> 2 He always enjoyed acting as a child, but didn't think he could do it as a career. He did economics at university but didn't enjoy it. Then he took acting classes and started to work as an actor.
> 3 Learning the lines.
> 4 He records other people's lines into a Dictaphone, then plays it back and pauses and says his lines.
> 5 Lines that are badly written.

4.23 CD3 Track 2

(tapescript in Student's Book on *p.126*)
I = interviewer, T = Trevor White

I Trevor White is a Canadian actor. Can you tell us a bit about the kind of acting you do?

T There isn't much I don't do, I guess, as far as acting goes. There's theatre, obviously, film work, television work, sometimes commercials and even voice-over work, which is for radio or for television or even sometimes animated shows where you lend your voice to those as well. So, I've rarely said 'no' to an acting job.

I Did you always want to be an actor?

T Well, it's something that I always loved to do, act, as a kid in high school, in school plays, and in my spare time, just playing around with friends. You know, acting and improvising and that kind of thing. But I don't think I ever believed that I could… or ever took it seriously to act as a profession for the rest of my life. So I went in to university and took economics as a more practical thing to do, but I didn't really enjoy it, I guess and ultimately, after university, I started taking some acting classes and really enjoyed that. And then started doing student films and fringe theatre and unpaid work just to get experience in acting and loved it and then started doing it more seriously and got an agent and started getting proper acting jobs and that was about 13 years ago.

I What's the most difficult thing about preparing for a new role?

T It really depends. When you do a play, for example, you have three, four, sometimes even six weeks to rehearse with the other people and the director and the props and everything, so you have a long time to learn your lines, to as it were find the character. The memorization is the most like real work, that can be difficult, you know, just memorizing lots of lines. In film and television you don't have the benefit of rehearsal. You just show up and you're expected to know all your lines and then you do it a few times and that's it. So you have to be very disciplined and get all that ready in advance.

I How do you learn your lines?

T I have a Dictaphone actually, which I just record the other people's lines, obviously in my voice, I don't do strange character voices because that would be weird, and, you know I just say their line, I stop it, I say my line, I play the next lines, so you just basically record all the other lines in any given scene and play it back and just work through it slowly. It's amazing the difference it makes when you, when the writing is good and it makes sense. It's much easier to memorize. But if sometimes you audition for a bad science fiction TV show or a horror movie or something, you often have a much harder time memorizing poorly written lines, because they're just bad. But of course it's your job so you do it.

Extra challenge

You could use the tapescript above to elicit more detailed answers from SS.

c • **4.24** Focus on the task and play the CD once (**Part 2**). Give SS time to discuss the questions and what they understood. Then play the CD once or twice more. Check answers.

1 (Earlier) this year he was in this play and he really enjoyed it. But the role he played was very demanding.
2 He had to do one in *Coriolanus* and found it very difficult. He injured the other actor who had to have three stitches (on his fingers).
3 He prefers theatre acting because you do it again and again in front of a live audience.
4 Good side: can be fun, you can work with famous people, you can shoot guns, be in car chases
Bad side: most of the time you are just waiting, not doing anything
5 He thinks it is probably glamorous but he hasn't been on one so he doesn't know.

4.24   CD3 Track 3

(tapescript in Student's Book on *p.126*)
I Is there any role you've particularly enjoyed?
T There's a few roles that I've played or oftentimes when you do something it's the whole experience of a job, not necessarily just the part you have in it. Earlier this year, I got to work for the Royal Shakespeare Company for the first time and we did *Coriolanus*, one of Shakespeare's lesser performed plays in Stratford, in Washington in America, also in Newcastle here in the United Kingdom and in Madrid in Spain for five months, which was amazing.
I What's the most difficult role that you've ever had to play?
T Well, I suppose, this last role that I played is one of the most difficult parts, Tullus Aufidius in *Coriolanus*, because there were lots of things that were very demanding about the part. We had to do a huge sword and axe fight in the middle of the play. Which… I'd done stage combat before, but never anything like this we were using actual… I mean they were blunt swords and axes, but they were still very large pieces of metal. And we had a couple of small accidents, but no major ones luckily I gave the other guy three stitches on his fingers at one point when he parried in the wrong place – that's my opinion anyway.
I Do you prefer working in the theatre or in film and TV?
T I think theatre is the most satisfying work in acting oftentimes, because you get to do it over and over again in front of a live audience, but it doesn't tend to pay as well as film and television, which is also fun, but not as glamorous as people might think it is, I guess.
I So being an actor isn't really glamorous?
T No, I don't think acting is a glamorous life, particularly in, well I guess in any way. In theatre it's you know, you don't really earn that much money and you work hard. Yeah, and film and television work is, you know, can be a lot of fun, you can get to work with some famous people sometimes or some very talented people that you admire and that's a thrilling thing and you get to shoot guns or, you know, go on car chases and all those things are really fun, but most of the time, the 90% of the day, even when you're doing exciting things, you're just sitting and waiting around, you're always waiting around, they're always fixing lights, setting up new camera positions, trying to figure out who's going where when and it takes them…to film a proper feature film takes months and maybe in all that time only two or three of those days all told is actually you doing anything. So yeah, I think a lot of people get into extra work and stuff because they think this will be really glamorous, but you end up sort of reading a book about nine hours a day. So, yeah. And I've never been on a red carpet so I suppose I can't judge. That looks glamorous.

d ● **4.25** This exercise gives SS intensive listening practice in deciphering phrases where words are often run together, and introduces them to some common English expressions. Focus on the phrases and give SS time to read them. Play the CD, pausing after the first phrase and replaying it as necessary. Elicit the missing words, and then the meaning of the whole phrase. Repeat for the other five phrases.

1 **as far as acting goes** (= related to acting)
2 **show up** (a phrasal verb = arrive somewhere where you are expected to be / do something, synonym *turn up*)
3 **that's it** (= informal way of saying *that's all there is, it's finished*)
4 **difference it makes** (= there is a big difference between good and bad writing)
5 **at one point** (= at one moment)
6 **over and over** again (= informal way of saying *many times one after another*, synonym *again and again*)

4.25   CD3 Track 4

1 There isn't much I don't do, I guess, as far as acting goes.
2 You just show up and you're expected to know all your lines.
3 You do it a few times and that's it.
4 It's amazing the difference it makes when the writing is good.
5 I gave the other guy three stitches on his fingers at one point when he parried in the wrong place.
6 You get to do it over and over again.

e ● Tell SS to go to *p.126* and to look at the tapescript for the interview. Play the CD (**Part 1** and **Part 2**) again and tell SS to read and listen at the same time. Deal with any vocabulary problems and get feedback from SS on what parts they found hard to understand and why, e.g. speed of speech, elision, pronunciation, etc.

● Finally, focus on the question. You could also ask SS *If you were an actor, do you think you would prefer acting on stage or in a film?* Get SS to answer in pairs or as a whole class. Then get feedback from the whole class.

IN THE STREET

a ● **4.26** Focus on the photos of the people and elicit impressions (e.g. *How old do they look? What job do you think they do?*, etc.) The two new people here are Louise and Ray as Ben, Mike and Cherry have appeared in Files 1 and 2. Tell SS that they were all interviewed in Covent Garden, a busy shopping area in Central London.

● Focus on the task. Point out that some of them may have done more than one. Play the CD once. Then play it again pausing after each speaker to check answers.

a musical 2 (Louise)
a music video 1 (Ben)
a play 2 (Louise), 4 (Cherry)
a school play 5 (Ray)
a show 3 (Mike)
Three of them mention feeling nervous. (Ben, Cherry, and Ray)

(tapescript in Student's Book on *p.127*)
**I = interviewer, B = Ben, L = Louise, M = Mike,
C = Cherry, R = Ray**

Ben

I   Have you ever acted?

B   I was in a music video once, and that's about as far as I've gone. But I mean, I'm a musician so I kind of appear on stage quite a lot.

I   How does it make you feel?

B   I suppose nervous at first but then you settle in and within a couple of minutes and before you know it you kind of lose any awareness of kind of any external factors or anything like that. And you're not aware of anything else outside of this kind of bubble that you've kind of managed to transport yourself into.

Louise

I   Have you ever acted?

L   Yes, I was in the Royal Shakespeare Company up in my area and did a few plays and a few musicals and I'm a specialist make-up artist, so I kind of work with actors, doing all their make-up, and zombies and that.

I   What do you like about it?

L   The buzz of it, being able to be someone else in front of people – just being someone else is good.

Mike

I   Have you ever acted?

M   Yes, I have. I'm studying acting now. I'm a student studying theatre and music. Er, I've been in a few things, when I was little, and I was, I've been in a few shows around London, things like that. But I plan to go further.

I   How does it make you feel?

M   I love it. I think it's really great. Because you don't have to be yourself for once. You're onstage and you can just be whoever your character is meant to be. And you can just sort of get taken away into this other world and you can get really into it. That's what I really like about acting.

Cherry

I   Have you ever acted?

C   Yeah, I'm in like a drama youth group so a couple of plays I've been in, like *Bugsy Malone* and *The Wizard of Oz*. A modernized one and stuff. So, yeah.

I   How does it make you feel?

C   Yeah, it is nerve-wracking just as you're about to go on, but apart from that, yeah, once you're on it's fine.

Ray

I   Have you ever acted?

R   Possibly not since I was at school. No, I don't think, not since I was at school, no.

I   How did it make you feel?

R   Very nervous beforehand, very apprehensive beforehand and then quite excited when it all went well, yes.

b ● Focus on the task and give SS time to go through the sentences. Play the CD once. Get SS to compare what they think. Play it again if necessary and check answers.

> 1   Cherry (*Bugsy Malone* and *The Wizard of Oz*)
> 2   Mike
> 3   Ray (since he was at school)
> 4   Louise (she's a make-up artist)
> 5   Ben (he's a musician)

c ●   **4.27**   Focus on the phrases and give SS time to read them. Play the CD, pausing after the first phrase and replaying it as necessary. Elicit the missing word, and then the meaning of the whole phrase. Repeat for the other four phrases.

> 1   **as far as** (= informal way of saying *that's all I've done*)
> 2   **buzz** (= informal way of saying *the excitement*)
> 3   **sort of** (= expression used when you are trying to think of the word / expression you want to use, or can't think what to say)
> 4   **a couple of** (= another way of saying *two*)
> 5   **you're about to** (= just before you walk on the stage. *nerve-wracking* (adj) = making you feel very nervous)

> 1   I was in a music video once, and that's about as far as I've gone.
> 2   The buzz of it, being able to be someone else in front of people.
> 3   And you can just sort of get taken away into this other world.
> 4   a couple of plays I've been in.
> 5   It is nerve-wracking just as you're about to go on.

d ● Tell SS to go to *p.127* and to look at the tapescript for **IN THE STREET**. Play the CD again and tell SS to read and listen at the same time. Deal with any vocabulary problems and get feedback from SS on what parts they found hard to understand and why, e.g. speed of speech, pronunciation, etc.

● Finally, focus on the two questions that the interviewer asked the people, and get SS to interview each other in pairs. Then get feedback from the whole class.

HOMEWORK

Study Link   **Workbook** *p.43*

Lesson plan

In this writing lesson SS learn to write an article giving advice, for example for a student magazine. The writing skills focus is on paragraphing.

a ● Focus on the pictures and elicit ideas from the class.

> They should have put the cleaning liquids in a cupboard which was out of reach of children.
> They shouldn't have left medicines where children could find them.
> They shouldn't have put the child's bed under the window.

● Now get SS to read the article and check.

b ● Focus on the instructions and get SS to see what they think first, and then compare with a partner.

> **New paragraphs begin with:**
> Next month…
> We started…
> Next was the bathroom…
> Finally, the kitchen…
> So we have three weeks…

c ● Focus on the instructions and the **Useful language** box. Go through them with SS and make sure they know how to use them.
● Focus on the picture and elicit that these might be useful things for them to include in their composition.

Extra support

For each object elicit why it might be useful, and demonstrate the use of *so that, in case,* etc.

WRITE an article

Go through the instructions. Then either get SS to plan and write the article in class (set a time limit of 20 minutes) or get them just to plan their composition in class and write at home, or set both planning and writing for homework.

If SS do the writing in class, get them to swap their article with another student to read and check for mistakes before you collect them all in.

Test and Assessment CD-ROM

CEF Assessment materials
File 4 Writing task assessment guidelines

For instructions on how to use these pages, see *p.33*.

GRAMMAR

a 1 hadn't found   4 had more time
    2 must have   5 can't have got
    3 should have told
b 1 c 2 a 3 c 4 b 5 c

VOCABULARY

a 1 relieved – the others are negative feelings
    2 anxious – the others mean surprised
    3 calf – the others are part of the hand / fingers
    4 hip – the others are organs
    5 nod – the others are gestures you do with your hand
b 1 remind   4 raise
    2 matter   5 argue
    3 stole
c 1 over   4 off
    2 up   5 down
    3 in
d 1 chew   4 frown
    2 yawn   5 stare
    3 scratch

PRONUNCIATION

a 1 notice (it's /s/)   4 comb (it's /əʊ/)
    2 delighted (it's /ɪ/)   5 chew (it's /tʃ/)
    3 frown (it's /aʊ/)
b ex<u>hau</u>sted, pre<u>vent</u>, ex<u>pect</u>, <u>kid</u>ney, <u>el</u>bow

CAN YOU **UNDERSTAND THIS TEXT?**

a 1 B 2 E 3 F 4 C 5 D
b **squeezes** = normally to press hard with your fingers, e.g. to get the juice out of a lemon. Here it means makes smaller.
trimmed off = cut a little bit off
doctored = changed in order to trick sb
flicked through = looked through quickly
within the grasp of = accessible to, within reach of

CAN YOU **UNDERSTAND THESE PEOPLE?**

a 1 c 2 c 3 b 4 b 5 c
b 1 B 2 N 3 B 4 C 5 N

1 There are some common sense precautions you can
   take if you want to avoid a snake bite when you are
   hiking in an area where you know there might be
   snakes. First, when choosing your campsite make
   sure you pitch your tent in a clearing, well away from
   long grass, trees or large rocks. Secondly, be very
   careful where you're treading – especially if there are
   fallen trees. Snakes like to hide behind these. This is
   the advice I would highlight most. Finally, and this
   is common sense, make sure you are wearing proper
   shoes – hiking or walking shoes. And of course never
   ever wear sandals or go barefoot.

2 Good morning and welcome on board this *Air
   Britannia* flight AB443 to Tunisia. My name is Steve
   Morris and I am your pilot today. First of all, I'd like
   to apologize for the forty-minute delay in boarding.
   This was due to the late arrival of the incoming
   flight. In a few minutes the cabin crew will be giving
   you instructions about what to do in case of an
   emergency. I would like to stress how important it
   is even for frequent flyers to pay attention to the
   safety demonstration. Every aircraft is different and
   emergency exits are located in different places. I
   would also like to recommend that you read the safety
   instructions card, which you'll find in your seat pocket.
   Flying time today will be approximately two hours and
   forty-five minutes, and we'll be taking off in a south-
   easterly direction, and flying over Brighton before we
   cross the Channel and head into France.

3 A What time is it?
   B It's 8.15. John should have been here by now. Are
      you sure you told him the dinner was tonight?
   A Of course I'm sure. I invited him when I saw him
      last Saturday.
   B So why isn't he here then? Is he usually late for
      things?
   A No, but he's a bit absent-minded. It's my fault. I
      should have reminded him today. I know what he's
      like. I'll give him a call on his mobile.
   B But if he's driving, he probably won't answer it.
      Something might have happened to him on the way.
      It's snowing very heavily now.
   A Relax. You don't know John as well as I do. Chances
      are it went right out of his mind. I think we ought
      to have dinner and not wait – everyone must be
      starving.

4 A OK, so you're getting the black dress, right?
   B I just can't make my mind up. I mean I know it's
      nice and it's not that expensive but I still think
      maybe the one I tried on in the last place was nicer, I
      mean it suited me better. What do you think?
   A I think they both looked great. Was the other one
      more expensive?
   B I can't remember… You know I think I need to just
      try it on again before I decide…
   A What, go back to the other shop now? But we've
      already spent an hour there and that means finding
      somewhere to park there again. If you really liked
      it, you should have bought it then. Couldn't you go
      back on your own tomorrow?
   B No, I really want to go back now. If I wait till
      tomorrow, it might be gone. Yes, I definitely need to
      try it on again. Come on!
   A Oh please…

5 A What do you think of it?
   B I love it. I think the expressions on their faces are
      incredible. Look at the way the child is looking
      at him, as if he had the most beautiful face in the
      world. The old man is ugly, but she can see right
      past his ugliness.
   A Actually, it's a boy, the child I mean, not a girl. The
      title is *Old man with a young boy*. It's just with those
      wonderful golden curls he looks like a girl. I agree
      with you though, it's an amazing painting. I guess
      the child must be the man's grandson. What do you
      think could have happened to the old man's nose?
   B It looks as if he had some sort of illness, I suppose
      – maybe it was the plague or something – there was
      a lot of it around at the time…

I = interviewer, C = Caroline, B = Ben

I And on today's *Holiday programme* we have Caroline
   and Ben to tell us about their experiences backpacking
   in their gap year. Caroline, if I can start with you, you
   spent three months in South America. Is that right?
C Yes. I started in Argentina and then went to Chile,
   Peru, Bolivia and Ecuador. I stuck to Spanish speaking
   countries because my Spanish is good but my Portuguese
   is non-existent. So that's why I didn't go to Brazil.
I Did you go on your own?
C No, I met up with some friends when I got there
   – they'd been working in Buenos Aires, and then we
   travelled together. I don't think I'd have felt completely
   safe travelling on my own.
I How about you, Ben?
B Yeah, I went on my own round Central and Eastern
   Europe. Czech Republic, Slovakia, Poland, Hungary,
   Slovenia, Croatia. Oh and Serbia.
I Could you speak any of the languages?
B No, but it wasn't a problem because everywhere I went
   I found people spoke really good English, especially
   the young people I met. I was amazed. Some of them
   actually sounded like native speakers.
I And did you ever feel unsafe or lonely travelling on
   your own?
B Well, I mean I was safety-conscious obviously, but it
   was more making sure I never lost anything like my
   phone, or my passport, or credit card – I'm usually
   not very good at that – but otherwise no it was great
   just being by myself because I could decide how long
   I wanted to stay anywhere and where I wanted to go
   next, I mean I had vaguely planned my route but I was
   free to change my mind whenever I liked.
C Yes that is definitely an advantage because sometimes
   one of us wanted to leave a place earlier or didn't like
   the hotel and wanted to move and there were a few
   arguments, not major ones but you know – arguments.
I So what kind of places did you both stay in?
B I stayed mostly in youth hostels. I'd thought of camping
   before I left but I decided the weather would probably
   be too cold – it was March and April. The hostels were
   pretty basic but great places to meet people.
C We stayed mainly either in budget hotels or sometimes
   in bed and breakfasts. They were all places we'd found
   on the Internet and generally speaking they were good.
   In fact we were often pleasantly surprised by how
   comfortable and clean places were.

Test and Assessment CD-ROM

File 4 Quicktest

File 4 Test

G gerunds and infinitives
V music
P *ch* and *y*

5A The psychology of music

File 5 overview

Lesson **5A** revises and extends the use of gerunds and infinitives. **5B** revises *used to* and introduces *be used to* and *get used to*. Lesson **5C** revises reported speech and introduces a variety of new reporting verbs, such as *advise, insist, apologize*. The lexical areas covered in this File are music, sleep and the media.

Lesson plan

This lesson revises the basic rules about when to use a gerund or an infinitive after a verb and introduces certain verbs (e.g. *remember, try*), which can be followed by either a gerund or infinitive but with a change in meaning. The topic of the lesson is music. SS listen to an interview with a music psychologist, who explains why we listen to music and how music can affect us emotionally. They also read an article based on recent research which suggests that someone's musical tastes may reflect their personality. The vocabulary focus is on words related to music (instruments, musicians, etc.) and pronunciation looks at spelling / pronunciation rules for *ch* and *y*.

Optional lead-in (books closed)

- Tell SS they are going to listen to ten short pieces of music and write the two questions in **1a** on the board.
- Play the extracts one by one. After each extract quickly elicit some answers to the first question and find out with a show of hands the majority view on the second question.

1 LISTENING & SPEAKING

a ● (**5.1**) Books open. Don't do this stage if you did the optional lead-in. If not, focus on the task and the two questions.

- Play the extracts one by one and elicit some answers to the first question. You could find out by a quick show of hands how many SS would like to carry on listening or not.

(**5.1**)   CD3 Track 9

Extracts from:
1 *Queen of the night* from Mozart's *Magic Flute*
2 Drum and bass
3 Strauss's *Blue Danube*
4 Messiaen's *Quartet for the end of time*
5 Traditional jazz
6 Experimental jazz
7 Country
8 Rap

- Focus on the **Taking notes** box and go through it with the class. Tell SS that they are going to listen to a short lecture and that they will try and complete some notes.

b ● (**5.2**) Tell SS that they are going to listen to a music psychologist talking about why we listen to music. Focus on the task and tell SS that the first time they listen they should try to complete sentences 1–3 with a phrase. The second time they should try to listen for at least one example.

- Play the CD twice and give SS time to write their notes. Then get them to compare what they understood / can remember with their partner. Feedback answers from the class.

---

1   to make us **remember important moments** in the past, e.g. when we met someone for the first time.

2   to help us **change activities**, e.g. we play a certain kind of music to prepare us to go out in the evening and another kind to relax us when we get home from work.

3   to **intensify the emotion** that we're feeling, e.g. if we're sad, we play sad music to make us even sadder; if we're feeling angry, we play angry music to make us angrier; we play romantic music to make a romantic dinner more romantic.

(**5.2**)   CD3 Track 10

(tapescript in Student's Book on *p.127*)

I think it is very interesting that human beings are the only animals which listen to music for pleasure. A lot of research has been done to find out *why* we listen to music, and there seem to be three main reasons. Firstly, we listen to music to make us remember important moments in the past, for example when we met someone for the first time. Think of Humphrey Bogart in the film *Casablanca* saying 'Darling, they're playing our song'. When we hear a certain piece of music, we remember hearing it for the first time in some very special circumstances. Obviously, this music varies from person to person.

Secondly, we listen to music to help us change activities. If we want to go from one activity to another, we often use music to help us make the change. For example, we might play a certain kind of music to prepare us to go out in the evening, or we might play another kind of music to relax us when we get home from work. That's mainly why people listen to music in cars, and they often listen to one kind of music when they're going to work and another kind when they're coming home. The same is true of people on buses and trains with their iPods.

The third reason why we listen to music is to intensify the emotion that we're feeling. For example, if we're feeling sad, sometimes we want to get even sadder, so we play sad music. Or we're feeling angry and we want to intensify the anger then we play angry music. Or when we're planning a romantic dinner, we lay the table, we light candles, and then we think what music would make this even more romantic?

c • **5.3** Focus on the task and give SS a few moments to look at the incomplete notes. To help SS you may want to pre-teach *pitch*, i.e. here, how high or low a musical note is.

• Play the CD twice and give SS time to complete their notes by pausing between each section. Then let them compare with a partner again to see how much they understood / can remember.

> **Three important human emotions**
> 2 sadness
> 3 anger
> **How we feel affects the way we speak, e.g.**
> 2 sad – speak more slowly / lower
> 3 angry – raise voice / shout
> **Music copies this, e.g.**
> 2 slow music with falling pitches sounds sad.
> 3 loud music with irregular rhythms sounds angry.
> **Examples:**
> 1 happy, e.g. *Seventh Symphony* (Beethoven)
> 2 angry, e.g. *Mars* (Holst)
> 3 sad, e.g. *Adagio for strings* (Albinoni)
> This is especially exploited in film soundtracks, e.g. the shower scene in *Psycho* (the woman is just having a shower but the music makes it terrifying).

5.3   CD3 Track 11

(tapescript in Student's Book on *p.127*)

Let's take three important human emotions: happiness, sadness, and anger. When people are happy they speak faster, and their voice is higher. When they are sad they speak more slowly and their voice is lower, and when people are angry they raise their voices or shout. Babies can tell whether their mother is happy or not simply by the sound of her voice, not by her words. What music does is it copies this, and it produces the same emotions. So faster, higher-pitched music will sound happy. Slow music with lots of falling pitches will sound sad. Loud music with irregular rhythms will sound angry. It doesn't matter how good or bad the music is, if it has these characteristics it will make you experience this emotion.

Let me give you some examples. For happy, for example, the first movement of Beethoven's *Seventh Symphony*. For angry, say *Mars*, from *The Planets* by Holst. And for sad, something like Albinoni's *Adagio for strings*. Of course the people who exploit this most are the people who write film soundtracks. They can take a scene which visually has no emotion and they can make the scene either scary or calm or happy just by the music they write to go with it. Think of the music in the shower scene in Hitchcock's film *Psycho*. All you can see is a woman having a shower, but the music makes it absolutely terrifying.

Extra support

If there's time, you could get SS to listen to the CD with the tapescript on *p.127* so they can see what they understood / didn't understand. Translate / explain any new words or phrases.

d • Focus on the questions and then set a time limit for SS to go through the questions together and compare answers and choices of music. When answering question 3 encourage SS to be as specific as possible in their answers, i.e. by specifying not just the kind of music they would play but also the name of the artist or song / piece of music.

• Get some quick feedback from around the class.

2 GRAMMAR   gerunds and infinitives

a • **Check what you know.** This exercise provides quick revision of what SS should already know about gerunds and infinitives.

• Focus on the task and sentences 1–5 and give SS a couple of minutes to put the verbs into the gerund or infinitive. Get them to compare their answers in pairs before checking answers. When you elicit an answer get SS to tell you why the gerund or infinitive form is used here (see key below).

> 1 Listening (gerund used as the subject of a sentence)
> 2 to feel (infinitive used after certain verbs, e.g. *want, need, would like*, etc.)
> 3 using (gerund used after a preposition), to create (infinitive used to express reason or purpose)
> 4 playing (gerund used after certain verbs, e.g. *enjoy, love, hate*, etc.)
> 5 to concentrate (infinitive used after adjectives)

• If SS are having problems, go to the Workbook *p.44*. Go through the rules and do the exercise.

b • **New grammar.** This exercise introduces the new grammar point which is that certain verbs can use either the gerund or infinitive but with a change in meaning.

• Focus on the task and give SS some time to try and circle the right form. Emphasize that they should use their instinct (what 'sounds right') if they aren't sure. Get SS to compare answers in pairs before checking answers.

> 1 hearing, to buy   3 to change, changing
> 2 to listen, going   4 plugging, to hear

c • Tell SS to go to **Grammar Bank 5A** on *p.140*. Go through the examples and the rules with the class, and drill the pronunciation of any new verbs.

Grammar notes

Previously SS have seen the basic rules governing the use of gerunds and infinitives (with and without *to*) after certain verbs. Here they revise and expand their knowledge of verbs and expressions which are followed by either form.

NB Other occasions when a gerund or infinitive is used, e.g. the infinitive after an adjective (*Pleased to meet you*) or the gerund after a preposition (*He left without saying goodbye*) are revised in **Check what you know** in the Workbook.

verbs followed by the gerund or the infinitive

- **rule 1:** Go through the list of verbs and expressions with SS making sure they know what they all mean, giving examples of new verbs, and expressions where necessary, e.g.

  I **can't help** laughing when he says that (= can't stop myself)

  I **can't stand** waiting for people (= I hate it)

  My job **involves** meeting people.

  We're going to **postpone** going to the coast until next week.

- **rule 2:** Go through the list of verbs and expressions with SS making sure they know what they all mean, giving examples of new verbs, and expressions where necessary, e.g.

  His leg **appears to be** broken (= seems to be)

  I **happened to see** him in the street (= I saw him by chance)

  I **pretended to be** ill (= I made people think I was ill but I wasn't)

- **rule 3:** You may want to point out that *have to* and *ought to* (= *should*) are exceptions to this rule.

  make and *let* Highlight that the verb form following *make* depends on whether the sentence is active or passive.

  like, love, hate In British English to describe a general feeling (*I like cooking*) the gerund is more frequent, although the infinitive is becoming increasing common, influenced by American English where the infinitive is preferred.

  verbs that can be followed by either gerund or infinitive with a change of meaning

  Before looking at the rules you may want to remind SS that *begin*, *continue* and *start* can be used with the gerund or infinitive with <u>no</u> change in meaning.

  This grammar rule will be new to most SS. In SS' L1 some of these concepts may be covered by using two different verbs, so if you know your SS' L1, you can use it to make the meanings clear.

  With *need to do / needs doing* highlight that *needs doing* is an alternative to a passive construction, e.g. *The house needs painting / to be painted*.

- Focus on the exercises for **5A** on *p.141* and get SS to do them individually or in pairs. Check answers after each exercise.

a			b		
	1	going out		1	seeing
	2	talking		2	to call
	3	do		3	reading
	4	waiting		4	locking
	5	to get		5	to turn
	6	tidy		6	painting
	7	not come		7	to send
	8	to go		8	to learn
	9	working			
	10	to know			

- Tell SS to go back to the main lesson on *p.69.*

d • Put SS in pairs for this oral grammar practice activity and focus on the task. Give SS a few minutes of thinking time before getting them to tell each other their true sentences.

Extra challenge

Alternatively, if you have time, you could get SS to develop these exchanges into mini conversations by asking each other further questions about each situation.

3 VOCABULARY music

a • **5.4** Tell SS they are going to hear some instruments being played which they have to identify. You could do this as a whole class activity and get SS to call out answers as you play each recording, or get SS in pairs to silently write down their answers and check answers at the end. SS may recognize the instrument but not know the word or pronunciation in English. Point out that the names of all of these instruments will be taught in the **Vocabulary Bank**.

- Play the CD once or twice as necessary and check answers.

5.4		CD3 Track 12
1 piano	3	violin
2 guitar	4	saxophone

b • Tell SS to go to **Vocabulary Bank** *Music* on *p.153*.

- Focus on section **1 Instruments and musicians** (**a** and **b**) and give SS time to match the words and pictures, and write the names of the musicians. Check answers, and model and drill pronunciation. When you check answers to **1b** ask SS which two words for musicians have a different syllable stress to the instruments they play (<u>pia</u>nist and sa<u>xo</u>phonist).

a	1	bass guitar	6	violin
	2	trumpet	7	saxophone
	3	piano	8	cello
	4	keyboard	9	organ
	5	drums		
b		bass gui<u>tar</u>ist, <u>cell</u>ist, <u>drum</u>mer, <u>key</u>board player, <u>or</u>ganist, <u>pia</u>nist, sa<u>xo</u>phonist, <u>trum</u>peter, vio<u>lin</u>ist		

- Now give SS time to do exercise **c** by matching the words and definitions. Check answers and model and drill pronunciation.

c	1	tenor	7	rapper
	2	bass	8	soloist
	3	soprano	9	lead singer
	4	orchestra	10	conductor
	5	choir	11	composer
	6	singer-songwriter	12	DJ (disc jockey)

- Focus on section **2 Adjectives and phrases to describe music** and give SS time to match the sentences. Check answers, and model and drill pronunciation.

1 D	2 E	3 F	4 A	5 B	6 C

- Now focus on section **3 Idioms** and give SS time to complete the sentences. Highlight that in each case the sentence without the idiom helps to explain what the idiom means. Check answers making sure that SS are clear about the meaning of each idiom.

1 C   2 E   3 A   4 B   5 D

- Finally, focus on the instruction 'Can you remember the words on this page? Test yourself or a partner'.

Testing yourself

For **Instruments and musicians** (**a** and **b**) SS can cover the words and look at the pictures and try to remember both the instrument and the musician. For **c** they can cover the definitions and remember the words. For **Adjectives and phrases to describe music** they can cover the sentences on the left and use definitions A–F to remember the adjectives. For **Idioms** they can cover sentences 1–5 and look at the phrases in the box and remember what each idiom means.

Testing a partner

See **Testing a partner** *p.20*.

Study Link SS can find more practice of these words and phrases on the MultiROM and on the *New English File Upper-intermediate* website.

- Tell SS to go back to the main lesson on *p.70*.

c ● **5.5** SS now recycle the vocabulary they have just learned. Play the CD, pause after the first part, and elicit from SS what they can hear – elicit the musicians / instruments they can hear and not the piece of music, e.g. *It's a cello soloist playing with an orchestra*. Write the answer on the board. Then carry on, pausing after each section for SS to write down what they hear. Check answers.

5.5	CD3 Track 13

1 a choir singing
2 a tenor singing
3 a DJ speaking between songs
4 a rapper rapping
5 a cello soloist, then an orchestra
6 an organ solo
7 a band: electric guitar, bass guitar, drums, and a lead singer

d ● Focus on the instructions, and make it clear to SS that they may not agree on, for example, who has a monotonous voice. Give SS time, in pairs, to write down names of songs, singers, etc. Get feedback by finding out what different pairs have written, and add ideas of your own.

Extra support

You could do this as a whole class activity eliciting ideas from SS.

4 PRONUNCIATION *ch* and *y*

a ● Focus on the instructions and give SS a few moments to complete the task. Don't check answers at this stage.

b ● Go through the rules with the class and make sure everything is clear. Check their answers to **a**.

/tʃ/ resear**ch**   /k/ **ch**aracter   /ʃ/ **ch**ef

c ● Give SS a few minutes to put the words in the list into the right columns in the chart in **a**. You could get them to do this in pairs or individually and then compare their answers with their partner.

d ● **5.6** Play the CD for SS to check their answers.

/tʃ/ change, cheerful choose
/k/ choir, chorus, orchestra, psychologist
/ʃ/ machine, moustache

5.6	CD3 Track 14

chess /tʃ/
change
cheerful
choose
key /k/
choir
chorus
orchestra
psychologist
shower /ʃ/
machine
moustache

- Give SS practice pronouncing the words by playing the CD again and pausing after each word for SS to repeat them.

Extra challenge

Alternatively, you could elicit some more examples of the three sounds by giving SS definitions of the words below:

/tʃ/ cheerful, chest, changeable, chin, chilly, scorching
/k/ charisma, chaos, chronic, chronological, headache
/ʃ/ chic

e ● Focus attention on the rules box and go through it with SS. Then give SS a couple of minutes to put the words in the list in the right columns. They could do this in pairs or individually, and then check their answers with a partner.

f ● **5.7** Play the CD for SS to check their answers. Then play the recording again, pausing for SS to listen and repeat the words.

/aɪ/ apply, lifestyle, psychiatrist, qualify, shy, try, type
/ɪ/ lyrics, physical, rhythm, symphony, typical
/i/ country, heavy

5.7	CD3 Track 15

/aɪ/
apply
lifestyle
psychiatrist
qualify
shy
try
type
/ɪ/
lyrics
physical
rhythm
symphony
typical
/i/
country
heavy

5 SPEAKING

- Focus on the **GET IT RIGHT** box and go through it with SS.
- Put SS in pairs and tell SS to read the questionnaire together and take turns to tell each other their answers to the questions (rather than do this as an interview).
- Finally, get some quick feedback from the class on some of the questions, e.g. find out how many SS can, for example read music, can play an instrument, what the best live concert was that they have seen, etc.

Extra idea

As a way of giving SS some 'live' listening comprehension you could tell them your own answers to some of the questions in the questionnaire, particularly if you have any interesting or amusing anecdotes.

6 READING

a ● Focus on the question and elicit answers from the class.

b ● Get SS to read the introduction to the article (the first paragraph) and elicit answers from the class.

c ● Now set a time limit for SS to read the article and to decide which category best describes their musical taste, and if they agree with the description it gives of the personality type associated with that kind of music.

d ● Focus on the task and make sure that SS know that A–D refers to the kinds of music. Set a time limit and then give SS a chance to compare their answers with a partner. Check answers.

| 1 B | 2 D | 3 B | 4 C | 5 A | 6 A | 7 D | 8 C |

e ● Give SS time to do this, then get some feedback on which words and phrases they have chosen.

f ● Do this as a whole class activity and feedback opinions from the class.

Extra photocopiable activities

Grammar
gerunds and infinitives *p.172*
Communicative
Gerund or infinitive? *p.210* (instructions *p.194*)

HOMEWORK

Study Link **Workbook** *pp.44–46*

G used to, be used to, get used to
V sleep
P linking words

5B Counting sheep

Lesson plan

This lesson revises the use of *used to* to talk about repeated past actions and introduces *be used to*, *get used to* (*doing something*) to talk about actions or activities which have become, or are becoming, familiar. The two contexts for this lesson are both to do with sleep. In the first half of the lesson SS do a questionnaire to see how sleep deprived they are and read about the effects of sleep deprivation in our daily lives. In the second half of the lesson SS listen to a true story about a girl who climbed a crane while sleepwalking. In vocabulary SS learn / revise words and phrases related to sleep (e.g. *oversleep*, *jet lagged*) and the pronunciation focus is on linking words.

Optional lead-in (books closed)

- Write on the board **count sheep** and ask SS when people might do this, and elicit that sometimes people do it in their head when they can't sleep. Then elicit other things you can do if you can't sleep (e.g. read, make yourself a drink, take sleeping tablets, watch TV, etc.). Ask if anyone in the class has problems sleeping and what they do to get to sleep.

- Then ask, with a show of hands, who in the class thinks that he / she <u>doesn't</u> sleep enough. Find out what percentage of the class think they don't sleep enough.

1 GRAMMAR used to, be used to, get used to

a ● Books open. Focus attention on the title of the questionnaire and elicit / teach the meaning of *sleep deprived* (= suffering negative effects from not sleeping enough).

  ● The questionnaire presents examples of the new grammar (*be used to / get used to something*); you will probably want to see if SS can guess the meaning from context. Go through the questions one by one stopping to focus on the new grammar and checking SS understand new vocabulary, e.g. *nap* = when you sleep (usually for a short time) during the day, *energetic* = full of energy, *refreshed* = feeling fresh and not tired.

  ● In question 3 elicit from / remind SS that *Did you use to...?* (interrogative form of *used to*) refers to past habits.

  ● In question 4 point out that *I'm used to it* does not refer to the past and elicit / teach that it means 'the situation is not unusual for me now and I have adapted to it.' If you know SS' L1, you could ask SS to tell you the equivalent form.

  ● In question 5 elicit / explain that *You get used to not sleeping enough* = not sleeping enough stops being a problem because your body adapts to it.

  ● Focus on the task and give SS time to interview each other. Encourage them to ask for, and give, as much information as possible.

b ● Now tell SS to go to **Communication** *Sleep p.118* to read the results of the questionnaire. Get feedback from

the class to find out how many people in the class are sleep deprived.

Extra idea

You could get the class to interview you to find out if you are sleep deprived or not and to give SS some 'live' listening comprehension.

c ● Now focus on the four sentences which contrast the meaning of *usually*, *used to*, *be used to* and *get used to*, and give SS time to match the sentence halves. Check answers.

> **1** D **2** A **3** B **4** C

d ● Tell SS to go to **Grammar Bank 5B** on *p.140*. Go through the examples and read the rules with the class.

Grammar notes

- **used to / didn't used to + infinitive**
  At this level SS should be confident about using *used to* (*do sth*) although they may still make mistakes like using *I use to...* instead of *I usually...* to describe a present habit. This can cause misunderstanding as a listener may understand *I used to...* (i.e. past habit). The use of *would* to refer to repeated actions in the past is referenced here but not practised in the grammar exercises. You may want to point out that *would* is used, especially in written English, as a variant to *used to*, e.g. *We **used to** spend all our holidays by the sea. We **would** get up early every morning and run to the beach...*

- **be used to / get used to + gerund**
  These structures are introduced for the first time. Their similarity in form to *used to* means that they sometimes get mixed up in SS' minds. A very common mistake is to use these structures with the infinitive instead of the gerund. Point out to SS that *to* here is a preposition, and can also be followed by a noun (e.g. *I'm used to the weather in London now*).

  The meaning of *be used to doing something* may not be immediately obvious to SS. A formal equivalent would be *be accustomed to doing something*.

  You may also want to point out that the difference between *be used to* and *get used to* is like the difference between *be angry* and *get angry*, and that *get* here = become.

- Focus on the exercises for **5B** on *p.141* and get SS to do them individually or in pairs. Check answers after each exercise.

> **a 1** ✗ usually go / 'm used to going
> **2** ✗ get used to drinking
> **3** ✓
> **4** ✓
> **5** ✗ used to have
> **6** ✗ I'm used to it
> **7** ✗ Did you use to wear

b
1	get used to getting up	5	is used to working
2	get used to eating	6	get used to wearing
3	I'm not used to having	7	used to have
4	used to spend	8	isn't used to sharing

- Tell SS to go back to the main lesson on *p.72*.

2 PRONUNCIATION linking words

Pronunciation notes

- SS should be very familiar by now with the fact that in spoken language words become joined or 'linked' together, especially in rapid speech. Learners naturally develop the ability to separate these linked words in their head as they hear them and also to link words together when *they* speak. This exercise gives SS practice in both these skills.

- Two of the most common rules for linking words are:
  1 When a word ends in a consonant sound and is followed by a word which begins with a vowel sound, e.g. *get up early*, the words are linked together and pronounced /getʌpɜːli/.
  2 When a word ends in a consonant sound and is followed by a word beginning with the same consonant sound, e.g. *used* (which ends in /t/) and *to* (which begins with /t/), the sounds are 'elided', i.e. they are linked together, and the /t/ sound is only made once, so *used to* = /juːstə/.

a • **5.8** Focus on the task and play the CD once telling SS to listen to the six sentences without writing anything.

- Now play the recording again, this time pausing to give SS time to write down the sentences. Then play the CD again for SS to check their sentences. Then check answers, eliciting the sentences onto the board.

5.8   CD3 Track 16

1 He used to get up at eight, but he doesn't any more.
2 I'm not used to sleeping until ten in the morning.
3 She usually switches on the TV as soon as she gets home.
4 I'll never get used to living alone.
5 He's not used to playing to big audiences.
6 It took me ages to get used to having lunch at twelve.

---

b • Get SS to do this activity in pairs while you move around monitoring pronunciation. Then you could choose individual SS to say the sentences.

c • Focus on the questions and then get SS to take turns to interview each other. Remind them to link words together when they can.

3 READING & SPEAKING

a • Focus on the instructions and then give SS two or three minutes to read the first paragraph. Then elicit answers to the questions.

The test involves going to bed holding a spoon in your hand. When you fall asleep the spoon falls onto a plate and wakes you up. If you are already sleeping so deeply that the spoon doesn't wake you up, then you are 'sleep deprived.'
The last sentence means that we need to give as much importance to sleeping enough as we do to taking exercise (because both are vital for good health).

- Ask SS some more questions on the first paragraph, e.g. *Who is Paul Martin? What is his book called? What is his theory?*

b • Before focusing on the task you may want to pre-teach *sleep debt* (= sleep owed to us, i.e. number of hours of sleep we haven't had in a week). Put SS in pairs and make sure they are clear exactly which part of the text they have to read. Set a time limit for them to do so. Tell them to read their two paragraphs first before they try to tick the questions which are answered in them. Then check answers by calling out the number of the questions one by one and asking SS to say if the answer was in student **A**'s part or student **B**'s part of the text.

A 1, 4, 6, 7, 9, 12	**B** 2, 3, 5, 8, 10, 11

c • Tell SS to read their paragraphs again and answer their six questions. They should do this in written or note form, or underline the relevant part of the text. Set a time limit for this.

d • Focus on the task. SS should go through the list of questions 1–12. Whoever has the answer to the question explains it to their partner as clearly as possible, using their own words and not just reading from the text.

e • Now give SS time to read the half of the article they haven't already read.

Extra support

At this point you could go through the four paragraphs with the class, highlighting useful expressions and eliciting / explaining the meaning of new words and phrases. You could also check the answers to questions 1–12.

1 Before the invention of the light bulb people slept during the hours of darkness.
2 Because doctors who are on 'night call' are more sleep deprived than doctors working during the day.
3 Yes. They are very effective in restoring our energy levels and making us feel happier, etc.
4 6.2 hours a night (during the week). Yes.
5 Because they often take important decisions when they are too tired.
6 The hours of sleep that we owe our body (i.e. the extra hours we need to sleep to feel at our best).
7 Caffeine.
8 Driving when you are tired isn't against the law (but is just as dangerous).
9 They sleep less because they have more reasons not to sleep (work, the Internet, TV, 24/7 society).
10 It shouldn't be hot, used as an office, or for watching TV.
11 Tired engineers made very serious mistakes with catastrophic consequences.
12 8–8.5 hours.

f • Do this as an open class activity and try to get some debate about each of the questions by asking SS to justify their opinions.

4 VOCABULARY sleep

a • **Vocabulary race**. Put SS in pairs. Focus on the task and set a time limit. SS should already know some of these words / phrases, others have come up earlier in the questionnaire and reading text, and others, e.g. *sleep like a log*, may be completely new. Point out to SS that all the missing words are above the exercise. Use the example word (*sleepy*) to demonstrate, and elicit / explain the difference between *sleepy* and *tired*.

b • **5.9** Play the CD for SS to check their answers. Feedback answers onto the board. Model and drill pronunciation of any words you think might be difficult, e.g. *duvet* /duːveɪ/.

2 yawn
3 set, alarm
4 pillow
5 duvet, sheets and blankets
6 fall
7 snore
8 dreams or nightmares
9 oversleep
10 keep you awake
11 insomnia
12 sleeping tablets
13 siesta or nap
14 log
15 jet-lagged

5.9   CD3 Track 17

1 Most people start feeling sleepy around 11.00 at night.
2 They often open their mouth and yawn.
3 They go to bed and set their alarm clock.
4 They get into bed and put their head on the pillow.
5 They cover themselves up with a duvet or with sheets and blankets.
6 Soon they fall asleep.
7 Some people make a loud noise when they breathe. They snore.
8 During the night people have dreams or nightmares.
9 If you don't hear your alarm clock in the morning, you might oversleep.
10 If you drink coffee in the evening, it might keep you awake.
11 Some people can't sleep because they suffer from insomnia.
12 These people often have to take sleeping tablets.
13 Some people have a siesta or nap after lunch.
14 A person who sleeps well 'sleeps like a log'.
15 Someone who is tired after flying to another time zone is jet-lagged.

---

c • Focus on the task and get SS to cover the words in the right-hand column, and then to try to remember them by reading sentences 1–15 again. If there's time, you could quickly elicit the words from the whole class to wrap up the activity.

5 SPEAKING

• Put SS in pairs. Quickly run through the questions and then set a time limit for SS to answer them. Then get some quick feedback from the class on some of the questions.

Extra idea

You could tell the class your answers to some of the questions to give them some listening practice.

6 LISTENING

a • Focus on the photo and the headline. Elicit the meaning of *crane*, and then ask the questions to the whole class. Elicit possible reasons without saying if they are right.

b • **5.10** Tell SS this is a true story. Then play the CD for SS to find out if they guessed correctly. Check answers.

The girl had been sleepwalking and had walked from her house to the building site. A fireman rescued her from the top of a crane.

c • Tell SS they are now going to read an article which is based on the same incident. Go through the text with the class dealing with any new vocabulary items such as *building site, crawled, safety harness, ladder*, etc.
• Tell SS that the newspaper article got eight pieces of information wrong. Give SS a few minutes to read the article and see if they can underline the eight mistakes.
• Play the CD again for SS to check their answers. Get SS to compare with a partner and then play the CD again.
• Finally, play the recording one more time for SS to try to correct all the information they have underlined. Then check answers.

1 a **40**-metre-high crane (not 30)
2 Dulwich, south-**east** London (not south-west)
3 The man called the **police** (not the fire brigade).
4 The fireman realized the girl was **asleep** (not drunk).
5 The **fireman** called the girl's parents (not the girl herself).
6 The rescue took **two and a half hours** (not two).
7 The security guard **wasn't asleep** (he was watching TV).
8 The girl had **never** left the house before when she was sleepwalking (not on several other occasions).

5.10   CD3 Track 18

(tapescript in Student's Book on *p.127*)
And finally on *News Today* the amazing story of a teenager who woke up this morning and discovered that she wasn't in bed – she was lying on top of a 40-metre-high crane!
In the early hours of this morning a man on his way to work was passing a building site in Dulwich, South-East London when he spotted the 15-year-old girl lying on the arm of the crane. He immediately called the police on his mobile phone. The police and fire brigade arrived on the scene at 1.30 and at first they were worried that the girl might be intending to commit suicide by throwing herself off the crane. But when a fireman climbed up the crane, he could see that the girl was asleep.

The fireman realized that it could be very dangerous if the girl woke up suddenly. So he crawled along the 21-metre arm of the crane and carefully wrapped the girl in a safety harness before waking her up gently. The girl had a mobile phone with her and the fireman was able to call her parents, who came to the building site straight away. Finally, the girl was brought down from the crane on a ladder.

The whole rescue operation had taken two and a half hours. Her parents were waiting for her on the ground and obviously they were very relieved to see her safe and well. The question everyone wanted to know was 'why did the girl go to sleep on the top of a crane?' Well, the answer is that she had been sleepwalking! She had walked out of her house during the night without her parents noticing and sleepwalked to the building site. There was a security guard but he didn't see her climbing the crane because he was watching TV. The girl's parents told the police that this wasn't the first time that she had sleepwalked but that she had never left the house before.

d ● Focus on the task and quickly run through the questions. Then give SS, in pairs, a few minutes to discuss whether sentences 1–10 are true or false.

e ● **5.11** Play the CD for SS to check their answers. Then play the recording again for SS to correct the wrong sentences. Get them to compare in pairs before playing the CD a final time.

1 T
2 F (sleepwalkers usually have their eyes open so they look awake)
3 F (It's very common. 18% of the population have a tendency to sleepwalk.)
4 T
5 T
6 F (You can wake up a sleepwalker without any problem, although they may be confused and not know where they are)
7 F (They can trip over chairs, fall down stairs, even fall out of a window)
8 T
9 T
10 F (A man in Canada was recently found not guilty of killing his mother-in-law because he was asleep at the time)

5.11   CD3 Track 19

(tapescript in Student's Book on *p.127*)
P = presenter, M = Professor Miller
P Now I imagine some of you are finding this story a bit difficult to believe, so I've invited into the studio Professor Miller, who is an expert in sleepwalking. Professor Miller, does this story surprise you?
M Not at all. I have treated people who have driven cars, ridden horses and I had one man who even tried to fly a helicopter while he was asleep.
P But how did this girl manage to climb a 40-metre crane?
M It would have been no problem for her. She would climb the crane just as easily as if she were awake.
P And would her eyes have been open?

M Yes, sleepwalkers usually have their eyes open. That's why sometimes it's difficult to know if someone is sleepwalking or not.
P Is sleepwalking very common?
M Yes. Research shows that about 18% of the population have a tendency to sleepwalk. In fact, it's much more common in children than in teenagers or adults. And curiously it's more common among boys than girls. Adults who sleepwalk are normally people who used to sleepwalk when they were children. Adult sleepwalking often happens after a stressful event, for example, after a road accident.
P People always say that you should never wake a sleepwalker up when they're walking. Is that true?
M No, it isn't. People used to think that it was dangerous to wake up a sleepwalker. But in fact this isn't the case. You *can* wake a sleepwalker up without any problem, although if you do, it is quite common for the sleepwalker to be confused, so he or she probably won't know where they are for a few moments.
P So if we see someone sleepwalking, should we wake them up?
M Yes, you should remember that another of the myths about sleepwalkers is that they cannot injure themselves while they are sleepwalking. But this isn't true. If a sleepwalker is walking around the house, they can trip or fall over a chair or even fall down stairs. The other day there was a case of a nine-year-old girl who opened her bedroom window while sleepwalking and fell ten metres to the ground. Luckily, she wasn't seriously injured. So you see it is definitely safer to wake a sleepwalker up.
P How long does sleepwalking last?
M It can be very brief, for example, a few minutes. The most typical cases are people getting up and getting dressed, or people going to the bathroom. But it can occasionally last much longer, maybe half an hour or even more.
P And what happens when sleepwalkers wake up? Do they remember the things they did while they were sleepwalking?
M No, a sleepwalker usually doesn't remember anything afterwards. So, for example, the girl who climbed up the crane will probably have no memory of the incident.
P So, is a sleepwalker responsible for his or her actions?
M A very good question, actually. A few years ago a man from Canada got up in the middle of the night and drove 20 kilometres from his home to the house where his parents-in-law lived and, for no apparent reason, he killed his mother-in-law. The man was charged with murder but he was found not guilty because he had been asleep at the time he committed the crime.

Extra support

If there's time, you could get SS to listen to both recordings again with the tapescripts on *p.127* so that they can see exactly what they understood / didn't understand. Explain / translate any words or phrases that SS aren't sure about.

7 (5.12) SONG ♫ *I don't want to miss a thing*

- *I don't want to miss a thing* was originally recorded by the American heavy rock band Aerosmith in 1998. For copyright reasons this is a cover version. If you want to do this song in class, use the photocopiable activity on *p.237*.

5.12   CD3 Track 20

I don't want to miss a thing

I could stay awake just to hear you breathing
Watch you smile while you are sleeping
While you're far away and dreaming
I could spend my life in this sweet surrender
I could stay lost in this moment forever
Where a moment spent with you is a moment I treasure

Chorus
Don't want to close my eyes
I don't want to fall asleep
'Cause I'd miss you baby
And I don't want to miss a thing
'Cause even when I dream of you
The sweetest dream will never do
I'd still miss you baby
And I don't want to miss a thing

Lying close to you feeling your heart beating
And I'm wondering what you're dreaming
Wondering if it's me you're seeing
Then I kiss your eyes
And thank God we're together
I just want to stay with you in this moment forever
Forever and ever

Chorus

I don't want to miss one smile
I don't want to miss one kiss
I just want to be with you
Right here with you, just like this
I just want to hold you close
And feel your heart so close to mine
And just stay here in this moment
For all the rest of time

Chorus

Extra photocopiable activities

Grammar
used to, be used to, get used to p.173
Communicative
usually, used to, get used to p.211 (instructions *p.194*)
Song
I don't want to miss a thing p.237 (instructions *p.232*)

HOMEWORK

Study Link Workbook *pp.47–49*

5 C

G reporting verbs; *as*
V the media
P word stress

Breaking news

Lesson plan

This lesson takes as its theme the media. The first half of the lesson looks at some true stories from the press which provide a context to revise the basic rules of reported speech and introduce reporting verbs, such as *offer, convince, admit, deny*, etc. which are followed by gerund or infinitive constructions. In the second half of the lesson SS read about, and listen to, real life journalists talking about the good and bad side of their job. The vocabulary focus of the lesson is the media and pronunciation looks at word stress in reporting verbs. Finally, there is a mini grammar focus on *as*.

Optional lead-in (books closed)

- Find out which English language news channels your SS ever watch, e.g. the BBC, CNN, Sky news, etc. and elicit opinions about them, e.g. how easy / difficult are they to understand and if they think that they provide a good coverage of the news.
- Find out if your SS have had any experience of reading English newspapers, magazines or websites, and elicit opinions.

1 GRAMMAR reporting verbs

a ● Books open. Focus on the headline and elicit opinions. The headline is ambiguous. It could mean that the man broke up with his wife at the petrol station or that he left her behind. Then set a time limit for SS to read the text. Elicit opinions about what happened (the man left his wife behind).

b ● **Check what you know**. Here SS quickly revise the basic rules for reported speech. Focus on the task and then give SS time to complete the sentences. Check answers.

> 1 if he was… he was
> 2 where he was… them… he was
> 3 hadn't noticed
> 4 would have

Extra support

If necessary, before SS do the exercise in **b**, remind them what reported speech is by giving this example: 'My name is Maria.' She said her name was Maria.

Remind SS that 'reported speech' is used when someone reports what someone else has said.

- If SS are having problems, go to the Workbook *p.50*. Go through the rules and do the exercise.
- Finally, write on the board: 'Don't talk.' I told you …, 'Please give me a pen.' She asked him …
- Ask SS how to complete the two reported sentences, and elicit that when you report an imperative or a request, you put the verb in the infinitive.

> I told you **not to talk**.
> She asked him **to give her a pen**.

c ● **New grammar**. Focus on the task and set a time limit for SS to quickly read all four stories to try to decide which one is <u>not</u> true (i.e. has been invented). Highlight that they have glossaries with some of the stories.

- When SS have read all four stories, get them to discuss with a partner which one they think is not true. You could have a class vote on this before giving the answer.

> *Locked out of her life* is an invented story.

d ● Focus on the instructions and the example, and give SS time to complete the task. It may be useful for SS to do this in pairs or compare their answers in pairs. Check answers, and for each one elicit the underlined part of the text. Elicit / explain the meaning of each reporting verb.

> 1 G have threatened to sue a neighbour
> 2 B refused to give back their balls
> 3 F had reminded her husband… to book a table
> 4 I promised not to forget
> 5 H have apologized for misspelling the word 'grammar'
> 6 D blamed the manufacturers for making the mistake
> 7 E have offered to make us a new sign
> 8 C asked the negotiators to talk to Dieter
> 9 A tried to convince him not to jump

- Finally, deal with any other vocabulary problems SS might have had in the stories.

e ● Tell SS to go to **Grammar Bank 5C** on *p.140*. Go through the examples and rules with SS.

Grammar notes

SS should be familiar with normal reported speech (statements, questions and imperatives with *say / tell / ask*) and this was quickly revised in **Check what you know**.

Here SS are introduced to a number of specific reporting verbs which can be used instead of *say / ask* + reported speech, and which are followed by either the infinitive or gerund. Some of these verbs and the structure following them have already been studied in lesson **5A**. Their previous study of reported imperatives (e.g. *he told me to open my suitcase*) will help SS with pattern **2** after verbs like *advise, invite*, etc.

Highlight that using these reporting verbs is an alternative and more exact way of reporting what someone says, e.g.

direct speech   'I won't go.'

reported speech He said that he wouldn't go.

reporting verb   He refused to go.

Emphasize the use of the negative infinitive (*not to do*) and the negative gerund (*not doing*) after these reporting verbs.

Some of these verbs can also be used with *that* + clause, often with a modal verb, e.g. *I convinced her to come.*

I convinced her that she should come. However, it is probably confusing to point this out at this stage and better to focus on getting SS to use the verbs correctly with either infinitives or gerunds.

- Focus on the exercises for **5C** on *p.141* and get SS to do them individually or in pairs. Check answers after each exercise.

a 1 paying
2 to go out
3 not to walk
4 stealing / having stolen
5 to give up
6 not to leave
7 taking
8 not remembering
b 1 suggested going
2 refused to eat
3 threatened to call
4 denied writing
5 invited me to have
6 reminded Jack to go

- Tell SS to go back to the main lesson on *p.77*.

2 PRONUNCIATION word stress

Pronunciation notes

- SS have, by now, built up an instinct for how words in English are pronounced and will know that many English two-syllable words are stressed on the first syllable. However, by coincidence, almost all the reporting verbs which SS learn in this lesson are stressed on the second syllable.
- Point out to SS the difference between the /s/ sound and the /z/ sound, e.g. *advise, accuse* and *refuse* are all /z/.

a • Focus on the task and give SS time to underline the stressed syllable in each verb. You could get them to do this with a partner.

b • **5.13** Play the CD for SS to check their answers, before giving the right answers.

See tapescript

5.13	CD3 Track 21

ac<u>cuse</u>
ad<u>mit</u>
ad<u>vise</u>
a<u>gree</u>
con<u>vince</u>
de<u>ny</u>
in<u>sist</u>
in<u>vite</u>
⟨offer⟩
per<u>suade</u>
⟨pro<u>mise</u>⟩
re<u>fuse</u>
re<u>gret</u>
re<u>mind</u>
su<u>ggest</u>
⟨<u>threaten</u>⟩

- Focus attention on the box and go through it with the class. As a contrast, point out to SS that with verbs like *offer* and *threaten*, where the stress is on the <u>first</u> ⟨syllable⟩, the final consonant is <u>not</u> doubled.

c • Focus on the task and give SS time to complete the sentences with the right reporting verb. You may need to explain in number 10 that *I wish I hadn't* = I'm sorry that I did (sth). This grammatical point is taught fully in lesson 7A. Check answers.

2	refused	8	denied
3	agreed	9	admitted
4	promised	10	regretted
5	reminded	11	suggested
6	advised	12	accused
7	invited		

d • **5.14** Focus on the task and explain that SS are going to hear the sentences on the left but in a different order and that they must respond with the corresponding reported sentence. Demonstrate the activity yourself before you play the recording.

- Play the CD pausing after each sentence for SS to call out the reported sentence.

Extra challenge

Alternatively, you could play the recording again and this time get individual SS to respond.

5.14	CD3 Track 22

Don't forget to do it!
I didn't do it!
You did it!
I wish I hadn't done it.
I'll do it, believe me.
Let's do it.
No, I won't do it.
OK, I'll do it.
I think you should do it.
Would you like to do it?
Yes, it was me. I did it.
You sit down. I'll do it.

3 VOCABULARY the media

a • Focus on the dictionary extract and the task. Elicit that [u] = uncountable. Give SS a few minutes to correct the sentences.

- Check answers, highlighting that although the word *news* has an *s* on the end, it is uncountable and so it is followed by a singular verb. To talk about individual items of news you have to use *some news* or *a piece of news*.

1 The news on TV **is** always depressing.
2 I have **some / a piece of** really exciting news for you!
3 It's 9.00. Let's watch **the** news.

b • Tell SS to go to **Vocabulary Bank *The media*** on *p.154*. Focus on section **1 Journalists and people in the media** and give SS time to match the words and definitions individually or in pairs. Check answers and drill pronunciation where necessary.

1	paparazzi	6	presenter
2	critic	7	freelance journalists
3	commentator	8	newsreader
4	reporter	9	press photographer
5	editor		

- Now focus on section **2 Sections of a newspaper or news website** and give SS time to match the words and pictures. Check answers. Elicit / explain that *ads* in *small ads* is short for *advertisements*.

1	review	5	small ads
2	crossword	6	horoscope
3	cartoon	7	weather forecast
4	advertisement	8	front page

- Focus on section **3 Adjectives to describe the media** and give SS time to match the sentences. Check answers. Then get SS to look at the words in bold and try to guess their exact meaning. In a monolingual class, and if you know the L1, elicit the meaning in your SS' language or get them to check with a dictionary.

1 D   2 E   3 B   4 A   5 C

- Now focus on section **4 The language of headlines**. This exercise focuses on the kind of language SS may see in headlines on newspaper websites and on TV news channels. Highlight that the language of headlines is quite specialized – words are usually short as the writers are always trying to save space. The same words tend to be used again and again, so it is worthwhile SS learning some very common ones here. Check SS' pronunciation of *row* /raʊ/.

- Give SS time to match the headline phrases with their meaning. Check answers.

1 A   2 D   3 B   4 G   5 E   6 C   7 H   8 F

⚠ Highlight that *wed* and *quiz* would not normally be used in conversation.

- Then look at the headlines again and ask SS to think how they would say them in normal English. *What kind of words get left out in headlines? What form or tense is used for a) the future b) the passive (all tenses)?*

> Articles and auxiliary verbs are often left out, e.g. *A man was run over by a bus* becomes *Man run over by bus*. The future is expressed by an infinitive, e.g. *Becks to go,* and passives by a past participle, e.g. *Man stabbed in Tube*.

Testing yourself

For **Journalists and people in the media** SS can cover the words and look at the definitions and try to remember the words. For **Sections of a newspaper and news website** they can cover the words and look at the photos, and try to remember the words. For **Adjectives to describe the media** they can cover 1–5, look at sentences A–E, and try to remember the adjectives. For **The language of headlines** they can cover the definitions A–H, read the headlines, and try to remember what the highlighted phrases mean.

Testing a partner

See **Testing a partner** *p.20*.

Study Link SS can find more practice of these words and phrases on the MultiROM and on the *New English File Upper-intermediate* website.

- Tell SS to go back to the main lesson on *p.78*.

---

c - The new vocabulary is recycled in this speaking activity. Put SS in pairs or small groups of three or four. Focus on the task and then set SS a time limit for them to read the questions and think about how they are going to answer them.

- Now set another time limit for the pairs or groups to discuss each question.

Extra support

Answer the questions yourself first to help SS with ideas.

4 READING & LISTENING

a - Put SS in pairs and focus on the task. Set a time limit for SS to discuss the good / bad side of the two jobs. Feedback some ideas onto the board in note form.

b - Emphasize that the two articles SS are going to read have been written by real journalists who both work for *The Times* newspaper.

- Focus on the instructions and set a time limit for SS to read both articles. Then compare what the journalists said with the ideas you elicited from the class about those two professions.

c - Focus on the task and set another time limit for SS to read both the articles again and choose the best option. Get SS to compare in pairs before checking answers.

Extra support

If there's time, you could go through both articles dealing with any vocabulary and comprehension problems.

**1 c   2 a   3 c   4 c   5 a   6 b   7 b   8 c
9 a   10 a**

d - Tell SS that they are now going to listen to two more journalists, a restaurant critic and a war reporter, talking about the good and bad sides of their jobs. SS should predict some of the things they might say. Feedback some ideas onto the board in note form.

e - **5.15 5.16** Play the restaurant critic **5.15** for SS to check their predictions. Then play the recording again and get SS in pairs to mark the sentences T or F, and say why the F ones are false. Check answers.

The restaurant critic
1 T
2 F (She can order them without worrying what they cost)
3 F (She can take a friend with her)
4 T
5 F (It's difficult for her to go back because the owner might recognize her)
6 T

- Then repeat the procedure for the war reporter **5.16**.

The war reporter
1 F (They usually chose to be war reporters because they wouldn't be happy with regular hours)
2 T
3 F (You work as part of a team)
4 T
5 T
6 F (Two colleagues were kidnapped and a very good friend was killed)

5.15 CD3 Track 23

(tapescript in Student's Book on *p.127*)

The best thing about my job is that I get to go to the best restaurants in England and sometimes abroad, and I don't get a bill at the end of the evening. I get the chance to eat the most wonderful, exquisite food in restaurants that I wouldn't normally be able to afford and I can order the most expensive dishes and wines without worrying about what it's costing me.

The other great side of the job is that I can take a friend with me so it's a good way of catching up with old friends, who I may not have seen for a while. And everyone loves a free meal in a posh restaurant so I rarely have to eat on my own.

The downside? Well, there are several. I often have to eat a lot when I'm not really hungry. To do my job properly, I have to try all the courses – you know starter, main course, dessert – and sometimes I don't feel like eating so much but I have to do it. I also have a problem with my weight now – it's very easy to put on weight when you eat out several times a week. In fact, most restaurant critics have a weight problem. Another problem is that if I write a bad review of a meal I have, it's difficult for me to ever go to that restaurant again, because the owner of the restaurant will probably recognize me. Another disadvantage of the job is that because I do it so often, eating out has lost a lot of its attraction for me. When the weekend comes I prefer to eat at home rather than go out for a meal.

5.16 CD3 Track 24

(tapescript in Student's Book on *p.128*)

Nearly all foreign correspondents and war reporters that I've met are people who were looking for adventure. They're not the kind of people who would be happy with a nine-to-five job. They are people who got into the job precisely because it has very weird hours and involves going to difficult places. I mean to some extent the things which are difficult and potentially dangerous about the job are also the things that made you want to do the job in the first place and the reason why the job is so exciting.

Something else I really like about the job is that I work as part of a team – you sit down and have dinner together at the end of the day and talk things through with other journalists and photographers, and you're talking to people who have experienced the same things as you, and seen the same things as you. And that's very important in this kind of work. One of the problems of the job is seeing a lot of horrific things and then going back home to normality. I remember a few years ago coming back from a war zone where I had been for a long time and I'd seen a lot of death and destruction, and I went to a friend's wedding in London. It was a beautiful day, everyone was drinking champagne and talking about unimportant things, and I wanted to say, 'Why can't you see that there is something awful happening in the world?'

Another major worry about my job these days is the risk of being killed. Journalists used to get killed by accident, but now there are more and more cases of journalists being killed simply because they are journalists, and they are also becoming the target of kidnappers. Two of my colleagues have been kidnapped recently and a very good friend of mine was killed last year.

Extra support

If there's time, you could get SS to listen to the two recordings again with the tapescripts on *p.127* so that they can see exactly what they understood / didn't understand. Explain / translate any words or phrases that SS aren't sure about.

- Finally, sum up by eliciting the good / bad sides of the two jobs.

> **Restaurant critic**
> Good side: can go to the best restaurants, it's free, can take a friend
> Bad side: has to eat even when not hungry, weight problem, can't go back to places where the review was bad, eating out at weekends isn't appealing
> **War reporter**
> Good side: weird hours, going to difficult places, part of team
> Bad side: see a lot of horrific things, contrast between war zones and home, risk of being killed / kidnapped

f • Do this as an open class activity by eliciting ideas.

5 SPEAKING

a • Focus attention on the task and on the topic SS are going to debate. If possible, give some examples of a famous recent case of the media publishing a story about the private life of a celebrity.

- Divide the class into groups of four, two **A**s and two **B**s, and make clear what each pair has to defend. Emphasize that SS should not worry if their real views are at odds with their role in the debate. The debate is purely to practise their English.

- Set a time limit to give pairs **A** and **B** time to think up the arguments that they will use in the debate.

b • The debate will work better if the two pairs of SS are sitting opposite each other. Focus on the instructions and stress that both sides are going to put forward their main points in turn. Get the **A**s to open the debate, and tell the **B**s to take notes of the points the **A**s make. Then the **B**s make their points and the **A**s take notes. Again, set a time limit for each side, but let the activity continue or cut it shorter according to how well the debates 'take off'.

c • Now tell both sides to check with the notes they made to see if there are any more points they would like to argue against. Set another time limit and encourage SS to use reported speech '*You said that…*'.

Extra idea

With a small class you could have a class debate by dividing the class in half. You could then judge one side or the other to be the winner of the debate according to how well they made their points.

- Finally, find out what SS <u>really</u> think by getting a show of hands.

MINI GRAMMAR as

- Focus on the example sentences, which come from the reading and listening, and go through the four different uses of *as*. In a monolingual class you could also contrast how the examples would be expressed in SS' own language.
- Focus on the task and give SS a couple of minutes to match sentences A–F with uses 1–4. Check answers.

> **A** 2 **B** 3 **C** 1 **D** 4 **E** 4 **F** 3

Extra support

If you think your class need more practice, use the extra photocopiable exercises on *p.187*.

- Finally, tell SS to go to *Phrasal verbs in context File 5* on *p.157* and complete the phrasal verbs which have come up in this File. (Answers *p.155*)

Extra photocopiable activities

Grammar
reporting verbs *p.174*
Communicative
Reporting verbs game *p.212* (instructions *p.194*)
Vocabulary
Revision race *p.227* (instructions *p.221*)

HOMEWORK

> **Study Link** Workbook *pp.50–52*

Lesson plan

In the first part of this lesson the person interviewed is Sir Nicholas Kenyon. He was the director of the Proms (the classical music festival held for two months in the summer at the Royal Albert Hall in London – www.bbc.co.uk/proms/2007) for twelve years and is now the managing director of the Barbican Centre in London, Europe's largest multi-arts centre. In the second part of the lesson, people in the street are asked if they've been to a music festival and what it was like.

> **Study Link** These lessons are on the *New English File Upper-intermediate* DVD / Video which can be used instead of the class CD (See Introduction *p.9*). SS can get more practice on the MultiROM, which contains more of the short street interviews with a listening task and tapescripts.

Optional lead-in (books closed)

- Tell SS to go to **Vocabulary Bank** Music on *p.153* and tell them to test themselves or each other on the words in section **1 Instruments and musicians**. Then ask them which of the words are used especially in the context of classical music.

  cello, organ, piano, violin, trumpet, bass, choir, composer, conductor, orchestra, soloist, soprano, tenor

THE INTERVIEW

a • Books open. Focus on the photos and get SS to tell you what they can see.

> A man (Sir Nicholas Kenyon), a bassoon, a circular building (the Royal Albert Hall), and a conductor.

- Now focus on the task and on the glossary. Go through it with the class eliciting from them how to pronounce the words and phrases.

b • **5.17** Focus on the task. Put SS in pairs and give them time to read the questions. Encourage SS not to write anything down when they listen the first time. They should listen and try to get the gist of what he is saying, and then discuss the questions with their partner.

- Play the CD once (**Part 1**). Give SS time to discuss the questions and tell each other what they understood. Then play the CD once or twice more. This time SS might want to jot down things they heard to help them remember the answers to the questions. Check answers.

> 1 Use the Queen's Hall for a series of popular concerts (to bring classical music to a wider audience).
> 2 Taking away the seats on the floor of the hall so that people could stand and walk around.
> 3 Because it is an abbreviation of Promenade concerts (people are able to walk around and stand during the music).
> 4 Two months.
> 5 They have to queue during the day.
> 6 They don't dress up and they behave how they want but they really listen to the music. There is an amazing level of concentration.

CD3 Track 25

(tapescript in Student's Book on *p.128*)

I = interviewer, N = Nicholas Kenyon

I Sir Nicholas Kenyon was the director of a festival of concerts called the Proms for 12 years. How did the Proms start?

N The promenade concerts started way back in 1895 when a brilliant impresario wanted to use a newly-built concert hall in London, the Queen's Hall, for a series of popular concerts that really brought classical music to the widest possible audience. There were important classical concerts during the year, but in the summer people tended to go away, society life finished and so he had the brilliant idea of taking away all the seats on the floor of the hall, where the expensive people usually sat and letting people come in and stand there and walk around and have a very informal experience of concert-going. The name 'Proms' is an abbreviation of 'Promenade concerts' and it basically means that people are able to walk around and stand during the music.

I How long do the Proms last?

N The Proms lasts for two months in the summer, from the middle of July to the middle of September and during that period there's one concert every day, two concerts on many days, three concerts on some days. So it's a very very intense period of music-making and people buy season tickets in order to be able to attend all the concerts, whether they do or not, very few people attend actually all of them, except me, and they come and they queue during the day in order to get the best places in the floor of the hall where they stand.

I World-class musicians perform at the Proms for much lower fees than they would expect to receive. Why do you think that is?

N I think the Proms has an absolutely unique atmosphere that's what orchestras and conductors and performers who come here say. And so people do want to come and perform. What you get at the Proms is a wonderful mixture of total informality and total concentration. So that although people don't dress up to come to the Proms, they behave how they want, they actually absolutely listen to the music and that is a feature that so many conductors and orchestras really comment on - the level of concentration is absolutely amazing.

Extra challenge

You could use the tapescript above to elicit more detailed answers from SS.

c ● **5.18** Focus on the task and play the CD once (**Part 2**). Give SS time to discuss the questions and what they understood. Then play the CD once or twice more. Check answers.

1 They changed the concert programme for that day and put in the Fauré Requiem.

2 He was going to conduct the Verdi Requiem later that season. He had been a friend of Diana's and wanted to dedicate the piece to her memory. But a week later he also died.

3 After Solti's death, Colin Davies conducted the Verdi Requiem and dedicated it to the memory of Diana and Solti.

4 The title of a piece of music by John Adams that had been programmed for the last night of the Proms and which they had to change (because Diana had been killed after a short ride in a fast car).

5 He was conducting this piece and, in a very quiet moment at the beginning, a mobile phone started ringing. He stopped the piece, looked angrily at the person, and then started from the beginning again.

6 Sir Nicholas Kenyon was interviewed on the BBC the next day about this incident, and in the middle of the interview <u>his</u> phone rang.

CD3 Track 26

(tapescript in Student's Book on *p.128*)

I There must have been many truly memorable concerts during your time as director of the Proms. Could you tell us about one of them?

N The death of Princess Diana was particularly difficult because of course she lived just across the road in Kensington Palace from where the Proms happened in the Royal Albert Hall. We changed some programmes to make them more appropriate. On the day of her funeral, we put in Fauré's Requiem to the programme. Very oddly we had programmed two or three requiems in that last two weeks of the season and they fitted very very well. We then lost another major figure of the musical world, the conductor Sir Georg Solti who was to have conducted the Verdi Requiem on the last Friday of the season and he had been a very good friend of Princess Diana and indeed had rung me up just after Diana's death to say that he wanted to dedicate this Verdi Requiem to her memory. As it turned out, he died just a week later and so another conductor, Colin Davies, took over that Verdi Requiem and dedicated it to both of them and it was a fantastically charged atmosphere in the hall. I can't remember such an electric occasion as that.

I I understand there was also another spooky coincidence in the programme at the time of Diana's death? Could you tell us about it?

N A wonderful American composer called John Adams had written an absolutely wonderful piece which we were going to do on the last night of the Proms in 1997. Unfortunately, I mean it could have been called absolutely anything this piece, it's a whirling abstract piece of fanfare music. Unfortunately he had called it *Short ride in a fast machine*. And so it was perfectly obvious from the first moment that we had to take that piece out and change the programme.

I Are there any embarrassing or amusing experiences you remember?

N One of the things that was a real challenge to the Proms was the arrival of the mobile phone, because in the beginning people didn't know how to use them, when to switch them off and the Albert Hall is a very very big space and mobile phones would go off in concerts and it could be very embarrassing. Usually, because they were in the middle of the music, conductors just ignored them and people got embarrassed and switched them off. But there was one particular incident that was just so awful because Stravinsky's *The Rite of Spring* starts with a very very exposed quiet bassoon solo and Simon Rattle and the

Berlin Philharmonic making one of their first appearances together at the Proms had just begun that piece when a mobile phone went off very loudly in the stalls and Simon Rattle stopped the bassoonist and turned round and glared at this person in the stalls and there was a round of applause and everything. So anyway, it restarted and the performance was a spectacular success and it was wonderful. But this was such an incident, that he had actually stopped it, that it became the subject of a lot of media attention and there were paragraphs in the papers and I had to go and be interviewed the next day at home for a Radio 4 programme about mobile phones going off in concerts, and in the middle of this interview, my own phone went off and it's a wonderfully classic little bit of tape. My embarrassment at the same thing happening to me.

d ● **5.19** This exercise gives SS intensive listening practice in deciphering phrases where words are often run together, and introduces them to some common English expressions. Focus on the phrases and give SS time to read them. Play the CD, pausing after the first phrase and replaying it as necessary. Elicit the missing words, and then the meaning of the whole phrase. Repeat for the other five phrases.

1 **way back in** (= informal way of saying *a long time ago*)
2 **walk around** (= walk here and there)
3 **except me** (= I am the only one)
4 **Very oddly** (= it was strange that)
5 **turned out** (= phrasal verb meaning *happened in the end*)
6 **I mean** (= I want to say – often used when speaking, to give yourself time when you want to rephrase something or before you explain something)

5.19   CD3 Track 27
1 The Promenade Concerts started way back in 1895.
2 …it basically means that people are able to walk around and stand during the music
3 Very few people attend actually all of them, except me.
4 Very oddly we had programmed two or three requiems in that last two weeks of the season.
5 As it turned out, he died just a week later.
6 Unfortunately, I mean it could have been called absolutely anything…

e ● Tell SS to go to *p.128* and to look at the tapescript for the interview. Play the CD (**Part 1** and **Part 2**) again and tell SS to read and listen at the same time. Deal with any vocabulary problems and get feedback from SS on what parts they found hard to understand and why, e.g. speed of speech, elision, pronunciation, etc.

● Finally, focus on the questions. You could also ask SS *Which of the anecdotes did you find most memorable?* Get SS to answer in pairs or as a whole class. Then get feedback from the whole class.

IN THE STREET

a ● **5.20** Focus on the photos of the people and elicit impressions (e.g. *How old do they look? What job do you think they do?*, etc). All the people have appeared in previous Files, except for Harley. Tell SS that they were all interviewed in Covent Garden, a busy shopping area in Central London.

● Focus on the task and the festivals, and ask SS if they have heard of any of them. The most famous is probably Glastonbury, which is one of the largest pop festivals in the world held every June near the town of Glastonbury. The Isle of Wight festival was held from 1968–70 and was the most important festival of that era. It was then revived in 2002 and has been held annually since then. The other three are also important music festivals.

● Play the CD once, and get SS to compare ideas. Then play it again pausing after each speaker to check answers.

Bath blues festival 4 (Ray)
The Big Chill 5 (Harley)
Glastonbury 3 (Mike)
Isle of Wight festival 1 (Anne)
Reading music festival 4 (Ray)
Rock festival in Ohio 2 (Jordan)

5.20   CD3 Track 28
(tapescript in Student's Book on *p.128*)
I = interviewer, A = Anne, J = Jordan, M = Mike, R = Ray, H = Harley
Anne
I Have you ever been to a music festival?
A Yes, Isle of Wight in the 70s.
I What was it like?
A There were just thousands and thousands of people just chilling out doing whatever you wanted to do. And it was just great fun – there was music, dancing, a great memory actually.
Jordan
I Have you ever been to a music festival?
J Yes, we have a rock festival back home in Ohio that we go to, a lot of my friends and I go to.
I What was it like?
J I don't know what it's called but it's just like a whole bunch of alternative music, it's like two days long and you all go and it's just a fun time – all outside. There's a ton of people and they're all usually younger, from like college age usually, and they just have a whole bunch of stages set up, and there's just bars in different places, and you can just go and hang out and listen to some music.
Mike
I Have you ever been to a music festival?
M Yes, I went to Glastonbury.
I What was it like?
M Incredibly muddy, incredibly muddy, but great fun, absolutely so much fun, I didn't get any sleep at all.
Ray
I Have you ever been to a music festival?
R Yes, not for many years. When I was much younger I went to Bath, Bath music blues festival, I've been to Reading music festival. I can't remember which other ones I've been to, but yes, in the 1970s, early 80s I went to quite a few.

113

I What was it like?

R From a 57-year-old's point of view? Well, at the time they were really exciting. I can remember a long journey down to Bath, sleeping in a field, I can remember expensive food, waiting up all night to the see the band that you wanted to see and then falling asleep. I can remember being taken back to sleep in somebody's tent then waking up and realizing we were in the wrong tent, and had no idea whose tent we were in the next morning. I can remember feeling slightly sort of sick and hungry all the time I was there, but yeah, it was good, it was exciting.

Harley

I Have you ever been to a music festival?

H No. Oh yeah, actually. The Big Chill? Yeah, we went to the Big Chill.

I What was it like?

H Yeah, it was really good. I went with my dad and my sister, and we went in a camper van. So we camped and yeah, it was good.

b • Focus on the task and give SS time to go through the sentences. Play the CD once. Get SS to compare what they think. Play it again if necessary and check answers.

1	Harley	4	Anne
2	Jordan	5	Mike
3	Ray		

c • **5.21** Focus on the phrases and give SS time to read them. Play the CD, pausing after the first phrase and replaying it as necessary. Elicit the missing word, and then the meaning of the whole phrase. Repeat for the other three phrases.

1 **chilling out** (informal = relaxing, taking it easy)
2 **hang out** (informal = spend a lot of time in a place, e.g. in a coffee bar).
3 **get any sleep** (= informal way of saying *I didn't sleep at all*)
4 **quite a few** (= a fairly large number)
5 We had no **idea** (= emphatic way of saying *We didn't know*)

5.21	CD3 Track 29

1 There were just thousands and thousands of people just chilling out.
2 You can just go and hang out and listen to some music.
3 I didn't get any sleep at all.
4 in the 1970s, early 80s I went to quite a few.
5 … and had no idea whose tent we were in the next morning.

d • Tell SS to go to *p.128* and to look at the tapescript for **IN THE STREET**. Play the CD again and tell SS to read and listen at the same time. Deal with any vocabulary problems and get feedback from SS on what parts they found hard to understand and why, e.g. speed of speech, elision, pronunciation, etc.

• Finally, focus on the two questions that the interviewer asked the people, and get SS to interview each other in pairs. Then get feedback from the whole class.

HOMEWORK

Study Link **Workbook** *p.53*

WRITING
A FORMAL LETTER

Lesson plan

In this writing lesson SS learn to write a formal letter (or email) of complaint. You may want to point out to SS that when writing an email they shouldn't include any addresses. The writing skills focus is on distinguishing between formal and informal register.

a • Focus on the picture of the family and elicit ideas for why they might look unhappy.

• Now focus on the task and set SS a time limit to read the letter and answer the questions. Tell them not to worry about the missing words at this point. Check answers. You could point out that the date would normally go under the sender's address and should be written out in full (date month year).

1 The head office of the Café Royale chain of restaurants.
2 Because he wants to complain about unsatisfactory service he and his family had at a Café Royale restaurant.
3 He wants an explanation and an apology.

b • Focus on the task and emphasize that when you write a formal letter / email you normally use a more formal kind of language. Give SS time to complete the letter with the more formal alternative in each case. Get them to compare their answers with a partner. Check answers.

2 on many occasions
3 pleasant
4 on this particular evening
5 an extremely rude
6 refused to
7 will not do so again
8 unacceptable treatment
9 Yours faithfully

c • Focus on the situation and the task.

Extra support

You could brainstorm typical problems you might have in a hotel, e.g. you didn't get the room you had booked / the room was dirty / the receptionist was rude, etc.

• Go through the **Typical openings** of the **Useful language** box and elicit possible continuations to the two sentences, e.g. *I am writing to complain about / to express my dissatisfaction with… the service / treatment I received in your hotel last week,* etc.

• Point out that we do not use *Dear Manager* to begin a letter, even if we do not know the person's name. *Dear Sir / Madam* should be used instead.

• Then focus on **Typical endings** and make sure SS are clear that you should only finish *Yours sincerely* if you know the name of the person. If not, *Yours faithfully* should be used.

WRITE a letter

Go through the instructions. Then either get SS to plan and write the letter in class (set a time limit of about 20 minutes) or get them just to plan in class and write at home, or set both planning and writing for homework.

If SS do the writing in class, get them to swap their letters with another student to read and check for mistakes before you collect them all in.

Test and Assessment CD-ROM

CEF Assessment materials
File 5 Writing task assessment guidelines

REVISE & CHECK

For instructions on how to use these pages, see *p.33*.

GRAMMAR

a	**1** used to driving	**4** killing her husband
	2 to have	**5** apologized for being
	3 Sarah to talk	**6** as a waiter
b	**1** meeting	**3** to get
	2 cleaning	**4** to be

VOCABULARY

a	**1** con<u>duc</u>tor	**6** <u>jour</u>nalist
	2 vio<u>lin</u>ist	**7** <u>so</u>loist
	3 <u>drum</u>mer	**8** re<u>por</u>ter
	4 <u>e</u>ditor	**9** pre<u>sen</u>ter
	5 com<u>po</u>ser	**10** <u>com</u>mentator
b	**1** weather forecast	**6** censored
	2 review	**7** pillow
	3 biased	**8** snore
	4 catchy	**9** nap
	5 tune	**10** insomnia

PRONUNCIATION

a	**1** whole (it's /h/)	**4** accurate (it's /æ/)
	2 convince (it's /s/)	**5** cartoon (it's /uː/)
	3 crossword (it's /ɜː/)	

b gui<u>tar</u>ist, <u>or</u>chestra, <u>bi</u>ased, sen<u>sa</u>tional, <u>cri</u>tic

CAN YOU UNDERSTAND THIS TEXT?

1 b   **2** a   **3** b   **4** b   **5** c   **6** a   **7** b   **8** c

CAN YOU UNDERSTAND THESE PEOPLE?

a	**A** not mentioned	**E** 1
	B 5	**F** 4
	C 2	**G** 3
	D not mentioned	

b **1** c   **2** b   **3** a   **4** b   **5** c

5.22   CD3 Track 30

1 The results of the tests have come back from the lab and they were positive. We'll have to wait until next week for the board to decide on how long he'll be suspended, but most people are predicting that his punishment will be quite tough in order to set an example to the younger players. So we definitely won't be seeing him in competition in the near future and he could be facing as much as a two-year ban.

2 Her nomination extends her lead as the most-nominated woman in the history of the Academy Awards. Her tally now extends to 14 nominations and two wins, and if she wins again in March, that will make it three. However, she faces strong competition this year, mainly from outside the USA.

3 After quite a chilly start to the day, tomorrow will be mild and overcast all over the country with the chance of scattered showers, especially later in the day.

4 An overturned lorry has completely blocked the northbound carriageway of the M6. Police advise motorists to find an alternative route if at all possible. However, the M40 is now clear in both directions. And delays are likely on the railway networks, due to major engineering work between Warwick and Birmingham.

5 A 45-year-old man has been charged with arson after a fire destroyed ten acres of woodland in Yorkshire last week. Nigel Slatterley from Leeds denies the charge and he will appear at Leeds Crown court at the end of this month.

5.23   CD3 Track 31

I = interviewer, J = John Sloboda

I Why can the same sound be beautiful music for some people and for others just noise – and probably unpleasant noise?

J Well, there are two main reasons. The first is to do with rules. Music has rules and you understand the rules, you enjoy the music. If you don't, for you it is noise. It's just like a language. If you listen to a language you don't understand, for you it is just noise. A good example is modern classical music. Most music over the last 500 years has been tonal. That means it has tunes, harmony, and so on, and those are the rules that most of us understand. But when some classical composers in the 20th century started writing atonal music, they 'broke the rules' and for most people this just sounds like noise – until you learn to understand the new rules of atonal music. The same is also true of a lot of experimental jazz, where players are improvising.

I And the second reason?

J The second reason is the cultural associations that music has for us. A lot of young people, for example, associate opera or classical music with boring older people, a stuffy concert hall, music that goes on forever. So for them it is noise. There is a shopping mall somewhere in the UK where they had a problem with a group of young people hanging around in the afternoons and evenings. So they decided to play classical music instead of playing the usual pop music. The teenagers found it so 'uncool' that they stopped coming. And of course for many older people, when they hear any music with a beat, they don't hear it as music, they just hear it as thump, thump, thump, and for them it also has negative associations.

6
A

G articles
V collocation: word pairs
P sentence stress

Speaking to the world

File 6 overview

Lesson **6A** consolidates and expands SS' knowledge of the rules governing use and non-use of definite and indefinite articles. **6B** deals with countable and uncountable nouns (e.g. *luggage* and *politics*) and there is a mini grammar focus on *have something done*. Finally, in **6C** SS revise and extend their knowledge of quantifiers, e.g. *all, both, neither*, etc. The lexical areas covered in this File are word pairs (*ladies and gentlemen*), towns and cities, and science.

Lesson plan

In this lesson SS revise and extend their knowledge of use and non-use of the definite and indefinite articles. The general topic of the lesson is public speaking. In the first part of the lesson the topic is famous speeches starting with the controversy surrounding Neil Armstrong's famous words when he stepped on the moon (Did he make a mistake by omitting an indefinite article?). SS will hear extracts from the original recordings of these famous speeches. In the second half of the lesson SS hear people talking about disasters that have happened to them when speaking in public and they also learn tips for giving a good presentation. The lesson finishes with SS preparing and giving a presentation. The vocabulary focus is on word pairs, e.g. *peace and quiet, now and again,* and pronunciation gives SS more practice with sentence stress.

Optional lead-in (books closed)

- Write the following on the board
  NASA   Apollo lift-off   Mission Control   countdown
- Ask SS what they have in common and elicit that they are all to do with space and space travel. Then elicit what each thing is.

> NASA = National Aeronautic and Space Administration (the US organization in charge of everything to do with space travel)
> Apollo = the name given to the program organized by NASA to put people on the moon, and also the name of the spacecraft used.
> lift-off (noun) = the moment when a spacecraft leaves the ground. A spacecraft *lifts off* (it doesn't *take off*).
> Mission Control = the people at NASA who control the spacecraft
> countdown = the counting backwards (10, 9, 8, etc.) which is done before lift-off

1 READING

a • Books open. Focus on the quiz and get SS to choose the answers with a partner. Get feedback and see what the most popular answers are, but don't tell them at this stage who is right.

b • Focus on the instructions. If necessary, explain *controversy* (= public discussion and argument about

sth that people strongly disagree about), and then set a time limit for SS to read and check their answers to the quiz, and to find out what the controversy is.

- Check answers to the quiz first, and elicit / explain the meaning of *a giant leap* (= a very big jump) and *mankind* = all humans. Then elicit from the class what the controversy was and why the missing *a* is important.

> **a** **1** c **2** b **3** c
> **b** The controversy was about what Neil Armstrong actually said when he landed on the moon. Did he say 'One small step for man…' or 'One small step for *a* man…'?
> The 'a' is important because the sentence makes good sense with it ('One small step for an individual man, but a giant leap for humans in general'). Without the article the sentence doesn't make sense as it means 'One small step for people in general, one giant leap for people in general'.

c • Focus on the task. Set a time limit for SS to re-read the article. Then put SS in pairs for them to say what they remember about each date, time, etc.
- Check answers.

Extra challenge

You could alternatively write the prompts (20th July 1969, etc.) on the board and get SS to do the task with their books closed.

> 20th July 1969 was the date of the first moon landing.
> 6 hours and 40 minutes is the time the astronauts spent in the spacecraft between landing on the moon and stepping out of the capsule.
> 500 million people watched or listened to the moon landing live.
> Buzz Aldrin was the second man to step on the moon.
> *First Man* is the name of Armstrong's biography.
> James Hansen is the author of his biography.
> Peter Shann Ford is the computer expert who discovered through sound analysis that Armstrong really did say the 'a'.

d • Focus on the task and make sure SS cover the article as all the words they have to make are in there. Highlight that they have to add something to the end of the word (a suffix) and maybe something to the beginning (a prefix). Check answers and elicit whether they are nouns or adjectives. Elicit which syllable is stressed and drill pronunciation.

> **2** mankind (noun) = people in general, humanity
> **3** momentous (adj) = very important or serious
> **4** meaningful (adj) = having a clear meaning
> **5** memorable (adj) = worth remembering
> **6** inaudible (adj) = can't be heard

Extra support

At this point you could go through the text with the class, highlighting useful expressions and eliciting / explaining the meaning of new words and phrases.

e • **6.1** Finally, tell SS that they are going to hear the original recording of Neil Armstrong speaking from the moon to see if they think he said 'One small step for man (or *a* man)'. Warn them that, understandably, the recording is quite crackly. They will almost certainly not hear the 'a'.

> **6.1**   CD3 Track 32
>
> *Neil Armstrong original recording*
> That's one small step for (a) man, one giant leap for mankind.

2 GRAMMAR articles

a • Focus on the task and make it clear to SS that the mistakes are all to do with using or not using *a* or *the*. Get SS to compare with a partner and then check answers getting SS to tell you why they think the wrong ones are wrong.

> 1 in the USA ✓
> 2 a shy boy ✓, ~~the~~ books and ~~the~~ music
> 3 at ~~the~~ university
> 4 the first man ✓, ~~a~~ **the** moon
> 5 ✓
> 6 ~~a~~ **an** astronaut, the US navy ✓
> 7 to give ~~the~~ autographs
> 8 some of ~~the~~ Armstrong's hair

b • Tell SS to go to **Grammar Bank 6A** on *p.142*. Go through the examples and rules with SS.

Grammar notes

Upper-intermediate SS should be familiar with the basic rules for using articles, but as this is an area that can be very difficult for some nationalities who don't have articles in their L1.

basic rules

The basic rules are revised here, as well as introducing SS to new areas such as the use of articles with institutions, e.g. *hospital*, and with geographical and other place names, e.g. *streets*, *hotels*, etc.

- **rule 2**: (non-use of the definite article when generalizing) is an area where SS often make mistakes, e.g. ~~*The men are better at parking...*~~

institutions

The use and non-use of *the* with *church*, *hospital*, and *school* is a tricky little point but with a clear rule. It will help to give SS other examples, e.g.

I'm studying at university (= I am a student there) NOT ... ~~at the university~~.

The university is in the centre of town. (= we are talking about the buildings).

I go to church every Sunday. The murderer is in prison (= no definite article)

Other words which are used like this are *college*, *mosque* / *synagogue* (and other places of worship).

geographical names

The number of rules here, most of which are new for SS, may seem overwhelming. Emphasize, however, that SS should already have a good instinct for whether they need to use *the* or not, and also that the easiest way to internalize the rules is by learning and remembering a clear example, e.g. *Fifth Avenue*, **the** *River Nile*, **the** *Mediterranean sea*, (*Mount*) *Everest*, **the** *Andes*, etc.

- Focus on the exercises for **6A** on *p.143* and get SS to do them individually or in pairs. Check answers after each exercise.

a	1	–	4	–	7	the	10	the
	2	The	5	a	8	–		
	3	–	6	–	9	a		
b	1	–, the	4	–	7	the	10	–
	2	the	5	–, the	8	the		
	3	the	6	the	9	The		

- Tell SS to go back to the main lesson on *p.85*.

c • Focus on the photos and elicit who the three people are, and if SS know anything about them. Then get SS to read the biographical data. If you have younger SS, you may need to highlight the historical importance of these people.

Extra support

You could check comprehension by asking them a few questions about each man, e.g. *When was Churchill the British Prime Minister? What did he mean by 'the iron curtain'?*, etc.

- Now tell SS that they are going to read three extracts from famous speeches made by these men. First, they should read the extracts and complete them with articles where necessary. Then SS will hear the original recordings of them speaking. Remind SS that they have glossaries to help them.

d • **6.2** Now play the CD. Pause after Churchill's extract and check answers. Repeat with the other two extracts. Then check answers.

> **Martin Luther King**
> 1 a   2 –   3 a   4 the   5 the
> **Churchill**
> 1 the   2 –   3 the   4 an   5 the   6 the
> 7 the   8 –   9 the   10 the
> **Edward VIII**
> 1 a   2 the   3 –   4 the   5 the

> **6.2**   CD3 Track 33
>
> *Martin Luther King original recording*
> I have a dream. That my four little children will one day live in a nation where they will not be judged by the color of their skin but by the content of their character.
> *Winston Churchill original recording*
> From Stettin in the Baltic to Trieste in the Adriatic, an iron curtain has descended across the continent. Behind that line lie all the capitals of the ancient states of Central and Eastern Europe. Warsaw, Berlin, Prague, Vienna, Budapest, Belgrade, Bucharest, and Sofia. All these famous cities, and the populations around them, lie in what I must call the Soviet sphere.

King Edward VIII original recording
At long last I am able to say a few words of my own.
I have never wanted to withhold anything, but until
now it has not been constitutionally possible for me to
speak. But you must believe me when I tell you that I
have found it impossible to carry the heavy burden of
responsibility, and to discharge my duties as King as I
would wish to do, without the help and support of the
woman I love.

● Finally, get SS to listen to the three speeches again
and ask who they think is the best / most charismatic
speaker.

Extra idea

Ask them who they think are good, charismatic speakers
among today's politicians and statesmen / women.

3 PRONUNCIATION sentence stress

Pronunciation notes

This exercise reminds SS of the weak pronunciation of
articles in general, and the difference between the two
pronunciations of *the* (depending on whether the article
precedes a word beginning with a vowel sound.)

a ● **6.3** **Dictation**. Focus on the task. Then play the CD
once the whole way through for SS to listen. Then play
it again, pausing after each sentence for SS to write.
Then play it again the whole way through for SS to
check. Check answers by writing the sentences on the
board.

6.3		CD3 Track 34

1 The <u>first</u> <u>man</u> on the <u>moon</u> was an <u>American</u>.
2 The <u>President</u> of the <u>company</u> is a <u>woman</u>.
3 There are some <u>beautiful</u> <u>lakes</u> in the <u>south</u>.
4 The <u>man</u> was <u>sent</u> to <u>prison</u> for <u>robbing</u> a <u>bank</u>.
5 The <u>twenty</u>-<u>fifth</u> of <u>December</u> is a <u>Thursday</u>.
6 The <u>Indian</u> <u>Ocean</u> is to the <u>east</u> of <u>Africa</u>.

b ● Focus on the task. Play the CD again for SS to underline
the stressed words. Check answers, and elicit answers to
the two questions.

The vowel sound of *a* / *an* / *the* in 1–5 is /ə/.
The is pronounced /ðiː/ in 6 because the following
word (*Indian*) begins with a vowel sound.

Extra support

Give SS some more examples of when *the* is pronounced
/ðiː/, e.g. *the end, the answer, the island, the umbrella, the
other one*, etc. and get SS to say them.

Remind SS that if a vowel is <u>not</u> pronounced as a vowel
sound, e.g. *the university*, then the article is pronounced
the /ə/.

c ● Give SS time to practise saying the sentences in pairs.
Monitor and check their rhythm and pronunciation of
the /ə/ sound.

4 ♫ SONG ♫ *Space Oddity* **6.4**

● *Space Oddity* was originally recorded by David Bowie
in 1969 coinciding with the first moon landing. For

copyright reasons this is a cover version. If you want
to do this song in class, use the photocopiable activity
on *p.238*.

6.4	CD3 Track 35

Space Oddity

Ground Control to Major Tom, Ground Control to Major
Tom:
Take your protein pills and put your helmet on
Ground Control to Major Tom, commencing
countdown, engine's on
Check ignition, and may God's love be with you

This is Ground Control to Major Tom, you've really made
the grade
And the papers want to know whose shirts you wear
Now it's time to leave the capsule if you dare

This is Major Tom to Ground Control, I'm stepping
through the door
And I'm floating in the most peculiar way
And the stars look very different today

For here am I sitting in a tin can, far above the world
Planet Earth is blue, and there's nothing I can do

Though I'm past one hundred thousand miles,
I'm feeling very still
And I think my spaceship knows which way to go
Tell my wife I love her very much – she knows

Ground Control to Major Tom
Your circuit's dead, there's something wrong
Can you hear me, Major Tom?
Can you hear me, Major Tom?
Can you hear me, Major Tom?
Can you…

Here am I floating round my tin can, far above the Moon
Planet Earth is blue, and there's nothing I can do.

5 LISTENING

a ● Either get SS to answer the questions in pairs and get
feedback, or do them as open class questions and elicit
SS' experiences. If you have a story of your own, tell it
to the class.

b ● Focus on the article and the task. Give SS a couple of
minutes to read the article and elicit the answer from
the class.

The speaker should have remembered to get to know as
much as possible about his / her audience beforehand
(tip 6).

c ● Focus on the pictures and give SS time to look at them.
Then elicit ideas as to what the problem was in each
one. Don't tell SS if they are right or wrong.

d ● **6.5** Play the CD once for SS to number the pictures.
Check answers. Did SS guess any of the situations
correctly?

A 5   B 1   C 4   D 2   E 3

6.5   CD3 Track 36

(tapescript in Student's Book on *p.128*)

1   I was giving a talk to about two hundred people in a large hotel room in Poland. About halfway through the talk, I realized that something was flying around the room. At first I just ignored it, as I thought it was probably a bird that had come in through the window, but after a while I noticed that the women in the audience were following its movements with their eyes and were not looking very happy. It was then that I realized that it was a large bat. The next moment I could see from the audience's eyes that it was directly above my head. I'm really frightened of bats, and I just panicked. I tried to carry on, but I couldn't concentrate and I kept forgetting what I was going to say. So I hurried through the last part of the talk, and then as soon as I finished, I rushed out of the room. It was awful, I'll never forget it!

2   I get invited to talk to teachers all around the world, and this time I was in Mexico giving a talk to some English teachers. Though I say it myself, I think I'm a good speaker and usually the audiences enjoy my talks and are interested in what I'm saying. But after about ten minutes, I realized that something was wrong. The audience weren't laughing at my jokes and some people were looking very unhappy. Then I saw several people get up and walk out of the hall. I just couldn't work out what was going on. I'd given a presentation there the year before and the audience had been really enthusiastic. In the end, I just stopped and asked them, 'Is anything the matter? You don't seem to be enjoying this.' And one teacher said 'Actually the problem is that you gave exactly the same talk last year, so we've heard it all before.' I didn't really know what to do at this point. I just apologized profusely and invited the people who had already heard the talk to leave, which, unfortunately, was almost everybody.

3   I was giving a presentation to a rather serious group of businessmen in Germany. They listened politely for 45 minutes, and at the end I asked for any questions. Nobody said anything. Then a young man stood up and said to me, 'Sir, you are open.' I looked down at my trousers and realized that I was.

4   I had to give a talk to some students at Imperial College in London. It's the science and technology department of London University, so I didn't think there would be any problems with the equipment. I'd seen the auditorium before and it was a nice room, good sound and screen, etc. But as soon as I began my talk, people started complaining that they couldn't see the slides – there was something wrong with the projector and the screen was too dark. So I started touching keys on my laptop, and I don't know what I did, but I managed to delete the whole presentation. So there I was with no presentation notes at all, nothing, and I had to improvise from what I could remember. It was all very embarrassing, I must say.

5   I had to give a business presentation to a company in Paris, and after I'd got there and checked into my hotel, I thought I'd go for a walk as it was such a beautiful day and I had plenty of time. My talk wasn't until one o'clock and I was well prepared. I was strolling along by the river enjoying the sunshine when I noticed that several people at the cafés were already having lunch. I thought it was a bit early for lunch and I checked my watch – it was only a quarter to twelve. And then I suddenly realized that I'd forgotten to change my watch. The UK is one hour behind France, so that meant it was in fact quarter to *one*. My presentation was supposed to start in 15 minutes' time. I desperately looked for a taxi to take me first back to my hotel and then to the company's offices where I was going to give the presentation. I finally arrived 20 minutes late and very stressed – and the worst thing of all was that the title of the talk I was giving was '*How to manage your time better!*'

e ● Focus on the questions A–E and play the CD again, pausing after each speaker to check the answer, and to elicit why the presentation was a disaster. Then do the same for the other four speakers.

A	**speaker 2**	He had given exactly the same presentation the year before.
B	**speaker 5**	He hadn't realized that Paris was one hour ahead of London, and arrived late for his presentation – which was about how to manage your time better.
C	**speaker 1**	A bat was flying around the room and she was scared of bats.
D	**speaker 4**	She touched the wrong button on the computer and deleted the presentation.
E	**speaker 3**	He didn't realize that the zip on his trousers was undone.

Extra support

If there's time, you could get SS to listen to the recording again with the tapescript on *p.128* so that they can see exactly what they understood / didn't understand. Explain / translate any words or phrases that SS aren't sure about.

Extra challenge

Alternatively, you could play all the speakers one after another and check answers, and elicit extra information about the disasters at the end.

f ● Focus on the questions and get SS to go back to the **Ten top tips**. Then put SS in pairs to discuss the three questions. Get feedback and elicit experiences.

1 Speaker 1: tip 3   Speaker 4: tip 10   Speaker 5: tip 5

Extra support

You could do these questions with the whole class.

6 VOCABULARY   collocation: word pairs

a ● Ask SS what would be the typical first words when someone makes a formal speech or presentation in English, and try to elicit *Ladies and Gentlemen*. Then ask SS if they think it is also OK to say *Gentlemen and Ladies*. Then focus on the information box and go through it with the class. Elicit the equivalent expressions in SS' languages and ask them which order the words come in.

b ● Focus on the instructions. Do one with the class. Ask SS which word (from circle B) often goes with *lemon* (from circle A) and elicit *ice*. Then ask SS if we say *ice and lemon* or *lemon and ice*, and elicit that it is the former. SS then continue matching the pairs. Don't check answers yet.

c ● Focus on the task and get SS to do it individually or in pairs.

d ● **6.6** Play the CD for SS to check. Then check answers, and get SS to compare the order in these expressions with their L1.

See tapescript

6.6	CD3 Track 37
ice and lemon	right or wrong
bread and butter	now or never
thunder and lightning	more or less
knife and fork	sooner or later
black and white	all or nothing
bed and breakfast	once or twice
backwards and forwards	
peace and quiet	

Extra idea

You could get SS to test each other by saying the first word from each pair for the partner to complete the expression, e.g. **A** *ice* **B** *and lemon*.

e ● Tell SS that they are now going to look at some more word pairs which are idioms. Focus on the task and give SS time to match the idioms and meanings. Check answers.

1 C	2 G	3 F	4 H	5 E	6 A	7 B	8 D

f ● This exercise recycles some of the expressions SS have just learnt. Focus on the sentences and give SS time to complete them. Check answers.

1	now and again
2	now or never
3	safe and sound
4	peace and quiet
5	Sooner or later
6	law and order
7	sick and tired
8	thunder and lightning

7 SPEAKING

a ● **6.7** Focus on the instructions and elicit / explain that a *chunk* is a reasonable amount of something, e.g. a chunk of cheese. Point out that there will always be a pause after full stops and commas, but that there are usually more pauses, which help the listener to follow what is being said.

● Play the CD once and get SS to compare with a partner. Then play it again and check answers.

See tapescript

6.7	CD4 Track 2

Good <u>afternoon everyone</u> / and <u>thank</u> <u>you</u> for <u>coming</u>. / I'm <u>going</u> to <u>talk</u> to you <u>today</u> / about <u>one</u> of my <u>hobbies</u>, / <u>collecting comics</u>. / <u>Since</u> I was a <u>child</u> / I've been <u>mad</u> about <u>comics</u> and <u>comic books</u>. / I <u>started</u> <u>reading</u> *Tintin* and *Asterix* / when I was <u>seven</u> or <u>eight</u>. / <u>Later</u> / when I was a <u>teenager</u> / some <u>friends</u> at <u>school</u> / <u>introduced</u> me to <u>manga</u>, / which are <u>Japanese</u> <u>comics</u>. / I've been <u>collecting</u> them now / for about <u>five</u> <u>years</u> / and I'm <u>also</u> <u>learning</u> to <u>draw</u> them. /

b ● Focus on the task and suggest SS do this lightly in pencil. This will also help SS to get the rhythm right in an extended piece of speaking. Play the CD again. Pause after each sentence for SS to underline the stressed words. Check answers.

See tapescript

Extra challenge

Alternatively, you could get SS to underline the stressed words before they listen again, and they then listen to check.

● Get SS in pairs to practise reading the speech making the right pauses and stressing the right words.

c ● Focus on the instructions. Set a time limit for SS to prepare their presentation, and monitor and help with vocabulary. Encourage SS to make a plan and write notes rather than writing the presentation out in full.

Extra support

Less confident / proficient SS might want to write up their presentation, perhaps for homework, and then read it in the following class.

d ● When SS are ready to give their presentations, go through the information in the **GET IT RIGHT** box. Then divide SS into groups of three or four to give the presentations to each other. Remind them of the question and answer session after each presentation.

● Try to listen to as many SS as possible, and to give positive feedback to the whole class, as this may be one of the most challenging speaking activities that they have done.

Extra idea

If you have a video camera, you could film some or all of the presentations to show later, provided SS feel comfortable with this.

Extra photocopiable activities

Grammar
articles *p.175*
Communicative
Test your general knowledge *p.213* (instructions *p.195*)
Song
Space Oddity p.238 (instructions *p.232*)

HOMEWORK

Study Link Workbook *pp.54–56*

6
B

G uncountable and plural nouns; *have something done*
V town and cities
P word stress in multi-syllable words

Bright lights, big city

Lesson plan

In this lesson SS extend their knowledge of uncountable nouns (e.g. *luggage, furniture,* etc.) and plural nouns (e.g. *news, politics*). The context is big cities. In the first half of the lesson SS read about a US reality show where five young people from the Amish community go to live with a group of sophisticated city kids in Los Angeles. In the second half, a British travel writer gives his own personal tips about things to see and do in London. The vocabulary focus is on language to describe cities, and the pronunciation is on word stress. There is also a mini grammar focus on *have something done*.

Optional lead-in (books closed)

- Find out how much SS know about the Amish. Write the following quiz on the board.

  Amish Quiz
  1   How do you pronounce 'Amish'? Who are they?
  2   What religion are they?
  3   Where do they live?
  4   Where did they originally come from?
  5   Which century does their lifestyle come from?
  6   What are they not allowed to do?

- Give SS a few minutes to answer the questions in pairs. Then elicit ideas from the whole class, and give them the answers.

  1   /ɑːmɪʃ/; they are a religious community.
  2   Christian
  3   Mainly in Pennsylvania in the USA.
  4   Switzerland and Germany. Today they still speak a dialect of German.
  5   the 19th century
  6   Use electricity or phones, drive cars, wear modern clothes, etc.

1 READING & SPEAKING

a • Books open. Focus attention on the photos and quote (from a TV review). Elicit that the city is Los Angeles, and you could ask SS where they think the idea for the title of the programme came from (from the very successful US TV series *Sex and the City*). Elicit which of the young people in the photo are Amish and what kind of clothes they are wearing (very old-fashioned clothes).

  • Then find out what they know about the Amish and get them to predict what they think the programme is about. If you didn't do the optional lead-in above, elicit that *Amish* is pronounced /ɑːmɪʃ/.

b • Focus on the text and set a time limit for SS to read it. Then in pairs get them to discuss the questions. Check they are clear what *Rumspringa* /ˈrʌmsprɪŋə/ is, and elicit ideas in answer to the other questions.

1   Rumspringa is a time when teenage Amish have to decide whether they want to stay in the community or leave.

c • Now focus on a review of the programme (written by a TV critic). Set a time limit for SS to read it, and then with a partner they should mark the sentences T or F. Encourage them not to look back at the text unless they have no idea at all. Check answers and get SS to explain why the F ones are false.

1   T
2   T
3   F (Ruth has never seen art before – they are not allowed to do art at school)
4   T
5   F (The people who are really learning something are the city kids)
6   F (He ignored him)
7   F (The majority choose to stay)
8   T
9   T
10 F (He / she says it depends on your point of view)

Extra support

At this point you could go through the text with the class, highlighting useful expressions and eliciting / explaining the meaning of new words and phrases.

d • Finally, elicit answers to the questions from the whole class.

Extra challenge

Alternatively, get SS to discuss the questions in pairs and then get feedback.

2 VOCABULARY towns and cities

a • Focus on the first highlighted word in the text (*skyscrapers*) and get SS to explain in their own words what they are (very tall / high buildings, typical in, e.g. New York). Then ask SS if there are any skyscrapers in their town or nearest big town.

  • Get SS to continue in pairs, and then check answers.

Extra support

You could do this stage with the whole class.

parking meters = machines you put money into when you park your car
elevators = machines that carry people or goods up and down different levels in a building
art gallery = a museum full of paintings or sculptures
pavement café = a café which has tables outside on the pavement
run-down neighbourhood = part of a town which used to be nice but is now dirty, poor, etc.
beggar = a person who asks for money in the street

b ● Tell SS to go to **Vocabulary Bank** *Towns and cities* on p.155. Focus on section **1 Buildings, landmarks, and getting around**. Elicit that a *landmark* is something such as a mountain or hill which you can see clearly from a distance and helps you to know where you are (elicit an example from SS' town). In a city *landmark* could refer, for example, to a very high building or to a bridge, etc.

● Give SS time, individually or in pairs, to put the words in columns. Point out that the words in the landmarks column here are not buildings, though obviously any of the buildings might also be a landmark. Stress that they should have four words in each column (except **other buildings**), although some of the words, e.g. *cathedral* and *town hall* may also be landmarks. Check answers. You could check the meaning of some words by asking SS for an example from their town if there are any. Highlight the difference between *harbour* (= a place on the coast where ships can tie up) and *port* (= a bigger area on a coast where ships load and unload goods and passengers).

● Model and drill pronunciation where necessary.

places of worship	landmarks and sights
chapel	harbour
mosque	hill
synagogue	square
temple	statue
other buildings	**getting around**
concert hall	cable car
football stadium	cycle lane
law courts	pedestrian street
skyscraper	taxi rank
tower	

Extra idea

You could elicit other buildings, sights, or forms of transport which you think are relevant to your SS, e.g. art gallery, conference centre, trams, etc.

● Now focus on section **2 Where people live / work** exercise **a**. When SS have finished check answers.

1 E	2 A	3 B	4 F	5 D	6 C

● Highlight that *the suburbs* does <u>not</u> have a negative connotation in English (which it does in some languages) and in fact the suburbs are often the nicest part of a city to live in. Then focus on **b** and ask a few SS where they live / work.

● Now focus on section **3 City problems** exercise **a** and give SS time to write the words in the column on the right. Check answers.

1 traffic jams	5 pollution
2 slums	6 homeless people
3 vandalism	7 Beggars
4 overcrowding	8 poverty

● Elicit that *poverty* is the noun from *poor* and that the adjective from *overcrowding* is *overcrowded* (e.g. *the train was very overcrowded*).

● Focus on **b** and ask the class which of these things are problems where they live.

● Focus on **4 Adjectives to describe a town / city**. Get SS to match the sentences and check answers.

1 C	2 F	3 G	4 A	5 D	6 B	7 E

● Finally, focus on the instruction 'Can you remember the words on this page? Test yourself or a partner'.

Testing yourself

For **Where people live / work** SS can cover the column on the left, look at the sentences and remember the bold words / phrases. For **City problems** SS can cover the column on the right, look at the sentences and remember the problems. For **Adjectives to describe a town / city**, they can cover the column on the right and remember the words.

Testing a partner

See **Testing a partner** *p.20*.

Study Link SS can find more practice of these words and phrases on the MultiROM and on the *New English File Upper-intermediate* website.

● Tell SS to go back to the main lesson on *p.89*.

c ● Go through the information in the box. Then get SS to complete the sentences with nouns. Check answers.

1 entertainment	6 sights
2 homelessness	7 admission
3 accommodation	8 height
4 community	9 performance
5 violence	10 exhibition

3 PRONUNCIATION word stress in multi-syllable words

Pronunciation notes

There are few rules regarding the stress pattern of multi-syllable words except that those ending in *-tion*, (e.g. *communication*), *-sion* (e.g. *decision*), and *-ssion* (e.g. *permission*) are always stressed on the penultimate syllable. Encourage SS to use their instinct (and their dictionaries) when they come across new multi-syllable words.

a ● Focus on the task and give SS a few minutes to do it. Encourage them to say the word out loud to help them. Get them to compare with a partner.

b ● **6.8** Play the CD for SS to check. Check answers, and then give SS time to practise saying the words.

See tapescript

6.8	CD4 Track 3
accommo<u>da</u>tion	<u>neigh</u>bourhood
ca<u>the</u>dral	over<u>crow</u>ding
com<u>mu</u>nity	pe<u>des</u>trian
cosmo<u>pol</u>itan	per<u>for</u>mance
enter<u>tain</u>ment	pol<u>lu</u>tion
exhi<u>bi</u>tion	<u>pov</u>erty
<u>gal</u>lery	pro<u>vin</u>cial
his<u>tor</u>ic	<u>sky</u>scraper
<u>home</u>lessness	<u>syn</u>agogue
in<u>dus</u>trial	<u>vio</u>lence

4 GRAMMAR uncountable and plural nouns

a • Focus on the task. Encourage SS to use their instinct if they are not sure. Check answers. Elicit why the other form is wrong and that these nouns (i.e. *hair, behaviour,* etc.) are uncountable and so can't be used with *a* or in the plural, although they may not be in SS' L1.

1 long hair
2 behaviour
3 terrible traffic
4 advice
5 some bad weather
6 hard work
7 too much luggage
8 piece of news

b • Tell SS to go to **Grammar Bank 6B** on *p.142*. Go through the examples and rules with SS.

Grammar notes

uncountable nouns

• **rules 1 and 2**: SS will be familiar with the concept of countable (C) and uncountable (U) nouns, especially in the context of food, e.g. *an orange* (C), *some water* (U), etc. However, there are many non-food nouns which are uncountable in English though they may be countable in SS' L1, e.g. *information, advice, furniture.* Other uncountable nouns can be confusing because they end in *s* and so would seem to be plural, e.g. *politics, news.* Here SS are introduced to the most common nouns of this type and shown to use some of them with *a piece of* to talk about individual items, e.g. *Do you want a piece of toast? / I'll give you a piece of advice. Some* can also be used with these words to mean an unspecified amount, e.g. *Do you want some toast? I want to buy some new furniture.*
As the list of nouns here is not very long encourage SS to learn them by heart.

• **rule 3**: SS probably already know the different uses of these words passively. Words like this include many materials, and also abstract nouns like *light* and *space* which are uncountable but have a different meaning when they are countable. Check that SS know the difference in meaning between the two forms, e.g.
glass (= the material windows are made of), *a glass* (= something you drink out of)
business (= general word to describe commercial activity), *a business* (= a company)
paper (= the material), *a paper* (= a newspaper)
light (= the energy from the sun), *a light* (= a lamp)
time (= what is measured in minutes, hours, etc.), *a time* (= an occasion)
space (= where the planets are), *a space* (= an area that is empty)

plural and collective nouns

• **rule 1**: Make sure SS know the meaning of these words, e.g. *belongings* = things that are yours. Remind SS that words that can be used with *a pair of* can also be used with *some.* Other words in this group are *jeans, pyjamas, pants / knickers, tights, (sun)glasses.*

• **rule 2**: These nouns, though singular, are always used with a plural verb.

• Focus on the exercises for **6B** on *p.143* and get SS to do them individually or in pairs. Check answers after each exercise.

a 1 ✗ ~~a~~ beautiful weather
2 ✗ some lovely furniture~~s~~
3 ✓
4 ✗ The police ~~has~~ have arrested
5 ✗ ~~a~~ some new trousers / a new pair of trousers
6 ✗ The staff ~~is~~ are
7 ✓
8 ✗ The homework~~s~~ ~~were~~ was

b
1	is	6	glass
2	✓	7	some
3	look	8	some
4	work	9	progress
5	✓	10	pair of glasses

• Tell SS to go back to the main lesson on *p.89*.

c • This is an oral grammar practice activity. Focus on the task and give SS a minute to read the topics. Put SS into groups of three or four and get them to decide which order they will go in. Stress that they have to try and keep going for a minute and not 'dry up'.

• Tell SS to start, and stop them after one minute. Then get the next student in the group to take the next topic. Stop the activity either when SS have been through all the topics or each student has spoken at least twice.

5 LISTENING

a • **6.9** Focus on the instructions and go through the questions. Give SS a moment also to look at the photos and discuss what they can see.

• Play the CD once. Get SS to discuss what they think the answers are, and play once more if necessary. Check answers, and elicit what each photo shows.

1	Hampstead	6	bagel shop
2	Parliament Hill	7	rowing boat on the
3	Westminster Bridge		Serpentine
4	St Paul's Cathedral	8	squirrel
5	sunset on the roof garden	9	nightingale

6.9   CD4 Track 4

(tapescript in Student's Book on *p.129*)
I = interviewer, S = Sebastian Hope

I What advice would you give to someone visiting London for the first time?
S It's often said that London is a city of villages, for example Hampstead, even Chelsea were all villages in the past; so take some time to get to know the village you are staying in before you start to explore the famous sights.
I What's the one thing you would say someone visiting London should do or see?
S Outdoors: walk up Parliament Hill – you get far and away the best view over the city. Indoors: the British Museum. When you see what the people of ancient times were capable of, it makes you feel humble about the achievements of our own age.
I And what's the best place to have your photo taken?
S I've always liked the classic view of the Houses of Parliament either from Westminster Bridge or from the other side of the river.

I   What's your favourite landmark?

S   St Paul's Cathedral. It is so hidden-away that when you catch your first sight of it, it's always a thrill. You just turn a corner and suddenly there it is.

I   What's the best place to watch the sunset?

S   Well, the views from the bridges are always spectacular. I imagine the London Eye, by Waterloo Bridge, would be a good spot, but I am ashamed to say I have never been on it. And on a summer evening I like the roof garden of The Trafalgar Hotel just off Trafalgar Square – you can watch the city lights come on as the sun sets.

I   What's the best place to be at dawn?

S   In the summer, almost anywhere. I love the city when it's completely deserted in the early morning light. One of my favourite places to be at that time is the all-night bagel shop on Brick Lane. I love queuing on the pavement outside for a salmon and cream cheese bagel in the early morning, because then it means I must have been out all night doing something fun or interesting. But in winter the best place to be at dawn is in bed – definitely!

I   What would be a good thing to do on a scorching hot day?

S   Getting a boat on the Serpentine or in Battersea Park is one of my favourite things, and another of my favourite places, the London Aquarium, is somewhere where you can escape from the heat into a world of water and air conditioning.

I   What's a good thing to do which is absolutely free?

S   Walking in the parks. London's parks deserve their fame. I love walking in Hyde Park. It always reminds me of my childhood – I have memories of feeding the squirrels there.

I   What do you think is the most romantic place in London?

S   In Kensington, Knightsbridge, and Chelsea, residential squares have enclosed gardens. They're magical places at any time of day, like secret gardens, but at night you can often hear nightingales singing – they're the only birds that sing at night. It's very romantic.

b ● Focus on the instructions and give SS time to read the questions. Then play the CD again. Pause at the end of each of Sebastian's answers, and check the answer to each question in turn. Ask SS follow-up comprehension questions where appropriate.

> 1   That many areas of London used to be villages. You should get to know the area you are in rather than trying to get to know the whole of London.
> 2   Go to the British Museum.
> 3   The Houses of Parliament.
> 4   It is hidden between other buildings so you walk round a corner and suddenly find it.
> 5   The bridges and the London Eye.
> 6   Because it's completely deserted.
> 7   Because it's air conditioned and there is a lot of water.
> 8   It reminds him of his childhood.
> 9   They are the only birds that sing at night. They sing in the enclosed gardens in residential squares.

c ● **6.10** Focus on the task. Play the CD and pause after the first extract. Elicit from SS what they think the word is, how they think it is spelt and what they think it means. Repeat with the other extracts.

> 1   humble (= not proud, not thinking that you are better than someone else)
> 2   hidden-away (= not easy to find)
> 3   ashamed (= feel very embarrassed about something)
> 4   queuing (= standing in a line waiting for something, e.g. in a shop)
> 5   feeding (= giving food to)

6.10   CD4 Track 5

> 1   When you see what the people of ancient times were capable of, it makes you feel humble about the achievements of our own age.
> 2   It's so hidden-away that when you catch your first sight of it, it's always a thrill.
> 3   But I'm ashamed to say I have never been on it.
> 4   I love queuing on the pavement outside for a salmon and cream cheese bagel in the early morning.
> 5   I have memories of feeding the squirrels there.

Extra support

At this point, if you have time, you may want to replay the interview (6.9) for SS to have a final listen with the tapescript on *p.129*.

d ● Put the SS in pairs and get them to answer the questions. Point out that if they live in a city, they can answer the questions about it; if not, about another one they know well. SS can either talk about different towns but preferably they should answer them together about one they both know well. Get feedback.

Extra support

You could do this as a whole class activity about the town / city you are in, eliciting ideas from SS and seeing if the others agree.

6 SPEAKING & WRITING

a ● Focus on the questionnaire and give SS time to go through the questions, and think about how they would answer them.

b ● Focus on the instructions and put SS in pairs, **A** and **B**. If you have uneven numbers, have a three with two local people talking to a tourist. Encourage SS to 'get into' the role of the tourist and to get the 'local person' to explain / give more information.

● Set a time limit for **A** to be the tourist with questions 1–3. Monitor and help **B** where necessary. Then get them to swap roles with **B** asking 4–6.

⚠ In a multilingual class get SS to talk about the place where they are studying.

Extra support

Demonstrate the activity first taking the role of the tourist and asking the class the first question. Then write some expressions for giving advice on the board, e.g. *If I were you, I'd...I think you should...Why don't you ...? I suggest you ...*, etc.

c • Focus on the instructions. Tell the **A**s first to say if they agreed with the information **B** gave them in questions 1–3, and then vice versa for questions 4–6.

• Finally, get some feedback about how SS answered some of the questions.

d • You could get SS to do this in class (as exam practice) or alternatively set it for homework as a mini project. If SS do it at home, encourage them to add in graphics, photos, etc. and to produce a mini brochure using the headings from the questionnaire.

MINI GRAMMAR *have something done*

• Focus on the examples and go through the rules. Highlight that *have something done* is usually when you pay someone else to do something for you, e.g. *have your car repaired*.

• Focus on the exercise and elicit from the class the answer to the first one. Then give SS a few minutes to complete the exercise and check answers.

> 1 We're **going to have** our flat **painted** / We're **having** our flat **painted**
> 2 **had** it **cut**
> 3 **have** it **cleaned**
> 4 **have** your car **serviced**
> 5 **have** it **repaired**
> 6 **have** my passport **renewed**
> 7 **having** a new garage **built**

• You may want to give your SS further practice with this structure. If so, there is a photocopiable activity on *p.188*.

Extra photocopiable activities

Grammar
uncountable and plural nouns *p.176*
Communicative
Talk for a minute *p.214* (instructions *p.195*)

HOMEWORK

Study Link **Workbook** *pp.57–59*

6 C   **G** quantifiers: *all* / *every*, etc.
      V science
      P changing stress in word families

Eureka!

Lesson plan

In this lesson SS learn the rules for using a variety of quantifiers correctly. Most of these SS will have seen before, so although rules are given, SS should be encouraged to use their instinct. The topic is a light-hearted look at science. In the first part of the lesson SS read and hear about so-called 'Eureka moments', and why some people are creative thinkers. In the second half of the lesson, they read extracts from the Bill Bryson book *A short history of nearly everything*, where he describes how scientists have historically suffered in order to make their discoveries. The vocabulary focus is on words related to science, and pronunciation deals with changing stress in words families (e.g. *science, scientist, scientific*).

Optional lead-in (books closed)

- Write on the board
  'Eureka!'
  1 Who said it?
  2 What was he doing at the time?
  3 What had he just discovered?
- Put SS in pairs to answer the questions. Check answers.

  > 1 Archimedes /ɑːkəmɪːdɪːz/ (a Greek mathematician)
  > 2 He was getting into the bath. The bath was quite full and the water overflowed.
  > 3 That the volume of an object can be calculated by the amount of water it displaces.

1 LISTENING & SPEAKING

a ● Books open. Focus on the text. Explain that it describes an experiment which involves the picture, and that they are going to do it. Set a time limit for SS to read the first paragraph and do the experiment themselves. Get feedback and ask whether the elephant 'disappeared' for them.

b ● Now focus on the instructions. Elicit ideas from SS, and then get them to read the second paragraph. (If you did the optional lead-in, just get SS to read to find out what kind of people have 'Eureka moments', and why most people don't.) Check answers.

  > Archimedes /ɑːkəmɪːdɪːz/ said it when he was having a bath. He realized that the volume of an object can be calculated by the amount of water it displaces.
  > People who are 'creative thinkers'.
  > Most people don't have them because they have 'psychological blind spots' which prevent them from seeing the obvious solution to a problem.

c ● **6.11** Focus on the photo and ask SS what they think is happening. Elicit ideas but don't tell them the answer.
  ⚠ If any of your SS know about this experiment, ask them not to tell the others yet.

- Focus on the three questions, and then play the CD once or twice if necessary. Check answers.

> 1 Because they concentrate too hard on the small job they are working on and don't see the bigger picture.
> 2 Volunteers were asked to watch a bit of a basketball match and count the number of passes made by one team. In the middle of the game somebody dressed as a gorilla walked in, but half of the volunteers didn't notice because they were just concentrating on counting the passes.
> 3 None of them saw the gorilla.

6.11   CD4 Track 6

(tapescript in Student's Book on *p.129*)
P = presenter, S = Steven Hutchinson
P And tonight on the book programme we're reviewing a book called *Did you spot the gorilla?* by Dr Richard Wiseman, who's an expert on creative thinking. With us tonight to talk about this book is Steven Hutchinson, a freelance journalist. So Steven, what exactly is Dr Wiseman's main message?
S Well, Dr Wiseman's theory is that most people don't think creatively because they concentrate so hard on the small, specific job that they are working on that they don't see the bigger picture. That's what the gorilla experiment proves.
P What was the gorilla experiment?
S Well, a study was carried out by Daniel Simons and Christopher Chabris at Harvard University in 1999. He got volunteers to watch a 45-second film of people playing basketball. There were two teams. One team were wearing black T-shirts and the other team were wearing white ones. He gave the volunteers a simple task: they just had to count the number of passes made by the white team. Afterwards, he asked them how many passes they had counted and most people got the answer right. Then he asked them if they had seen anything unusual and at least half of them said no. And that's really amazing. Because during the film, while the two teams were playing basketball, a woman dressed as a gorilla walked onto the court and she beat her chest at the camera, and then slowly walked off the court. And half the volunteers just didn't see it!
P That's incredible. Why not?
S Because they were so busy trying to count the passes that they didn't notice the gorilla! Dr Wiseman repeated this experiment many times and the result was always the same. In fact, he actually tried it on a group of top British scientists and not one of them saw the gorilla.
P How extraordinary!

---

d ● **6.12** Focus on the instructions and photos, and elicit what they are (Post-it™ notes, IKEA (a large furniture store) and an easyJet (a low-cost airline) plane). Ask SS why they think these ideas were innovative.

- Before SS listen, pre-teach *glue* (= a sticky substance used for joining things together), *weak* (= the opposite of strong) and *book token* (= a piece of paper that can be exchanged for books in a shop). Then play the CD once. Get SS to discuss the questions, and then play it again. Check answers.

1 That we normally only focus on what we're looking for and we don't see anything else.
2 Post-it notes were invented by someone who was trying to make a strong glue, but when the glue he made was not strong enough, he didn't throw it away but simply thought of a good use for the weak glue. IKEA sells cheap furniture but which is well designed, something that people thought was not possible, and easyJet is an example of a low-cost airline which people also thought was an impossible concept.
3 To do the opposite of what they normally do, e.g. try to think of articles that nobody will find interesting. Maybe this will actually give them an idea for something really interesting.
4 A book containing the first chapters of 15 other books, and a book token with which you can buy the book you like best.

6.12   CD4 Track 7
(tapescript in Student's Book on *p.129*)
s The gorilla experiment is a perfect demonstration that we normally only focus on what we're looking for, and don't see outside it, so we sometimes miss really important discoveries which are right in front of us, we just don't see them. That's why when something is invented people often say, 'Why didn't anybody think of that before?' – well, they didn't because they didn't think creatively.
P Dr Wiseman gives some examples of people who he says *are* creative thinkers, doesn't he?
s Yes, people like the man who invented Post-it™ notes. He was actually trying to develop a really strong kind of glue, but he could only manage to make a very weak one. But instead of just thinking, 'Oh that's no good' he actually thought of a way of using the weak glue to make Post-it™ notes, notes that would stick to something but not too much. Or the man who set up IKEA, the furniture company – I mean for years people had been wanting cheap furniture that was well designed, but nobody did it. Or the idea of cheap air travel. People just accepted that it was impossible. But then somebody said 'It *is* possible, and I'm going to do it'. And that's how we got low-cost airlines like easyJet.
P Can we make ourselves creative thinkers?
s Yes, Dr Wiseman has lots of tips on how we can become more creative. One of the things he recommends is to try to do the *opposite* of what you normally do. For example, he told a group of journalists to try to think of articles that *nobody* would find interesting – he said that from that, possibly a brilliant idea for something interesting will come up. His book is full of tips – it's really worth reading.
P Has he had any 'Eureka moments' himself?
s Yes, actually he's thought up a great idea for book lovers. His idea is to print a book which contains the first chapters of 15 other different books. This book has a book token in the back, a voucher that you can use to buy another book. The idea is that you read the beginnings and then choose which book you want to read more of and buy it with the book token.
P What a great idea! That's creative thinking for you.

Extra support

If there's time, you could get SS to listen to the two recordings again with the tapescripts on *p.129* so that they can see exactly what they understood / didn't understand. Explain / translate any words or phrases that SS aren't sure about.

e ● Focus on the test **Are you a creative thinker?** Set a time limit for the first two parts of the test of, e.g. two minutes, for SS to do it individually. Then set a time limit of three minutes for SS to do the drawing question and then give them a few moments to fill in the clock. Get SS to compare with a partner.

f ● Now tell SS to go to **Communication** *Are you a creative thinker?* on *p.118* and check their results. Get feedback to find out which SS seem to be creative thinkers, e.g. ask what their score was for 1, what number they had chosen for 2, etc.

2 GRAMMAR   quantifiers: *all / every*, etc.

a ● Focus on the instructions. Point out to SS that they are going to be looking at a lot of quantifiers, all of which they have seen before but haven't studied the rules of use, but they may instinctively know what sounds right.
  ● Give SS a few minutes to circle the right form and then check answers. If SS ask why, say that they are now going to the **Grammar Bank** to find out.

1 every year	4 all
2 All living things	5 Everything
3 Both	6 nor

b ● Tell SS to go to **Grammar Bank 6C** on *p.142*. Go through the examples and rules.

Grammar notes

quantifiers
SS will have frequently seen and heard all the quantifiers they learn here and should know what they mean. They should also have an instinct for how to use them correctly. For example, a phrase like *every animals* should *sound* wrong even if they don't know why.
The rules here have been simplified (i.e. there are some other uses or positions which we haven't referred to). If SS find so many rules a bit overwhelming, focus particularly on the examples and encourage them to use their instinct when they do the exercises and are not sure which form to choose.

all, every, most
● **rule 3**: Point out that *most* can't be used in mid-position, e.g. NOT ~~the people in this class are most women.~~

no, none, any
SS should know the difference between *no* and *none*, but the use of *none of* + pronoun / noun and *any* meaning it doesn't matter what / who, etc. may be new.
SS may confuse *none* and *any*, e.g.
A *How many chocolates are there?*
B *None* (NOT ~~Any~~). *Any* cannot be used on its own like this to mean zero quantity.
SS may also confuse *none* with the other meaning of *any* (= it doesn't matter which).
Compare two possible answers to this question:
Which of your sweaters can I borrow? *None of them* (= not one of them) and *Any of them* (= it doesn't matter which one you borrow. I don't mind).

C

both, neither, either

You may also want to point out that you can use *not* + *either* instead of *neither … nor*, e.g. *Neither Tim nor Andrew can come. Tim can't come and Andrew can't (come) either.* This is also more informal than *neither … nor* which can sound quite formal in spoken English.

- Focus on the exercises for **6C** on *p.143* and get SS to do them individually or in pairs. Check answers after each exercise.

> **a** 1 Most of   5 every
> 2 no   6 any
> 3 Everything   7 None
> 4 Most   8 Anybody
>
> **b** 1 … to either Greece or Italy.
> 2 Neither of us…
> 3 either the 6th or the 7th of May. (either on the 6th or the 7th)
> 4 Both (of) my children could read… (My children could both read…)
> 5 Neither my brothers nor my sisters…

- Tell SS to go back to the main lesson on *p.93*.

c - This is an oral grammar practice activity. Focus on the quiz and give SS a few minutes to do it with a partner. Check answers.

> 1 c – figures vary, but it's about 97%
> 2 a – together they make up 71% of air
> 3 c – we only absorb a part of the oxygen in the air, so we can breathe some out again
> 4 b – about 90–120 minutes in total
> 5 a
> 6 a

3 READING

a - Focus on the instructions and pictures. Set a time limit for SS to read and match the paragraphs and pictures. Check answers.

> 1 C   2 A   3 B   4 D
> Two (Karl Scheele and Marie Curie) died as a result of their research.

b - Focus on the questions and set another time limit for SS to re-read the texts and answer the questions. Get SS to compare with a partner and then check answers.

> 1 B   2 A   3 C   4 D   5 A   6 D   7 B   8 C

c - **6.13** Focus on the instructions and give SS time to look at the words with a partner. Then play the CD, pausing after each word. Get SS to practise the pronunciation and then elicit / explain the meaning, and ask if the word is similar in SS' L1. Get SS to underline the stressed syllable.

lenses = curved pieces of glass or plastic that make things larger, smaller, or clearer
phosphorus = a chemical (element)
elements = simple chemicals which consists of atoms of only one type, e.g. oxygen
chlorine = a chemical (element) often used to keep swimming pool water clean
substance = a type of solid, liquid, or gas that has particular properties, e.g. a chemical substance
mercury = a poisonous chemical element that used to be used in thermometers
cyanide = another highly poisonous chemical
toxic = containing poison
radiation = powerful and very dangerous rays that are sent out from radioactive substances
radioactive = sending out radiation
lead /led/= a chemical element, which is a heavy soft grey metal used especially in the past for water pipes.
craters = large holes in the top of a volcano or holes in the ground caused by, e.g. a bomb explosion
comets = masses of ice and dust which moves around the sun and looks like a bright star with a tail

- Highlight that the spelling of *lead* is the same as the verb *lead* /liːd/, but the pronunciation is different.

Extra support

Deal with any other vocabulary problems that SS have and ask them which words, apart from the ones in exercise **c**, they would like to try and remember from the text.

> **6.13**   CD4 Track 8
> lenses
> phosphorus
> elements
> chlorine
> substance
> mercury
> cyanide
> toxic
> radiation
> radioactive
> lead
> craters
> comets

4 VOCABULARY & PRONUNCIATION   science; changing stress in word families

a - Focus on the words in the list and elicit that they are all words for people who study or work in a certain area of science (highlight the *-ist* ending). Then give SS time to match them to what they study. Check answers.

> 1 a physicist
> 2 a biologist
> 3 a chemist
> 4 a geneticist
> 5 a geologist

b - Now focus on the table and get SS to complete the adjective and subject columns.

Pronunciation notes

The stress pattern in multi-syllable words does not normally change when a prefix (e.g. *un-*, *dis-*) is added. However, when a suffix is added to change the part of speech (e.g. to make a verb into an adjective), the stressed syllable sometimes changes.

c • **6.14** Go through the ⚠ box. Then play the CD for SS to check and underline the stressed syllable. Check answers, and elicit that the adjectives from *science*, *biology* and *geology* have the stress on a different syllable from the base word.

1 scientist	scientific	science
2 chemist	chemical	chemistry
3 biologist	biological	biology
4 physicist	physical	physics
5 geneticist	genetic	genetics
6 geologist	geological	geology

6.14   CD4 Track 9

1 scientist
  scientific
  science
2 chemist
  chemical
  chemistry
3 biologist
  biological
  biology
4 physicist
  physical
  physics
5 geneticist
  genetic
  genetics
6 geologist
  geological
  geology

---

d • Get SS to practise saying the word families aloud.

Extra support

Drill the pronunciation with the whole class first and them get them to practise in pairs.

e • Now focus on the verbs in the list and elicit that, apart from *make* and *do*, the others are all regular. Give SS time to complete the sentences. Remind them that they may have to put the verb in the past, and underline the stressed syllable in the new verbs and words in bold.

1 discovered radiation	6 Pharmaceutical ...
2 do experiments in a	develop
laboratory	7 do ... research
3 made ... discovery	8 do tests and trials
4 proved his theory	9 volunteer to be guinea
5 invented	pigs

f • **6.15** Play the CD for SS to check. Elicit / explain *laboratory* (= the place where scientists work), *theory* (= a formal set of ideas which is intended to explain why sth happens or exists), *trials* (= the process of testing sth), *guinea pigs* /ˈɡɪni pɪɡz/ (= a person used in medical or other experiments).

• Then get SS to practise saying the sentences.

6.15   CD4 Track 10

1 Pierre and Marie Curie discovered radiation in 1900.
2 Scientists do experiments in a laboratory.
3 Archimedes made an important discovery in his bath.
4 Isaac Newton's experiments proved his theory that gravity existed.
5 The telephone was invented in the 1870s.
6 Pharmaceutical companies try to develop new drugs to cure illnesses and diseases.
7 Scientists have to do a lot of research into the possible side effects of new drugs.
8 Before a company can sell a new drug they have to do tests and trials to make sure they are safe.
9 People can volunteer to be guinea pigs in clinical trials.

---

5 SPEAKING

• Focus on the instructions and put SS in pairs. Give them time to read the questions.

Extra idea

Get SS to choose two or three questions to ask you.

• Then get SS to answer the questions together. Encourage them to ask each other for more information where relevant. Monitor and correct pronunciation where necessary.

• Get feedback from the whole class on some of the questions, especially the last two.

• Finally, tell SS to go to *Phrasal verbs in context File 6* on *p.157* and complete the phrasal verbs which have come up in this File. (Answers *p.155*)

Extra photocopiable activities

Grammar
quantifiers *p.177*
Communicative
Biology quiz *p.215* (instructions *p.195*)
Vocabulary
Alphabet race *p.228* (instructions *p.222*)

HOMEWORK

Study Link **Workbook** *pp.60–62*

Lesson plan

In the first part of this lesson the person interviewed is John Bigos, the managing director of London Duck Tours limited, which offer guided tours of the city of London. Duck Tours, which originated in the USA, are so called because they use World War II amphibious vehicles called DUCKs, which can travel on land and water. In the second part of the lesson, people in the street are asked what their favourite city is, and which city they would most like to visit.

Study Link These lessons are on the *New English File Upper-intermediate* DVD / Video which can be used instead of the class CD (See Introduction *p.9*). SS can get more practice on the MultiROM, which contains more of the short street interviews with a listening task and tapescripts.

Optional lead-in (books closed)

- Write on the board

  What big cities have you visited as a tourist?

  Did you go on any kind of guided tour? Did you enjoy it? Why (not)?

  Put SS in pairs and give them a few moments to answer the questions, or do them with the whole class.

THE INTERVIEW

a • Books open. Focus on the photos and get SS to tell you what they can see.

> A vehicle that can travel on land and water, Nelson's Column, a statue of Nelson Mandela, and the Houses of Parliament.

- Ask if anyone has ever been on a Duck tour and explain why the boats are called Ducks (Their official name in World War II was DUKWs but they were nicknamed Ducks because they could go on land and water).

- Now focus on the task and on the glossary. Go through it with the class eliciting from them how to pronounce the words and phrases.

b • **6.16** Focus on the task. Put SS in pairs and give them time to read the questions. Encourage SS not to write anything down when they listen the first time. They should listen and try to get the gist of what he is saying, and then discuss the questions with their partner.

- Play the CD once (**Part 1**). Give SS time to discuss the questions and tell each other what they understood. Then play the CD once or twice more. This time SS might want to jot down things they heard to help them remember the answers to the questions. Check answers.

> 1 You go both on land and on the river in one tour. There are only 30 people on each tour so it is quite intimate.
> 2 They have to drop the anchor and then wait to be rescued, sometimes by another Duck.
> 3 People who have fallen or jumped off one of the bridges.

> 4 Her coat got wet and she complained, and wanted the company to have it cleaned for her. Luckily she had to return home soon after and so there wasn't time to have the coat cleaned.

6.16 CD4 Track 11

(tapescript in Student's Book on *p.129*)

I = interviewer, J = John Bigos

I John Bigos is the managing director of London Duck Tours Limited. This company use Ducks, renovated World War II amphibious vehicles, which can travel on land and water. What makes a Duck tour better than a normal sightseeing tour?

J What makes Duck tours more interesting in terms of the tour as opposed to other tours is the ability to be able to go on the land and the river in one tour at the same time. That has a great benefit for all our clients. We also have a very small vessel which only takes 30 people and that allows you to have a much more intimate relationship with your clients, which makes it a wonderful experience, which you don't get when you go on ordinary, pre-determined computerized tours.

I Some people might say that taking tourists on such a busy river is a bit dangerous. Have you ever had any accidents?

J In terms of accidents, we have had breakdowns, that means that we have to drop the anchor in the river which is similar to having to use the brake on the land and we've had to recover both our boat and our passengers, but that fortunately is quite a rare thing, but it adds to the fact that the tour is unique and no one else can do it. It's an experience, which can include being recovered by another Duck.

I Do you ever have to rescue other people on the river?

J When we are on the river, we are one of the most frequent users of this part of the river and people will often fall or jump off Westminster Bridge, Lambeth Bridge… or indeed Vauxhall Bridge and therefore we will be within the vicinity and often have to rescue people who have either fallen off accidentally or who have deliberately tried to commit suicide, so in terms of the river it is a very serious river with a very fast-flowing tide and we treat it with the utmost respect.

I Do you have many difficult customers?

J We do have people who come in a very unprepared manner, for example a lady in a mink coat who then gets wet and she asks for the mink coat to be specifically cleaned, which would cost us a whole day's revenue, which, the coat was very expensive and the good news is that she was travelling abroad back to her homeland and unfortunately we were unable to get it cleaned within the time that she asked, and in the circumstances, it didn't cost us any money. So those sort of people can be difficult as well as your normal customers who either don't think they've had the service they requested or the tour was not up to a standard that they thought they would like, probably because they're afraid of water.

Extra challenge

You could use the tapescript above to elicit more detailed answers from SS.

c ● **6.17** Focus on the task and play the CD once (**Part 2**). Give SS time to discuss the questions and what they understood. Then play the CD once or twice more. Check answers.

> 1 It's one of the most popular sights. It's in Parliament Square. It's the first statue that has been erected while someone is still alive.
> 2 It's another very popular sight. People like the fountains and Nelson's Column.
> 3 It's another popular sight and is the place where the Duck boats go into the water.
> 4 This is one of his personal favourite sights – he thinks it's a beautifully designed building.
> 5 The year when women got the vote – quite recent, he thinks. He mentions this in the context of the statue of Emmeline Pankhurst.
> 6 He thinks the fact that there are over 200 different cultures is one of the best things about London.
> 7 The standard of service in London isn't as high as in other big cities. For him this is one of the worst things.
> 8 An example of the bad service which needs to be improved – there are a lot of delays.

6.17   CD4 **Track 12**

(tapescript in Student's Book on *p.130*)

I What are the most popular sights?

J The most popular sights that get people really excited are Parliament Square, where we have the new Nelson Mandela statue, and that's the first statue that I'm aware of that has been erected whilst someone is still alive, and that's very exciting. Additionally we have a number of heroes in our country and Trafalgar Square with all the fountains and Nelson and Nelson's Column, really excite people, and finally we obviously have MI6, which is where our vessels go into the water and it is also where the film *The Living Daylights* and *The World is not Enough* started where the boat came out of a second floor window and as a 'Duck' we replicate that in our own style.

I What are your personal favourite sights on the tour?

J I personally like the Houses of Parliament, because I think it is a beautifully designed building and it's got some very very interesting features. I also favour the statue of Emmeline Pankhurst because that is quite interesting in so much as it was only in 1928 that women were given the vote and yet it seems so many years ago, and then in terms of large sights, obviously things like Buckingham Palace and Horse Guards are very interesting as well, because of the history.

I What do you think is the best and worst thing about London for a tourist?

J I think the best thing is the fantastic variety and depth of culture that we have in our capital city here. We have over 200 different cultures and nations who live here in the centre of London, and it makes for a fantastic cosmopolitan city with so much variety that it is impossible to get bored. It is a fabulous capital to come to as a tourist.
In terms of the worst things for tourists in London, I don't think our capital has yet reached the standards of service that a lot of other cities have, where you don't get good quality food at a reasonable price on time quite often and you have a lot of delays in terms of travel and congestion and therefore there are many things that can still be done to improve the quality of service for a fantastic capital city.

---

d ● **6.18** This exercise gives SS intensive listening practice in deciphering phrases where words are often run together, and introduces them to some common expressions often used in spoken English. Focus on the phrases and give SS time to read them. Play the CD, pausing after the first phrase and replaying it as necessary. Elicit the missing words, and then the meaning of the whole phrase. Repeat for the other three phrases.

> 1 as **opposed to** (= compared with)
> 2 **quite a** rare thing (= something which is quite rare. We often use *quite a / an* before a noun + adjectives, e.g. *It's quite a nice day today. We watched quite an interesting film last night.*)
> 3 **aware** of (= that I know about)
> 4 **a number** (= some, several)

6.18   CD4 **Track 13**

1 What makes Duck tours more interesting in terms of the tour, as opposed to other tours…
2 …but that fortunately is quite a rare thing
3 that's the first statue that I'm aware of that has been erected whilst someone is still alive…
4 Additionally, we have a number of heroes in our country…

---

e ● Tell SS to go to *p.129* and to look at the tapescript for the interview. Play the CD (**Part 1** and **Part 2**) again and tell SS to read and listen at the same time. Deal with any vocabulary problems and get feedback from SS on what parts they found hard to understand and why, e.g. speed of speech, elision, pronunciation, etc.

● Finally, focus on the question. Get SS to answer in pairs or as a whole class. Then get feedback from the whole class.

IN THE STREET

a ● **6.19** Focus on the photos of the people and elicit impressions (e.g. *How old do they look? What job do you think they do?*, etc.). All the people have appeared in previous Files, except for Matandra. Tell SS that they were all interviewed in Covent Garden, a busy shopping area in Central London.

● Focus on the task and on the cities and ask them where, e.g. Cape Town, Stockholm and Delhi are (South Africa, Sweden, India). Play the CD once, and get SS to compare ideas. Then play it again pausing after each speaker to check answers. Elicit which was their favourite city, and which they would like to visit. Elicit that Harley only mentions London (she then says anywhere in Australia, but doesn't mention a city).

> Barcelona 2 (Anne, would like to visit)
> Cape Town 1 (Theresa, would like to visit)
> Casablanca 4 (Matandra, would like to visit)
> Delhi 2 (Anne, favourite)
> London 5 (Harley, favourite)
> New York 3 (Agne, favourite)
> Rome 4 (Matandra, favourite)
> Stockholm 1 (Theresa, favourite)
> Sydney 3 (Anne, would like to visit)
> Harley only mentions one city.

(tapescript in Student's Book on *p.130*)
**I = interviewer, T = Theresa, A = Anne, Ag = Agne,
M = Matandra, H = Harley**
Theresa
I   What's your favourite city?
T   I would have said Prague actually, but I've recently
    been to Stockholm a couple of times and I loved it.
    Stockholm is fantastic. It's built on 14 islands, lots
    of water, which I love, lots of interesting museums,
    Stockholm's lovely.
I   Which city would you most like to visit?
T   I went to Cape Town earlier on this year and we were
    only there for five days and there was so much that I
    didn't see that I would love to go back to Cape Town
    and see Robben Island and some of the apartheid
    museums and learn more about Nelson Mandela.
Anne
I   What's your favourite city?
A   Probably Delhi, because of the difference in culture
    and the monuments that are there and the people, and
    looking at the cultural differences of how we live and
    how they live. And I just find everyone so nice and so
    friendly.
I   Which city would you most like to visit?
A   I would most like to visit Barcelona because I've heard
    the shopping's very good.
Agne
I   What's your favourite city?
AG It would be New York. I like the hustle and bustle and
    the 'busyness' and just the overall feeling of being in
    that city – it's just really nice, it just makes you feel
    really alive all the time, lots and lots of things to do
    and it just goes on, it just doesn't stop.
I   Which city would you most like to visit?
AG I'd like to go to Sydney, see what that's like.
Matandra
I   What's your favourite big city?
M   My favourite big city. I risk sounding partial but it
    would have to be my home town, it would have to
    be Rome. I think it's, you know, a lot of the reasons
    are... no need to explain. I think it's very happening,
    more than people think and it's the right compromise
    between a laid-back lifestyle and, you know, the
    positive aspects of living in a metropolis.
I   Which city would you most like to visit?
M   Either Casablanca or a place like that. I'm just
    fascinated with that part of the world.
Harley
I   What's your favourite city?
H   Em. London. Because it's got all the shops. So I can
    come here and go shopping.
I   Which city would you most like to visit?
H   Any, really, any, I'd like to go to Australia, anywhere
    hot, anywhere with shops. Anywhere.

b ● Focus on the task and give SS time to go through the
    sentences. Check SS understand *change their mind* (=
    think sth different) in question 3. Play the CD once. Get
    SS to compare what they think. Play it again if necessary
    and check answers.

1   Anne
2   Harley (for shopping)
3   Theresa (it used to be Prague)
4   Agne (it makes her feel alive)
5   Matandra

c ● **6.20** Focus on the phrases and give SS time to read
    them. Play the CD, pausing after the first phrase and
    replaying it as necessary. Elicit the missing word, and
    then the meaning of the whole phrase. Repeat for the
    other three phrases.

1   **would most like** (= Barcelona is the city I would like
    to visit the most.)
2   **hustle and bustle** (= idiomatic expression meaning
    busyness, lots of people and noise)
3   **laid-back lifestyle** (= a relaxing lifestyle)
4   **Anywhere** hot, **anywhere** (= any place, I don't mind
    which)

1   I would most like to visit Barcelona.
2   I like the hustle and bustle
3   It's the right compromise between a laid-back lifestyle
    and you know, the positive aspects of living in a
    metropolis.
4   Anywhere hot, anywhere with shops.

d ● Tell SS to go to *p.130* and to look at the tapescript for
    IN THE STREET. Play the CD again and tell SS to read
    and listen at the same time. Deal with any vocabulary
    problems and get feedback from SS on what parts they
    found hard to understand and why, e.g. speed of speech,
    elision, pronunciation, etc.

  ● Finally, focus on the two questions that the interviewer
    asked the people, and get SS to interview each other in
    pairs. Then get feedback from the whole class.

HOMEWORK

Study Link **Workbook** *p.63*

6 WRITING A REPORT

Lesson plan

In this writing lesson SS learn to write a short report. The writing skills focus is on using headings to separate out paragraphs.

a ● Focus on the report. Highlight the fact that one paragraph (the second) has a heading, and tell SS to read the report and then in pairs invent headings for the other three paragraphs. Encourage SS to try to copy the style of the heading that is there.

Extra support

Suggest that SS begin the headings for 1 and 3 with *When…* and point out that section 4 is different from the first three as it is more general.

● Get feedback and write the different suggestions on the board. You could get SS to vote for the best heading.

> **Possible answers**
> 1 When you want to eat out cheaply / When you don't want to spend much money
> 3 When you are celebrating something / When it's a special occasion
> 4 Some general advice / Things to remember about eating out in London

b ● Focus on the **Useful language** box. Then get SS to scan the report to find synonyms for the expressions in the box. Tell them not to write them in until they are sure they are right. Check answers.

> Most / **The majority of**
> (Cinemas) are usually / **tend** to be
> In general / **Generally speaking**
> Almost always / **nearly always**

c ● Focus on the instructions. Get SS to brainstorm useful information in both categories. Elicit feedback and write their ideas on the board.

WRITE a report

Go through the instructions. Then either get SS to plan and write the report in class (set a time limit of about 20 minutes) or get them just to plan in class and write at home, or set both planning and writing for homework.

If SS do the writing in class, get them to swap their reports with another student to read and check for mistakes before you collect them all in.

Test and Assessment CD-ROM

CEF Assessment materials
File 6 Writing task assessment guidelines

---

6 REVISE & CHECK

For instructions on how to use these pages, see *p.33*.

GRAMMAR

> 1 b 2 a 3 b 4 b 5 a 6 c 7 c 8 a
> 9 c 10 c

VOCABULARY

> **a** 1 provincial   4 genetics
>   2 poverty   5 scientific
>   3 government
> **b** 1 quiet   4 twice
>   2 sound   5 pieces
>   3 forwards
> **c** 1 do   4 made
>   2 made   5 do
>   3 do
> **d** 1 harbour – the others are places of worship
>   2 cable car – it's a form of transport, and the others are places where you can get a taxi / bus / plane
>   3 landmark – the others describe areas in a town
>   4 square – the others are buildings
>   5 genetics – it is the subject and the others are people

PRONUNCIATION

> **a** 1 neighbourhood (it's /eɪ/)   4 both (it's /θ/)
>   2 prove (it's /uː/)   5 synagogue (it's /g/)
>   3 research (it's /ɜː/)
> **b** bio<u>log</u>ical, <u>phys</u>icist, cosmo<u>pol</u>itan, <u>out</u>skirts, in<u>dust</u>rial

CAN YOU UNDERSTAND THIS TEXT?

> **a** 1 B 2 F 3 D 4 E 5 C 6 A
> **b** **about to** = going to
>   **devastating** = extremely shocking
>   **overuse** = use too much
>   **counteract** = to do sth to reduce or prevent the bad effects of sth
>   **podium** = a small platform that a person stands on when giving a speech or conducting an orchestra

CAN YOU UNDERSTAND THESE PEOPLE?

> **a** 1 c 2 c 3 b 4 b 5 a
> **b** 1 F 2 T 3 T 4 F 5 F

1 **A** Excuse me, are you one of the conference organizers?

   B Yes, I am. Is there anything you need?

   A Yes, I'm giving a presentation here in half an hour and I'm just trying out the equipment. There seems to be something wrong with the projector. Do you see? The image is very dark. I've been trying to increase the contrast but it's not really any better. I'm not sure what the problem is. Is there anyone here who could have a look at it, a technician or someone?

   B Well, there is a technician, but actually he already had a look at it for the previous speaker and there wasn't anything he could do. He suggested drawing all the curtains so that less light comes into the room. Would you like us to do that for you?

   A Well, if nothing else can be done, yes.

2 **A** So what made you move here?

   B I love my country and my city, but it's not an easy place to live. We have a lot of problems there.

   A What kind of problems?

   B For a start it's very overcrowded and there's a real housing shortage. As a result, there are a lot of homeless people, a lot of beggars on the streets and, unfortunately, a lot of muggings. There are many car accidents too – nobody ever stops at traffic lights and people drive much too fast.

3 Right, now remember the bus will be leaving to go back to the hotel in two hours. Now first I'd like to give you a bit of advice. Three hours isn't enough to see everything – you'd need at least two days for that or more. Some of you have told me that you want to see the Roman room – that's room 49 but there's so much to see that I don't really want to confuse you by recommending anything specific. What I suggest is that you get an information leaflet from the ticket office and have a look at what there is in each room and decide what you're *most* interested in seeing, and leave the rest for another time. You're sure to come here again. But do leave yourselves time to have a look at the shop, which is on the right of the entrance, as there are lots of really interesting and imaginative gifts, apart from the usual postcards.

4 Now science is all about testing – and about looking closely at things. Some scientists use microscopes to take a close look. Do you know what a microscope is? Well, we're just going to use a simple piece of paper. Like this. We're going to cut out a square in the middle to make a window, which we'll do like this by folding the piece of paper in half, and then we're going to look at a leaf through the window we've made. Then later we're going to go outside and have a look at a tree trunk. So have you all got your piece of paper? Right, now fold it in half…

5 This next painting is of Sir Isaac Newton, the famous physicist and mathematician. Newton was born in 1643 at Woolsthorpe Manor in Woolsthorpe-by-Colsterworth, a small village in the county of Lincolnshire. He was born to a family of farmers who owned animals and land, thus making them fairly wealthy. According to his own later accounts, Newton was born prematurely and no one expected him to live. His father, also named Isaac Newton, had been a yeoman farmer and had died three months before Newton's birth, at the time of the English Civil War. When Newton was three, his mother remarried and went to live with her new husband, leaving her son in the care of his maternal grandmother, Margery Ayscough.

P = presenter, L = Lucy

P According to a recent survey, we are a nation on the move. 115,000 people a year are leaving the city and heading to the country in search of a better life. It seems like a logical thing to do, less crime, better health, less stress, and lower house prices. Six years ago Lucy Beck, a 41-year-old IT consultant made a life-changing decision and moved from a flat on a busy road in town, to a house with four acres of land in the middle of the country. Hello Lucy.

L Hi.

P So, what did your friends think when you told them you were moving?

L They all thought I was mad. They thought I'd have a nightmare journey getting to work, for example, and that I'd be lonely, miss my friends, things like that.

P And has any of that happened?

L Not at all. I made an arrangement with my company to work from home more, so I only have to go into the office once a week. And my friends come and stay with me at weekends, so in many ways I see them more often. Besides, I've made friends with the locals in the village here and it's great. I mean it's one of the benefits I hadn't expected. I'd always thought about the obvious things, such as beautiful countryside and a better standard of living, but one of the things I value most is the fact that the village seems to keep hold of the traditional values in life. We all try to help each other as much as we can. For example if I do something for someone in the village, then they'll probably give me eggs or potatoes as a thank you. I certainly never had that when I lived in town.

P There must be some disadvantages though, a downside?

L Well, in the early days I had a few problems. I wasn't on mains electricity and there were a lot of power cuts. Also at that time the local shop didn't open on Sunday – and the pub doesn't serve food. So, I had to learn to be much more organized than before. When I lived in town if I hadn't had time to go shopping, I just used to order a takeaway or go out to eat. But that's not an option these days.

P Anything else?

L Yes, I do think that if you move to live in the country, you need your own car. Public transport isn't that good in my village. The bus comes through here only two or three times a day depending if it's a weekday or weekend, so you really do need to have your own transport.

P But otherwise it's all positive?

L Absolutely. It was the best decision I've ever made.

Test and Assessment CD-ROM

File 6 Quicktest
File 6 Test

7
A

G structures after *wish*
V *-ed / -ing* adjectives and related verbs; expressions with *go*
P sentence rhythm

I wish you wouldn't…!

File 7 overview

Lesson **7A** introduces the construction *I wish…!* to talk about present and past regrets, and to express annoyance. Lesson **7B** looks at clauses of contrast (e.g. *Even though… In spite of…*) and clauses of purpose (e.g. *so that…, in order to…*), and there is a mini grammar focus on *whatever, whenever,* etc. Finally, lesson **7C** revises and extends SS' knowledge of relative clauses. The vocabulary areas in this File are *-ed / -ing* adjectives, business and advertising, and prefixes.

Lesson plan

The grammatical aim of this lesson is to teach SS to be able to use the construction *I wish…* to express annoyance (*I wish my sister wouldn't borrow my clothes*) and to express present and past regrets (*I wish I were taller, I wish I hadn't said that*). The topic in the first half of the lesson is things which annoy us in our daily lives, e.g. shop assistants talking on the phone while you are waiting to be served. In the second half of the lesson SS read about, and listen to, people talking about things they regret. The vocabulary focus is different ways of expressing feelings, with a verb or with an *-ed* or *-ing* adjective, e.g. *It annoys me / I'm annoyed / It's annoying*. The pronunciation focus is on sentence rhythm.

Optional lead-in (books closed)

- Write on the board **THINGS THAT REALLY ANNOY US**
- Explain to the class that there are things that other people do which really annoy us. Give an example of your own, e.g. *people who drive too close behind you* and write it on the board.
- Then elicit more ideas from the class, e.g. six sentences, and leave them on the board.

1 SPEAKING

a ● Books open. Focus on the magazine article and the task. Point out that 'pet hates' is a colloquial expression for things that annoy you. If you did the optional lead-in, tell SS to read the list of annoying things to see if any of the ideas you elicited are on the board.

- Put SS in pairs. If you didn't do the optional lead-in, focus on the task and give SS a few minutes to discuss the things in the list and to choose their top three.

- Get feedback from the class. Tell the class your 'Top three' too. You could find out which is the top annoying habit for the whole class.

- Focus on the **GET IT RIGHT** box and go through the list of expressions. Highlight that all the expressions are more or less synonymous, but that *It drives me mad…* and *It drives me up the wall…* are more colloquial and are used when something seriously annoys us.

b ● Focus on the task. Tell SS individually to think of three more things which annoy them in their daily life, e.g. at home, at school, at work, in the street, driving, on public transport, etc. Help with any vocabulary SS may need.

- Then put SS in groups of three to compare their answers with other SS using the expressions in **GET IT RIGHT**. Get feedback from the whole class. You could tell SS some of your own personal 'pet hates'.

2 GRAMMAR *wish* + past simple and *would*

a ● ⬤ **7.1** Focus on the instructions. Explain that SS are going to hear four short conversations and the first time they listen they have to decide which of the annoying habits in the magazine article the people are talking about.

- Play the CD once, pausing after each conversation for SS to write their answers. Play the recording again if necessary.

> 1 People reading over your shoulder on a bus or train.
> 2 When you get a trolley in the supermarket and one of the wheels is broken.
> 3 When you get a taxi and the driver asks <u>you</u> the best way to go.
> 4 Cyclists who ride on the pavement and nearly knock you over.

7.1   CD4 Track 18

1 A I wish you wouldn't do that!
  B Do what? I'm not doing anything.
  A You know perfectly well. You can read the paper when I've finished with it.

2 A Oh that's so typical!
  B Is it broken?
  A Yes, can't you see – one of the wheels doesn't work. I wish I had a pound for every time I've chosen the one broken one. I'd be a millionaire by now.

3 A Which way do you want to go? Through the centre of town or on the ring road?
  B I don't know. Whichever way's the quickest.
  A I wish I knew, but it depends on the traffic.
  B Well, you decide. You're the expert.

4 A Oh my God. He nearly hit me.
  B Yes, he was going a bit fast.
  A I wish they would ride in the road. I mean the pavement's supposed to be for pedestrians. I'm sure it's illegal.
  B Yeah but he was only a child. It's a bit dangerous for him to ride in the road.

---

b ● Focus on sentences 1–4 which have been taken from the four conversations. Play the CD again pausing to give SS time to try and complete the sentences. Play the recording again for SS to check their answers. Elicit the missing words from the class.

1	you wouldn't do	3	I knew
2	I had	4	they would ride

c ● Focus on the task and give SS a few moments to decide their answers. Check answers.

speakers **1** and **4**

d ● Tell SS to go to **Grammar Bank 7A** on *p.144*. Go through the examples and rules with the class for *wish* + past simple and + *would* only. Model and drill the example sentences.

Grammar notes

These structures after *wish* are new for SS and have been separated in two parts. First, SS learn to use *wish* to refer to the present / future, and later to refer to the past to express regrets.

wish* + past simple, *wish* + *would* / *wouldn't

The first thing to establish is the meaning of *wish* (= to want sth to happen or to be true, even through it is impossible / unlikely, e.g. I *wish I was taller, I wish my hair wasn't so curly*). Depending on SS' L1 you may want to contrast *wish* and *hope*. For something more likely to happen we use *hope*, e.g. I *hope I'll pass the exam*. NOT *I wish I passed the exam*.

● **rule 1**: In the first person *wish* is often used as an exclamation. You can use *that* after *wish*, e.g. *I wish that I had more money*, but it is nearly always left out, especially in speech.

● **rule 2**: Highlight the information in the ⚠ box as *I wish I would be…* is a typical mistake.

The information about *If only* in the box applies to all uses of *wish*. *If only* is simply a stronger expression, e.g. *If only it would stop raining!* is stronger than *I wish it would stop raining*. We normally use an exclamation mark after *If only…!*

● Focus on the exercises on *p.145* and get SS to do exercise **a** only, individually or in pairs. Check answers.

a	1	had	5	would buy
	2	lived	6	knew
	3	would drive	7	had
	4	would stop	8	would turn

● Tell SS to go back to the main lesson on *p.100*.

e ● This is an oral grammar practice activity. Focus on the task and demonstrate the activity by giving personal examples for each of the sentences. Give SS time to complete the sentences and monitor while they do this making sure they are writing sentences which are grammatically correct and which make sense. Remind SS not to use *would* after *I wish I…*

Extra support

Write your personal examples on the board.

● Now get SS to compare what they have written with their partner. Then get some quick feedback from the class.

3 VOCABULARY *-ed / -ing* adjectives and related verbs

a ● Focus on the information box and go through the examples with the class.

Extra support

Give SS another example as follows:

verb: *to bore*, adjectives: *bored / boring*, e.g. *This programme bores me. / It's a boring programme* = *it's a programme which makes me feel bored*.

● Then focus on the instructions to the exercise and give SS time to do the task either individually or in pairs. Check answers, modelling pronunciation where necessary.

1	frustrated	7	worries
2	embarrassing	8	amused
3	irritates	9	disappointed
4	depressing	10	thrilling
5	terrified	11	shocked
6	tiring	12	exhausting

b ● Focus on the instructions and on the example (number 1). Drill pronunciation of the two adjectives and elicit the meaning (very happy). SS learnt this adjective in **Vocabulary Bank** *Feelings*. Elicit that *She was a delightful person* here = that 'She made me feel delighted'.

● Give SS time to do the task. They have seen *scary* before (lesson 3C) and should know *stressful*. They may not know *impressive* and *offensive*. Check answers and elicit which syllable is stressed.

2	<u>scar</u>y	4	<u>stress</u>ful
3	im<u>press</u>ive	5	of<u>fen</u>sive

Extra challenge

Alternatively, you could call out the sentences in **a** and **b** in random order saying 'blank' instead of the adjective / verb and getting the class to call out the missing word, e.g. *Jack wasn't very BLANK when we laughed at his new tie. I'm very stressed by my new job. My job is very BLANK.*

c ● Put SS in pairs. Focus on the task which activates orally some of the adjectives in **a** and **b**. Give SS a couple of minutes to think about which of the subjects they can talk about and then tell SS to take turns to talk. You could tell SS some of your own experiences too.

4 READING

a ● Focus on the task and elicit ideas from the class. Some older SS may remember seeing Paula Wilcox in the TV series *Man about the house*.

In the first photo she is in her fifties and in the second she is 19. Her hair is lighter and thinner, and she has wrinkles.

b ● Focus on the instructions. Tell SS to read the text once all the way through before doing the task. Then get them to compare their answers with a partner and then check answers.

A 4	**B** 2	**C** 1	**D** 6	**E** 3	**F** 5

c ● Now tell SS to read the article again and give them time to do the task. Point out that the numbers in brackets refer to the paragraph numbers in the article. Check answers and drill pronunciation where necessary. Highlight that *loads of* is a very commonly used colloquial expression.

1 reminds
2 gorgeous
3 a waste
4 loads of
5 witty
6 the life and soul (of the party)
7 gentle
8 challenges

d ● Do this as a whole class activity. Give SS time to quickly read the first paragraph again and then elicit SS' ideas for a sentence which sums up her advice. Write two or three of these on the board and get the class to decide which they think is best. Then repeat this process for the other paragraphs.

Possible answers
1 Be happy with the way you look when you are young.
2 If you become famous, enjoy it – don't be embarrassed by it.
3 Be a good listener, not just a good talker.
4 Try to understand <u>why</u> someone is treating you badly. It's probably because they are unhappy.
5 Make the most of your time when you are young enough to learn things.
6 If you are offered the chance to do something, go for it!

5 GRAMMAR *wish* + past perfect

a ● Focus on the task and give SS time to find the six examples first.
  ● Elicit the sentences onto the board.

Here she talks about things she wishes she had known then… (intro)
I wish I'd known what I was going to look like thirty years later…(para 1)
I wish I'd known that it's possible to enjoy the good things about fame… (2)
I wish I had learned sooner how to listen to people properly… (3)
I wish I had been more gentle with people in that situation… (4)
I wish I'd spent more time on my piano lessons. (5)
I wish I had always said yes to challenges. (6)

  ● Now ask SS the two questions and elicit answers.

The tense is the past perfect.
The wishes refer to the past.

b ● Tell SS to go to **Grammar Bank 7A** on *p.144*. Go through the examples and rules with the class for *wish* + past perfect. Model and drill the example sentences.

Grammar notes

wish + **past perfect**
Here SS extend their knowledge of how to use *I wish* and learn to use it with the past perfect to express a regret. With this meaning *wish* can be used with all persons (*I wish I had…, I wish you had…*, etc.)

● Focus on the exercises for **7A** on *p.145* and get SS to do exercise **b**, individually or in pairs. Check answers.

b	1 I wish I hadn't left my camera in the car.
	2 I wish I had set my alarm clock.
	3 I wish I hadn't bought a house in the country.
	4 I wish I hadn't dropped my phone in the bath.
	5 I wish I had been able to go to your party.
	6 I wish I'd had a holiday last year.

● Tell SS to go back to the main lesson on *p.102*.
c ● This is an oral grammar practice activity. Focus on the task and get SS to do it with a partner. Highlight that they should write sentences referring to the past using *I wish* + the past perfect (<u>not</u> *wish* + past simple) Tell them to try and think of at least two sentences for each situation. Get feedback.

Possible answers
1 I wish I had saved a bit of money. / I wish I hadn't spent so much.
2 I wish I hadn't had my hair cut so short. / I wish I hadn't changed the colour.
3 I wish I had learned more English at school. / I wish I had been to extra classes.
4 I wish she hadn't left me. / I wish we hadn't had an argument.

6 PRONUNCIATION sentence rhythm

Pronunciation notes

This exercise gives practice in using correct stress and rhythm in *wish* sentences. Remind SS that the key to speaking English with a good rhythm is stressing the information carrying words in a sentence more strongly and the other words, e.g. articles, less strongly.

a ● **7.2** Focus on the task. Tell SS to close their books. Play the CD once the whole way through. Then play it again pausing after each sentence to give SS time to write the sentences. Finally, play the CD once more for SS to check their sentences. Elicit the sentences onto the board.

7.2	CD4 Track 19
1 I wish I hadn't eaten all the chocolates.	
2 I wish you wouldn't drive so fast.	
3 I wish it wasn't my turn to cook tonight.	
4 I wish it would stop raining.	
5 I wish we didn't have to go to the party.	
6 I wish I'd bought that jacket I saw yesterday.	

b ● Now play the CD again, pausing between each sentence for SS to underline the stressed words. Play the recording again if necessary. Check answers.

1 I <u>wish</u> I <u>hadn't eaten all</u> the <u>chocolates</u>.
2 I <u>wish</u> you <u>wouldn't drive</u> so <u>fast</u>.
3 I <u>wish</u> it <u>wasn't my turn</u> to <u>cook tonight</u>.
4 I <u>wish</u> it <u>would stop raining</u>.
5 I <u>wish</u> we <u>didn't have</u> to <u>go</u> to the <u>party</u>.
6 I <u>wish</u> I'd <u>bought</u> that <u>jacket</u> I <u>saw yesterday</u>.

Extra support

Play the CD for SS to listen and repeat the sentences
trying to copy the rhythm.

c ● Focus on the task and give SS time to match the six *I
      wish* sentences to sentences A–F. Do the first one with
      the class as an example.

| A 5 | B 2 | C 4 | D 1 | E 6 | F 3 |

● Put SS in pairs and get them to practise the six two-
  lined dialogues. Encourage SS to concentrate on getting
  the rhythm right, especially in the *I wish…* sentences.

7 LISTENING & SPEAKING

a ● (7.3) Focus on the task and go through sentences A–E.
   ● Tell SS just to listen the first time and try to get the gist
     of what they hear without writing anything.
   ● Play the CD all the way through once. Then play it
     again pausing after each speaker giving SS time to
     choose their answer. Get SS to compare with a partner.
     Elicit the answers from the class.

| A 5 | B 4 | C 1 | D 3 | E 2 |

7.3   CD4 Track 20

(tapescript in Student's Book on *p.130*)
1 When I was a young man, about 17, I was working
in Spain as an electrician for the German car company
Mercedes. A man from the engineering company,
Bosch, visited Mercedes and he liked the way that I
worked and he offered me a job in Germany. I suppose
it is what you would call 'an apprenticeship'. I would
have learnt to become an engineer. I really wanted to
do it, but my parents didn't want me to leave home
and go and work in a foreign country. In those days
not many people did that. So in the end I didn't go. But
I really wish that I'd taken that job because I think it
would have opened doors for me and my professional
life would have been more fulfilling.
2 Three years ago I was going to take part in a dance
competition. I was a bit pale so I decided to go to
a suntan studio the day before the competition. As
I didn't have much time and I wanted to get a nice
tan really quickly, I stayed under the lamp about 20
minutes. Unfortunately, that was too long and I got
burnt. The top and skirt I wore the next day for the
competition were really skimpy and so everyone in the
audience could see how red my skin was. I felt really
stupid and really wished I hadn't done it.
3 I really wish I'd been able to know my grandmother
better. She died when I was 12, and since then I've
discovered that she must have been a fascinating
person, and there are so many things I would love to
have been able to talk to her about. She was Polish but
she was in Russia, in St Petersburg, during the Russian
Revolution, and she knew all sorts of interesting

people at the time, painters, writers, people like that. I
was only a child so I never asked her much about her
own life. Now I'm discovering all about her through
reading her old letters and papers, but I wish she had
lived longer so that I could have talked to her about
those times face-to-face.
4 The only thing I really regret is not having had
the courage to chat up a guy who I saw at a party last
summer. I really fancied him – he was very good-
looking – but I just wasn't brave enough to start a
conversation. I wish I'd tried. I'm absolutely positive
we would have got on well. And now it's too late – he's
engaged to another girl!
5 My biggest regret is how I spent my time at
university. I studied English Literature, which was
something I was quite interested in, but it certainly
wasn't the most important thing in my life. I played
a lot of sport, I played in a band, and listened to a
lot of music, but I also spent most of my time either
socializing or asleep. And in terms of studying, I just
did the bare minimum – I read what I had to, but
never anything more. I only went to the compulsory
lectures, never the optional ones and I left all my essays
until the last minute and kept them as short as I could.
OK, I passed my exams and I got my degree in the end,
but I've always regretted not taking more advantage
of those three years. I wish I'd realized at the time that
this was a unique opportunity to read lots of novels, to
learn about great writers and to listen to people who
really knew what they were talking about. Now I'm
working and have small children, I don't have time to
read anything.

b ● Focus on the task. Check SS understand *skimpy* in 2
     (= very small and not covering much of your body),
     fancied in 4 (= was attracted to) and *the bare minimum*
     in 5 (= a colloquial expression meaning as little as
     possible). Play the CD again pausing after each speaker
     to give SS time to compare with a partner. Play each
     part again if necessary. Check answers.

1 *Mercedes and Bosch* – He was working for Mercedes
   (the German car company) when a man from Bosch
   (the German engineering company) offered him a job.
   It would have opened doors for me – Taking the
   job would probably have given him better work
   prospects when he came back to Spain.
2 *The top and skirt I wore were really skimpy.* – Her
   clothes didn't cover much of her body so everyone
   could see how burnt she was.
3 *The Russian Revolution* – Her (Polish) grandmother
   was in Russia during the revolution and met
   many interesting people (painters, writers). Her
   granddaughter wishes she could have talked to her
   about this time.
   Old letters – By reading her old letters the
   granddaughter is discovering about her life.
4 *I really fancied him.* – She was attracted to the man.
   Now it's too late. – It's too late because the man she was
   too afraid to chat up is now engaged to be married.
5 *I just did the bare minimum.* – He studied as little as
   possible, just doing enough to pass his exams but
   not more.
   This was a unique opportunity. – Being a student was
   a once in a lifetime chance to learn about literature

from people who really knew about the subject and a chance to read a lot of novels.

Extra support

If there's time, you could get SS to listen to the CD with the tapescript on *p.130* so they can see what they understood / didn't understand. Translate / explain any new words or phrases.

c ● Focus on the instructions and on the web page. When SS have read it, tell them if you identify with any of the regrets, and elicit from SS whether any of them do.

d ● Focus on the task, and give SS time to think of three regrets. Emphasize that they should all be about something which happened (or didn't happen) in the past. Then get SS to work with a partner and compare regrets. Encourage SS to ask each other for more information.

● Get some feedback from the class about some of the SS' regrets. Tell SS about some of your regrets too.

8 VOCABULARY expressions with *go*

a ● Focus on the two sentences in the box and elicit what they mean from the class.

going on = happening
go for it = take the opportunity (that is being offered to you)

b ● Focus on the task and give SS time to complete the sentences. Check answers and get SS to say what the expression means in each case.

1 go through = look at again, revise
2 goes wrong = stops working normally
3 gone back on = not keep a promise or your word
4 go without = live without having
5 go with = match, complement
6 go to sleep = fall asleep
7 go far = be successful
8 gone off = stop liking something / someone
9 go for it (see **a**)
10 going on (see **a**)

c ● Now get SS to ask and answer the questions with a partner.

9 🔘 7.4 SONG 🎵 *If I could turn back time*

● This song was originally recorded by the American singer Cher in 1989 and was a worldwide hit. For copyright reasons this is a cover version. If you want to do this song in class, use the photocopiable activity on *p.239*. The song links to the lesson as the singer regrets something she did in the past and wishes she could 'turn back time.'

7.4   CD4 Track 21

If I could turn back time

If I could turn back time
If I could find a way
I'd take back those words that have hurt you
And you'd stay

I don't know why I did the things I did
I don't know why I said the things I said
Pride's like a knife it can cut deep inside
Words are like weapons, they wound sometimes

I didn't really mean to hurt you,
I didn't want to see you go
I know I made you cry, but baby

Chorus
If I could reach the stars
I'd give them all to you
Then you'd love me, love me
Like you used to do
If I could turn back time

My world was shattered, I was torn apart
Like someone took a knife and drove it deep in my heart
You walked out that door, I swore that I didn't care
But I lost everything darling then and there

Too strong to tell you I was sorry
Too proud to tell you I was wrong
I know that I was blind, and darling...

Chorus

Extra photocopiable activities

Grammar
wish p.178
Communicative
Wishes A *p.216* (instructions *p.196*)
Wishes B *p.217* (instructions *p.196*)
Song
If I could turn back time p.239 (instructions *p.232*)

HOMEWORK

Study Link **Workbook** *pp.64–66*

G clauses of contrast and purpose; *whatever, whenever,* etc.
V business and advertising
P changing stress in nouns and verbs

A test of honesty

Lesson plan

This lesson introduces clauses of contrast after expressions like *Even though… In spite of …,* etc. and clauses of purpose or reason after expressions like *so that…, in order to…,* etc. There is also a mini grammar focus on using *whatever; whenever;* etc. The topic and lexical area of the lesson is business and advertising. In the first half of the lesson SS read and listen about a man who set up a business selling bagels in companies and unintentionally designed an interesting test of honesty. The honesty link is continued in the second half of the lesson where the focus is on honesty (or dishonesty) in advertising and how companies try to trick us through the use of misleading advertisements.

Optional lead-in (books closed)

- Write the word **HONEST** and elicit the grammar (it's an adjective), the pronunciation (/ɒnɪst/ – stress that the *h* is not pronounced) and the meaning (always telling the truth / never stealing or cheating). Then elicit the opposite adjective (*dishonest*), and the noun (*honesty*).

- Then ask the class if they are usually honest about the following…

  1 not cheating in an exam
  2 playing a game (e.g. cards) or in sport
  3 saying what they really think if someone asks their opinion about, e.g. their clothes

1 READING & LISTENING

a ● Books open. Focus SS' attention on the photos and the title of the article, and quickly elicit ideas from SS as to what the article could be about.

b ● Set SS a time limit to read the text to find out what it is about. Quickly go through sentences 1–7 so that SS know what they will later be trying to remember. Tell SS not to worry at this stage about unknown words but just to try to get the gist of the article.

- When SS have finished reading the text put them in pairs and tell them to cover the article, and together discuss what they can remember about the article using sentences 1–7 to help them. Check answers.

> 1 He worked in Washington for the US navy (analysing weapon expenditures). / He was senior level / He earned good money. / He was head of the public research group.
> 2 At the office Christmas party his colleagues introduced him as 'the guy who brings in the bagels' (instead of 'the head of the public research group').
> 3 It started as a way of rewarding his employees when they won a contract. Then it became a habit. Every Friday he bought in bagels and cream cheese.
> 4 People from other departments wanted bagels too. Finally he was bringing in so many bagels that he needed to charge to cover his costs. 95% of people paid.

> 5 They thought he was mad ('had lost his mind').
> 6 Within a few years he was delivering thousands of bagels (8,400) a week to many companies (140).
> 7 He discovered how honest his customers were and what kind of people and companies stole more or less.

- There is some new vocabulary in this text and you might want to point out / elicit some of this to the class, e.g. *tackle* (line 2) = try and solve, *treating his employees* (line 9) = rewarding, *recoup his costs* (line 14) = cover his costs, *oversight* (line 17) = when you forget to do something, *quit his job* (line 19) = leave his job, *pitch* (line 22) = sales idea, *leftovers* (line 25) = food which isn't eaten, *versus* (line 32) = compared with.

c ● Focus on the task and give SS time, in pairs, to predict the answers to questions 1–6. They can do this orally. Get some feedback from the class on what they think the right answers will be.

d ● [7.5] Tell SS that they are now going to listen to the economist. You may want to point out before they listen that he often says *an office* when he is referring to a department in a company. Play the CD. Pause after the first section, and give SS a few moments to circle a, b, or c. Check the answer and find out how many SS had guessed correctly. Then repeat with the next section, until they have answered all five questions.

> 1 b (80–90%)
> 2 Smaller offices were more honest.
> 3 The cash box has hardly ever been stolen.
> 4 They cheated more during bad weather.
> 5 They cheated more before Christmas because many people often feel anxious and stressed before this holiday and don't look forward it.
> 6 Executives cheated more than lower status employees.

> [7.5]   CD4 Track 22
>
> (tapescript in Student's Book on *p.130*)
>
> When Paul Feldman started his business, you know, he really thought that at least 95% of the people would pay for their bagels. This was presumably because that was the payment rate that he got in his own office. But in fact this rate wasn't representative at all. I mean in his office, most people paid probably just because Feldman worked there himself, and they knew him personally, and probably liked him.
> So when Feldman sold his bagels in other offices, he had to accept less. After a while, he considered that a company was 'honest' if over 90% of the people paid. Between 80 and 90% was what he considered to be normal, you know, the average rate. He didn't like it, but he had to accept it. It was only if a company habitually paid less than 80% – which luckily not many did – that he would feel he had to do something. First he would leave a note, sort of giving them a

141

warning, and then, if things didn't improve, he would simply stop selling there. Interestingly, since he started the business, the boxes he leaves to collect the cash have hardly ever been stolen. Obviously in the mind of an office worker, to steal a bagel isn't a crime – but to steal the money box is.

So what does the bagel data tell us about the kind of offices that were not honest, the ones that *didn't* pay? Well, first of all, it shows that smaller offices are more honest than big ones. An office with twenty to thirty employees generally pays 3 to 5% more than an office with two to three hundred employees. This seems to be because in a smaller community people are more worried about being dishonest – probably because they would feel worse if they were caught.

The bagel data also suggests that your mood, how you feel, affects how honest you are. For example, the weather is a really important factor. When the weather is unusually good, more people pay, but if it's unusually cold or rainy, fewer people pay. And people are also affected by public holidays, but in different ways – it depends *which* public holiday. Before Christmas and Thanksgiving, people are *less* honest, but just before the 4th of July and Labour Day they are *more* honest. This seems to be because holidays, like the 4th of July, are just a day off work, and people always look forward to them. But Christmas and Thanksgiving are holidays where people often feel quite stressed or miserable. So their bad mood makes them less honest.

The other thing Feldman believes affects how honest people are, is the morale in an office. When employees like their boss and like their job, then the office is more honest. He also thinks that the higher people are promoted, the less honest they are. He reached this conclusion because over several years he'd been delivering three baskets of bagels to a company that was on three floors. The top floor was the executive floor, and the lower two floors were people who worked in sales, and service, and administrative employees. Well, it turned out that the least honest floor was the executive floor! It makes you wonder whether maybe these guys got to be executives because they were good at cheating!

But in general the story of Feldman's bagel business is a really positive one. It's true that some people *do* steal from him, but the vast majority, even though no-one is watching them, are honest.

e ● Focus on the task and quickly run through the sentences. Play the CD again, pausing after each paragraph to give SS time to choose the right answer. Then play it again the whole way through for SS to check their answers. Elicit answers from the class.

> 1 c 2 a 3 b 4 c 5 c

Extra support

If there's time, you could get SS to listen to the CD with the tapescript on *p.130* so they can see what they understood / didn't understand. Translate / explain any new words or phrases.

f ● Focus on the first question and elicit answers from the class. Is there consensus of opinion about what proportion would pay?
 ● Ask the other question (*How do you feel about people …?*) one by one to the class and elicit opinions. Again try to find out what the majority opinion is. Give your opinion too.

Extra challenge

Alternatively, you could get SS to discuss the answers to these questions in pairs before getting open class feedback of opinions.

2 VOCABULARY business and advertising

a ● Focus on the task and give SS a couple of minutes or so to do this. Check answers.

> 1 head
> 2 colleague
> 3 boss
> 4 employees
> 5 customers

b ● Tell SS to go to **Vocabulary Bank** *Business and advertising* on *p.156*. Focus on section **1 Verbs and expressions** and give SS time to do exercise **a** individually or in pairs. Check answers, and model and drill pronunciation where necessary.

> 1 set up   6 expand
> 2 manufacture   7 become
> 3 market   8 take over
> 4 import   9 launch
> 5 export   10 merge

 ● Now focus on **b**. Give SS time to put the word(s) into the right column. Check answers and drill pronunciation where necessary. Highlight that *a deal* = a business agreement and *make somebody redundant* = to take somebody's job away from them because he / she isn't needed any more or because, e.g. the company is losing money and needs to cut down on staff. Compare this with *sack somebody*, which SS learnt in *New English File Intermediate,* which means take someone's job away from them because they have done something wrong.

> **do**   business (with), a deal, a job, market research
> **make**   a decision, money, a profit, somebody redundant

 ● Now focus on section **2 Organizations and people a** and **b**, and give SS time to match the words and definitions. Check answers and drill pronunciation. You might also want to teach the word *worker* which is often used to describe someone who works in an office or factory, etc.

> **a** 1 a chain
>   2 a business / company / firm
>   3 a multinational
>   4 head office
>   5 a branch

b 1 the staff
2 an employee
3 an employer
4 a customer
5 a client
6 a colleague
7 the (managing) director (MD)
8 the owner
9 a head of department
10 a manager

- Now focus on section **3 Advertising** and give SS time to match the words and pictures. Check answers and drill pronunciation. Make clear the difference between *slogan*, which is something which is written or spoken, and *logo*, which is a design or symbol which companies use to identify their product.

1 logo   **4** slogan
2 commercial   **5** junk mail
3 advertisement **6** cold-calling

- Finally, focus on the instruction 'Can you remember the words on this page? Test yourself or a partner'.

Testing yourself
For **Verbs and expressions a** SS can cover the words on the left and try to remember them by reading the words on the right. For **b** they can look at the words in the box and remember if they are *do* or *make*. For **Organizations and people** they can cover the words on the left and read the definitions to remember the words. For **Advertising** they can cover the words / phrases and look at the pictures to remember.

Testing a partner
See **Testing a partner** *p.20*.

Study Link SS can find more practice of these words and phrases on the MultiROM and on the *New English File Upper-intermediate* website.

- Tell SS to go back to the main lesson on *p.105*.

c • This is an oral grammar practice activity. Focus on the quiz and give SS time to do this with a partner before feeding back answers from pairs. In the second part where they tell you names of companies or businesses, get them to tell you what the company or business does.

1 *an employer* is the person who employs other people to work for him / her. *An employee* is the person who is contracted to work for someone else.
2 *a customer* is normally used for someone who buys a product (e.g. in a shop) or a service (e.g. a meal in a restaurant). *A client* is normally used for someone who pays a professional for a service, e.g. a lawyer or accountant.
3 *the boss* is the person in charge of a group of people. *The staff* are a group of people who work for a business / company.
4 *set up* a company = start a company; *take over* a company = when one company takes control of another
5 *sack somebody* = tell somebody to leave their job because they work badly or have done something wrong; *make somebody redundant* = tell somebody to leave their job because there is not enough work for them

6 *export a product* = selling a product to another country, *import a product* = buying a product from another country

3 PRONUNCIATION   changing stress in nouns and verbs

a • Focus on the information box and go through it with the class highlighting the two examples. Then get the class to practise saying the nine words (*increase, decrease*, etc.) both ways, first as a noun then as a verb, e.g. noun: <u>increase</u>, verb: in<u>crease</u>.

b • Focus on the task and give SS time to mark the stress on the highlighted words. Don't check answers at this stage as SS are going to hear the words.

c • **7.6** Now play the CD for SS to check their answers. You could pause after each sentence and elicit the right answers as you go or check answers after you have played the recording.

1 <u>progress</u>
2 pro<u>gress</u>ing
3 ex<u>port</u>
4 <u>export</u>s
5 A re<u>fund</u>   B <u>refunds</u>
6 in<u>creased</u>, <u>increase</u>
7 pro<u>duce</u>
8 pro<u>duced</u>
9 tran<u>sport</u>
10 <u>transport</u>

7.6	CD4 Track 23

1 We're making good progress with the report.
2 The new building is progressing well.
3 We export to customers all over the world.
4 One of our main exports is wine.
5 **A** Can you refund me the cost of my ticket?
   B Sorry, we don't give refunds.
6 Sales have increased by 10% this month, so there has been an increase in profits.
7 The demand for organic produce has grown enormously.
8 Most toys nowadays are produced in China.
9 They are planning to transport the goods by sea.
10 There has been a rise in the number of people using public transport.

Extra support
You could get SS to listen and repeat after the CD.

MINI GRAMMAR   *whatever, whenever*, etc.

- Focus on the example from the article (*Honest workers or thieves?*) and on the explanation. Then go through the rules with the class regarding *whatever, whichever*, etc. giving SS these examples.
*You can have **whatever** you want* = it doesn't matter what you want you can have it.
*He offered me two watches and said I could have **whichever** one I wanted.* = it doesn't matter which one
*I'll buy it **however** much it costs* = The price doesn't matter.

However hard I try, I can never remember birthdays. =
It doesn't matter how hard I try…
I always take my identity card **wherever** *I go.* = it doesn't
matter where I go…

- Highlight that *whichever* is used instead of *whatever*
  when there is a very limited choice, usually two or three.
- Focus on the exercise and give SS a couple of minutes or
  so to do it. Check answers.

1	wherever	4	however
2	whoever	5	Whatever
3	Whenever	6	whichever

Extra support

If you think your class need more practice, use the extra
photocopiable exercises on *p.189*.

4 GRAMMAR clauses of contrast and purpose

a • Focus on the advert and the questions, and set SS a
time limit to read it and decide if they would buy the
product. Elicit answers from the class.

> SS will probably say they wouldn't try the product as it
> seems to be very unlikely that it would work.

- Then ask SS if they think it's a real advert, and explain
  that in fact it isn't a real advertisement (*Pumavite*
  doesn't exist), but it was produced by the British
  Advertising Standards Authority to draw attention to
  fraudulent adverts.

b • Focus attention on the magazine article. Set SS a time
limit to read it once quite quickly and to tick the
paragraphs which talk about a trick that the *Pumavite*
advert used. Tell SS not to worry about the gaps in the
text at this stage and not to use the glossary yet.

> Buy now while stocks last! ✓
> The camera never lies, or does it? ✓
> Trust me I'm a doctor (or a celebrity) ✓

c • Focus on the task and on the phrases which SS have
to try and insert in the text. Suggest that SS read each
paragraph carefully one by one, using the glossary to
help with new words, and completing the gaps as they
go. Although this is 'new grammar', SS should have seen
most of the highlighted expressions before, and the
context will help them to gap fill the text even if they are
unsure of the exact meaning of some of the highlighted
phrases. Get SS to compare their answers in pairs before
checking answers.

1 H	2 G	3 A	4 D	5 C	6 E	7 F	8 B

Extra support

You could do the first paragraph with the class as an
example.

d • Focus SS' attention on the eight clauses in the text
(which begin with the highlighted phrases) and ask
them to decide if they express a contrast or a purpose
(= the aim or function of something). Check answers.

A contrast:	A purpose:
In spite of…	for
Even though…	so as to
Although…	In order to
	so that
	to

e • Tell SS to go to **Grammar Bank 7B** on *p.144*. Go
through the examples and rules with SS.

Grammar notes

clauses of contrast

- **rule 1:** SS should be familiar with the meaning and use
  of *although*. Here they are introduced to *though* and
  even though.
- **rule 2:** SS will have seen *in spite of* or *despite*, e.g. in
  reading texts, but in this lesson they learn how to use
  them.

clauses of purpose

SS have previously learned to use *to* + infinitive to express
purpose. Here they learn other ways of expressing the
same idea.

- **rule 1**: *So as to* and *in order to* are more formal than *to*
  (but see **rule 4**). Make sure SS don't use *for* + infinitive
  here. ~~I went to the bank for to talk to my bank manager.~~
- **rule 2**: Stress that *for* + gerund is only used to describe
  the purpose of a thing (often in answer to the question
  What's it for?). It can't be used for the purpose of
  an action, e.g. NOT ~~I come to this school for learning
  English.~~
- **rule 3**: Point out that when there is a new subject in a
  clause of purpose we <u>must</u> use *so that* (and not *to*, *in
  order to*, *so as to*), e.g. *We bought a big car so that the
  children would have more space.* NOT …~~in order to the
  children have more space.~~
- **rule 4**: The main point to stress here is that the most
  common way of expressing purpose in spoken English
  (*to* + infinitive) <u>can't</u> be used to express negative
  purpose; however, you can use *in order not to* and *so as
  not to*.

- Focus on the exercises for **7B** on *p.145* and get SS to do
  them individually or in pairs. Check answers after each
  exercise.

a	1	despite	6	spite
	2	even	7	that
	3	to	8	Although
	4	as	9	for
	5	order	10	Despite
b	1	we wouldn't be late		
	2	she earns a fortune…		
	3	the terrible reviews / the reviews being terrible /		
		the fact that the reviews were terrible		
	4	the fog was very thick		
	5	not to offend her		
	6	to explain the new policy		

- Tell SS to go back to the main lesson on *p.107*.

f • **Sentence race.** Put SS in pairs. Focus on the task and make sure SS know what they have to do. Monitor while pairs are writing their sentences and point out any incorrect sentences you see but don't correct them. When the time limit is up, elicit several possible answers for each sentence and write them on the board.

Extra idea

Stop the activity as soon as one pair has ten correct sentences and declare them the winners.

> **Possible answers**
> 1 change them.
> 2 didn't say anything to me.
> 3 she could be nearer her boyfriend.
> 4 not being very good at his job.
> 5 personally I think she's very nice.
> 6 get a better job.
> 7 he was the first to be made redundant.
> 8 the new product didn't sell very well.
> 9 a meeting.
> 10 encourage young people to smoke and drink.

5 SPEAKING

• Focus on the **GET IT RIGHT** box and give SS a few moments to underline the stressed syllable on the four words. Check answers and highlight that *advertisement* is the word which has a different stress pattern. Model and drill pronunciation.

> ad<u>ver</u>tise   ad<u>ver</u>tisement / <u>ad</u>vert   <u>ad</u>vertiser

• Put SS in small groups of three or four and quickly run through the questions making sure SS understand everything. Then give SS time to discuss each question. Go around monitoring, helping with vocabulary and prompting where necessary. If there's time, get some feedback from the class on how they answered some of the questions.

Extra photocopiable activities

Grammar
contrast and purpose *p.179*
Communicative
Guess the sentence *p.218* (instructions *p.196*)

HOMEWORK

Study Link **Workbook** *pp.67–69*

G relative clauses
V prefixes
P word stress

Tingo

Lesson plan

In this final lesson SS revise and extend their knowledge of relative clauses, both defining and non-defining. The context of the lesson is words. In the first half of the lesson SS read an extract from a book called *The meaning of Tingo*, where the author takes a humorous look at words from other languages which have no exact equivalent in English. The second part of the lesson looks at the origins of several common English words. The vocabulary focus is on making new words by adding prefixes which add extra meaning, e.g. *over-*, *under-*. Pronunciation focuses on word stress in words with prefixes.

Optional lead-in (books closed)

- Write the following words on the board.
  kindergarten chef siesta pasta karaoke
- Ask SS what they have in common and elicit that they are all foreign words which English has 'borrowed' and incorporated into the language.
- Then elicit what languages the words have been borrowed from, and ask if any of these words are used in their L1.

> kindergarten – German; chef – French; siesta –
> Spanish; pasta – Italian; karaoke – Japanese

1 GRAMMAR relative clauses

a • Books open. Focus on the instructions and give SS a few minutes to match the words. Check answers For each word get SS to pronounce it correctly using the phonetics, and ask SS if they use a similar word in their L1.

> **1** D **2** F **3** C **4** E **5** A **6** B **7** I **8** H
> **9** G **10** J

b • **Check what you know.** Here SS quickly revise the use of *who, which, whose,* and *that* in defining relative clauses. Give them a few minutes to complete the definitions and match them to the words. Check answers, getting SS to tell you why they used *which, who,* or *whose*.

> **2** igloo – whose   **5** chauffeur – whose
> **3** muesli – which   **6** graffiti – which
> **4** tycoon – who

c • Elicit that you could use *that* instead of *who / which*.
d • Then get SS to write short definitions for the other four words. Check answers.

> **Suggested answers**
> **shampoo** – a liquid which you use to wash your hair
> **algebra** – a type of mathematics which uses letters and symbols to represent quantities
> **macho** – an adjective which describes a man (or his behaviour) that is very masculine in an aggressive way
> **yogurt** – a kind of food made from milk which people often eat with fruit for dessert

- If your SS seem to be having problems with relative clauses, go to the Workbook *p.70*. Go through the rules and do the exercise. However, if your SS seemed comfortable with exercise **1b**, let them do the Workbook exercise as part of their homework.

e • **New grammar.** Focus on the instructions and the book extract. Tell SS that the book *The meaning of Tingo* was an amusing book, which looked at words which exist in other languages but not in English. Set a time limit for SS to read the introductions and definitions but not to complete the gaps at this point. Then ask if they have a word in their L1 for any of these things.

Extra challenge

Alternatively, you could ask SS why they think English doesn't have these words. In some cases it is probably because a particular concept doesn't exist, e.g. pavement cafés are not as common in Britain as in France so we do not have an equivalent expression for *Seigneur-terrasse*.

f • Now focus on the task. If SS have never seen *whom* before, get them to try to work out what it means and where it goes. Check answers, and elicit that we use *whom* for people after a preposition, and that *what* = the thing(s) which.

> **1** who   **8** who
> **2** which   **9** whom
> **3** who (whom)   **10** who
> **4** which   **11** what
> **5** which   **12** what
> **6** whose   **13** who
> **7** which   **14** whose

g • Focus on the questions and get SS to answer them with a partner. Check answers and elicit why.

> **1** The first two sentences in the introduction. The commas round the relative clauses show they are non-defining.
> **2** 3, 4, 5, 7, 8, 10, and 13, i.e. instead of *who* or *which* in defining relative clauses
> **3** 3, 4, 5, and 8. You can leave out *which / who / that* when the subject of the relative clause is a <u>different</u> person / thing. Compare. *A woman (**who**) you think is pretty…* and *a man **who spends** a lot of time…*
> **4** If the preposition comes at the end of the relative clause, after the verb, the relative pronoun is *who, which* or *that*. If the preposition comes at the beginning of the relative clause and the relative pronoun comes directly after it, you must use *whom* for people or *which* for things.

Extra support

You could do the questions with the whole class.

h • Tell SS to go to **Grammar Bank 7C** on *p.144*. Go through the examples and rules with SS.

Grammar notes

defining relative clauses

SS at this level should be fairly confident with basic defining relative clauses, i.e. with *who / which / that* (**rule 1**). They have also been introduced to the use of *whose*, and relative clauses where the relative pronoun is left out (**rules 2** and **3**), but will still need practice of these kinds of sentences.

● **rule 4**: Here SS learn two ways to say the same thing. *Whom* + preposition is rather more formal than using *who / which* and a verb + preposition.

Whom is still used sometimes when the person it refers to is the object of the relative clause, e.g. *The person whom I saw yesterday*, but this is very formal and normally we would either use *who / that* or leave the relative pronoun out altogether.

● **rule 5**: This use of *what* (= the thing / things that) was introduced at the end of *New English File Intermediate* but SS may still confuse *what* and *that* as relative pronouns, often because of L1 interference.

non-defining relative clauses

SS have already been introduced to non-defining relative clauses but will probably need reminding of what they are and how to use them (**rule 1**).

● **rule 2**: This use of *which* is probably new for SS, who may try to use *what* in these kinds of sentences.

● Focus on the exercises for 7C on *p.145* and get SS to do them individually or in pairs. Check answers after each exercise. Remind SS before they do exercise **b** that they have to decide if the relative clause is defining or non-defining, and use commas accordingly.

> **a** 1 ✓
> 2 ✗ ~~it~~ that goes
> 3 ✗ ~~that~~ which was absolutely true
> 4 ✗ ~~that~~ who is very tall
> 5 ✗ to ~~who~~ whom
> 6 ✗ ~~that~~ what I cook
> 7 ✓
> 8 ✗ ~~who~~ whose suitcase
> 9 ✗ what I just said
> 10 ✗ ~~what~~ that I bought last week
>
> **b** 1 His girlfriend, who is an architect, is very intelligent. (His girlfriend, who is very intelligent, is an architect.)
> 2 They gave us a present, which was a complete surprise.
> 3 I didn't understand what he was saying.
> 4 The car which / that crashed into mine was a Mini.
> 5 The police officer (who / that) I spoke to was working on the reception desk / The police officer to whom I spoke …
> 6 Our computer, which we bought two months ago, keeps on crashing.
> 7 The things (which / that) I left on the table aren't there any more.
> 8 It's too hot in my flat, which makes it impossible to sleep.

● Tell SS to go back to the main lesson on *p.108*.

i ● Put SS in pairs, **A** and **B**. Tell them to go to **Communication** *What's the word?* **A** on *p.118*, **B** on *p.120*, and go through the instructions.

● SS define their words to each other alternately (**A** defines his / her first one, then **B** defines his / her first one). Make sure SS don't say the word itself.

● When SS have finished, they go through the words to see which ones have also been 'borrowed' by their language. Get feedback to find out.

2 SPEAKING

● Focus on the **GET IT RIGHT** box and go through it with the class. Point out to SS that *for example, for instance,* and *such as* can all be used to introduce an example(s), e.g. There are many foreign words in English, *for example / for instance / such as* 'pasta'.

● However, you cannot use *such as* to introduce a clause, e.g. *If you can't sleep, there are many things you can do. For example / instance, you can read a book.* NOT ~~Such as, you can read a book~~.

● Then put SS in groups of three or four and get them to go through the questions discussing each one in turn. Tell SS that each group will have to report back its answers to the class at the end.

● Get feedback eliciting examples from each group.

3 READING & LISTENING

a ● Tell SS to cover the bottom part of the page (exercises **b**, **c**, and **d**) Focus on the article and the instructions. Set a time limit for SS to read the article. Then ask them if they could guess any of the words. Elicit ideas but don't tell them if they are right or wrong.

b ● Tell SS to uncover the exercise. Focus on the words in the box and get them to match each word to its origin. Check answers and now find out how many SS guessed.

> | | | | |
> |---|---|---|---|
> | 1 | husband | 6 | hooligan |
> | 2 | cab | 7 | broke |
> | 3 | alarm | 8 | genuine |
> | 4 | jeans | 9 | tip |
> | 5 | escape | 10 | addict |

c ● Focus on the instructions. Get SS to underline any other words they didn't know, compare with a partner to see if he / she can help, and finally check with you.

Extra idea

While SS are doing this, you could write the ten words in the list up on the board in preparation for the next stage.

d ● Now either get SS to cover the article and focus on the words, or if you have written them on the board, to close their books. In pairs, SS try to remember the origin of each word.

Extra support

Do this as a whole class activity.

e ● **7.7** Focus on the instructions and on the three questions. Play the CD once and then check answers.

> | | | |
> |---|---|---|
> | 1 orange | 2 ketchup | 3 tennis |

7.7   CD4 Track 24

(tapescript in Student's Book on *p.131*)

J = John, S = Sally

J   Now it's time for our regular Wednesday afternoon spot about words and their origins. And I have with me, as usual, our English language expert, Sally Davies. So what are the three words you are going to tell us about today, Sally?

S   Hello, John. My three words today are 'ketchup', 'orange', – that's the fruit, the colour came later – , and 'tennis'.

J   Let's start with 'ketchup' then.

S   Yes, well, the Chinese invented a sauce called 'ke-tsiap', spelled K-E-hyphen-T-S-I-A-P in the 1690s. It was made from fish and spices, but absolutely no tomatoes. By the early eighteenth century, its popularity had spread to Malaysia, and this is where British explorers first found it, and obviously really liked it. By 1740 the sauce was part of the English diet – people were eating a lot of it and it was also becoming popular in the American colonies. And they renamed the sauce 'ketchup', because it was a bit easier for the English to pronounce. Then about fifty years later, in 1790, some American colonists in New England mixed tomatoes into the sauce and it became known as 'tomato ketchup'.

J   So it is American after all?

S   Well, tomato ketchup is.

J   So, tell us about 'orange'?

S   Well, it's very interesting that neither 'orange' in English nor 'naranja' in Spanish or 'arancia' in Italian, come from the Latin word for 'orange', which was 'citrus aurentium'. Instead they, they all come from the ancient Sanskrit word 'narangah'. There is also an interesting story about where this word, 'narangah', comes from. It's said that it comes from 'naga ranga', which literally means 'poison for elephants.'

J   Poison for elephants?

S   Yes, apparently, one day in around the 7th or 8th century BC an elephant was passing through the forest, when he found a tree which he had never seen before. This tree was full of beautiful, tempting oranges; as a result, the elephant ate so many that he died. Many years later a man came to the same spot and noticed the remains of the elephant with some orange trees growing from what had been its stomach. The man then exclaimed, 'These fruit are naga ranga' that is, 'poison for elephants'.

J   So is this true?

S   Well, I don't know, but it's a nice story!

J   And finally our last word is 'tennis'.

S   This is my favourite one, and it shows that the English have always had their own special way of pronouncing foreign languages. Tennis is a sport which first developed in France. The name was originally 'tenez', which is from the French verb 'tenir', which means in this case, something like 'Here you are'. Players used to say 'tenez' when they hit the ball meaning something like 'there, try to get this one'. But the sport lost popularity in France and gained popularity in England at the same time. So, English people were still using the word 'tenez' each time they hit the ball, but they were saying it with the English accent which sounded more like 'tennis', and eventually it took this new spelling. Then the sport gained popularity worldwide and was taken up by many nationalities, including the French – but they now had to call it 'le tennis'!

J   Fascinating! Well, thank you very much for those three words, Sally, and we'll look forward to next week's programme.

f   • Now focus on the instructions and the notes. Give SS time to read through the notes and think about what's missing.
   • Play the CD again. Pause after the origin of ketchup. Get SS to try to complete the notes with a partner.
   • Do the same with the next two words. Then play the whole thing again for SS to check. Check answers.

   1 the Chinese
   2 fish and spices
   3 18th
   4 America / the USA / New England
   5 tomatoes
   6 Spanish
   7 Italian
   8 Latin
   9 poison for elephants
   10 elephant
   11 died
   12 stomach
   13 France
   14 originally
   15 'Here you are'
   16 lost popularity
   17 England
   18 English accent

4 VOCABULARY & PRONUNCIATION prefixes and word stress

a   • Focus on the information box and go through it with SS. Highlight that prefixes always change the meaning of a word, e.g. *pronounce* – **mis**pronounce (= to pronounce wrongly).
   • You could remind SS that suffixes on the other hand change the grammar of a word, e.g. *communicate* (verb) – *communication* (noun).
   • Then focus on the words in the list and tell SS to decide what the word means, and then think what the bold prefix has added to the base word. Give SS time to match the prefixes to their meaning and then check answers.

1 post	8 multi
2 re	9 under
3 anti	10 auto
4 mis	11 mono
5 pre	12 micro
6 ex	13 over
7 semi	14 bi

   • Highlight that most words with prefixes are not hyphenated but a few are, e.g. *semi-final, ex-husband,* and SS will need to learn them as they come up.

b   • **7.8** Focus on the information box and go through it with SS. Remind them that most words only have a main stress (indicated in the dictionary by an apostrophe <u>above</u> and <u>before</u> the syllable to be stressed). However, some words, including most prefixed words, also have secondary stress indicated by an apostrophe <u>below</u> and <u>before</u> the syllable to be stressed, e.g. semi-final /ˌsemiˈfaɪnl/. Secondary stress is not as strong as main stress.

- Play the CD once for SS just to listen. Then play it again, pausing after each word for SS to underline the stressed syllable(s). Check answers. Highlight also that the prefix *mis-* is pronounced /mɪs/, not /mɪz/.

7.8	CD4 Track 25

,anti'social
'autograph
,ex-'husband
bi 'annual
,mis'spell
,micro'scopic
'monosyllable
,multi'national
,over'worked
,post'graduate
,precon'ceived
,re'wind
,semi-'final
,under'paid

- Now give SS time to practise saying the words.

Extra support

You could replay the CD and pause after each word for SS to repeat.

c • Focus on the task. Get SS to do it in pairs and then check answers.

1 undercooked
2 oversleep
3 autopilot
4 post-Impressionists
5 misunderstand
6 semicircle

d • Focus on the questions and quickly go through the bold words to make sure SS understand them. Then put SS in pairs and get them to ask and answer the questions. Encourage them to ask for more information for each one.
- Get feedback from different pairs.

Extra support

Get a few SS to choose questions to ask you.

- Finally, tell SS to go to *Phrasal verbs in context File 7* on *p.157* and complete the phrasal verbs which have come up in this File. (Answers *p.155*)

Extra photocopiable activities

Grammar
relative clauses *p.180*
Communicative
Grammar Auction *p.219* (instructions *p.196*)
Vocabulary
Describing game *p.229* (instructions *p.222*)

HOMEWORK

Study Link **Workbook** *pp.70–72*

7 COLLOQUIAL ENGLISH WORDS

Lesson plan

In the first part of this lesson the person interviewed is Susie Dent. She is an English lexicographer (= writer and editor of dictionaries), and is the resident expert and adjudicator on British TV's *Channel 4*'s long-running quiz show *Countdown*, where contestants have to make words from a number of letters they are given. She is also the author of a series of annual *Language Reports* for *Oxford University Press* on new words which have entered the English language.
In the second part of the lesson, four non-native speakers of English are asked what English words have been 'imported' into their language, and if they think it would be better to have their own words for these.

Study Link These lessons are on the *New English File Upper-intermediate* DVD / Video which can be used instead of the class CD (See Introduction *p.9*). SS can get more practice on the MultiROM, which contains more of the short street interviews with a listening task and tapescripts.

Optional lead-in (books closed)

- Write on the board

carbon footprint   **a hoody**   **road rage**

Tell SS that these are new words which have come into English in recent years. Ask them if they can try to guess what they mean. Elicit ideas and then tell them.

carbon footprint = the total amount of carbon dioxide that a person produces, e.g. by driving, flying, using energy at home, i.e. it is a measure of the impact your activities have on the environment
a hoody = a young person (usually male) who wears a hooded top with the hood up, often used to describe delinquents who wear their hood up so as not to be recognized if filmed on closed circuit television while committing a crime
road rage = a situation in which a driver becomes extremely angry or violent with the driver of another car because of the way they are driving

THE INTERVIEW

a • Books open. Focus on the photos and get SS to tell you what they can see.

A woman (Susie Dent) and The *Oxford English Dictionary*

- Now focus on the task and on the glossary. Go through it with the class eliciting from them how to pronounce the words and phrases.

b • 7.9 Focus on the task. Put SS in pairs and give them time to read the questions. Encourage SS not to write anything down when they listen the first time. They should listen and try to get the gist of what she is saying, and then discuss the questions with their partner.
- Play the CD once (**Part 1**). Give SS time to discuss the questions and tell each other what they understood. Then play the CD once or twice more. This time SS might want to jot down things they heard to help them remember the answers to the questions. Check answers.

1 No one knows – thousands and thousands of new words are made up every second.
2 On average about 900.
3 To see if a new word will survive.
4 It was invented by a rapper (called Baby Gangsta or BG) in the USA.

7.9 CD4 Track 26

(tapescript in Student's Book on *p.131*)
I = interviewer, S = Susie Dent

I Susie Dent is a well-known English lexicographer who also appears in the popular British TV quiz *Countdown*. Could you give us an estimate of how many new words come into the English language each year?

S A lot of people ask me how many new words are born in any particular year and the quick answer to that is no one knows, because thousands and thousands and thousands of new words are made up every second. What we do know is that in the twentieth century about 900,000 new words went into the *Oxford English Dictionary*, which is the vast vast dictionary that Oxford keeps going, basically constantly, tracking current language and historical language, so that means on average about 900 words each year made it in a significant enough way to get into the dictionary.

I How does a new word or expression get into the dictionary?

S Normally dictionary makers will wait about five years to see whether or not a word will survive before they put it in. They have quite strict criteria. There are exceptions to that and 'bling' is a prime example. It went into the dictionary very very soon.
'Bling' is a wonderful word that is used by journalists particularly to sum up the sort of celebrity obsessed, very materialistic opening years of the 21st century, but in fact is was coined in 1999 and it was coined by a rapper and I think it's an absolutely beautiful example of how US black slang particularly and hip hop and rap have had a major influence on British slang particularly today, and it was used by the rapper Baby Gangsta or BG and it was probably suggestive of light flashing off jewellery so it was 'bling' and that's how it was taken up and it went into the mainstream incredibly quickly.

Extra challenge

You could use the tapescript above to elicit more detailed answers from SS.

c ● **7.10** Focus on the task and play the CD once (**Part 2**). Give SS time to discuss the questions and what they understood. Then play the CD once or twice more. Check answers.

---

1 They are new words made by combining two words. 'Chofa' means a mixture of a chair and a sofa; 'Waparazzi' (a mixture of 'WAP' and 'paparazzi') means a person who takes photos of celebrities on their mobile phone, and 'mandals' (a mixture of 'man' and 'sandals') are men's sandals.
2 'Cool' (= good, trendy) is a word which people think is new but in fact it has existed with this meaning since the late 19th century. It was made popular by the jazz singer Charlie Parker.

---

3 'Wireless' is an example of an old word which now has a different meaning. It used to mean radio, but now it means Internet connection with no cables.
4 'Sushi' and 'sashimi' are examples of foreign words which have come into English. They are both Japanese dishes.
5 'Kleenex' and 'Hoover' are two words which are brand names but are now often used to describe all tissues and vacuum cleaners.
6 'A marmalade dropper' is one of her favourite new words. It means a piece of news which is so surprising that when you read it in the papers in the morning you drop your toast (and marmalade). In the USA they use a similar expression, 'a muffin choker' (because there they have muffins for breakfast, and the surprising news makes them choke on their muffins).

7.10 CD4 Track 27

(tapescript in Student's Book on *p.131*)

I Where do new words come from?

S One of the main processes by which new words come about today is one called 'blending' where you put two words together to form a new one. And one of my favourites is 'chofas' which is a cross between a chair and a sofa and 'waparazzi' as well which I think is really clever and 'waparazzi' is basically citizen journalists, if you like, going around snapping celebrities with their WAP (WAP) enabled phone, and so people thought, 'Oh, we'll call them the 'Waparazzi'. So that's quite a good example of how new words are coming about. 'Mandals' is another one, male sandals or 'man sandals' is another one that has been doing the rounds in Britain anyway. And another process by which new words are born is by bringing older words back. And so 'cool' for example was around probably in the late nineteenth century, then it was popularized by jazz circles, Charlie Parker and people like that and now, you know, it's used by young people everywhere. Another way in which new words are coined if you like is when old words come back and take on a slightly different meaning. So again they're not completely new at all but we've adapted them to our new environment. A great example of this is 'wireless'. Whereas our grandparents certainly in Britain used to listen to the wireless and it meant a portable radio, today 'wireless' has everything to do with broadband and the way we use our computers in a cable-free way.

I Any other ways?

S English has long been a 'hoover', really, of foreign languages and it is made up of so many different words from different cultures, right back from Latin and Greek to modern influences now. Food is a wonderful example of that where we just take different cuisines from around the world and we introduce obvious examples, like 'sushi', 'sashimi', that sort of thing, into our language. Brand names, another key way in which we generate new words if you like. If you think about 'Kleenex' or 'Hoover' as I mentioned. Those used to be brand names, they are still brand names, but we've somehow imported them so that we know exactly what we're talking about and they mean anything generic.

I Do you have any favourite new words of the last few years?

S I have so many favourites from the last few years, ever since I've been first writing the *Language reports*, I have to collect my favourite new words of the year. I loved the idea of a 'marmalade dropper', which was basically a news item that made you drop your toast in the morning. In America it was called a 'muffin choker'.

d ● **7.11** This exercise gives SS intensive listening practice in deciphering phrases where words are often run together, and introduces them to some common English expressions. Focus on the phrases and give SS time to read them. Play the CD, pausing after the first phrase and replaying it as necessary. Elicit the missing words, and then the meaning of the whole phrase. Repeat for the other five phrases.

1 **whether or not** (a word will survive) (= if a word will survive or not)
2 **into the mainstream** (= ideas, opinions or words which are accepted as normal because they are shared or used by most people)
3 **a cross between** (= half one thing and half another)
4 **snapping** (= informal way of saying *taking photos*)
5 **was around** (= informal way of saying *existed*)
6 **somehow** (= in some way)

7.11 CD4 Track 28

1 Normally dictionary makers will wait about five years to see whether or not a word will survive.
2 And it went into the mainstream incredibly quickly.
3 One of my favourites is 'chofas', which is a cross between a chair and a sofa
4 …basically citizen journalists, if you like, going around snapping celebrities with their WAP (WAP) enabled phone.
5 So 'cool', for example, was around probably in the late nineteenth century.
6 They are still brand names, but we've somehow imported them.

e ● Tell SS to go to *p.131* and to look at the tapescript for the interview. Play the CD (**Part 1** and **Part 2**) again and tell SS to read and listen at the same time. Deal with any vocabulary problems and get feedback from SS on what parts they found hard to understand and why, e.g. speed of speech, elision, pronunciation, etc.

● Finally, focus on the question. You could also ask SS *Which of the new words do you like best? Why?* Get SS to answer in pairs or as a whole class. Then get feedback from the whole class.

IN THE STREET

a ● **7.12** Focus on the photos of the people. Tell SS they are not British and elicit how old they think they are and what nationality they might be. Matandra appeared in the previous File. Tell SS that they were all interviewed in Covent Garden, a busy shopping area in Central London.

● Focus on the task. Play the CD once, and get SS to compare ideas. Then play it again and check answers.

Most positive: Victoria (speaker 2) – she says it brings nations and people closer
Most negative: Volke (speaker 4) – he thinks you should keep your own culture

7.12 CD4 Track 29

(tapescript in Student's Book on *p.131*)
I = interviewer, M = Mateusz, V = Victoria, Ma = Matandra, Vo = Volke
Mateusz
I Are there any English words that are used in your language?
M Yes, for example, hamburger. It is used I think worldwide, but in Poland we say *hamburger*. Yes, maybe computer, in Poland *komputer*, there are plenty of words like that, plenty of words that are about cuisine, hot dog, *hot dog* in Polish. Really, plenty of words like that.
I Do you think it would be better to use your own words?
M No, I don't think so, because they are used everywhere in this world and why not in Poland?
Victoria
I Are there any English words that are used in your language?
V Erm yes. Like, well, no I don't think there are a lot of English words, but there are French words that sound English like *parking* which actually doesn't make sense in English. But it's a car park and we call it *parking* and it's not French at all. But we have a lot of things like that because English is cool so we try to make our words sound English.
I Do you think it would be better to use your own words?
V No, no, we should… I like the idea that there are words that you can, yeah, understand in every country, it makes us, brings nations, people closer, you know.
Matandra
I Are there any English words that are used in your language?
MA An English word that is used in the Italian language well, everything to do with technology, everything to do with the Internet, and Internet itself, well someone could argue that Internet is actually Latin but… say *download*, we've given up saying the Italian version of downloading which is *scaricare* and most people just go with *downloadare* which sounds very odd to the Italian ear, but we, we're going with it.
I Do you think it would be better to use your own words?
MA I don't think it's necessary to to set off on a crusade to defend language in so much as, you know, as specific areas which are just the domain of another language. Italian is the main domain in say music. No one complains around the world because you say *pianissimo* when you have to play softly.
Volke
I Are there any English words used in your language?
VO Too many, too many, I must say. We forget a lot of German words and replace them by English words and they are pronounced in the same way. I miss that, because I like Spanish as well and they have so many, they have like, words for computer or skateboard and things like that which we don't have and we take all the English words. And if there are new inventions and stuff like that we don't invent new words – we just take them and I think it's a pity not to do the opposite.
I Do you think it would be better to use your own words?
VO It's part of culture and I think we should maintain that. You can be open to other languages and cultures but at the same time you should keep your own one, I think.

b • Focus on the task and give SS time to go through the sentences. Check they understand this meaning of *field* (= area of knowledge or expertise). Play the CD once. Get SS to compare what they think. Play it again if necessary and check answers.

> 1 Matandra (speaker 3) – he says Italian is dominant in the field of music.
> 2 Volke (speaker 4) – he says Spanish has its own words for computer and skateboard.
> 3 Victoria (speaker 2) – she explains that the French say *parking* meaning *car park*.
> 4 Mateusz (speaker 1) – he mentions hamburger and hot dog.

c • **7.13** Focus on the phrases and give SS time to read them. Play the CD, pausing after the first phrase and replaying it as necessary. Elicit the missing word, and then the meaning of the whole phrase. Repeat for the other four phrases.

> 1 **worldwide** (= all over the world)
> 2 **doesn't make sense** (= doesn't have a meaning that you can easily understand)
> 3 **to do with** (technology) (= everything related to technology)
> 4 **go with** (= accept, choose to use)
> 5 **stuff like that** (= informal for *things like that*)

> **7.13**   CD4 Track 30
> 1 It is used, I think worldwide
> 2 …which actually doesn't make sense in English.
> 3 …everything to do with technology…
> 4 Most people just go with *downloadare.*
> 5 And if there are new inventions and stuff like that we don't invent new words

d • Tell SS to go to *p.131* and to look at the tapescript for **IN THE STREET**. Play the CD again and tell SS to read and listen at the same time. Deal with any vocabulary problems and get feedback from SS on what parts they found hard to understand and why, e.g. speed of speech, pronunciation, elision, etc.

• Finally, focus on the two questions that the interviewer asked the people, and get SS to interview each other in pairs. Then get feedback from the whole class.

HOMEWORK

Study Link **Workbook** *p.73*

7   WRITING: 'FOR AND AGAINST'

Lesson plan

In this last writing lesson SS learn to write a 'for and against' composition, where they put both sides of an argument and then say which side they agree with. This is quite a formal kind of writing task, and one which often comes up as an exam composition title. The writing skill focused on here is linking expressions.

a • Focus on the composition title and ask the class what they think and why. Then tell them to quickly read the composition and find out what the writer thinks (that there are advantages and disadvantages, and it depends on each individual). Elicit a few advantages and disadvantages mentioned in the composition.

• Now focus on the words in the list and elicit that they are used to connect either parts of a sentence or one sentence to another. Give SS a few minutes to complete the gaps. Check answers.

> 1 The main advantage
> 2 such as / for example
> 3 Another advantage
> 4 also
> 5 on the other hand
> 6 for example / such as
> 7 Although
> 8 because of
> 9 To sum up

b • Focus on the instructions and the chart. Then elicit where the first expression from the list (*also*) should go (*To add more points to the same topic*). Then get SS to continue individually or in pairs.

• Check answers.

> **To list advantages / disadvantages**
> Another advantage
> The main advantage
> **To add more points to the same argument**
> In addition
> Furthermore
> Also
> **To introduce an example**
> For instance
> For example
> such as
> **To make contrasting points**
> However
> In spite of (the fact that)
> Although
> on the other hand
> **To give a reason**
> Because (+ clause)
> Because of (+ noun)
> **To introduce the conclusion**
> In conclusion
> To sum up

- Highlight that:
  – *furthermore* and *in addition* normally come at the beginning of a sentence or phrase and are often followed by a comma. However, *also* usually comes before the main verb or after *be*.
  – *However* and *On the other hand* are always followed by commas if they come at the beginning of sentences. *On the other hand* is also sometimes used when we want to express an advantage and a disadvantage in the same sentence together with *on the one hand*, e.g. *On the one hand you earn a lot of money, but on the other hand the job is very boring.* However, we often use *On the other hand* alone to introduce a contrasting point.

c • Focus on the composition title and the planning stages.

WRITE a composition

Go through the instructions. Then either get SS to plan and write the composition in class (set a time limit of about 20 minutes) or get them just to plan in class and write the composition at home, or set both planning and writing for homework.

If SS do the writing in class, get them to swap their composition with another student to read and check for mistakes before you collect them all in.

Extra support

If you are getting SS to plan in class, you could get them to also write the first paragraph with a partner, and then compare what different pairs have written.

Test and Assessment CD-ROM

CEF Assessment materials
File 7 Writing task assessment guidelines

For instructions on how to use these pages, see *p.33*.

GRAMMAR

a	1	I had	4	not having
	2	you would	5	to work for
	3	had spoken		

b 1 c 2 c 3 a 4 b 5 a

VOCABULARY

a	1	exhausting	4	do
	2	shocked	5	clients
	3	employees		
b	1	profit	4	launch
	2	slogan	5	branches
	3	redundant		
c	1	up	4	as
	2	over	5	for
	3	up		
d	1	mispronounce	4	underpaid
	2	postgraduate	5	autobiography
	3	rebuilt		

PRONUNCIATION

a	1	misunderstand (it's /s/)	4	irritate (it's /ɪ/)
	2	launch (it's /ɔː/)	5	shocked (it's /ɒ/)
	3	colleague (it's /ɒ/)		

b dis**a**pp**oi**nted, **in**crease, **ex**port, emplo**yee**, **au**tograph

CAN YOU UNDERSTAND THIS TEXT?

a 1 b 2 a 3 c 4 b 5 b

b **mainly** = more than anything else
restricted = limited in size or amount
To the untutored ear = to someone who is not used to hearing it
humming = low continuous sound
Their culture is similarly constrained = their culture is also very limited
keen to learn = wanting to, enthusiastic to learn
beyond them = too difficult for them
disprove = prove that sth is wrong
enables = permits, allows

CAN YOU UNDERSTAND THESE PEOPLE?

a 1 b 2 c 3 c 4 c 5 c

b 1 *A Tale of Murder, Madness and the Love of Words.*
2 An American army surgeon and a millionaire.
3 The *Oxford English Dictionary.*
4 He found that Minor was living in a hospital for mentally ill criminals.
5 He had shot a man.

1 **A** I wish you wouldn't do that.
    B Do what?
    A Take my plate to the kitchen the minute I've finished eating.
    B But I don't like seeing dirty plates in front of me.
    A Yes, but I feel as if you're watching me, waiting for me to finish so you can take my plate away. It stresses me out. I can't enjoy what I'm eating.
    B Well, maybe I wouldn't if you helped clear the table after the meal!
    A OK, no problem. I'll do it.

2 **A** Did you go to university?
    B No, but I wish I had. It's one of the things I really regret. Not so much because of the qualifications, I mean I don't necessarily think I would have got a better job, although I suppose I *might* have a slightly higher salary, but it's more for the people you meet and the extra-curricular things people do, you know the whole 'university life' thing. I think I missed out on something by starting work straight after school.

3 Get the slim, toned body you've always dreamed of with the Feelgood Fitness Program! The Feelgood Fitness Program is designed to tone and sculpt your entire body and help you lose weight, all at the same time. And all from the comfort of your own home! For just 159 dollars and 99 cents you will receive an exercise DVD accompanied by a 20-page diet plan, and access to a fitness trainer you can email every time you have a problem. The first 50 people to sign up will also receive a free set of weights, so hurry and contact us at www.feelfit.com. We're waiting to hear from you.

4 The Japanese computer company has seen its profits jump in the nine months from April to December, thanks to the popularity of its new games machine. Profits for the period reached 132 billion yen (that's approximately £550m), which is up 43% on last year. The firm, whose new product was launched in November, said that they had met their target to ship four million units by the end of the year.

5 **A** So what is your new boss like, Karen?
    B Well, at first I thought she was nice, but now I find her a bit patronizing.
    A Sorry, what does 'patronizing' mean?
    B Well, a person who's patronizing is someone who seems to be sort of friendly, but by the way they treat you or speak to you, you know that actually they think they are much better than you are.
    B So like 'arrogant' then.
    A Well, not so much 'arrogant', more sort of looking down on you.
    B I see.

I On the Book programme today John Sampson is going to talk about a book with the rather unpromising title of *The Surgeon of Crowthorne*. So John, what made you want to read it and what is it really about?

J Well, you mentioned the title, which it's true doesn't sound very exciting, but the book has a subtitle which is *A Tale of Murder, Madness and the Love of Words*, and that certainly does draw you in. This book is a remarkable account of the life of a man called W.C. Minor. Not a famous name, but as it happens, a quite extraordinary man. William Chester Minor was an American army surgeon and a millionaire. He was also one of the keenest volunteers involved in the making of the *Oxford English Dictionary*. The *Oxford English Dictionary*, or the *OED* as it is usually called, is one of the largest and most encompassing dictionaries in the world. It took almost 70 years to complete the first epic edition. During those years, thousands of volunteers searched through newspapers, and journals and new and old books to find new words, or new meanings of words. They then sent their findings to the people in Oxford who were working on the dictionary. W.C. Minor was one of the people who sent in most contributions, and during the 20 years that he collaborated, he developed a friendship with the editor of the *OED*, the formidable James Murray. But they had never met, as Minor never agreed to travel to Oxford for a meeting, and all that Murray knew was that he lived in the country in Berkshire. So then in 1896 Murray decided to travel to Berkshire to find this elusive man. To his absolute amazement he found that Minor was a patient in Broadmoor Asylum, a hospital for mentally ill criminals. He turned out to be an educated American gentleman, who had been a surgeon in the Civil War, but who also happened to be a psychopathic killer. He had shot a man in the London streets because he believed, mistakenly and for no reason that anyone could discover, that his victim was Irish and a terrorist who wanted to kill him. The author is Simon Winchester, and although perhaps his prose style is not always as elegant as it could be, he has found a strange and extraordinary life story and turned it into an intriguing piece of historical detective work. Once you start reading it you can't put it down.

Extra photocopiable activities

Grammar
revise and check: verb forms *p.181*
Communicative
Revision *p.220* (instructions *p.196*)
Vocabulary
Revision *p.230* (instructions *p.222*)

Test and Assessment CD-ROM

File 7 Quicktest
File 7 Test
Progress test 4–7
End-of-course test

File 1

1 up
2 back
3 up
4 down
5 up
6 down

File 2

1 burst
2 turn
3 leave
4 knock
5 put

File 3

1 D
2 E
3 B
4 A
5 C

File 4

1 out
2 off
3 down
4 on
5 off

File 5

1 lie
2 fall
3 fill
4 catch
5 put, eat

File 6

1 D
2 E
3 C
4 B
5 A

File 7

1 going
2 ended
3 pick
4 take

CONTENTS

Photocopiable material

- There is a **Grammar activity** for each main (A, B, and C) lesson of the Student's Book.
- There is a **Communicative activity** for each main lesson of the Student's Book.
- There is a **Mini grammar activity** for every Mini grammar item in the Student's Book (one per File).
- There is a **Vocabulary activity** for each File of the Student's Book.
- There are seven **Song activities**. These can be used as part of the main lesson in the Student's Book or in a later lesson. The recording of the song can be found in the main lesson on the Class CD.
- There is a photocopiable page of **irregular verbs**.

Using extra activities in mixed-ability classes

Some teachers have classes with a very wide range of abilities, and where some students finish Student's Book activities much more quickly than others. You could give these fast-finishers a photocopiable activity (either Communicative or Grammar) while you help the slower students. Alternatively, some teachers might want to give faster students extra oral practice with a communicative activity while slower students consolidate their knowledge with an extra grammar activity.

Tips for using Grammar activities

The Grammar activities are designed to give students extra practice in the main grammar point from each lesson. How you use these activities depends on the needs and abilities of your students and time you have available. They can be used in the lesson if you think all of your class would benefit from the extra practice or you could set them as homework for some or all of your students.

- All of the activities start with a writing stage. If you use the activities in class, get students to work individually or in pairs. Allow students to compare before checking the answers.
- Many of the activities have a final section that gets students to cover the sentences and to test their memory. If you are using the activities in class, students can work in pairs and test their partner. If you set them for homework, encourage students to use this stage to test themselves.
- If students are having trouble with any of the activities, make sure they refer to the relevant Grammar Bank in the Student's Book.
- Make sure that students keep their copies of the activities and that they review any difficult areas regularly. Encourage them to go back to activities and cover and test themselves. This will help with their revision.

Tips for using Communicative activities

- We have suggested the ideal number of copies for each activity. However, you can often manage with fewer, e.g. one copy per pair instead of one per student.
- When students are working in pairs, if possible get them to sit face-to-face. This will encourage them to really talk to each other and also means they can't see each other's sheet.
- If your class doesn't divide into pairs or groups, take part yourself, get two students to share one role, or get one student to monitor, help and correct.
- If some students finish early, they can swap roles and do the activity again, or you could get them to write some of the sentences from the activity.

Introduction

2 decided to move   3 is five / five years old   4 who are
5 the oldest / eldest child   6 He used to be   7 in charge of
8 to meet   9 I've been learning   10 went to   11 as a
waiter   12 very hard work / a very hard job   13 had
improved   14 to be able to speak   15 good at reading
16 is good enough   17 have very little   18 I'd learn

1A   question formation

a   1 Who paid for it?
2 Do you know who that man is over there?
3 Where are they going on their honeymoon? How long
are they going for?
4 Who did James come with? Why did she leave him?
5 How long have Matt and Claire known each other?
Where did they meet? Who told you that?

b   2 Do you know why Sarah didn't come to the wedding?
3 Do you know if / whether that tall woman over there is
Claire's mother?
4 Do you remember what Molly's husband does?
5 Do you have any idea if / whether I can get a taxi after
midnight?
6 Do you remember if / whether Claire's sister got
married here?
7 Do you think they'll be happy?
8 Do you know where they put our coats?

1B   auxiliary verbs

2 do   3 isn't   4 Do   5 aren't   6 do   7 aren't   8 are
9 do   10 would   11 am   12 are   13 do   14 Did
15 did   16 do   17 didn't   18 was   19 Couldn't
20 aren't   21 will

1C   present perfect simple and continuous

a   2 Have you been eating   3 haven't had   4 haven't
wanted   5 Have you had / Have you been having
6 've taken   7 Have you been working   8 have been
9 've been getting   10 haven't been sleeping / haven't
slept   11 've been overworking   12 've just been
promoted

   2 have you been waiting   3 have you known   4 have you
had   5 have you been learning   6 have you been
coming

2A   adjectives

2 the long one or the short one   3 The Irish   4 homeless
people   5 Japanese man / woman   6 ✓   7 the poor /
poor people   8 the dead   9 ✓   10 rich / a rich man

2 blue denim   3 awful gold   4 big dark   5 long black
silk   6 beautiful old wooden   7 small black leather
8 delicious spicy Thai   9 short brown curly
10 new blue and white striped

2B   narrative tenses

1 hadn't noticed, had stopped
2 had been (carefully) saving, had been concentrating,
had been watching, had (only) been looking
3 was leaving, was happening, were looking

b   2 asked   3 mentioned   4 had been looking
5 had accused / accused   6 had searched / searched
7 made   8 had said   9 jumped up   10 made
11 had never seen   12 drove   13 parked   14 had taken
place   15 came   16 started   17 had never stolen
18 made   19 found   20 had stopped
21 were watching

2C   adverbs

a   2 Do you really mean that; their defence was absolutely
awful   3 played well   4 Unfortunately England never
play well   5 were incredibly lucky   6 do you ever
have   7 To be honest England were quite lucky
8 were extremely lucky   9 Personally I thought both
teams defended badly; England were a bit better,
especially in attack

b   2 slowly   3 quickly   4 already   5 before   6 obviously
7 actually   8 angrily   9 nearly   10 just   11 badly
12 just   13 always   14 well   15 naturally

3A   passive

a   2 have been stolen   3 are being forced   4 was being
driven   5 were discovered, was stopped   6 be taken
7 are caught   8 has been vandalized   9 had been
left   10 Being burgled   11 to be sent

b   2 is understood to   3 is believed (that)   4 are reported
to   5 is thought (that)   6 is expected (that)

3B   future perfect and future continuous

2 'll (still) be working   3 'll have been promoted
4 'll be earning   5 'll have found   6 'll have beaten
7 'll have equalled   8 won't be playing   9 won't be
watching   10 'll be lying   11 won't have arrived
12 'll have just got off   13 'll be driving   14 'll have
gone   15 won't have finished   16 'll be watching
17 'll be using   18 'll be arriving   19 'll have finished

3C   conditionals and future time clauses

2 a and b   3 a   4 b   5 b and c   6 c   7 a and c   8 b
9 a   10 c   11 c   12 a and c   13 b and c   14 a and b
15 c

4A   unreal conditionals

2 hadn't been   3 were   4 would kill   5 didn't give
6 hadn't found   7 would have eaten   8 hadn't been
9 would have died   10 would have been
11 would you do   12 would have given

4B   past modals

a   2 might have been expecting   3 must have just come
back   4 can't have been   5 must have heard
6 might not have known   7 might have been surprised
8 must have known   9 can't have been   10 might have
wanted

b   2 shouldn't have used   3 shouldn't have broken up
4 should have come   5 should have waited
6 shouldn't have worn   7 should have told
8 shouldn't have bought

4C verbs of the senses

2 smells   3 smells as if   4 smells like   5 feels
6 feels like   7 feels as if   8 feels   9 tastes
10 tastes like   11 tastes as if   12 tastes   13 look as if
14 look   15 look as if   16 look   17 look like   18 look
19 sounds   20 sounds   21 sounds as if   22 sound like

5A gerunds and infinitives

a 2 seeing   3 go out   4 to have   5 not stay   6 working
7 to wear   8 live   9 laughing   10 to finish   11 seeing
12 not to tell   13 work   14 not seeing   15 to help
16 waiting   17 to park   18 speaking   19 getting up /
to get up   20 not come   21 spending   22 to give

b 2 not to be   3 changing   4 meeting   5 arriving
6 to revise   7 to tell   8 turning

5B used to, be used to, get used to

a 2 get used to   3 usually   4 was used to being able
5 used to be   6 usually go

b 2 am used to   3 get used to   4 used to   5 usually
6 get used to   7 am used to   8 get used to
9 get used to   10 used to

c 2 being   3 seeing   4 get up   5 eating

5C reporting verbs

a 2 having   3 to explain   4 of stealing   5 to wait
6 to release   7 not to say   8 for interrupting
9 buying   10 to get

b 2 not to try to influence the accused
3 buying a more expensive apartment
4 to go to the bank that day
5 to give you $200,000
6 to lend me the money
7 keeping money in the bank
8 to come to court
9 for not coming

6A articles

2 –   3 –   4 a   5 The   6 the   7 –   8 The   9 the
10 –   11 a   12 –   13 The   14 the   15 the   16 the
17 a   18 The   19 –   20 the   21 –   22 –   23 the
24 the   25 –   26 the   27 –   28 a   29 –   30 the
31 –   32 the   33 the   34 –

6B uncountable and plural nouns

2 some jeans   3 says   4 is   5 housework   6 rubbish
7 business   8 the research   9 equipment
10 a piece of   11 some   12 is   13 is   14 some advice
15 –   16 some   17 those scissors   18 them   19 the
20 homework   21 some

6C quantifiers

a 2 Most   3 both   4 everything   5 none   6 all

b 7 anyone   8 anything   9 all   10 Neither   11 no
12 Either   13 most of   14 Both of   15 every

7A wish

a 2 would leave   3 had   4 wouldn't borrow
5 earned   6 would stop raining   7 didn't have to
8 wouldn't wear

b 2 hadn't told   3 hadn't broken   4 had bought
5 had had   6 had been born

7B contrast and purpose

a 2 j   3 h   4 i   5 f   6 e   7 a   8 c   9 d   10 b

b 2 The company have reduced staff in order to save
money.
3 Despite the long flight she felt great when she arrived.
4 He didn't tell her so as not to hurt her feelings.
5 She bought the bag even though it was ridiculously
expensive.
6 The company have a big market share in spite of doing
very little advertising.
7 They had to make a lot of workers redundant so that
the company would survive.
8 Although she smoked 40 cigarettes a day my granny
lived until she was 96.

7C relative clauses

a 2 whose   3 who   4 whose   5 whose   6 whom
7 which   8 which   9 who   10 which

b 8

c 2 The man who / that I was talking to is a colleague of
mine / The man to whom I was talking is a colleague
of mine.
3 I didn't understand what you said.
4 She looks ill, which is a bit worrying.
5 He's the famous politician whose wife left him last
week.
6 This house, which was built in 1534, is one of the oldest
houses in the village.

The relative pronoun can be left out in sentence 1 and the
first possibility of 2 (i.e. with the preposition at the end of
the clause).

revise and check: verb forms

2 have you been feeling
3 've had
4 had been driving
5 had been damaged
6 is thought
7 'll have finished
8 'll be putting
9 doesn't pass
10 have spoken
11 weren't
12 wouldn't have survived
13 have been
14 have seen
15 seeing
16 meeting
17 being
18 not to take
19 was / were
20 had warned

Grammar **introduction**

a Read about Arnost. Then correct the **bold** phrases 1–18.

My name's Arnost and I'm from Prague in the Czech Republic. I was born there, and [1] **I have lived there** until I was 15, but then my family [2] **decided move** to Brno, and that's where I live now.

I'm divorced and I have a daughter called Eliska who [3] **is five years**. She spends two weeks a month with me and two weeks with her mother. I have two sisters, [4] **which are** both studying at university. I am [5] **the older child** in the family. My mother works in the tourist office and my father is retired. [6] **He use to be** a computer consultant.

I work for a big supermarket chain. I am [7] **on charge of** foreign suppliers which means that I have to use English when I talk to them on the phone, and sometimes I travel to other countries such as The Netherlands and Italy [8] **for to meet** suppliers.

[9] **I am learning** English for about eight years. I studied it at school and then when I left school I spent six weeks in England. During the day I [10] **was going to** English classes and in the evening I worked [11] **like a waiter** in a restaurant. It was [12] **a very hard work**. When I came home my English [13] **has improved** a lot but I still need to learn more. My main aim this year is [14] **to be able speak** more fluently and to improve my writing. I think I am quite [15] **good at read** in English. As soon as my level of English [16] **will be good enough**, I'll take the Cambridge First Certificate exam.

I [17] **have very few** free time but when I can, I go swimming. If I had more time, [18] **I 'll learn** another language, maybe Spanish or Italian.

1 *I lived there*	10 _____
2 _____	11 _____
3 _____	12 _____
4 _____	13 _____
5 _____	14 _____
6 _____	15 _____
7 _____	16 _____
8 _____	17 _____
9 _____	18 _____

b Write a similar text about yourself, in five paragraphs.

a Complete the questions.

1 A I don't like her dress.

  B What _don't_ _you_ _like_ about it?

  A The style. I think it's awful.

  B It must have cost a fortune though.

  A Yes. Who _____ _____ _____?

  B Her parents paid. It was a wedding present.

2 A Do you know _____ _____ _____ _____ over there?

  B That man there? I think he's Matt's brother.

3 A Where _____ _____ _____ on their honeymoon?

  B On a Mediterranean cruise, I think.

  A How _____ _____ _____ going _____?

  B Three weeks!

4 A Who _____ James _____ _____?

  B Nobody. He came on his own. His girlfriend left him last month.

  A Why _____ _____ _____ him?

  B I think she met someone else.

5 A _____ long _____ Matt and Claire _____ each other?

  B For about a year, I think.

  A Where _____ _____ _____?

  B Someone told me they met at a speed dating evening.

  A Speed dating? Who _____ _____ that?

  B I think Jane told me. She's Claire's best friend.

b Change the direct questions to indirect questions.

1 'Where are the toilets?' 'Could you tell me _where the toilets are_ _____?'

2 'Why didn't Sarah come to the wedding?' 'Do you know _____?'

3 'Is that tall woman over there Claire's mother?' 'Do you know _____?'

4 'What does Molly's husband do?' 'Do you remember _____?'

5 'Can I get a taxi after midnight?' 'Do you have any idea _____?'

6 'Did Claire's sister get married here?' 'Do you remember _____?'

7 'Will they be happy?' 'Do you think _____?'

8 'Where did they put our coats?' 'Do you know _____?'

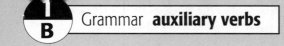

New English File Teacher's Book Upper-intermediate
Photocopiable © Oxford University Press 2008

● Complete the dialogue with auxiliary verbs.

A Hello.

B Good morning. Are you here for an interview too?

A Yes. They say it's a good company to work for, [1] *don't* they?

B Yes, they [2]_____. Let's hope we're both lucky.

A I'm Adam Matejko.

B That's a Polish name, [3]_____ it?

A Yes. I live in Cracow.

B [4]_____ you? I've got a friend who lives there. Anyway, I'm Blanca Cuellar, from Bogotá, in Colombia.

A Nice to meet you.

B You're a bit nervous, [5]_____ you?

A A little. Don't you get nervous before interviews?

B Not really. I [6]_____ get nervous before exams, but not interviews. What's the time now?

A 11.00. They're making us wait a long time, [7]_____ they?

B Yes, they [8]_____. They always [9]_____.

A I wouldn't mind a coffee.

B Neither [10]_____ I. Where are you staying, by the way?

A At the Hotel Europe.

B Ah, so [11]_____ I. The rooms aren't very nice, [12]_____ they?

A No. But I [13]_____ like the restaurant. I had a good meal there last night.

B [14]_____ you? I just had room service. Are you working at the moment?

A No, I resigned last week.

B Why? Didn't you like the company you were working for?

A I [15]_____ like the company but to be honest I couldn't stand my boss! Anyway, I think I need a new challenge.

B So [16]_____ I. That's why I'm here. Ah, it's your turn now. Good luck.

Half an hour later…

A You look confident. It went well, [17]_____ it?

B Quite well, I think.

A How many interviewers were there?

B Three men and a woman. One of the men was a bit unfriendly, and so [18]_____ the woman. But the other two were OK. I couldn't always understand the woman either.

A [19]_____ you? Why not?

B She had a really difficult accent. You're next, [20]_____ you?

A Yes. I'll go down to the café on the corner when I finish.

B OK, so [21]_____ I, and we can compare notes. Good luck!

a Complete the dialogue with the verbs in brackets in the present perfect simple or continuous.

DOCTOR   So, what seems to be the problem?

PATIENT   Well, for about a week now I ¹*'ve been feeling* quite dizzy. I even thought I was going to faint once or twice. (**feel**)

DOCTOR   I see. ²_____ normally? (**you / eat**)

PATIENT   Well, to tell you the truth I ³_____ much of an appetite recently. I'm just not hungry. (**not have**)

DOCTOR   You need to try to eat regularly, you know, even if you're not hungry.

PATIENT   I know, but I ⁴_____ to eat anything. (**not want**).

DOCTOR   Hmm. Any other symptoms? ⁵_____ headaches or any other aches or pains? (**you / have**)

PATIENT   Well, I ⁶_____ my blood pressure three times this week, and it's a little bit high. (**take**)

DOCTOR   I'll check that in a minute. ⁷_____ harder than usual? (**you / work**)

PATIENT   Yes, I suppose I have. This is a very important time of the year for us and things ⁸_____ incredibly busy recently. I ⁹_____ home very late, and to be honest I ¹⁰_____ very well for the last few days. (**be, get, not sleep**)

DOCTOR   I think you ¹¹_____. I want you to take a week off work, and have a complete rest. (**overwork**)

PATIENT   I can't possibly have a week off at the moment. I ¹²_____ to head of department. (**just / be promote**).

DOCTOR   Well, I'm afraid they'll just have to manage without you. You can't play around with your health.

b Write questions with either the present perfect simple or continuous.

1 I didn't know Agnes was ill. How long *has she been* in hospital? (**be**)

2 Sorry I'm late! How long _____ you _____? (**wait**)

3 So Jack is your oldest friend? How long _____ you _____ him? (**know**)

4 Is that your new car! How long _____ you _____ it? (**have**).

5 Your English is very good. How long _____ you _____ it? (**learn**).

6 I haven't seen you before. How long _____ you _____ to this school? (**come**)

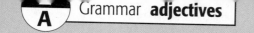

A Grammar **adjectives**

a Tick (✓) the highlighted phrases that are right and correct the wrong ones.

1 The unemployed can apply to do these training courses free of charge. ✓

2 Which of these skirts suits me best, the long or the short?

3 The Irishes are very proud of their culture and their sense of humour.

4 There are a lot of homeless sleeping in the park at night.

5 I met a really friendly Japanese last year when I was learning English in Bath.

6 When you wash the shirts make sure you separate the white ones and the coloured ones.

7 Prime Minister, a lot of people say that your government just doesn't care about poor.

8 Don't talk like that – you should show more respect for the deads.

9 The Turks adopted the Roman script early in the 20th century.

10 My uncle buys and sells property – he's a rich!

b Complete the sentences with the adjectives in brackets in the correct order. Use your instinct if you are not sure.

1 **A** Can I help you?
  B Yes, I'm looking for some _smart_ _high-heeled_ sandals. (**high-heeled** / **smart**)

2 **A** Did you see either of the robbers?
  B It all happened so fast. I saw a young man wearing a _____ _____ jacket running out of the restaurant. (**blue** / **denim**)

3 **A** I don't really like these pictures, do you?
  B No. And I can't bear those _____ _____ picture frames. (**gold** / **awful**)

4 **A** Your son looks really like you – he has your _____ _____ eyes. (**dark** / **big**)
  B Do you think so? I think he looks more like my husband.

5 **A** Are you looking for something?
  B Yes. I've lost a _____ _____ _____ scarf. Have you seen it? (**silk** / **long** / **black**)

6 **A** We used to live in a _____ _____ _____ house near the river. (**wooden** / **beautiful** / **old**)
  B How lovely. Could you swim in the river?

7 **A** I've just arrived on the flight from Athens, but my suitcase hasn't arrived.
  B What's it like?
  A It's a _____ _____ _____ case. (**black** / **leather** / **small**)

8 **A** Ever since Simon came back from Bangkok he's been cooking me _____ _____ _____ curries. (**spicy** / **Thai** / **delicious**)
  B Lucky you! I love curries.

9 **A** What does Simon's wife look like?
  B She's quite slim and she has _____ _____ _____ hair. (**brown** / **curly** / **short**)

10 **A** I'm going to wear my _____ _____ _____ shirt. (**new** / **striped** / **blue and white**)
   B Yes, do. It really suits you.

a Read the first part of the story and find examples of each tense below.

1 the past perfect _had finished_ _____ _____

2 the past perfect continuous _____ _____ _____ _____

3 the past continuous _____ _____ _____

The most embarrassing moment of my life …

When I was about nine years old I used to go to the cinema every Saturday morning. After the film _had finished_, I would go to a toy shop and look at model planes and trains and sometimes I bought them with the pocket money that I had been carefully saving. One day after the film I went to a big department store to have a look at the model planes they had. I didn't buy anything, but as I was leaving a very large man grabbed my arm quite violently and accused me of shoplifting. The man said that he was a store detective. As I had been concentrating on the toys, I hadn't noticed that he had been watching me. He made me empty my pockets and he went through my coat, searching for stolen goods, even though I told him very clearly that I had only been looking. Of course he didn't find anything but by this time several people had stopped to see what was happening. I felt very embarrassed and humiliated that so many people were looking at me and I was very glad to leave the shop when it was all over.

b Complete the second part of the story with the correct form of the verbs in brackets: past simple, past continuous, past perfect, or past perfect continuous.

An hour or so later, when my family [1] _were having_ (**have**) lunch at home, my father [2] _____ (**ask**) me about the film. I then [3] _____ (**mention**) that I [4] _____ (**look**) at toys in a department store when a store detective [5] _____ (**accuse**) me of shoplifting and [6] _____ (**search**) me in the middle of the shop. My father [7] _____ (**make**) me repeat what I [8] _____ (**say**), and then immediately [9] _____ (**jump up**) from the table. Without either of us having finished our lunch, he [10] _____ (**make**) me get into the car. I [11] _____ (**never see**) my father so angry! He [12] _____ (**drive**) quickly to the store, [13] _____ (**park**) outside and marched me to where the incident [14] _____ (**take place**). He then demanded to see the manager and the store detective. When the manager [15] _____ (**come**), my father [16] _____ (**start**) shouting at him and he told him that I [17] _____ (**never steal**) anything in my life. He [18] _____ (**make**) the manager and store detective apologize to me for having accused me of shoplifting, and for embarrassing me. But the thing is, I [19] _____ (**find**) this scene even more embarrassing than the first one, especially as I could see that a lot of customers [20] _____ (**stop**) and [21] _____ (**watch**) us.

a Put the adverbs in the best place in the dialogue.

GARY   So, what did you think of the match?

CRAIG   ¹Even though they lost, I think Scotland played ^brilliantly^ again ^tonight^. (**brilliantly** / **tonight**)

JOHN   ²Craig, do you mean that? (**really**) Their defence was awful. (**absolutely**)

CRAIG   ³I suppose you think England played? (**well**)

JOHN   ⁴England play these days. (**unfortunately** / **never** / **well**)

CRAIG   ⁵But even you must admit that England were lucky. (**incredibly**)

GARY   ⁶Craig, do you have anything good to say about England? (**ever**)

JOHN   ⁷England were lucky with the second goal. (**to be honest** / **quite**)

CRAIG   ⁸Come on, John, England were lucky with both the first <u>and</u> second goals! (**extremely**)

GARY   ⁹I thought both teams defended (**personally** / **badly**), but at the end of the day, Craig, I'd say England were better, in attack. (**a bit** / **especially**)

b Complete the dialogue with the correct adverbs from the list.

~~absolutely~~   already   always   angrily   badly   before   actually
just (×2)   naturally   nearly   obviously   quickly   slowly   well

DIRECTOR   Jason. That was ¹ _absolutely_ marvellous, but you've got to get to centre stage.

JASON   But I have to wait for Tanya to finish her line, and she's doing it too ²_____.

TANYA   I could try saying it more ³_____ if you want me to.

DIRECTOR   Yes, could you? Now, Jason, remember when Tanya tells you she's going to marry Henry, you ⁴_____ know about it, because you heard them talking in the garden ⁵_____, so you aren't at all surprised.

JASON   Well, ⁶_____ I know about it, but I thought maybe I should pretend at first that I didn't know.

DIRECTOR   No, we want to see your emotion! You reacted very calmly, but ⁷_____ you're not a calm person at all. I want you to react ⁸_____, OK? Now the next scene. Sally, you were great. But, when you've ⁹_____ finished reading Tanya's letter, when you're on the last couple of lines, ¹⁰_____ look up at the audience. Let them feel how ¹¹_____ you've been treated by her.

SALLY   Do you want me to cry?

DIRECTOR   Not yet. Look out at the audience, ¹²_____ like this.

TANYA   Can I just ask why you ¹³_____ ask me to play horrible characters?

DIRECTOR   Because you do it so ¹⁴_____, darling. It just comes ¹⁵_____ to you. Right everyone, let's take it again from the beginning…

3A Grammar **passive**

a Complete the sentences by putting the verbs into the correct passive tense.

1 Three men were arrested this evening and _will be questioned_ by police tomorrow morning. (**question**)

2 Oh no. My car isn't here! It must _____. (**steal**)

3 At the moment the hostages _____ to remain in the plane. (**force**)

4 The accident happened because the car _____ at 180 kph. (**drive**)

5 The drugs _____ when the lorry _____ at the border. (**discover, stop**)

6 Strong measures must _____ to reduce the number of knife crimes. (**take**)

7 People who _____ shoplifting often turn out to have some kind of psychological problem. (**catch**)

8 The graffiti is particularly annoying as it is the third time the building _____ so far this year. (**vandalize**)

9 As soon as we got home we could see that the front door _____ open and that there were two men in the living room. (**leave**)

10 _____ is a deeply unpleasant experience. (**burgle**)

11 Sarah used _____ to her room without food when she really naughty. (**send**)

b Complete the police officer's statement with the verbs in brackets in the passive. Add any other necessary words.

Ladies and gentlemen, I can now confirm that two dangerous criminals, Roberto Floriano and Walter Hacker, have escaped from Florida State Prison. Security arrangements at the prison are being investigated to find out exactly how they escaped, but they [1] _are thought to_ (**think**) have escaped through the air-conditioning system. Floriano [2] _____ (**understand**) be one of the engineers who installed the air-conditioning system five years ago. This afternoon a semi-automatic rifle was stolen from a pet shop near the main highway, so I must warn members of the public not to approach these men, as it [3] _____ (**believe**) they are armed. According to witnesses the two men [4] _____ (**reported**) be still wearing prison clothes. It [5] _____ (**think**) they are heading in the direction of the Everglades swamp to make it harder for tracker dogs to find them. The public should not panic – it [6] _____ (**expect**) these two dangerous men will be recaptured within the next 24 hours.

Thank you, ladies and gentlemen.

● Complete the dialogues with the verbs in brackets in the future perfect or future continuous.

1

SARAH I wish I could find another job. What do you think
you [1] _'ll be doing_ (**do**) this time next year?

LISA Unfortunately I think I [2] _____ still _____ (**work**)
here. But I hope I [3] _____ (**be promoted**) to
assistant manager by then, so at least I [4] _____
(**earn**) a bit more money.

SARAH Well, I really hope that I [5] _____ (**found**) a more
interesting job by then. I'm so bored – I suppose I've just
been here too long!

2

DAVE If Jimmy Brent scores in this match he [6] _____
(**beat**) Golding's record of 24 matches for the club in a season.

CHRIS No, he [7] _____ (**equal**) it. To beat it he'll need to
score another one. But he [8] _____ (**not play**) next
week, because he's already got two yellow cards.

3

SOPHIE Just imagine it. This time tomorrow we [9] _____
(**not watch**) the rain, we [10] _____ (**lie**) on a
tropical beach!

BERT No, not at 3.00 we won't. Don't forget the time difference.
We [11] _____ (**not arrive**) at our hotel yet. Let's see.
I think we [12] _____ (**just / get off**) the plane and
we [13] _____ (**drive**) to our hotel.

4

NIGEL Is it too late to call Hannah and Sam? Do you think
they [14] _____ (**go**) to bed yet?

ANNA What's the time? 11.00. That's fine. Knowing them,
they [15] _____ (**not finish**) their dinner yet.
They [16] _____ (**watch**) a film.

5

JOE Can I borrow the car this afternoon?

MOTHER What time do you need it? I [17] _____ (**use**) it
myself until about 4.00.

JOE Natalie [18] _____ (**arrive**) at the bus station
around 5.00. I want to pick her up.

MOTHER Oh, that's fine. I [19] _____ (**finish**) with it by then.

● Circle the correct answer. Sometimes two answers are possible.

1 I'll have my mobile phone with me in case _____ later.

  a you need to call me
  b you'll need to call me
  c you've needed to call me

2 Phone him as soon as _____ that report.

  a you finish
  b you've finished
  c you'll finish

3 I'll play football with you when _____ my dinner.

  a I've had
  b I'll have
  c I have

4 I'm not going to go to the party unless _____ too.

  a you'll go
  b you go
  c you've gone

5 Could you get me some milk if _____ to the supermarket?

  a you'll go
  b you go
  c you're going

6 If the weather _____ we'll be able to eat outside tonight.

  a will have improved
  b will improve
  c improves

7 I'm not going to tell my boss I'm leaving until _____.

  a I find a new job
  b I'm finding a new job
  c I've found a new job

8 If we don't start using less petrol it _____ by the end of the century.

  a is running out
  b will have run out
  c runs out

9 Please come in quietly because _____ when you arrive.

  a we'll be sleeping
  b we'll sleep
  c we're sleeping

10 Take a jacket in case _____ when you come out of the cinema.

  a it'll have been cold
  b it's being cold
  c it's cold

11 If he _____ by 6.00, we'll go without him.

  a won't have arrived
  b isn't arriving
  c hasn't arrived

12 We're going to have a picnic tomorrow unless _____.

  a it rains heavily
  b it will be raining heavily
  c it's raining heavily

13 I _____ apologize until he apologizes to me.

  a don't
  b am not going to
  c won't

14 If you want to speak English well, _____ practise.

  a you'll have to
  b you have to
  c you've had to

15 Come and say goodbye tomorrow before _____.

  a you'll leave
  b you've left
  c you leave

> **11–15** **Excellent.** You can use conditionals and future time clauses very well.
> **8–10** **Quite good**, but check the rules in the Grammar Bank (Student's Book p.136) for any questions that you got wrong.
> **0–7** **This is difficult for you.** Read the rules in the Grammar Bank again (Student's Book p.136). Then ask your teacher for another photocopy and do the exercise again at home.

● Complete the dialogue with the correct form of the verbs in brackets to make conditional sentences.

STEVE So where are you going next?

EMILY We're not sure. We might carry on into the interior. Have you been there?

STEVE Yes, and I ¹*wouldn't go* (**not go**) there again if you paid me!

EMILY Why not?

STEVE Well it's pretty dangerous. I had a really bad experience there. If I ²_____ (**not be**) really lucky, I wouldn't have survived. If I ³_____ (**be**) you, I'd think twice about going there.

CARL Really? What happened to you?

STEVE I was camping near a river and I got attacked in the middle of the night by thieves.

EMILY Oh no! What happened?

STEVE They made me give them my rucksack which had my map, all my food, my passport, and my money. They said they ⁴_____ (**kill**) me if I ⁵_____ (**not give**) them everything I had, so I had no choice. After that I wandered in the jungle for two days and then I must have fainted from the heat and exhaustion. Luckily, two American backpackers found me. If they ⁶_____ (**not find**) me, the ants and mosquitoes ⁷_____ (**eat**) me alive! The Americans helped me get to the nearest village but then I fell ill with a terrible fever. To be honest with you, if it ⁸_____ (**not be**) for the local doctor I ⁹_____ (**die**). It was three weeks before I was well enough to travel home.

EMILY Weren't your family worried about you?

STEVE No, because I was able to send a message to the British Embassy and they contacted my parents. If not, they ¹⁰_____ (**be**) worried sick!

EMILY Wow! What a trip! What ¹¹_____ (**you / do**) if we got attacked by thieves, Carl? You wouldn't do anything silly, would you?

CARL Don't worry. If I had been in the same situation as Steve I ¹²_____ (**give**) the thieves everything! I'm not stupid. Anyway, don't worry, after hearing that story I don't think we'll be going into the interior!

4
B Grammar **past modals**

ⓐ Complete the dialogue. Rewrite the phrases in brackets using *might (not) have*, *must have* or *can't have* + past participle.

SANDY Jack, come over here!

JACK What is it?

SANDY There's a bottle of champagne in the fridge.

JACK What's strange about that?

SANDY It's not very cold yet. So, it ¹ *can't have been*_____ in the fridge for very long.
I can't be sure, but I think the victim ²_____ a visitor.
(**I'm sure it hasn't been / perhaps the victim was expecting**)

JACK Look! He ³_____ from holiday. See that suitcase with clothes on the bed? (**I'm sure he has just come back**)

SANDY Yes, he was very suntanned. He ⁴_____ in England. He was definitely on holiday somewhere very sunny. (**I'm sure he wasn't**)

JACK Oh, you're right. Look at this – Mexican currency in his wallet.

SANDY Now, we know he was getting ready for a bath. Then he ⁵_____ a noise downstairs. He quickly put on a dressing gown and came out of the bathroom into the bedroom. (**I'm sure he heard**)

JACK The intruder ⁶_____ the victim was at home. He ⁷_____ when he found the victim here, and then he lost his nerve and killed him.
(**perhaps the intruder didn't know / maybe he was surprised**)

SANDY You know, I don't think that's right. I think the intruder ⁸_____ the victim. I think this was a murder. (**I'm sure the intruder knew**)

JACK Are you saying it ⁹_____ a burglary? (**you're sure it definitely wasn't**)

SANDY That's right. But I think the killer ¹⁰_____ it to look like a break-in and not a murder. (**perhaps the killer wanted**)

ⓑ Complete the sentences with *should / shouldn't have* and the past participle of a verb from the list.

break up	buy	come	~~take~~	tell	use	wait	wear

1 We're lost. I knew we *should have taken*___ a map!

2 This tastes really spicy. You _____ so much curry powder.

3 You _____ with James. He was such a nice guy.

4 The film was fantastic. You really _____ with us.

5 Jim's already left! I can't believe it – he _____ for us.

6 I'm afraid we can't exchange the jacket. You _____ it.

7 You _____ us you wanted to come. We would have got you a ticket.

8 I knew I _____ those jeans. They were a complete waste of money.

170

New English File Teacher's Book Upper-intermediate
Photocopiable © Oxford University Press 2008

Complete the dialogue with *smells*, *smells like*, or *smells as if*.

CUSTOMER   I'm looking for a perfume for my wife. Something that
           smells nice and fresh.

ASSISTANT What about this one. It _____ very fragrant.

CUSTOMER   No, I don't like it. It _____ it's for a teenager.

ASSISTANT Try this one then, sir – 'Fatal attraction'.

CUSTOMER   Yes, that ⁴_____ another one she's got, but
           fresher. Very nice. I'll take two of them.

Complete the dialogue with *feels*, *feels like*, or *feels as if*.

ASSISTANT This one is very good quality. Here, touch it and see.

TOURIST 1 Hmm, It ⁵_____ very smooth. I'd say it ⁶_____ silk. Is it silk?

TOURIST 2 No, it's cotton, but it ⁷_____ it's made of silk.

ASSISTANT It ⁸_____ very soft but it's very strong material. I can give
           you a very good price.

Complete the dialogue with *tastes*, *tastes like*, or *tastes as if*.

ASSISTANT   Please try this one. It ⁹_____ very different from the last one.

CUSTOMER 1 Mmm. This one ¹⁰_____ a Beaujolais to me. What do you think?

CUSTOMER 2 Yes, it does. It's very light. It ¹¹_____ it would go really well
            with chicken.

CUSTOMER 1 Yes. It ¹²_____ much smoother than the others we've tried.

Complete the dialogue with *look*, *look like*, or *look as if*.

WOMAN You shouldn't have said you wanted to come if you didn't.

MAN   Why do you say that?

WOMAN You ¹³_____ you are totally bored.

MAN   I <u>did</u> want to come. It's just that they all ¹⁴_____ fine to me.

WOMAN Even the ones that make me ¹⁵_____ I'm 60 years old?

MAN   OK, those ones <u>do</u> ¹⁶_____ a bit old fashioned.

WOMAN And these ones that ¹⁷_____ something a 13-year-old would wear?

MAN   They ¹⁸_____ OK to me.

WOMAN Oh you're so helpful!

Complete the dialogue with *sound(s)*, *sound(s) like*, or *sound(s) as if*.

ENGINEER Wait, wait, wait!

GUITARIST What is it now?

ENGINEER The bass guitar is coming in too soon. It ¹⁹_____ wrong.

GUITARIST It ²⁰_____ OK to me.

ENGINEER No, it ²¹_____ you're rushing in.

BASS   Well how should it sound?

ENGINEER It should ²²_____ an early 70s rock band, remember?

ⓐ Complete the sentences with the verbs in brackets in the infinitive (with or without *to*) or the gerund.

1 I learned _to speak_ French when I was at school. (**speak**)

2 Do you fancy _____ a film tonight? (**see**)

3 Laura's mother doesn't let her _____ when she wants. (**go out**)

4 I can't afford _____ a holiday this year. (**have**)

5 It's getting late. We'd better _____ much longer. (**not stay**)

6 I'm going to carry on _____ until 8.00 tonight. (**work**)

7 What are you planning _____ to the party? (**wear**)

8 Would you rather _____ in the country or in a town? (**live**)

9 I couldn't help _____ when my brother fell off his bicycle. (**laugh**)

10 Did you manage _____ all the homework I gave you? (**finish**)

11 We're really looking forward to _____ you again. (**see**)

12 If I tell you, do you promise _____ anybody? (**not tell**)

13 My boss made me _____ late last night. (**work**)

14 Since I've moved abroad I really miss _____ my friends. (**not see**)

15 Would you like me _____ you with the dinner? (**help**)

16 I don't mind _____. I'm not in a hurry. (**wait**)

17 You're not allowed _____ here. (**park**)

18 You need to practise _____ if you want to pass your English exam. (**speak**)

19 I like _____ early in the morning in the summer. (**get up**)

20 Monica might _____ tomorrow. She's ill. (**not come**)

21 I enjoy _____ time with my grandparents. (**spend**)

22 Will you be able _____ me a lift to work tomorrow? (**give**)

ⓑ Complete the sentences with the verbs in brackets in the gerund or the infinitive with *to*.

1 You forgot _to buy_ the milk. (**buy**)

2 Could you try _____ late tomorrow? (**not be**)

3 The sheets on this bed are dirty. They need _____. (**change**)

4 Don't you remember _____ his wife at that party at Christmas? (**meet**)

5 I'll never forget _____ in New York for the first time. (**arrive**)

6 I think you need _____ the irregular verbs. (**revise**)

7 Did you remember _____ James about the meeting tomorrow? (**tell**)

8 If the computer doesn't work, try _____ it off and switching it on again. (**turn**)

25–30	**Excellent.** You can use gerunds and infinitives very well.
16–24	**Quite good,** but check the rules in the Grammar Bank (Student's Book p.140) for any questions that you got wrong.
0–15	**This is difficult for you.** Read the rules in the Grammar Bank again (Student's Book p.140). Then ask your teacher for another photocopy and do the exercise again at home.

a Circle the correct form.

Inge,
Madrid, Spain

I come from Germany, and I ¹ (used to live) / **am used to living** in the north, in Hamburg, but then I moved to Madrid about five years ago. I had to ² **be used to / get used to** having lunch quite late, at about 2.00 p.m., and dinner as late as 9.00 or 10.00 p.m. I love the weather in Spain – there are more sunny days and it's a lot warmer. In Germany, things ³ **usually / use to** happen exactly on time but here things are much more relaxed. I like that too. The only thing I really miss is the bread! I ⁴ **was used to being able / was used to be able** to choose from between 20 or 30 different kinds of bread but here it's more like two or three, and white, not wholemeal. And sometimes I have problems with noisy neighbours, especially at night. That never ⁵ **used to be / was used to being** a problem in Hamburg. People there ⁶ **usually go / are used to going** to bed at 10.30 at the latest.

b Complete the text with *used to*, *am used to*, *get used to*, or *usually*.

I ¹ _used to_ live in Sweden, but now I live in Parma, Italy. I've been here for six years now so I ² _____ the lifestyle. Life is more hectic here than in Sweden. You also have a wider choice of things to do in your free time and I really enjoy that. I had to ³ _____ eating lots of pasta, particularly *tortelli*, which are Parma's local speciality. In Sweden I ⁴ _____ eat pasta once or twice a month, and now I ⁵ _____ have it once or twice a week! I also had to ⁶ _____ the different mentality. For example people here are very family-orientated. This was new to me and hard to understand at first. But now I ⁷ _____ having lunch every Sunday with my in-laws! It was also quite hard for me to ⁸ _____ the dialect they speak in Parma. I still sometimes have to ask people to repeat things. The only thing I can't ⁹ _____ is the coffee. I know, *espresso* is supposed to be the best coffee in the world, but it's just too strong for me. In Sweden I ¹⁰ _____ drink a lot of coffee, but it was much less strong. Still, I do love the smell.

Lennart,
Parma, Italy

c Complete the text with a verb from the list in the correct form.

Neil and Shirley,
Queensland, Australia

| be | eat | get up | ~~live~~ | see |

We used to ¹ _live_ in England but we've been living in Queensland, Australia, since 1997. We're used to ² _____ here now, but at first it was quite hard. We live in the country, and when we first moved into the house I just couldn't get used to ³ _____ snakes in the garden, but now it's not a problem. We just leave them alone. Although we speak the same language, there are still some things here that are strange. People here usually ⁴ _____ really early, at about 5.00 a.m., which we still haven't got used to. Christmas doesn't feel right either – I haven't got used to ⁵ _____ roast turkey in 40 degrees of heat!

New English File Teacher's Book Upper-intermediate
Photocopiable © Oxford University Press 2008

a Circle the correct form.

MS BEAL (DEFENCE LAWYER) Your honour, my client admits
  ¹**to be** / **being** at the scene of the crime, but he denies
  ²**to have** / **having** anything to do with the crime.

JUDGE Yes, but you're going to have to explain what the accused
  was doing there, with a weapon and $200,000 in cash.

MR LUSKIN (PROSECUTION LAWYER) And she will also have to
  explain why her client refused ³**to explain** / **explaining** his
  presence, the weapon, or the money, to the police.

MS BEAL My client is accused ⁴**to steal** / **of stealing** this money,
  but I will ask you ⁵**that you wait** / **to wait** until you have heard
  all the evidence. The evidence will convince you ⁶**to release** /
  of releasing him as an innocent man. It is true that I advised
  my client ⁷**not to say** / **not say** anything until I arrived at the
  police station. But that is his legal right…

JUDGE I apologize ⁸**for interrupting** / **interrupting** you Ms Beal,
  would you mind beginning your defence now?

MS BEAL Thank you, your honour. Now Mr Dykes, let's go
  back to the morning of the crime. Your girlfriend suggested
  ⁹**to buy** / **buying** a new house that she had seen, did she not?

MR DYKES (THE ACCUSED) Yes, she's been trying to persuade me
  ¹⁰**getting** / **to get** an apartment in a better neighbourhood…

b Complete the dialogue by reporting the phrases in brackets.

MR LUSKIN Mr Dykes, may I remind you ¹ _to tell the truth_____.
  ('**Please remember you must tell the truth.**')

JUDGE I have already warned you ²_____.
  ('**You must not try to influence the accused.**')

MR LUSKIN Very well. So, Dykes, your girlfriend at the time insisted on ³_____,
  and you promised ⁴_____ and take out $200,000 – is that right?
  ('**I really want to buy a more expensive apartment.**' / '**I'll go to the bank today.**')

MR DYKES Not exactly, I didn't go to the bank.

MR LUSKIN Oh, so somebody you met in the street simply offered
  ⁵_____? ('**Shall I give you $200,000?**')

MR DYKES No, a friend had agreed ⁶_____ a couple of months ago.
  ('**I'll lend you the money.**')

MR LUSKIN I see. And this friend just happened to have lots of money at home in cash?
  Clearly, your friends don't recommend ⁷_____. It's interesting, ladies and
  gentlemen, that the defence didn't invite this friend ⁸_____ today as a
  witness to tell us how he lent you the money.
  ('**You should keep money in the bank.**' / '**Please come to court as a witness.**')

MR DYKES Well, my friend apologized ⁹_____. He's out of the country at the
  moment, so he couldn't be here today. ('**Sorry, I can't come.**')

● Complete the sentences with *a*, *an*, *the*, or – (no article).

1 [1] *The* population of [2]_____ South Africa is approximately 47 million.

2 My father is in [3]_____ hospital because he had [4]_____ heart attack.

3 [5]_____ first state in [6]_____ USA where [7]_____ women could vote was Wyoming.

4 [8]_____ Louvre is probably [9]_____ most famous museum in [10]_____ Paris.

5 Although there is [11]_____ good university in Bristol where we live, my daughter decided to go to [12]_____ Edinburgh University.

6 [13]_____ River Ebro in Spain flows into [14]_____ Mediterranean Sea.

7 When we went to [15]_____ wedding we couldn't park near [16]_____ church, so we had to get [17]_____ taxi.

8 [18]_____ quickest way to get from London to Oxford by [19]_____ car is to take [20]_____ M40.

9 [21]_____ Lake Superior, in [22]_____ Canada, is [23]_____ biggest lake in [24]_____ world.

10 I don't usually enjoy [25]_____ films with subtitles but I absolutely loved [26]_____ German film which won the Oscar for 'Best Foreign Language Film' this year.

11 The man was sent to [27]_____ prison for robbing [28]_____ bank in London.

12 [29]_____ Mont Blanc is the highest mountain in [30]_____ Alps.

13 Whenever I go to London, I alway go shopping at [31]_____ Harrods.

14 When we went to Morocco on our honeymoon, we camped in [32]_____ Sahara desert. It was so romantic!

15 She decided not to go to the top of [33]_____ Eiffel Tower because she's so scared of heights.

16 My brother loves eating at [34]_____ Mario's. He thinks it's the best Italian restaurant in the city centre.

14–16	**Excellent.** You can use articles very well.
9–13	**Quite good**, but check the rules in the Grammar Bank (Student's Book p.142) for any questions that you got wrong.
0–8	**This is difficult for you.** Read the rules in the Grammar Bank (Student's Book p.142). Then ask your teacher for another photocopy and do the exercise again at home.

New English File Teacher's Book Upper-intermediate
Photocopiable © Oxford University Press 2008

● Circle the correct option.

Daniel! Bertha! I want to see you out of your [1] **pyjama** / (**pyjamas**)
and in [2] **a jeans** / **some jeans** and a T-shirt in two minutes
– OK? Your breakfast is on the table. The news [3] **says** / **say**
there's been an accident on the motorway so the traffic
[4] **is** / **are** sure to be bad. Hurry up!

Right, Susana, the most important [5] **housework** / **houseworks**
to do today is the washing and ironing. Leave the beds and
the floors until all the washing and ironing is done. Oh, and
please take the [6] **rubbish** / **rubbishes** out. Thanks a lot.

That's great! We're going to be doing [7] **a business** / **business**
with the Central Sports Arena people! They must have
been impressed with [8] **the research** / **the researches**
we did for them about new sports [9] **equipment** / **equipments**.

OK everybody, listen, I've got [10] **a** / **a piece of** very good news.
We've got the marketing contract for the Central Sports Arena.
You'll remember that we did [11] **a** / **some** very helpful research
for them three months ago. Well, they were very pleased.

So, Kevin, Economics [12] **is** / **are** what you did at university,
and athletics [13] **is** / **are** what you spend your time doing
at the weekend? What practical skills could you bring
to this company?

I know what you're going to say, doctor. You're going to give
me [14] **some advices** / **some advice** about reducing stress
in my life, and tell me that I need to take [15] **an** / **–** iron more
often. But I read [16] **an** / **some** information on the Internet
which said it didn't really help.

Bertha, come and sit down and eat, please. And put
[17] **that** / **those scissors** down – you could hurt yourself with
[18] **it** / **them**, or scratch [19] **a** / **the** furniture. Good girl. You can watch
TV afterwards if you've finished your [20] **homework** / **homeworks**.
Oh, and could you bring me [21] **a** / **some** paper? I need to make
a shopping list.

a Circle the correct form.

b Complete the dialogues with words from the list.

most of	every	anything	anyone	both of	all	neither	either	no

A Could ⁷_____ have put ⁸_____ into your baggage?
B No, absolutely not. I packed it ⁹_____ myself.

A ¹⁰_____ of us eat meat. Can we get vegetarian meals on the plane?
B No problem. On your flight to New Delhi you will be offered a vegetarian option.

A Sorry, ¹¹_____ drinks are allowed past this point.
B But I've just bought this water!
A Sorry, madam. ¹²_____ you drink it now, or you put it in this bin.

A I've missed my flight back to Los Angeles! What can I do?
B Not much today, sir. I'll see if I can find you an alternative, but I'm afraid ¹³_____ the flights are full.

A ¹⁴_____ us have heart conditions. Do we have to go through that machine?
B Don't worry. It won't do you any harm.

A Excuse me, sir, could you take off your belt and walk through again?
B Oh, ¹⁵_____ time I fly I forget!

New English File Teacher's Book Upper-intermediate
Photocopiable © Oxford University Press 2008

a Complete the sentences with a verb from the list in the past simple or add *would* / *wouldn't* + infinitive.

not have to	leave	stop raining	not borrow	earn	not wear	~~be taller~~	have

1 I wish I _were taller_____. Then maybe I could be a model.

2 I wish my mum _____ me alone! She's always interfering in what I do.

3 I wish I _____ the latest version of this game. This one is two years old!

4 I wish my sister _____ my clothes. She never puts them back.

5 I wish Mum and Dad _____ more money. Then we could go on better holidays.

6 I wish it _____! Then I could go out and play ball.

7 I wish I _____ share a room with Allie. She's such an irritating little kid.

8 I wish my dad _____ that awful jacket! My friends think he looks really strange.

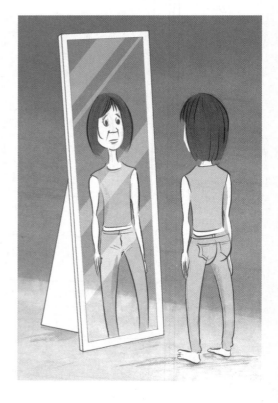

b Complete the sentences with a verb from the list in the past perfect.

not break	be born	~~not fight~~	buy	not tell	have

1 I wish I _hadn't fought_____ with Kate and Helen. Now I've got no one to go out with.

2 I wish I _____ Mum and Dad about my school results. Now they're worried I won't get into university.

3 I wish Allie _____ my iPod. She's so annoying.

4 I wish I _____ the other jeans. These ones just aren't right.

5 I wish I _____ the courage to phone Sam last week. Maybe he would have asked me out.

6 I wish I _____ in another family! Mine are so awful.

ⓐ Match 1–10 with a–j to make complete sentences.

1 ⟦g⟧ We went to New York to…   a be late.
2 ⟦ ⟧ She flew to Amsterdam for…   b the terrible storm.
3 ⟦ ⟧ Although Josh played really well,… c the fact that he hadn't studied at all.
4 ⟦ ⟧ They bought a guide book so that…   d avoid the traffic.
5 ⟦ ⟧ Despite losing the first set,…   e he still took the exam.
6 ⟦ ⟧ Even though he was feeling sick,…   f he beat his opponent.
7 ⟦ ⟧ I took a taxi so as not to…   g ~~see the sights.~~
8 ⟦ ⟧ His English marks were good in spite of…   h he lost the match.
9 ⟦ ⟧ They left early in order to…   i they would know what to see.
10 ⟦ ⟧ The men went out fishing in spite of…   j her sister's wedding.

ⓑ Rewrite the sentences using the words in brackets so that both sentences mean the same.

1 In spite of the cold weather, the barbecue was a success. (**although**)

   Although the weather was cold, the barbecue

   was a success. _____

2 The company have reduced staff so that they can save money. (**in order to**)

   _____

   _____ .

3 Even though the flight was long, she felt great when she arrived. (**despite**)

   _____

   _____ .

4 He didn't tell her because he didn't want to hurt her feelings. (**so as**)

   _____

   _____ .

5 She bought the bag in spite of the ridiculously expensive price. (**even though**)

   _____

   _____ .

6 The company have a big market share even though they do very little advertising. (**in spite of**)

   _____

   _____ .

7 They had to make a lot of workers redundant. If not the company wouldn't have survived. (**so that**)

   _____

   _____ .

8 In spite of smoking 40 cigarettes a day my granny lived until she was 96. (**although**)

   _____

   _____ .

a Complete the article with *which*, *who*, *whose*, or *whom*.

■ Freud painting tops Tate Gallery card sales

A painting by the British artist Lucian Freud is now the top-selling postcard at the Tate Britain gallery in London. The sales of Freud's *Girl with a White Dog* have now overtaken the previous top-selling work of art, ¹ *which* was *Ophelia*, by John Everett Millais. Lucian Freud, ² _____ grandfather Sigmund Freud is known as the father of psychoanalysis, was born in Berlin. The family moved to England in the 1930s, when his father, ³ _____ was an architect, decided to escape the threat of Hitler's Germany.

Lucian Freud, ⁴ _____ paintings sell for huge sums of money, is regarded as one of the world's most brilliant figurative artists. He tends to concentrate on portraits, ⁵ _____ subjects are often friends or relatives. These non-professional models, many of ⁶ _____ remain anonymous, are

Self Portrait by Lucian Freud

painted with an intensity that is often shocking and disturbing.

Although he works in a figurative style, Freud's work cannot be categorized easily. His importance, ⁷ _____ had been recognized for a long time in Britain, turned into super-celebrity status after a retrospective exhibition ⁸ _____ was held in Washington, DC in 1987. Robert Hughes, ⁹ _____ was the art critic for TIME magazine, described Freud as 'the greatest living realist painter.'

Even more fame came later, when a portrait by Freud sold for £7.86 million at an auction in 2007. The painting, ¹⁰ _____ is a 1992 portrait of his friend Bruce Bernard, broke the record for a work sold by a living European artist.

b In which gap(s) could you also use *that*? _____

c Link the sentences using a relative clause. In which ones do you not need to use a relative pronoun?

1 That's the book. I told you about it.
   That's *the book which / that I told you about* .

2 I was talking to a man. He is a colleague of mine.
   The man _____
   _____ .

3 You said something. I didn't understand it.
   I didn't understand _____
   _____ .

4 She looks ill. It's a bit worrying.
   She looks _____
   _____ .

5 He's a famous politician. His wife left him last week.
   He's the _____
   _____ .

6 This house was built in 1534. It is one of the oldest houses in the village.
   This house, _____
   _____ .

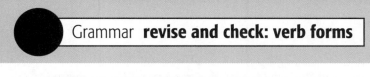

Grammar **revise and check: verb forms**

● Put the verbs in brackets in the correct form.

1 How many people _went_____ to the concert last weekend? (**go**)

2 How long _____ ill? If you don't feel better tomorrow, you really must go to the doctor's. (**feel**)

3 I _____ three cups of coffee already today. I'd better not have any more. (**have**)

4 We _____ for over an hour before we realized we'd left the map at home. (**drive**)

5 They arrived back from holiday to the terrible news that their house _____ by the heavy storms. (**damage**)

6 It _____ that house prices will continue to go up in the next five years. (**think**)

7 I _____ all my exams by the end of July – I can't wait. (**finish**)

8 Don't phone me between 7.00 and 7.30 as I _____ the children to bed. (**put**)

9 If he _____ his driving test, I'll be really surprised. (**not pass**)

10 As soon as I _____ to him, I'll let you know what he's going to do. (**speak**)

11 If you _____ so untidy, you'd be able to find things in your room. (**not be**)

12 If the rescuers hadn't found him so quickly, he _____. (**not survive**)

13 The match can't _____ very exciting – the final score was 0–0. (**be**)

14 She was standing at the traffic lights when the accident happened, so she must _____ whose fault it was. (**see**)

15 Do you remember _____ my glasses on the table? I'm sure I left them there. (**see**)

16 My ex-boyfriend is very friendly with my brother, so I can't avoid _____ him from time to time. (**meet**)

17 She apologized for _____ so rude on the phone. (**be**)

18 My parents persuaded me _____ the job in the USA. (**not take**)

19 I wish I _____ a more patient person – I think I take after my father. (**be**)

20 I wish you _____ me that the book was going to be so sad. I burst out crying on the train – it was very embarrassing. (**warn**)

1B *the...the...* + comparatives

a 2 a 3 g 4 b 5 d 6 f 7 e 8 c

b 2 The sooner we start, the sooner we'll finish.
3 The older you get, the wiser you become.
4 The faster people drive, the more accidents they have.
5 The hotter the weather is, the more you need to drink.
6 The better you know her, the more you'll like her.
7 The more slowly you cook it, the better it'll taste.
8 The more work we do now, the less we'll have to do later.

c Possible answers
2 ...the sooner we'll arrive.
3 ...the fitter / healthier you'll be.
4 ...the more clothes I wear.
5 ...the meaner they are.

2B *so / such...that*

a 2 such a 3 so 4 such 5 so 6 so 7 such a 8 such

b 2 It was such a bad film (that) we left after half an hour.
3 The food was so disgusting (that) nobody could eat it.
4 He made so many mistakes (that) the boss sacked him.
5 It was such beautiful music (that) everyone stopped to listen.
6 They were such good seats (that) we had a perfect view.

c Possible answers
2 ...we had to put on the air conditioning.
3 ...I can't go out this weekend.
4 ...we went straight to bed.
5 ...we left the restaurant.

3C *likely* and *probably*

a 2 probably 3 probably 4 likely 5 likely 6 probably
7 likely 8 probably

b 2 The builders aren't likely to finish before the summer.
3 The meeting is likely to finish late.
4 The jury will probably find him guilty.
5 There's likely to be a lot of traffic this evening.
6 We'll probably never know what really happened.
7 We aren't likely to be here at the weekend.

4B *would rather, had better*

a 2 better 3 better 4 rather 5 better 6 better
7 rather 8 rather

b 2 I'd rather go shopping now.
3 I'd rather not go out tonight.
4 We'd better hurry.
5 You' better not go to work today.
6 Would you rather eat in or go out tonight?

d Possible answers
1 stay in / revise tonight; not go out tonight
2 drive carefully / drive slowly; not go too fast

5C *as*

a 2 f 3 h 4 c 5 g 6 i 7 a 8 j 9 d 10 e

b 2 as 3 like 4 like 5 as, as 6 as 7 as 8 like

c Possible answers
2 it's a public holiday 3 it's going to rain
4 a TV presenter 5 tall as my sister

6B *have something done*

a 2 He needs to have his coat / jacket cleaned. 3 She needs to have her shoe repaired. 4 She needs to have her hair / fringe cut. 5 He needs to have his eyes tested.

b 2 had my portrait painted
3 having my photo taken
4 are having our kitchen redecorated
5 have your blood pressure checked
6 had your fortune told
7 I'm having my car serviced / going to have my car serviced
8 to have my watch repaired
9 have the big tree cut down
10 have our house repainted
11 I'm having the brakes tested/ I'm going to have the brakes tested
12 had a burglar alarm installed

7B *whatever, whenever*, etc.

a 2 Whenever 3 Whoever 4 however 5 whatever
6 wherever 7 Whenever 8 however 9 whichever
10 Whoever 11 whichever 12 wherever

b Possible answers
2 they never think they have enough money 3 you have some money 4 you prefer 5 a McDonald's 6 you are

a Match 1–8 with a–h to make complete sentences.

1 | h | The more dangerous the sport,...
2 | ☐ | The longer I waited,...
3 | ☐ | The more you work,...
4 | ☐ | The younger you are,...
5 | ☐ | The older you are,...
6 | ☐ | The earlier we leave,...
7 | ☐ | The longer I stay in bed,...
8 | ☐ | The faster I speak,...

a the angrier I got.
b the easier it is to learn something.
c the more mistakes I make.
d the harder it is to find a job.
e the worse I feel.
f the less traffic there will be.
g the more you earn.
h ~~the more I enjoy it.~~

b Rewrite the sentences using *The...the...* + a comparative.

1 If a car is big it uses more petrol.   *The bigger a car is, the more petrol it uses.*

2 If we start soon we'll finish soon. _____

3 When you get old you become wiser. _____

4 If people drive fast they have more accidents. _____

5 If the weather is hot you need to drink more. _____

6 When you know her well you'll like her more. _____

7 If you cook it slowly, it'll taste better. _____

8 If we do a lot of work now, we'll have less to do later. _____

c Complete the sentences with your own ideas.

1 The more you practise your English, *the better you will get* _____.

2 The sooner we leave, _____.

3 The more exercise you do, _____.

4 The colder the weather is, _____.

5 The more money people have, _____.

a Complete the sentences with *so*, *such*, or *such a*.

1 My case is _so_____ heavy (that) I can hardly pick it up.

2 It was _____ long flight (that) the children got very bored.

3 There were _____ many people at the airport (that) we couldn't see him.

4 It was _____ awful weather (that) we couldn't leave the hotel.

5 We had _____ much luggage (that) we had to ask a porter to help us.

6 Jim is _____ selfish (that) he can't think about anybody else.

7 Jim is _____ selfish person (that) he can't think about anybody else.

8 They were _____ cheap tickets (that) we decided to buy them.

b Rewrite the sentences using *so*, *such*, or *such a*.

1 I played badly. I lost 6–0, 6–0.

I played _so badly (that) I lost 6–0, 6–0_____.

2 The film was very bad. We left after half an hour.

It was _____.

3 The food was disgusting. Nobody could eat it.

The food _____.

4 He made a lot of mistakes. The boss sacked him.

He made _____.

5 The music was beautiful. Everyone stopped to listen.

It was _____.

6 They were good seats. We had a perfect view.

They were _____.

c Complete the sentences with your own ideas.

1 She has so many clothes (that) _she never knows what to wear_____.

2 It was such a hot day (that) _____.

3 I have so much work (that) _____.

4 We were so tired (that) _____.

5 They were playing such loud music (that) _____.

a Complete the sentences with *likely* or *probably*.

1 My mother's _likely_ to be in the garden watering the plants.
2 I'll _____ be very busy tomorrow.
3 The missing plane _____ crashed in the sea.
4 There's _____ to be a hurricane later this month.
5 They aren't very _____ to raise our salary, are they?
6 James will _____ be late. He always is.
7 I'm _____ to be very busy tomorrow.
8 The police say that the burglars were _____ local people.

b Rewrite the sentences changing from *probably* to *likely* or vice versa.

1 The weather forecast said it's likely to snow tonight.
   The weather forecast said it _will probably snow tonight_____.
2 The builders probably won't finish until the summer.
   The builders aren't _____.
3 The meeting will probably finish late.
   The meeting is _____.
4 The jury are likely to find him guilty.
   The jury will _____.
5 There will probably be a lot of traffic this evening.
   There _____.
6 It's likely that we'll never know what really happened.
   We'll _____.
7 We probably won't be here at the weekend.
   We aren't _____.

c Ask a partner the questions.

1 What will you probably do next summer?
2 Are you likely to be living in this town in five years' time? Why / Why not?
3 Do you think you will probably pass the end of course exam?
4 Where are you likely to be this evening at 9.30?

New English File Teacher's Book Upper-intermediate
Photocopiable © Oxford University Press 2008

ⓐ Complete the sentences with *rather* or *better*.

1 Would you _rather_ walk or go by car
tonight?

2 You'd _____ not forget Jane's birthday
this year!

3 We'd _____ reserve a table. It's a very
popular restaurant.

4 I'd _____ go to Ireland than England
for a holiday.

5 I'd _____ write that down. I'm very
forgetful.

6 We'd _____ not be late for class. We're
having a test today.

7 Wouldn't you _____ go to the cinema
than rent a DVD?

8 I'd _____ not meet my ex-boyfriend, so
I'm not going to the party.

ⓑ Rewrite the sentences using *would rather* or
had better.

1 You should take an umbrella in case it rains.

You *'d better take an umbrella in case it rains.*

2 I'd prefer to go shopping now. There won't
be so many people.

I _____.

3 I'd prefer not to go out tonight. I'm
exhausted.

I _____.

4 We ought to hurry. The film starts in ten
minutes.

We _____.

5 You shouldn't go to work today. You don't
look well.

You _____.

6 Would you prefer to eat in or go out
tonight?

Would _____?

ⓒ Ask a partner the questions.

1 Would you rather go on holiday
with friends or with your family?

2 Would you rather work for yourself
or for a company? Why?

3 Would you rather live in your town
or somewhere else? Why?

4 Would you rather be an only child
or have brothers and sisters? Why?

ⓓ Complete the sentences with your own ideas.
Make one negative and one positive.

1 I have an exam tomorrow, so I'd better

_____

_____.

2 It's very foggy tonight, so we'd better

_____

_____.

5C Mini grammar *as*

a Match 1–10 to a–j to make complete sentences.

1 [b] You're nearly as tall…
2 ☐ The burglar was arrested…
3 ☐ He's very well known…
4 ☐ We'll have to use this scarf…
5 ☐ I didn't go and see that film…
6 ☐ As I wasn't feeling very well…
7 ☐ It isn't as foggy…
8 ☐ Turn the light off…
9 ☐ I never read that newspaper…
10 ☐ As I was coming here…

a as it was yesterday.
b ~~as me.~~
c as a bandage.
d as it's too biased.
e I met an old friend.
f just as he was leaving the house.
g as the reviews were awful.
h as a composer and conductor.
i I didn't go to work.
j as you go out.

b Complete the sentences with *like* or *as*.

1 This tastes _like_ chicken, or is it turkey?
2 My brother works _____ a freelance journalist.
3 He looks _____ my father. They have the same mouth and nose.
4 That sounds _____ thunder. Do you think it's going to rain?
5 It's not _____ cold today _____ yesterday.
6 Please don't use that glass _____ an ashtray!
7 Teresa is late _____ usual.
8 I'm not sure what it is, but it smells _____ petrol.

> **Remember:**
>
> Use **like** to say things are similar.
> *My jacket is **like** yours.*
> *He looks **like** a basketball player.*
>
> Use **as** for comparisons and to describe
> somebody's job or something's function.
> *I'm **as** tall **as** my father.*
> *He works **as** a waiter.*

c Complete the sentences with your own ideas.

1 As I was coming out of the cinema _I met an old school friend_____.
2 All the shops will be shut tomorrow as _____.
3 It's very cloudy. It looks as if _____.
4 I would love to work as _____.
5 I'm not as _____ as my _____.

a Look at the pictures. What do these people need to have done?

1 _They need to have the_
window mended.

2 _____

3 _____

4 _____

5 _____

b Complete the sentences with the correct form of *have*, the past participle, and the words in brackets.

1 I need _to have my suit cleaned_ before my cousin's wedding. (**suit / clean**)

2 When we were in Paris I _____ by a street artist. (**my portrait / paint**)

3 I absolutely hate _____. I always look awful! (**my photo / take**)

4 We _____ at the moment. (**our kitchen / redecorate**)

5 If you are feeling dizzy you should _____. (**blood pressure / check**)

6 Have you ever _____? (**your fortune / tell**)

7 I _____ tomorrow. Could you give me a lift to work? (**my car / service**)

8 I need _____ – it's not working properly. (**my watch / repair**)

9 They had to _____ in their garden. It was damaged in a storm. (**the big tree / cut down**)

10 We usually _____ every five years. (**our house / repaint**)

11 My car makes a funny noise when it stops. I _____ tomorrow. (**brakes / test**)

12 Our neighbours _____ last month. (**a burglar alarm / install**)

c Ask a partner the questions.

1 Where do you go to have your hair cut?

2 Do you mind having your photo taken?

3 When was the last time you had your blood pressure checked?

4 How often do you have your eyes tested?

5 Have you ever had your portrait painted? If not, would you like to?

New English File Teacher's Book Upper-intermediate
Photocopiable © Oxford University Press 2008

a Complete the sentences with *whatever, whichever, whoever, whenever, however,* or *wherever.*

1 *Whatever* I do my boss always finds something wrong with it.
2 _____ I see Nelly she's always in a good mood.
3 _____ broke the window must come and see me after school.
4 I never put on weight _____ much I eat.
5 We've decided that we are going to go _____ happens.
6 People were really friendly to us _____ we went.
7 _____ I go to New York on business I always see a show.
8 I never seem to get better at tennis _____ much I practise.
9 You have _____ one you want and I'll have the other one.
10 _____ said 'it's better to be poor but happy' was wrong!
11 We could fly or get the train, _____ is quicker.
12 I'm sure the police will find him _____ he's hiding.

b Complete the sentences with your own ideas.

1 I'll always love you whatever *you do* _____ .
2 However rich people are _____ .
3 You can pay me back whenever _____ .
4 Let's buy this one or that one, whichever _____ .
5 Wherever you go in the world you'll always find _____ .
6 I'm not going to let you in whoever _____ .

Introduction

A pairwork activity

This photocopiable 'getting to know you' activity can be used together with the Grammar activity on *p.159* for a first-day class, especially if your SS do not yet have the Student's Book. It should help you and your class remember each other's names.

SS talk about names through a names quiz, read and discuss an article about the importance of names, and answer questions with their partner.

Copy one sheet per student.

> **LANGUAGE** Vocabulary related to names:
> *nickname, name…*, etc.

- Put SS in pairs and give each student a sheet.
- Focus on **a** (the names quiz). Give SS five minutes to answer the questions with a partner. Point out that (**M**) and (**F**) in question 4 mean male, female. Check answers.

> 1 b
> 2 **a** Katherine (or Catherine), **b** William, **c** Richard,
> **d** Robert, **e** Samuel (male) or Samantha (female),
> **f** Elizabeth
> 3 **a** Harry Potter or Prince Harry **b** Keira Knightley
> **c** Brad Pitt **d** Kylie Minogue **e** Victoria Beckham
> 4 Gwyneth Paltrow and Chris Martin – Apple
> Angelina Jolie and Brad Pitt – Shiloh
> Victoria and David Beckham – Romeo
> Tom Cruise and Katie Holmes – Suri

- Ask SS if any celebrities in their country have given their children strange names, and also ask them to give you some examples of what names are currently popular (or unpopular) and why.
- Now focus on **b**, which is a pre-reading task. Give SS, in pairs, time to discuss whether they think the statements are true or false and why. Elicit answers, but don't say whether they are right or wrong at this stage as that is what they will find out when they read the text.
- Now focus on **c**, and set a time limit for SS to read the article and check their answers. Check answers.

> 1 F   2 T   3 F   4 T   5 F

- Go through the text and deal with any vocabulary problems. Finally ask SS if they agree what the article says, and ask them why / why not.
- Finally focus on the questions in **d**. You could get SS to interview you first, and then they interview each other.
- Get feedback from as many SS as possible, particularly about why their parents chose their names as these anecdotes often help SS to remember each other's names.

1 A Q and A

A pairwork question formation and fluency activity

SS revise question formation by ordering jumbled questions and then interview each other. Copy one sheet per pair and cut into **A** and **B**.

> **LANGUAGE** Word order in questions:
> *What makes you want to learn English?*
> *What don't you like about where you live?*
> *Would you mind telling me what you are afraid of?*

- Put SS in pairs, ideally facing each other, and give out the sheets. **Make sure SS can't see each other's sheets.**
- Focus on **a** and give SS time to reorder the words to make their questions. Go around monitoring and helping. Check answers orally, first for **A**, then for **B**.

> **A**
> 1 Could you tell me if you speak any other languages?
> 2 How do you spend your weekends?
> 3 What's your idea of a perfect holiday?
> 4 Do you come from a big family?
> 5 What kind of food don't you like?
> 6 Have you ever been to an English-speaking country?
> 7 What did you want to be when you were a child?
> 8 What do you use the Internet for?
> 9 What kind of things annoy you in a restaurant?
> 10 Do you mind telling me where you bought those shoes?
> 11 Can you remember the first time you travelled by plane?
> 12 What music do you like listening to in the car?
>
> **B**
> 1 Can you remember the last time you bought a DVD?
> 2 What would be your ideal evening?
> 3 What kind of things are you good at?
> 4 What don't you like about where you live?
> 5 What made you want to learn English?
> 6 What were you doing this time yesterday?
> 7 Do you know how long this school has been open?
> 8 Would you like to go and live in a foreign country?
> 9 Have you ever broken your arm or leg?
> 10 Would you mind telling me what you are afraid of?
> 11 What most irritates you / What irritates you most about people from your country?
> 12 When was the last time you went to the cinema?

- Focus on **b** and get SS to sit facing each other. They then take it in turns to ask each other their questions. Emphasize that SS should listen actively to their partner's answers and show interest, e.g. *Really? That's interesting. Me too!* and ask follow-up questions where possible to get more information and make the activity more like a real conversation.

1 B A walk through the forest

A psychological test and free-speaking activity

SS use their imagination to describe a walk through a forest and then interpret each other's descriptions, revising vocabulary of personality.

Copy one sheet per student and cut into two separate pieces, **The story** and **The interpretation**.

<table>
<tr><td>LANGUAGE</td><td>Present tense (narrative):
It's a very dark forest. It makes me feel afraid. I start to walk more quickly.
The…the + comparatives: The darker the forest is, the more negative you feel about your life.
Vocabulary: personality</td></tr>
</table>

- Tell SS that they are going to use their imagination to describe a walk in a forest. They will describe the situation to each other, and then ask their partner to imagine the details.

- Put SS in pairs, ideally facing each other, and give out a sheet to each (just **The story** part, not **The interpretation**), and give them time to read it. You may need to pre-teach / elicit *forest* = a large area of trees, *scary* = frightening, *fence* = wooden wall around a house, a *bear* = large, heavy wild animal with thick fur often found in forests, *gate* = small door in a wall or fence, *wild* (garden) = not cultivated or tidy, e.g. with very long grass.

- Tell the **A**s to put their sheet face down. They have to answer **B**'s questions about the walk **in as much detail as they can**. **B** begins by reading the introduction to **A** (*It's a beautiful summer's day…*) and then asks **A** the questions and takes notes of **A**'s answers.

- When **B** has finished they change roles: **B** turns the sheet over and **A** asks all the questions and takes notes of his / her answers.

- When both students have described their walk to each other, tell SS that this was a psychological personality test and that now they are going to interpret each other's answers. Give out the other half of the photocopied sheet: **The interpretation**.

- Give SS time to read the interpretation and then tell them to take turns to use the information to interpret their partner's description. Encourage them to do this in as imaginative a way as possible!

- Get some quick feedback from pairs to find out if SS agreed with the interpretation of their personality.

Doctor, doctor

Two roleplays

SS take the parts of doctor / patient and revise the grammar and vocabulary of the lesson.

Copy one sheet per pair and cut into **A** and **B**.

<table>
<tr><td>LANGUAGE</td><td>Present perfect:
How long have you been feeling like this?
Vocabulary: illness and medicine</td></tr>
</table>

- Put SS in pairs, ideally facing each other, and give out the sheets. **Make sure SS can't see each other's sheets.** If you have odd numbers make one pair a three and have two **A**s (or take part in the roleplay yourself).

Extra support You could pre-teach the meaning and pronunciation of *alternative medicine* = non-traditional medicine, *acupuncture* /ˈækjʊpʌŋktʃə/ = a way of treating illness or stopping pain by inserting thin needles into the body; *hypochondriac* /ˌhaɪpəˈkɒndriæk/ = a person who is always worried about his / her health, even when there is nothing wrong with them; *diagnosis* /daɪəgˈnəʊsɪs/ = what a doctor thinks is wrong with a patient.

- Give SS time to read the instructions for **Roleplay 1**.

SS should think about their role and what they are going to say. Encourage the patients and doctors to be as imaginative and inventive as possible in their questions and answers. Tell the patients to invent a new *persona* (age, job, etc.).

- When SS are ready, tell the **B**s to begin. Give SS time to act out the roleplay. While they do this move around the class monitoring and noting down anything you might want to draw their attention to afterwards.

- Repeat the process for the second roleplay, but with **A** starting. If a pair finishes really fast, you could get early finishers to repeat the roleplay, but changing roles.

- Finally get feedback from some pairs on what the outcome of the patient / doctor conversation was.

 ## Spot the difference

A pairwork information gap activity

SS describe their pictures to each other to find twelve differences between them. Copy one sheet per pair and cut into **A** and **B**.

<table>
<tr><td>LANGUAGE</td><td>Adjective order:
She's wearing a long patterned skirt and flat sandals.
He has long fair hair and a short beard.
Vocabulary: clothes and appearance</td></tr>
</table>

- Put SS in pairs, ideally facing each other, and give out the sheets. **Make sure SS can't see each other's sheets.**

- Focus on the instructions and explain that they both have the same picture, but it has been changed and there are twelve differences. Encourage SS to try to use adjectives in pairs when they describe the people, getting the order right, i.e. to say, *My first person is a tall slim woman. She has long dark hair…* (rather than *She's tall and slim. Her hair is long and dark*).

- Get **A** to start by describing the first person on the left (*My first person is a girl. She's quite tall and slim, and she has very long dark hair.*). **B** should listen, and ask questions if necessary, to see if there are any differences. Then **B** describes the next person.

- SS continue in pairs. When they have described all the people and found the differences they can finally show each other the pictures to check.

- Check the differences, correcting any mistakes with adjective order.

1 In A woman 1 is wearing a long patterned skirt, in B it's plain.
2 In A woman 1 is wearing a long sleeved sweater, in B it's short sleeved.
3 In A man 2 is wearing smart jeans, in B they are scruffy.
4 In A man 2's top hasn't got a pocket, in B it has.
5 In A woman 3 is wearing a jacket with a fur collar, in B the collar isn't fur.
6 In A woman 3's boots are flat, in B they have high heels.
7 In A man 4 is wearing a black and white striped football shirt, in B it's a plain one.
8 In A man 4 has short fair hair, in B he has short dark hair.
9 In A woman 5 has long curly hair, in B she has long straight hair.
10 In A woman 5 is wearing a short tight cardigan, in B she's wearing a loose long one.
11 In A man 6 is wearing a checked shirt, in B it's a patterned one.
12 In A man 6 is wearing long baggy trousers, in B he's wearing baggy shorts.

2 B Did it really happen to you?

Question prompts for SS to tell anecdotes in small groups

SS are dealt cards with prompts for anecdotes. They plan what they are going to say, inventing details if they haven't had the experiences. Copy and cut up one set of cards per group of three.

LANGUAGE	Narrative tenses: past simple, past continuous, past perfect (simple and continuous)

- Put SS in groups of three, and give each group a set of cards, face down. The cards are then dealt out between them, and each student looks at his / her cards. Now set a time limit, e.g. two minutes, for SS to plan what they are going to say. Stress that if they have had the experience to tell the truth, if not to invent the details. Help SS with the vocabulary they need if necessary.

  Extra support SS may want to make notes on their cards to help them tell their anecdotes.

- Suggest that each student starts with '*I'm going to tell you about a time when…*' Then SS take turns to tell their first anecdote. After each person has spoken, the other two decide if what they have said is true or not. Monitor, help, and correct any misuse of narrative tenses.

- If there is time, let each student tell three anecdotes. Get feedback to find out who was able to convince the group of a story that wasn't really true.

  Non-cut alternative Make one copy per pair. Put SS into pairs and give them a few moments to read through the cards. Tell SS to choose two anecdotes each to tell each other. Give them a few minutes to plan what they are going to say. They then tell alternate anecdotes. Encourage SS to ask for more information where appropriate.

2 C Guess my adverb

A pairwork activity

SS practise using adverbs by trying to guess the missing adverb in their partner's sentences. Copy one sheet per pair and cut into **A** and **B**.

LANGUAGE	Adverbs: *Unfortunately, I didn't pass my driving test.*

- Put SS in pairs **A** and **B** and give out the sheets. If possible sit **A** and **B** face to face so that they can't see each other's sheet.

- Demonstrate the activity. Write these two sentences on a piece of paper:

  *I lived in Brazil for three years so I speak Portuguese **fluently**.*
  *The exam was **incredibly** difficult.*

  Then write them on the board with the bold adverbs gapped, and get SS to suggest adverbs that could go in the gaps. If they say the wrong one, say *Try again*. When they get the right one say: *That's right*. Highlight that there are often several possibilities, but that SS have to try to say the same sentence that their partner has.

  Focus on the sentences and explain that half of their sentences have gaps, and that the missing words are adverbs. Where **A** has a gapped sentence **B** has the completed sentence and vice versa. The aim of the activity is for SS to try and guess the missing adverbs by making guesses. They

should continue guessing until they say **the exact adverb** their partner has in his / her completed sentence. Their partner should help and prompt as necessary, but not give away the answers if possible.

- Give SS a few minutes to read their sentences and try to think of possible adverbs to fill their gaps.

- Student **A** begins by trying to guess the missing adverb in his / her first sentence. Emphasize that when SS make their guesses they should say **the whole sentence**. If the adverb is wrong, **B** should say: *Try again*, and **A** has another guess. When **A** correctly guesses the missing adverb, he / she writes it in the gap.

- Now **B** tries to guess his / her first adverb, etc.

  Extra challenge At the end of the activity you could get SS to turn over the sheets and try to recall the adverbs by reading out the sentences one by one, saying 'blank' or making a noise where the missing adverb is and letting the class call it out.

3 A Crime and punishment

A pairwork information gap speaking activity

SS read about laws in different countries, some of which are true and some false. They then tell each other about them, and together decide which they think are true. Copy one sheet per pair and cut into **A** and **B**.

LANGUAGE	Passive (all forms) Vocabulary: crime and punishment

Extra support You could pre-teach some of the new vocabulary in the texts, e.g. *litter* = rubbish, *cactus* = a plant which grows in the desert, *the state* = the government, *to be released from prison* = allowed to leave prison, *whistle* /ˈwɪsl/ = make a noise by blowing air through your lips. You could also revise the crime-specific vocabulary, e.g. *commit a crime, be arrested, be charged with a crime, be found guilty, be sentenced, be fined*, etc.

- Put SS in pairs **A** and **B** and give out the sheets. **Make sure SS can't see each other's sheets.**

- Focus on the instructions and go through them. Then set a time limit for SS to read their laws, and underline the key points, i.e. the country, the crime, and the punishment. Move round and help with any vocabulary or pronunciation problems.

- Now get **A** to tell **B** about his / her five laws. Encourage SS to improvise / rephrase this from memory and to only look at their sheet if absolutely necessary. Then **A** and **B** should decide together which **two** laws are true. **A** can remind **B** of the five laws as necessary and **B** can note down the main points for each law as a memory aid.

  Extra challenge You could get SS to do this completely from memory by getting them to turn their sheets over and writing the names of the countries on the board.

- **B** now tells **A** about his / her five laws and together they decide which **three** are true.

- Now get feedback to find out which laws SS think are true. You could write A 1, 2, 3, 4, 5 on the board and record which laws most SS think are true, and then do the same for **B**. Finally tell them which are true and which are invented.

True laws:	A 1 and 3	B 1, 3, and 4

- Finally ask SS if they would like any of the laws (both real or invented) to be laws in their country and why.

3 B In twenty years' time…

A pairwork activity

SS revise the two new future tenses by discussing predictions and deciding whether they think the things will happen, and whether they think it will be a good or bad thing. Copy one sheet per pair.

LANGUAGE	Future perfect and future continuous

- Put SS into pairs and give out the sheets. Go through the predictions and make sure SS understand them all. SS then discuss each one in turn, first saying whether they think the predictions will be true in 20 years' time, and secondly saying whether they think it will be a good thing.

Extra support Discuss the first prediction with the whole class eliciting opinions and giving your own opinion.

- Stop the activity when SS have discussed all the predictions or when you think it has gone on for long enough. Get feedback from different pairs, and find out which prediction SS think is the most positive and which is the most negative.

3 C Are you a risk-taker?

A pairwork questionnaire

SS interview each other with a questionnaire to find out if they are risk-takers. Copy one sheet per student.

LANGUAGE	General vocabulary: *do a parachute jump, hitch hike, sunbathe,* etc.

- Put SS into pairs **A** and **B** and give out the questionnaires.
- Go through the questions and make sure SS understand and can pronounce any new vocabulary, e.g. *do a parachute jump, charity* = an organization that collects money to give to people who are poor, ill etc., *hitchhike* = to travel by getting free rides in other people's cars, *second hand* = not new, *past its sell-by-date* = when a food item has passed the date by which it should be eaten, *drastically* = in a very noticeable way, etc.
- Focus on instruction **a**. Then tell **B** to put his / her questionnaire face down. **A** interviews **B** and makes notes of the answers. Then they swap roles.
- Focus on instruction **b**. Tell SS to read through the notes they made of their partner's answers, and assess how much of a risk-taker he / she is. Tell SS to try to assess whether their partner is prepared to take risks in some areas of life but not in others, e.g. relationships, money, physical risk, etc.
- Get feedback from the class to find out which SS are real risk-takers.

4 A Snakes and ladders

A group board game

SS revise the second and third conditional by completing sentences and moving around a board. Copy one sheet per group of three or four.

LANGUAGE	Second and third conditionals:
	If I found some extra money in my bank account, I'd spend it.
	If you had told me what time your plane was arriving, I would have picked you up.

- Put SS into groups of three or four players. Each group needs counters, e.g. bits of paper or small coins and a dice. If you don't have a dice put 1–6 on small pieces of paper inside an envelope for SS to pick. Give each group a board.

- Focus on the board and highlight that some of the sentences to be completed are second conditionals and some are third conditionals.
- Each player puts a counter on the **Start** square. S1 throws the dice and moves according to the number they get.
- Explain the rules of the game: if a player lands on the foot of a ladder he / she goes up the ladder to the square at the top. If a player lands on the head of a snake they go down the snake to the square at the bottom. If a player lands on a square with an unfinished sentence he / she has to complete the sentence in a way which is grammatically correct and makes sense. The other SS in the group have to decide if the sentence is a valid one. You should be the judge if there is a dispute. If the sentence is valid, the player **moves forward three squares**. If not, he / she **moves back three squares**. If a player lands on a square where another player has been before, he / she must complete the sentence in a different way. The first player to reach **Finish** is the winner.
- While SS play the game monitor to help them with the rules and check that they are making correct sentences. If a group has an early winner, let them play again until each group has had at least one winner.

4 B Communication breakdown!

A pairwork roleplay activity

A free-speaking activity to promote fluency. SS roleplay being a young married couple who need to try and solve some very typical problems and differences of opinion that have arisen. Copy one sheet per pair and cut into **A** and **B**.

LANGUAGE	All tenses

- Put SS in pairs, ideally facing each other, and give out the sheets. Try to pair SS with someone of the opposite sex. If you have an uneven gender split, get women to play men or vice versa. If you have odd numbers make one pair a threesome and have two **A**s or two **B**s (or take part in the roleplay yourself).
- First set the scene. Explain that you have two friends, Emma and Martin. Tell SS that they got married five years ago and at first they were very happy but now they are having some problems. Tell SS that they are going to take the parts of Emma and Martin and that they are going to talk about their problems and to try and find solutions.
- Put SS in pairs **A** and **B** and give out the copies. Give SS 5 minutes to read their instructions. **They must not look at their partner's sheet at all.** Tell them to highlight what they think is key information and try to memorize it.

Extra support As a memory aid they could write down the four points they are going to discuss on the back of the sheet and just use this as a memory aid.

- When SS are ready, get them to sit face to face and tell them to imagine that they have just finished dinner and that they are going to discuss the four points on the sheet – remind them of the difference between *discuss* and *argue*. Set a nominal time limit (but be flexible depending how the conversations are going), and highlight the instruction: **Keep calm and don't lose your temper.** However, if your SS get into their roles, you should be prepared for some animated conversations.

Emphasize that they should go through the points one by one, first giving their own points of view and then trying to reach agreement. Go around monitoring, making sure that SS don't get stuck for too long on one topic and not leaving themselves enough time to discuss all the points.

- Emma begins the conversation, e.g. *Martin, I think we need to talk… Let the discussion / argument carry on until you think most pairs have discussed all the points. Give a two-minute warning for SS to be able to try to reach agreement on whatever point they are discussing before saying: *Stop!*

- Get feedback from as many pairs as you can to find out if they managed to reach agreement and what decisions they took.

4 C What is it?

A group card game

SS play a definitions guessing game in small groups of 3–4. Copy and cut up one set of cards per group.

LANGUAGE	*It sounds / looks / feels / tastes / smells (like / as if …)*
	relative clauses

- Put SS into small groups of 3–4. Give each group a set of cards face down.

- Demonstrate the activity. Pick a card. First use the prompts on the card to define it. Then add more information to help SS guess the word, e.g. for *velvet*: *It's a material. It feels very soft and smooth. It's often used to make dresses and jackets, especially for the winter and for special occasions, when people want to dress up. It's not usually patterned but in plain strong colours like black, red, etc.*

- Highlight that SS mustn't say the word on the card but must describe it, first using the prompts on the card and then adding more clues. Remind them that if they have *sounds / feels /tastes*, etc. they must add an adjective; if they have *sounds / feels / tastes like*, they must add a noun and if they have *sounds / feels / tastes as if* they must add a verb phrase.

- S1 picks up a card and describes the word. The first person in the group to say the word gets the card. Then S2 takes the next card and so on, SS taking turns to pick a card until they are all used up. The person with most cards is the winner.

- Set a time limit, e.g. five minutes, for SS to play the game, though you may want to let it go on longer if SS are enjoying it and they still have several cards left to define.

- When SS have finished find out who the winner was in each group.

5 A Gerund or infinitive?

A pairwork activity

SS complete questions with gerunds or infinitives, and then ask them to each other. Copy one sheet per pair and cut into **A** and **B**.

LANGUAGE	Verbs + gerund or infinitive (with or without *to*)

- Put SS into pairs, **A** and **B**, and give out the sheets. Focus on instruction **a**, and explain that SS should write the verbs in the verb column on the right (not in the sentences). Give SS time to write the verbs in and then check answers, first **A**'s then **B**'s.

> **A 1** meeting **2** play **3** to worry **4** to drive
> **5** to buy **6** doing **7** going **8** going out
> **9** to pack **10** to be **11** to look after
> **12** being able to
>
> **B 1** watching **2** to charge **3** studying **4** to buy
> **5** see **6** to swim **7** repairing **8** to learn
> **9** to live **10** speaking **11** to do **12** eating

- Focus on instruction **b**. Tell SS to fold their sheet on the fold line so they cannot see the verbs in the **verb** column, and to remember the right form of the **bold** verb in brackets. **A** asks **B** the questions, and then they swap. Encourage SS to react to what their partner says and ask for more information when they can.

- Monitor and correct any mistakes with gerunds and infinitives. Finally, get feedback on some of the more interesting answers.

5 B usually, used to, get used to

A pairwork activity

SS practise asking and talking about things people used to do, usually do, or could / couldn't get used to doing. Copy one sheet per pair and cut into **A** and **B**.

LANGUAGE	*Did you use to…?*
	Do you usually…?
	Do you think you could get used to…?

- Put SS into pairs, **A** and **B**, and give out the sheets. Focus on the instructions and on the three possible questions forms in the speech bubble. Highlight that for each prompt SS must use the most appropriate question form. Ask an **A** student to ask the first question: *Do you think you could get used to always working at night?* Then elicit **B**'s first question: *Do you usually celebrate your birthday?* Ask first the **A**s then the **B**s which questions they will need to use, *Do you think you could get used to…?* (**A**: numbers 1, 7, 9, and 12; **B**: numbers 4, 8, and 12).

 Remind SS that after *get used to* they will need to put the verb in the *-ing* form.

Extra support You could give SS time to decide which question form they will use for each prompt before they start asking them. Check these by asking: *What about Number 1?* Then elicit first from the **A**s then the **B**s which of the three forms they think they should use, e.g. *Did you use to…?* However, don't call out the whole question.

- In pairs, SS take turns to ask and answer the questions. Remind them that the 'questioner' should show interest and ask follow-up questions wherever possible to make the exchanges into mini-conversations.

- Get some feedback from individual pairs.

5 C Reporting verbs game

A pairwork activity

SS dictate sentences to each other, and then put them into reported speech. Copy one sheet per pair and cut into **A** and **B**.

LANGUAGE	Verbs + gerund or infinitive (with or without *to*)

- Put SS into pairs, **A** and **B**, and give out the sheets. Focus on instructions **a** and **b**, and tell SS to write their eight sentences on a piece of paper or in their notebook.

- Tell SS that they should dictate their eight sentences slowly and clearly **twice**, pausing to give their partner time to write them down. Long sentences could be broken down into two parts. They should then show their partners what they have written, to check if they have made any spelling mistakes or missed words out. Get feedback to find out how many SS wrote down all their sentences correctly.

- Now focus on instruction **c**. Set a time limit for SS to put the sentences they wrote down into reported speech using the beginnings 1–8 they have been given, and using a reporting verb from the list. Then give pairs time to look at each other's reported sentences to check for mistakes. Check answers.

Extra support You could get SS to do stage **c** together, i.e. change A's sentences to reported speech and then B's.

A

1 The little girl refused to eat the cabbage.
2 The teacher reminded them to bring their dictionaries to class.
3 The boy admitted breaking the window.
4 A young man offered to help me with my case.
5 His friend advised him to go to the doctor.
6 Anya suggested going to a Chinese restaurant.
7 My brother insisted on paying for the drinks.
8 He recommended seeing the Tower of London.

B

1 The teacher apologized for being late.
2 Jane denied breaking the vase.
3 The bride promised to love her husband / him for ever.
4 The policeman warned her not to walk on her own at night.
5 Mark invited Miriam to come to a concert.
6 I regretted not buying the jacket.
7 She accused her brother of eating all the biscuits.
8 The robbers threatened to kill me if I didn't give them the money.

---

6 A Test your general knowledge

A general knowledge quiz

SS revise articles by complete quiz questions and and try to answer them in pairs. Copy one sheet per pair.

LANGUAGE	Definite and indefinite articles

- Put SS into pairs and give out the sheets. Focus on instruction **a**, and set a time limit for SS to complete the questions. Check answers.

1	the	8	–	15	a	22	a (*or* the),
2	a	9	the, –	16	the, the		an
3	the	10	the, –	17	–, the	23	the, a
4	the	11	–	18	–, –	24	the, –
5	–, –	12	the, the	19	a, –	25	–, –
6	the, the	13	a	20	the		
7	–	14	the, the	21	–		

- Focus on instruction **b**. Set a time limit, e.g. 5 minutes, for SS to try to answer as many questions as possible.
- When the time is up check answers, making sure SS use the article correctly in their answers, and see which pair had most correct answers.

1	Mercury	14	Buzz Aldrin
2	a melon	15	6
3	50	16	Cancer
4	the Mediterranean	17	New Zealand
5	men	18	dogs
6	the panda	19	Switzerland
7	blue	20	The Great Wall of China
8	16	21	potatoes
9	the letter N	22	No – it's an arachnid
10	Cheeta(h)	23	orange
11	Italy	24	The Ganges
12	Mount Everest	25	light
13	4		

6 B Talk for a minute

A group card game

SS revise countable and uncountable nouns by trying to talk for a minute about the topic on the card they pick. Copy and cut up one set of cards per group of three or four SS.

LANGUAGE	Nouns: uncountable and plural nouns

- Put SS into small groups of 3–4. Give each group a set of cards face down.
- SS pick a card in turn and try to talk for a minute about the subject on the card. They should first say what the subject is, and then say what they think. Ask someone in each group to monitor the time.

Extra support You could demonstrate by picking a card yourself and talking for a minute about the subject.

- Tell SS that if they can carry on for a minute, they keep the card. If they 'dry up', then the student on their left can try to carry on. Whoever is talking when a minute is up keeps the card. The student with the most cards at the end is the winner.
- Either set a time limit for the game, or stop it when you think SS have had enough.

6 C Biology quiz

A quiz about animals

SS revise quantifiers by doing a true / false biology quiz based on animals. Copy one sheet per pair.

LANGUAGE	Quantifiers: *each*, *all*, *neither*, etc. animal vocabulary

- Put SS into pairs and give out the sheets. Focus on instruction **a**, and on the first picture and letters. Elicit the answer from the class. Then let SS try to work out the other words. Check answers.

1	toad	2	jellyfish	3	bat	4	bear
5	alligator	6	clam				

- Focus on instruction **b** and give SS, in pairs, time to answer the questions. Encourage them to discuss each question before choosing their answers.
- Check answers and see which pair got most right answers.

1 T
2 F – they all have six legs but not all insects have wings, e.g. lice, fleas.
3 F – all elephants are great swimmers, and can swim for up to 48km, at a speed of up to 2.70km/h
4 T – they wouldn't be able to survive the low temperatures.
5 F – they have both.
6 T
7 F – e.g. lizards can regrow their tails, and if you cut a starfish into pieces, each piece will grow into a whole new starfish.
8 T – there are polar bears in Alaska and in Greenland.
9 F – most can see either two or three colours.
10 T – most bats aren't able to walk, but vampire bats can both walk and run.
11 F – crocodiles have 68–70 and alligators 80–88.
12 T
13 F – pandas don't hibernate at all.
14 F – toads can only hop (take very small jumps), whereas frogs can jump quite far.
15 F – they communicate by emitting low-frequency sounds which most humans can't hear.

A pairwork activity

SS write about their wishes into a chart. They then swap charts with a partner and ask each other to explain the information. **This is a two-page activity**. Copy an **A** and a **B** page for each pair.

| LANGUAGE | *wish* + past simple, *would*, or past perfect |

- Put SS in pairs, **A** and **B**, and give each student their corresponding sheet.
- Focus on **a** and the instructions for the circles. Point out that **they each have different instructions for what to write**. Make it clear too that SS should just write words in the circles, not sentences with *wish*, e.g. in **A**'s circle 1 he / she should write: *to play the piano* – not *I wish I had learned to play the piano*.
- Give SS five minutes to write answers in at least seven circles. When they have finished, focus on **b** and **c**, and tell them to fold their sheet in half (or tear off the instructions).
- Now get SS to swap circles. Demonstrate the activity by taking a copy from one student and asking him / her: *Why did you write…?* and elicit: *Because I wish…* Ask follow-up questions too to continue the conversation.
- SS now do the activity in pairs. Tell SS that they can ask about the information in any order. Monitor and help where necessary, correcting any errors SS make using *wish*.

7 B Guess the sentence

A pairwork activity

SS practise using linkers of contrast and purpose by trying to guess the missing part of their partner's sentences. Copy one sheet per pair and cut into **A** and **B**.

| LANGUAGE | Clauses of contrast and purpose: *even though…*, *despite…*, *so as to …*, etc. |

- Put SS in pairs, **A** and **B**, and give out the sheets.
- Demonstrate the activity. Write these two sentences as large as possible on two pieces of paper.
  I'm going to the supermarket to <u>buy some eggs</u> *because I want to make a cake.*
  We enjoyed our holiday, even though <u>the weather was bad</u>.
  Then write them on the board **with the underlined phrases gapped**, and get the class to suggest which words could complete the gaps. Tell them that they have to guess your sentence, i.e. what you have written on a piece of paper. If they guess wrongly, say: *Try again*. When they get the right one say: *That's right*, and show them the piece of paper.
- Focus on the activity and tell SS that half of their sentences have gaps and that where **A** has a gapped sentence **B** has the completed sentence and vice versa. The aim of the activity is for SS to try and guess the missing phrases. They should continue trying until they say **the exact phrase** their partner has in his / her completed sentence. Highlight that there are often several possibilities, but that SS have to try to say the same sentence that their partner has. Their partner should help and prompt as necessary.
- Give SS a few minutes to read their sentences and try to think of possible phrases to fill their gaps.
- Student **A** begins by trying to guess the missing phrase in his / her first sentence. Emphasize that when SS make their guesses they should say **the whole sentence**. If it is wrong, **B** says: *Try again* until **A** gets the right phrase, which he / she writes it in the gap.
- Now **B** tries to guess his / her first phrase, and they continue alternately.
- Find out which phrases SS found hard to guess.

7 C Grammar Auction

A class grammar game

SS revise the main grammar points of the book by playing a game where, in pairs, they have to bid to try to 'buy' correct sentences. Copy one sheet per pair.

| LANGUAGE | General revision |

- Put SS in pairs. Give each pair the list of 21 sentences. Elicit what an auction is = a public sale where things are sold to the person who offers most money. Explain that SS have 1,000 euros (or dollars, depending on which currency they are most familiar with). They have a list of sentences, some of which are correct and some incorrect. They have to bid to 'buy' as many correct sentences as they can. Bids start at 50, the next bid is 100, then 150, etc. SS must record on their sheet how much they have spent on a sentence, in order to calculate how much money they have left. The pair which buys the most correct sentences is the winner.
- Start with the first sentence and invite bids. Make the activity more fun by using typical language of an auctioneer, e.g. *How much am I offered for this fantastic sentence? 50 euros, 100? Do I hear 150? Going, going, gone to Marc and Andrea for 150 euros.*
- When you have 'sold' all the sentences, go through each one eliciting whether it is correct or not and what the mistake is. Then find out who bought the most correct sentences.

1 ✓		11 ✗	He can't have seen you or he would've said hello.
2 ✗	Her name's Marta, isn't it?	12 ✗	It looks as if it's going to rain.
3 ✓		13 ✗	We'd better go now.
4 ✗	She has beautiful long dark hair.	14 ✓	
5 ✓		15 ✓	
6 ✗	She's a wonderful student and she works hard.	16 ✓	
		17 ✗	I need to buy some new furniture for my living room.
7 ✗	The missing man is thought to be from Manchester.		
8 ✓		18 ✓	
9 ✓		19 ✗	I wish I had more free time!
10 ✗	I would have enjoyed the film more if it hadn't had subtitles.	20 ✓	
		21 ✓	

7 Revision

Questions to revise vocabulary, verb forms, and tenses

SS ask each other questions about the main vocabulary areas from *New English File* Upper-intermediate using a range of tenses and verb forms from Files 1–7. This could be used as a final 'pre-test' revision. Alternatively it could be used as an oral exam. Copy and cut up one set of cards per pair.

| LANGUAGE | Grammar and vocabulary of the book |

- SS work in pairs. Give each pair a set of cards. Set a time limit, e.g. ten minutes. SS take turns to take a card and talk to their partner about the topic on the card, using the prompts. Encourage SS to ask follow-up questions. Monitor, help, and correct.

a In pairs, do the names quiz.

> **1** 'What's in a name?' is a quotation from which Shakespeare play?
>   **a** *Hamlet*   **b** *Romeo and Juliet*   **c** *Othello*
>
> **2** 'Tom' is short for Thomas. What are these names short for?
>   **a** Kate   **b** Bill   **c** Dick   **d** Bob   **e** Sam   **f** Liz
>
> **3** In the UK, parents often name their children after celebrities or TV/film characters. Who do you think might have inspired these names which have been popular in the UK in the last few years?
>   **a** Harry   **b** Keira   **c** Bradley   **d** Kylie   **e** Victoria
>
> **4** Match the celebrity couples to their children:
>
> | | |
> |---|---|
> | ☐ Gwyneth Paltrow and Chris Martin | **a** Romeo (M) |
> | ☐ Angelina Jolie and Brad Pitt | **b** Suri (F) |
> | ☐ Victoria and David Beckham | **c** Apple (F) |
> | ☐ Tom Cruise and Katie Holmes | **d** Shiloh (F) |

b Talk to a partner. Do you think the following are true or false?

1 Your name doesn't have any influence on how happy you are.
2 Your name could prevent you from getting a job.
3 People with attractive names work harder than people with unattractive ones.
4 An actor called Norman might want to change his name.
5 Being named after a celebrity probably makes you more popular when you are a teenager.

c Read the article and check. Do you agree with what it says?

What's in a name?

'What's in a name?' asked Shakespeare's Juliet. 'A rose by any other name would smell as sweet…', that is to say, the name of a person is irrelevant. However, research by psychologists suggests that our names can have a direct effect on our happiness.

Having a popular name, it seems, can make other people think you are intelligent and attractive even before they have met you. This is because, according to psychologist Dr Philip Erwin, people associate a particular name with a stereotyped image. However, having an unpopular name can have the opposite effect. 'It can even affect your employment prospects,' says Dr Erwin. 'The first thing employers read is your name on your CV, which may immediately create a negative stereotype in their mind.'

As a result, people with less attractive names tend to work harder to get on in life. According to Dr Erwin's research, students with unpopular old-fashioned names did significantly better in exams. This suggested that they were aware they had an unattractive name and were working harder to overcome negative attitudes. Names considered to be less attractive were, for example, Norman, Ronald, and Albert for men, and Gillian, Pauline, or Agnes for women. Actors and pop stars certainly seem to take this into account, and they often swap the name they were born with for a more glamorous stage name. Elton John, for example, was born Reginald Dwight.

In the last two decades there has been a definite tendency both in the UK and USA for parents to choose unusual names, or to name their child after a celebrity. But the question is, will these names still be considered attractive when the children grow up? 'When I was at school there was no one in my class with the same name as me,' says 30-year-old Farrah Stephens, who was named after the Charlie's Angels actress, Farrah Fawcett-Majors. 'By the time I was 15, everybody had forgotten about the actress, and I was left with this really stupid name. In the end I decided to use my middle name.'

Dr Erwin's advice is: 'Choose names for your children which they will be happy with in 20 years' time, and choose a second name in case your child doesn't like the first one.'

d Talk to your partner.

- What's your first name? Do you have any others?
- Do you like your first name? Why (not)?
- Do you know why your parents chose it?
- Do you have a nickname?

- Do people have a stereotype which they associate with your name?
- Do you think your name has had an effect on your life?
- Would you like to change your name?

a Reorder the words to make the questions.   **A**

b Interview your partner. Remember to ask for more information.

1   languages you me any Could other speak if you tell ? _____

2   you your How weekends spend do ? _____

3   holiday idea of What's a perfect your ? _____

4   family you Do a from big come ? _____

5   food of kind you like What don't ? _____

6   ever country you Have been an to English-speaking ? _____

7   want when were you What a child be to you did ? _____

8   for Internet What you the use do ? _____

9   restaurant kind things a of What annoy you in ? _____

10   bought Do shoes you where mind me you those telling ? _____

11   first Can plane by remember the you travelled you time ? _____

12   car listening What in do like to the music you ? _____

---

a Reorder the words to make the questions.   **B**

b Interview your partner. Remember to ask for more information.

1   time last you Can DVD the you remember bought a ? _____

2   would your be ideal What evening ? _____

3   things you kind of at good What are ? _____

4   like you don't What about you live where ? _____

5   made you learn want What to English ? _____

6   you were What yesterday doing this time ? _____

7   school you long know open how Do this has been ? _____

8   to a country like you in Would go and foreign live ? _____

9   broken you your or ever Have arm leg ? _____

10   afraid Would me of telling you what are you mind ? _____

11   country What you people most about from irritates your ? _____

12   cinema was time When you the went to the last ? _____

198

The story

It's a beautiful summer's day and you decide to go for a long walk. After a short while you reach a forest, and you decide to walk through it.

1 Describe the forest in as much detail as you can.

- Is it dark or light?
- Is it beautiful or scary?
- What are the trees like?
- What else can you see?
- How does the forest make you feel?

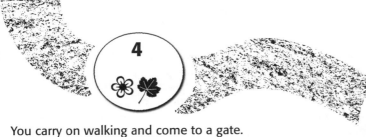

2 You start walking through the forest, and you come to a house. **Describe the house in as much detail as you can.**

- What style is it?
- Is it light or dark?
- How many bedrooms are there?
- Is there a fence? If yes, what is it like?

3 You continue walking, and go deeper into the forest. Suddenly you see a bear. **Describe the bear in as much detail as you can.**

- How big is it?
- Is it friendly or unfriendly?
- What does the bear do? What do you do?

4 You carry on walking and come to a gate. You open the gate, and find yourself in a garden. **Describe the garden in as much detail as you can.**

- Is it wild or tidy?
- Is it well looked after or abandoned?
- What's in it?

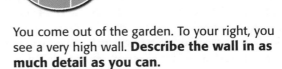

5 You come out of the garden. To your right, you see a very high wall. **Describe the wall in as much detail as you can.**

- Can you hear anything behind it? If yes, what?
- How does it make you feel?

The interpretation

1 The forest = how you see your life at the moment, e.g. the darker and scarier the forest is, the more negative you feel about life right now.

2 The house = how you see yourself, e.g. the lighter the house, the more optimistic and positive your personality. The number of bedrooms = the number of people you want close to you in your life. No fence = open-minded and extrovert.

3 The bear = your attitude to love and relationships. The smaller and friendlier the bear, the more affectionate you are, and the more positive you feel about love. Running away from the bear = you are frightened of commitment.

4 The garden = how you see your country at the moment. The more cultivated and bright the garden, the more positive your view about your country.

5 The wall = the way you see the afterlife (i.e. life after death). If you hear happy voices singing behind the wall, you have an optimistic view of the afterlife.

A Roleplay 1

You're a family doctor. B is your patient. You're new to this surgery and so you haven't met him/her before. When you meet a new patient, you like to find out as much as you can about them. Although you're in favour of traditional medicine too, you've recently become very interested in alternative medicine like acupuncture and massage. You think that some conditions can be better treated using alternative medicine, e.g. acupuncture for people with phobias or weight problems.

- Find out as much information as you can about the patient e.g. age, job, family life, previous illnesses, operations.
- Ask the reason for today's visit. Find out how long he/she's had this problem.
- You don't like the medicine the patient usually takes, Calmozene. You prefer a natural one called Tranquil.

B will start.

Roleplay 2

You're a patient. B is your family doctor. You know your doctor very well and you think that he/she likes you. That's why you call him/her by his/her first name (Paul/Paula) and not Dr Woods.

- Today you've made an appointment with the doctor because you have some very strange symptoms (what are they?), and you are convinced that you have a problem with your heart. You want the doctor to take you seriously and confirm your suspicions!
- Explain all your symptoms to the doctor.
- Ask the doctor to take your blood pressure and temperature.
- Tell him/her that you would like to see a specialist. Be prepared to argue with him/her if necessary.

You start the conversation.
Hello Paul/Paula. How are you?

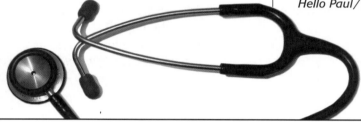

B Roleplay 1

You're a patient. A is your family doctor. You haven't been to the doctor's for some time so you're quite surprised to see that you have a new family doctor. You had known the previous doctor all your life. He knew all about your fear of flying and was very sympathetic to the problem. He also knew about your fear of needles and injections. You're going on holiday next week – by plane. Your old doctor always prescribed Calmozene – a tablet which relaxes you when you fly. If you take two before the plane takes off, you simply fall asleep and don't feel afraid. You know what you want – Calmozene! If you don't get it, you can't go on holiday. You are not very convinced by alternative medicine!

- Answer any questions the doctor asks you about your age, job, family life, previous illnesses, operations. Explain the reasons for today's visit.
- Ask the doctor to prescribe Calmozene and explain why you need it.
- Only accept an alternative form of treatment you feel completely happy with.

You start the conversation.
Good morning doctor. You're new, aren't you?

Roleplay 2

You're a family doctor. A is your patient. You've been working for seven hours and you're very tired. Your last patient is a man/woman who comes to see you very often, always with a different problem. You think he/she might be a hypochondriac. For some reason, this patient always calls you by your first name. You hate that!

- Ask him/her not to call you by your first name. Ask him/her to call you Dr Woods.
- Ask what his/her symptoms are (this week) and how long he/she has had them.
- Give your diagnosis (a virus) and refuse to send him/her to a specialist.
- Prescribe some painkillers.

A will start.

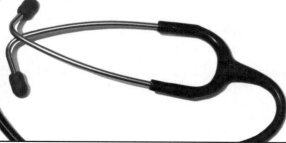

A

Describe your picture to **B**. Find twelve differences. Mark the differences on your picture.

B

Describe your picture to **A**. Find twelve differences. Mark the differences on your picture.

New English File Teacher's Book Upper-intermediate
Photocopiable © Oxford University Press 2008

A time you met (or were very close to) a celebrity

- Where were you? Who with? What had you been doing?
- Who was the celebrity? What was he/she doing there? What did he/she look like?
- Did you speak at all? What about?
- Did he/she seem different in any way in real life?

A time when you read something in your horoscope and it came true

- Where did you read it? What did it say?
- How much later did it come true? What exactly happened?
- Had anything like this ever happened before?
- Do you still read your horoscope regularly?

A time when you overslept and missed something important

- What were you supposed to be doing?
- Had you gone to bed very late the night before? Why?
- Had you set an alarm clock?
- How late did you wake up? What did you do?
- What happened in the end?

A time when your parents were very angry with you about something

- How old were you? What had you been doing? Who with?
- How did your parents find out?
- Did they punish you? How?

An important exam or test you failed

- When did you take it?
- What kind of exam/test was it?
- Had you revised before you did it?
- How did you feel on the day of the exam/test?
- Were a lot of people doing it at the same time as you?
- How did you find out that you had failed? Were you surprised?

A time when you lost something important

- What was it? When?
- What had you been doing when you realized you had lost it?
- How did you find out you'd lost it? How did you feel?
- What action did you take?
- Did you ever find it again?
- Did losing it cause you any problems?

A time when you had a very disappointing birthday

- How old were you? Where were you?
- What had you been expecting to happen?
- Why was the birthday so disappointing?
- How did it end?
- Did you tell anybody that you hadn't enjoyed it?

A time you won something

- What was it?
- When? Where? How old were you?
- Were you expecting to win?
- How did you feel when you realized you'd won?
- Did you celebrate? What did you do?

A family holiday you didn't enjoy

- Where/When was it? Who went?
- Had you been there before?
- What did you do there?
- Why didn't you enjoy it?

A

1 _____, I didn't pass my driving test.

2 Could you speak more slowly? I don't understand what you're saying.

3 **I hope you get better _____ .**

4 I used to drink a lot of coffee but lately I've started drinking tea.

5 **We _____ missed the start of the film but we got there just in time.**

6 I never eat meat as I'm a vegetarian.

7 **Living alone isn't easy. _____, it can be difficult at times.**

8 Ideally, we're looking for someone between 18 and 20 to do the job.

9 **She looks quite arrogant but _____ she's very friendly.**

10 I'm so tired I can hardly keep my eyes open.

11 **The vet picked up the injured dog _____ and put it on the table.**

12 Your room is in a terrible mess. Go and tidy it immediately!

13 **She'll _____ pass her driving test. She's had loads of lessons.**

14 It was a very bad accident but luckily no one was hurt.

15 **He's _____ good-looking. Is he a model?**

16 I love all kinds of foreign food, especially Vietnamese. That's my favourite.

17 **She doesn't have any money and she's _____ had to sell her car.**

18 Jake looks exhausted, doesn't he? He's been working too hard recently.

- -

B

1 Unfortunately, I didn't pass my driving test.

2 **Could you speak more _____? I don't understand what you're saying.**

3 I hope you get better soon.

4 **I used to drink a lot of coffee but _____ I've started drinking tea.**

5 We nearly missed the start of the film but we got there just in time.

6 **I _____ eat meat as I'm a vegetarian.**

7 Living alone isn't easy. In fact, it can be difficult at times.

8 **_____, we're looking for someone between 18 and 20 to do the job.**

9 She looks quite arrogant but actually she's very friendly.

10 **I'm so tired I can _____ keep my eyes open.**

11 The vet picked up the injured dog carefully and put it on the table.

12 **Your room is in a terrible mess. Go and tidy it _____!**

13 She'll definitely pass her driving test. She's had loads of lessons.

14 **It was a very bad accident but _____ no one was hurt.**

15 He's incredibly good-looking. Is he a model?

16 **I love all kinds of foreign food, _____ Vietnamese. That's my favourite.**

17 She doesn't have any money and she's even had to sell her car.

18 **Jake looks exhausted, doesn't he? He's been working too _____ recently.**

A **ⓐ** Read about five laws in different countries. **Two** are true and **three** are false.

ⓑ Tell **B** about each law, using your own words. Then discuss each one together and decide whether you think it's true or false.

ⓒ Listen to **B**'s laws and say whether you think they're true or false.

Things you probably didn't know about the law in…

1 Singapore If you are caught dropping litter on three different occasions, you could get a very embarrassing sentence. You could be arrested and sentenced to cleaning the streets on Sundays. While you are cleaning, you have to wear a big sign saying 'I'm a litter bug' (= a person who frequently drops rubbish in the street).

2 Bolivia Kidnapping is considered to be a very serious crime in this South American country. However, if you are found guilty of this crime, the length of your prison sentence will vary depending on whether the person you kidnapped was male or female. A kidnapper will get a much longer prison sentence if the victim is a woman.

3 The USA The Arizona Desert is the only place on the planet where the Saguaro cactus grows. Cutting down one of these plants without a special permit is considered an act of vandalism under Arizona law, and you could be heavily fined if you're found guilty.

4 Brazil If a man is caught wearing a skirt in this country, he can be charged with immoral conduct and fined. However, if this crime is committed at Carnival time – then the police usually turn a blind eye (= pretend they haven't seen you).

5 The Netherlands The Dutch are a nation of dog lovers. If you are a dog owner and you commit a crime and are sentenced to go to prison, you do not need to worry about what will happen to your pet in your absence. The dog will be looked after by the state until you are released from prison.

- -

B **ⓐ** Read about five laws in different countries. **Three** are true and **two** are false.

ⓑ Tell **A** about each law, using your own words. Then discuss each one together and decide whether you think it's true or false.

ⓒ Listen to **A**'s laws and say whether you think they're true or false.

Things you probably didn't know about the law in…

1 France The French are well known for being very protective of their language and culture. Under French law 70% of music on the radio must be by French artists between 8.00 a.m. and 8.00 p.m. Any radio station not obeying this law could be investigated, charged, and fined.

2 Japan One of the most popular presents for children is a robot pet, for example a robot dog. As these 'pets' have artificial intelligence, and behave like real animals, they are included in the Animal Protection Laws, and it is a crime to damage or mistreat one. If you are caught doing this you may be banned from ever owning a pet again, either real or robot.

3 Switzerland Many Swiss people live in blocks of flats and each building has a president who is responsible for the smooth running of this building. If you visit this country and stay in a flat, be careful! If you need to go to the toilet after 10.00 p.m. it's illegal to flush the toilet. If another neighbour hears you flushing, he or she can report you to the president of the building and you may even be fined by the police.

4 Scotland In England, if someone has been charged with a crime and has to go to court, he or she is considered innocent until proved guilty. However in Scotland the opposite is true – a suspect is considered guilty until proved innocent.

5 England One of the best ways to travel around London is on the Tube (the London Underground). But have you ever noticed that nobody ever whistles? This is because although you can read a book or talk to a friend while you're travelling, it is against the law to whistle. If a London Underground employee hears you, you could be reported to the police and even charged.

Discuss each prediction with a partner.

a Do you think it will be true in twenty years' time?

b Do you think it will be a good thing? Why / Why not?

- We will be paying much more for water than for electricity.

- We will be living in a 'cashless' society, and will pay for everything with credit cards, or with a credit chip implanted under our skin.

- Most people will be living until they are 90 or longer.

- We will have lost our ability to socialize and interact with other human beings because of the time we spend on 'individual' hobbies.

- The idea of a retirement age will have disappeared. People will be able to work for as long as they want.

- Shops will have disappeared and all shopping will be done on the Internet.

- Some countries will have disappeared because of flooding.

- Women's football will have become nearly as popular as men's football.

- Everybody will be travelling far less by plane and car in order to reduce CO₂ emissions.

- Sunbathing on the beach will have been banned, and people found lying on the beach will be fined.

New English File Teacher's Book Upper-intermediate
Photocopiable © Oxford University Press 2008

a Interview your partner using the Risk Questionnaire. Ask for more information.

b In general, do you think your partner is a risk-taker? Why / Why not?

The **Risk** Questionnaire

1 Would you do a parachute jump for charity?

2 Have you ever been out with someone you met on the Internet? Would you do it?

3 Would you try to cheat in an exam if you knew you weren't well prepared for it?

4 If you had missed the last bus home, would you consider hitchhiking?

5 If you fell in love with a person who lived in another country, would you move with him / her to that country?

6 Would you ever buy a second-hand car or motorbike on eBay?

7 Would you go on holiday to a foreign country on your own?

8 If you find some food in your fridge which is a couple of days past its sell-by date, do you still eat it?

9 Do you start revising as soon as you know you have an exam coming up or do you leave your revision until the night before?

10 Would you drastically change your hair colour or hair cut? Have you ever done it?

11 Would you still sunbathe if you arrived at the beach without any suncream?

12 If there was a job you really wanted, would you lie about your experience or qualifications at the interview?

13 If you have a flight to catch, do you leave your house in good time or do you leave at the last possible moment?

14 Do you always put on your seat belt in the car? Do you wear a helmet on a bike / motorbike?

15 Would you lend a lot of money to a very close friend?

16 When you are abroad do you tend to try foreign dishes that you haven't had before?

17 Would you fly with a low-cost airline that you had never heard of?

18 Do you ever drive at more than 30 kilometres per hour over the speed limit?

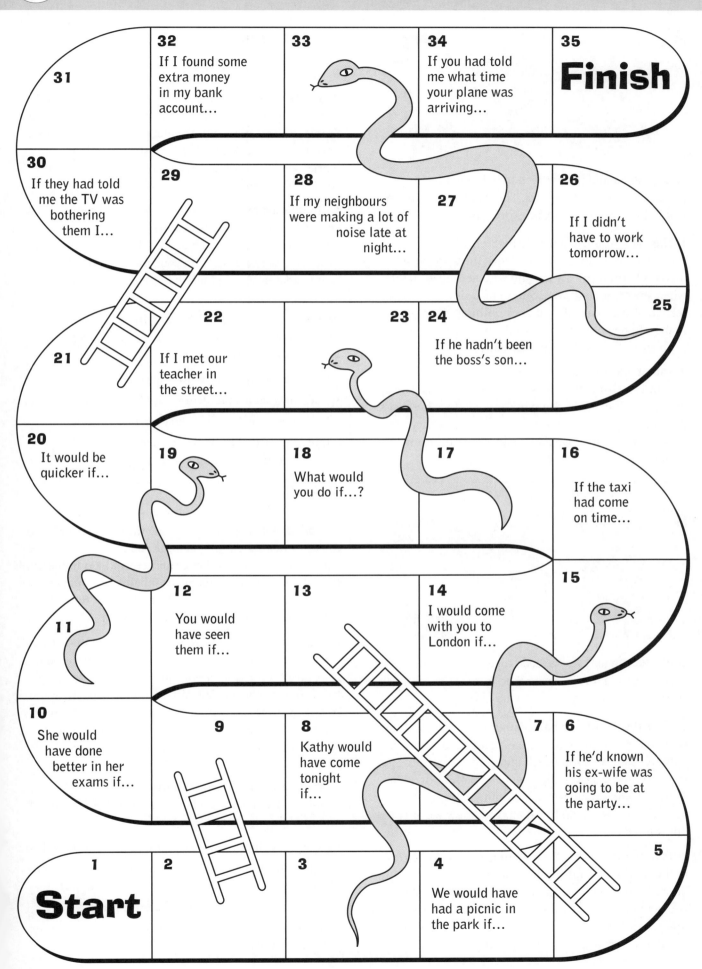

31

32 If I found some extra money in my bank account…

33

34 If you had told me what time your plane was arriving…

35 **Finish**

30 If they had told me the TV was bothering them I…

29

28 If my neighbours were making a lot of noise late at night…

27

26 If I didn't have to work tomorrow…

21

22 If I met our teacher in the street…

23

24 If he hadn't been the boss's son…

25

20 It would be quicker if…

19

18 What would you do if…?

17

16 If the taxi had come on time…

11

12 You would have seen them if…

13

14 I would come with you to London if…

15

10 She would have done better in her exams if…

9

8 Kathy would have come tonight if…

7

6 If he'd known his ex-wife was going to be at the party…

1 **Start**

2

3

4 We would have had a picnic in the park if…

5

A

You're **Emma** and you've been together with your partner Martin for five years. There are several things you've been wanting to talk to him about.

1 The baby You had a baby daughter, which you both wanted, 11 months ago. Since then, you've felt incredibly tired (it's always <u>you</u> who gets up at night when she cries), and you seem to be doing everything related to the baby. Martin does nothing. You want Martin to help you more with the baby but the only problem is that he's completely useless!

2 Your mum Your mum (a widow) lives in the same city and she usually visits you most afternoons, and at weekends. She's great company and you love her visits. She also helps you a lot with the baby. Recently you've noticed that Martin isn't as friendly to your mum as he used to be.

3 Money Before having the baby you had a well-paid job. You think a baby should be with its mother until it is at least three years old. You definitely don't want to go back to work but Martin's salary isn't enough. He only works seven hours a day in a bank so maybe he could work longer and earn more money.

4 His Internet obsession Martin loves his computer! The computer is in the study and Mark spends hours there when he comes home from work. Why doesn't he sit and talk to you or watch TV with you? You've heard a lot about Internet dating. Could Mark have a cyber girlfriend?

Tonight after dinner talk to Martin about these problems and try to reach an agreement. Keep calm and don't lose your temper.

• Try to get Martin to agree to help you more with the baby.
• Find out what the problem is with Martin and your mum.
• Try to persuade Martin to do overtime at work.
• Try to persuade Martin to spend less time on the computer in the evening.

B

You're **Martin** and you've been together with your partner Emma for five years. There are several things you've been wanting to talk to her about:

1 The baby You had a baby daughter, which you both wanted, 11 months ago. Emma's completely obsessed with the baby and you've felt ignored since she was born. If you try to feed the baby, give her a bath or dress her, Emma always says that you are doing it wrong! Now, you just don't try and help her at all. You know when you're not wanted!

2 Your mother-in-law Emma's mum (a widow) lives in the same city. Your mother-in-law is always at your house in the evenings, and at the weekend too. When you get home you just want to relax but you can't if your mother-in-law's there too! Also, she's incredibly bossy. She doesn't let you do anything with the baby either.

3 Work and money Before having the baby, Emma used to have a well-paid job. When she had the baby you both agreed that it would be better for her to stay at home until the baby was at least three years old. But it's impossible for you to live on just your salary. You think that Emma will have to go back to work as soon as possible.

4 Your computer hobby You often go to the study and use the computer in the evening. You need some time to yourself to relax after working all day, and to escape from your mother-in-law. You enjoy 'chatting' with the friends you've made on the Internet – none of them are women. Recently Emma has been getting very angry about you spending time on the computer.

Tonight after dinner talk to Emma about these problems and try to reach an agreement. Keep calm and don't lose your temper.

• Try and convince Emma to let you do more with the baby.
• Suggest to Emma that her mother could visit less often. Be careful! She's very sensitive about this subject.
• Try to persuade Emma to go back to work.
• Explain your reasons for wanting to use the computer in the evening.

New English File Teacher's Book Upper-intermediate
Photocopiable © Oxford University Press 2008

1 flamenco

It's a kind of music.
It sounds…
It sounds like…

2 velvet

It's a material.
It feels…

3 cauliflower

It's a vegetable.
It tastes…
It smells…

4 roast turkey

It's something you eat.
It tastes like…

5 dirty socks

You have worn them.
They smell…
They smell like…

6 a panda

It's a kind of animal.
It looks like…

7 a lift

It's a kind of machine.
It makes some
 people feel…

8 vinegar

It's a liquid.
It tastes / smells…
It tastes / smells like…

9 chilli peppers

They're a kind of vegetable.
They taste…

10 a dentist's drill

It's a machine.
It sounds…

11 a mosquito

It's an insect.
It sounds like…

12 a teddy bear

It's a toy.
It feels…
It looks like…

13 an open fire

It's something in a house.
It makes you feel…
It smells…

14 the Mona Lisa

It's a woman.
She looks…
She looks as if…

15 a grapefruit

It's a fruit.
It looks like…
It tastes…

16 the London Eye

It's a London tourist attraction.
It looks like…

17 yogurt

It's a kind of food.
It looks like…
It tastes…

18 petrol

It's a liquid.
It looks like…
It smells…

A

a Complete the verb column with the correct form of the verbs in brackets.

b Ask your partner the questions in **a**.

VERB

1 Do you remember _____ your best friend for the first time? (**meet**) _____

2 Did your parents let you _____ in the street when you were young? (**play**) _____

3 What kind of things do you tend _____ about? (**worry**) _____

4 When did you learn _____? (**drive**) _____

5 What's the next thing you really need _____? (**buy**) _____

6 Have you ever tried _____ a winter sport, e.g. skiing or ice skating? (**do**) _____

7 Would you avoid _____ to a party if you knew your ex–partner was going? (**go**) _____

8 Would you ever risk _____ and leaving your front door unlocked? (**go out**) _____

9 Have you ever forgotten _____ something important for a holiday? (**pack**) _____

10 If you didn't want to go to school / work one day, would you pretend _____ ill? (**be**) _____

11 Would you agree _____ a friend's dog for the weekend? (**look after**) _____

12 Can you imagine _____ speak English totally fluently? (**be able to**) _____

FOLD

B

a Complete the verb column with the correct form of the verbs in brackets.

b Ask your partner the questions in **a**.

VERB

1 Are there any programmes you really can't stand _____ on TV? (**watch**) _____

2 Do you always remember _____ your mobile phone? (**charge**) _____

3 Do you think you'll carry on _____ English here next year? (**study**) _____

4 What is there that you would really like to have but can't afford _____? (**buy**) _____

5 Would you rather _____ a film at the cinema or on DVD? (**see**) _____

6 Who taught you _____? (**swim**) _____

7 Is there anything at your home which needs _____? (**repair**) _____

8 Have you ever tried _____ something but then given up? (**learn**) _____

9 Would you or your family manage _____ without a car? (**live**) _____

10 What can you do to practise _____ English outside the class? (**speak**) _____

11 Do you sometimes forget _____ things or have you got a good memory? (**do**) _____

12 Could you give up _____ chocolate if your doctor told you to? (**eat**) _____

FOLD

A

Choose questions to ask your partner.
Ask for more information.

> *Do you usually…?*
> *Did you use to…?*
> *Do you think you could get used to…?*

1 (always work) at night?

2 (behave) well at primary school?

3 (hate) any particular food when you were a child?

4 (have) a favourite toy?

5 (have) a siesta after lunch?

6 (have) breakfast in the mornings?

7 (live) in the UK or the USA?

8 (remember) your friends' birthdays?

9 (not eat) any sweet things?

10 (prefer) playing indoors or outdoors when you were a child?

11 (read) a daily newspaper or news website?

12 (live) without your mobile phone?

B

Choose questions to ask your partner.
Ask for more information.

> *Do you usually…?*
> *Did you use to…?*
> *Do you think you could get used to…?*

1 (celebrate) your birthday?

2 (cheat) in exams?

3 (download) films from the Internet?

4 (drive) on the left?

5 (fight) with your brothers and sisters when you were little?

6 (get up) as soon as you wake up?

7 (go) to the hairdresser's more than once a month?

8 (live) without credit cards?

9 (have) a favourite TV programme when you were a child?

10 (keep) a diary when you were younger?

11 (have) lunch at home?

12 (not have) Internet access?

A

a Dictate these sentences to **B**.

1 Sorry I'm late.
2 I didn't break the vase!
3 I'll love you for ever.
4 Don't walk on your own at night.

5 Would you like to come to a concert?
6 I was sorry I hadn't bought the jacket.
7 You ate all the biscuits!
8 We'll kill you if you don't give us the money.

b Now **B** will dictate eight sentences to you. Write them down.

c Now change the sentences **B** dictated to you into reported speech. Use a reporting verb from the list.

| admitted | advised | insisted on | offered | recommended | refused | reminded | suggested |

1 The little girl _____.
2 The teacher _____ them _____.
3 The boy _____.
4 A young man _____ with my case.
5 His friend _____ him _____.
6 Anya _____ a Chinese restaurant.
7 My brother _____ the drinks.
8 He _____ the Tower of London.

- -

B

a **A** will dictate eight sentences to you. Write them down.

b Now dictate these sentences to **A**.

1 I won't eat the cabbage!
2 Remember to bring your dictionary to class.
3 I broke the window.
4 I'll help you with your case.

5 I think you should go to the doctor.
6 Let's go to a Chinese restaurant tonight.
7 I'm going to pay for the drinks – it's my turn.
8 You must see the Tower of London!

c Now change the sentences **A** dictated to you into reported speech. Use a reporting verb from the list.

| accused | apologized | denied | invited | promised | regretted | threatened | warned |

1 The teacher _____.
2 Jane _____.
3 The bride _____ her husband for ever.
4 The policeman _____ her _____.
5 Mark _____ Miriam _____.
6 I _____.
7 She _____ her brother _____.
8 The robbers _____ if I didn't give them the money.

New English File Teacher's Book Upper-intermediate
Photocopiable © Oxford University Press 2008

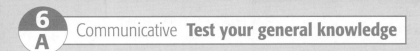

ⓐ Complete the quiz with *a*, *an*, *the*, or – (no article).

ⓑ In pairs, see how many questions you can answer.

1 Which planet is nearest to _____ sun?

2 What type of fruit is _____ cantaloupe?

3 How many states are there in _____ USA?

4 In which sea can you find _____ Balearic Islands?

5 Who are more numerous in the world, _____ men or _____ women ?

6 Which animal is _____ symbol of _____ WWF?

7 What colour are _____ babies' eyes at birth?

8 What is _____ 40% of 40?

9 What letter is on _____ right of _____ 'B' on a keyboard?

10 What was _____ name of _____ Tarzan's monkey?

11 What country is _____ Lake Como in?

12 What's _____ highest mountain in _____ Himalayas?

13 How many strings does _____ bass guitar have?

14 Who was _____ second person to walk on _____ moon?

15 How many players can be on court in _____ volleyball team?

16 What is _____ fourth sign of _____ zodiac?

17 Which nation first gave _____ women _____ right to vote?

18 Which animals were domesticated first, _____ cats or _____ dogs?

19 Which European country hasn't fought in _____ war since _____ 1815?

20 What is _____ largest man-made structure on Earth?

21 What vegetable is _____ vodka often made from?

22 Is _____ spider _____ insect?

23 What colour is _____ black box on _____ plane?

24 What's _____ sacred river in _____ India called?

25 Which travels faster, _____ light or _____ sound?

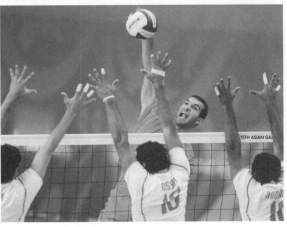

1

Nowadays it's perfectly acceptable to wear jeans in all situations.

2

People should pay extra for all the luggage they check in with them on flights.

3

The best place to find accurate information about something is on the Internet.

4

Politics should be a compulsory subject at secondary school.

5

Having good health is more important than having a lot of money.

6

When you need advice, your family are usually more helpful than your friends.

7

The weather can affect the way we feel on a specific day.

8

It's hard for a student to see any kind of progress when they get to a certain level of English.

9

A person studying a foreign language doesn't need to do any homework. Going to class is enough.

10

You can't be good at sport unless you have the right equipment.

11

It's impossible to get an unbiased view of what is happening in the world from the news on TV. Newspapers are far more objective.

12

Luck is something you're born with. Some people are just 'naturally' lucky.

13

People's manners are much worse nowadays than they were 50 years ago.

14

The clothes you wear are a reflection of what you're like as a person.

15

Traffic should be banned from all city centres. Only public transport, bikes, and pedestrians should be allowed in them.

6C Communicative **Biology quiz**

a Reorder the letters to name the animals.

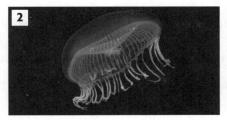

1 | **2** | **3**

o d t a _____   f s i l y j l h e _____   a b t _____

4 | **5** | **6**

r a e b _____   r a t l i a g l o _____   m l a c _____

b Look at the sentences. In pairs, decide if the sentences are true or false.
You get one point for each correct answer.

1 **Every** animal belonging to the reptile family has cold blood.

2 **All** insects have six legs and wings.

3 **Neither** African **nor** Indian elephants can swim.

4 There are **no** snakes in Iceland.

5 Jellyfish don't have **either** a mouth **or** a sense of smell.

6 **All** clams start as males and then some decide to become females at some point in their lives.

7 **No** animals can regrow any part of their bodies.

8 Polar bears can live **both** in the USA and Greenland.

9 **All** monkeys are colour blind.

10 **No** bats can walk, because their leg bones are too thin.

11 **Both** crocodiles **and** alligators have the same number of teeth.

12 **Few** wild birds live for more than a year.

13 **All** bears hibernate **every** winter.

14 **Both** toads **and** frogs can jump well, but toads can jump higher.

15 Giraffes do not have **any** vocal chords. They **all** communicate with their tails.

New English File Teacher's Book Upper-intermediate
Photocopiable © Oxford University Press 2008

A

a Write something in at least seven of your circles.

In circle **1**, write something you wish you had learned to do when you were younger.

In circle **2**, write something annoying you wish someone in your family wouldn't do.

In circle **3**, write something you wish you hadn't bought recently.

In circle **4**, write something you wish you could change about your personality.

In circle **5**, write the name of a famous person you wish you could meet.

In circle **6**, write the name of a language you wish you could speak.

In circle **7**, write somewhere you wish you could go on holiday, but probably won't be able to.

In circle **8**, write something you wish you had more of.

In circle **9**, write an activity you wish you didn't have to do in your English class.

In circle **10**, write the name of a film you wish you had seen at the cinema (not on DVD).

b Give your sheet to **B**. He / She will ask you to explain what you have written.

c Ask **B** to explain what he / she has written.

FOLD

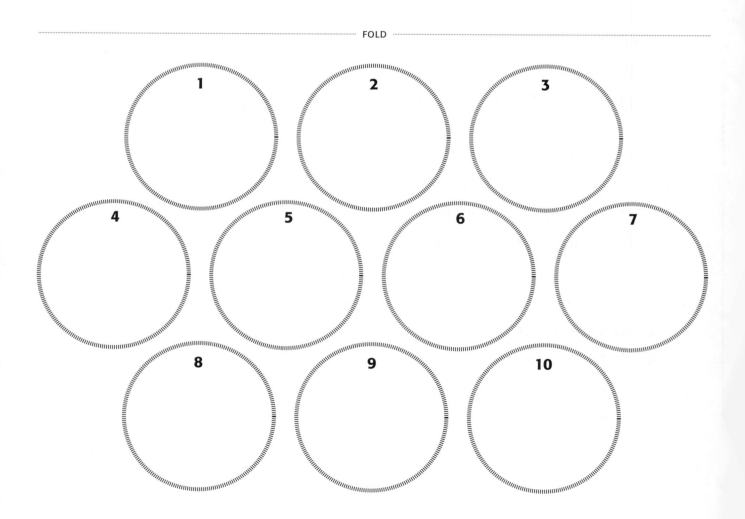

B

a Write something in at least seven of your circles.

In circle **1**, write something you wish you could do more often.

In circle **2**, write something in modern life you wish hadn't been invented or discovered.

In circle **3**, write an activity you wish you could be better at.

In circle **4**, write the name of a person you wish you saw more often.

In circle **5**, write something you wish you could eat / drink less of.

In circle **6**, write the name of a singer / pop group you wish you had seen in concert.

In circle **7**, write something you wish people wouldn't do in the cinema.

In circle **8**, write something you wish they would do to improve your town / city.

In circle **9**, write something you wish you had done when you were younger.

In circle **10**, write a name you wish your parents had called you.

b Give your sheet to **A**. He / She will ask you to explain what you have written.

c Ask **A** to explain what he / she has written.

---- FOLD ----

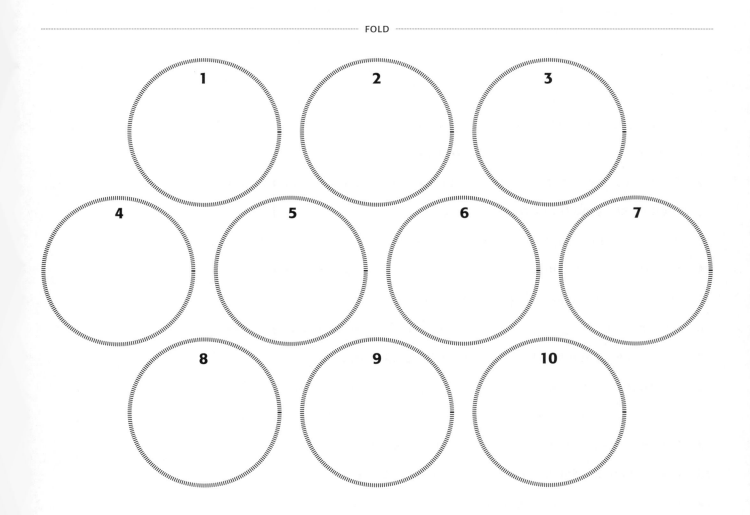

A

1   **Even though _____, he isn't very generous.**

2   Despite going on a diet, he's still a bit overweight.

3   **Despite the fact that he's _____, he's had two accidents this year.**

4   I felt so stressed that I went to a spa for a massage.

5   **You should turn off your TV and DVD player at night so as to _____.**

6   In spite of the fact that he doesn't speak English, he still found a good job.

7   **I'm going to work late tonight so that _____ tomorrow.**

8   I'm saving to buy a new car. The one I have now is ten years old.

9   **Cats make great pets although personally _____.**

10 She took a taxi so as to be on time for her first day at work.

11 **My sister's gone to New York for _____ with an American company.**

12 You need to go to the UK for a month so that you can practise your English.

13 **I'm _____ in spite of knowing that it's safer than driving.**

14 My mum looks as if she's in her forties even though she's in her sixties.

B

1   Even though he's rich, he isn't very generous.

2   **Despite _____, he's still a bit overweight.**

3   Despite the fact that he's a very good driver, he's had two accidents this year.

4   **I felt so stressed that I went to a spa for _____.**

5   You should turn off your TV and DVD player at night so as to save electricity.

6   **In spite of the fact that he _____, he still found a good job.**

7   I'm going to work late tonight so that I can leave early tomorrow.

8   **I'm saving to _____. The one I have now is ten years old.**

9   Cats make great pets although personally I prefer dogs.

10 **She took a taxi so as to _____ for her first day at work.**

11 My sister's gone to New York for an interview with an American company.

12 **You need to go to the UK for a month so that you _____.**

13 I'm terrified of flying in spite of knowing that it's safer than driving.

14 **My mum looks as if she's in her forties even though _____.**

Grammar Auction

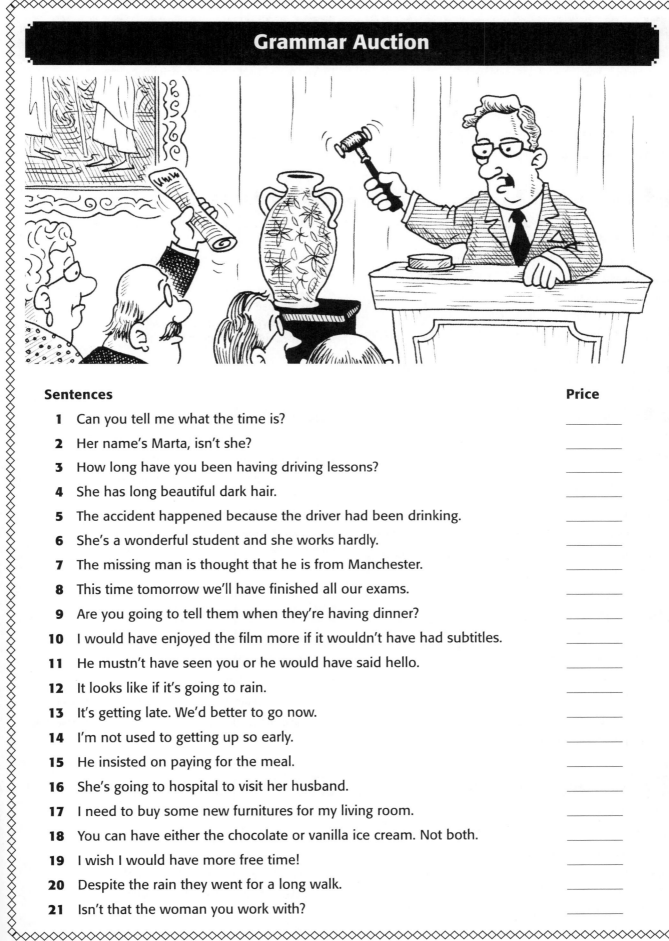

Sentences	Price
1 Can you tell me what the time is?	_____
2 Her name's Marta, isn't she?	_____
3 How long have you been having driving lessons?	_____
4 She has long beautiful dark hair.	_____
5 The accident happened because the driver had been drinking.	_____
6 She's a wonderful student and she works hardly.	_____
7 The missing man is thought that he is from Manchester.	_____
8 This time tomorrow we'll have finished all our exams.	_____
9 Are you going to tell them when they're having dinner?	_____
10 I would have enjoyed the film more if it wouldn't have had subtitles.	_____
11 He mustn't have seen you or he would have said hello.	_____
12 It looks like if it's going to rain.	_____
13 It's getting late. We'd better to go now.	_____
14 I'm not used to getting up so early.	_____
15 He insisted on paying for the meal.	_____
16 She's going to hospital to visit her husband.	_____
17 I need to buy some new furnitures for my living room.	_____
18 You can have either the chocolate or vanilla ice cream. Not both.	_____
19 I wish I would have more free time!	_____
20 Despite the rain they went for a long walk.	_____
21 Isn't that the woman you work with?	_____

1 Personalities

Tell your partner about…

■ somebody you know who is quite vain
■ somebody you know who is always very cheerful
■ somebody you know who is extremely stubborn
■ somebody you know who is often bad-tempered
■ somebody you know who is very wise

2 Your style

Do you dress up often or do you tend to wear casual clothes?

Do you prefer wearing plain or patterned clothes?

Do you consider yourself to be quite trendy?

What are your three favourite items of clothing?

Where do you tend to buy most of your clothes? Why?

3 Your town

In which part of your town / city do you live? (in the centre, on the outskirts, etc.)

What do you like best / least about your neighbourhood?

Are there any famous landmarks or sights in your town?

Are there any problems with…?
  a homeless people **b** pollution **c** crime

If you had to choose one adjective to describe your town / city, what would it be?

Are you happy living there or would you like to move?

4 Your health

Tell your partner about a time when you or someone you know well…

■ needed stitches
■ fainted
■ had food poisoning
■ had very bad flu
■ had an allergic reaction to something
■ had to spend some time in hospital

5 Music

When and where do you normally listen to music?

What kind of music do you listen to?

Did your parents listen to a lot of music when you were growing up? What kind?

Is your taste in music similar in any way to your parents'?

Do you tend to have friends who share your musical tastes?

If you could be a world-class musician, what exactly would you choose to be?

6 The media

How up to date are you with what's going on in the world?

Where do you usually get the news from?

Do you think news reporting in your country is objective or biased?

What's the biggest story in the news at the moment?

What kind of reviews do you usually read? Do you take any notice of them?

7 Feelings

Tell your partner about a time you felt…

■ really disappointed about something
■ a bit homesick
■ over the moon about some news
■ furious with someone in your family
■ scared stiff before you had to do something

8 The weather

Tell your partner about…

■ the kind of weather you enjoy
■ the kind of weather you hate
■ the most extreme weather you have ever experienced
■ a holiday or trip that was a disaster because of the weather

9 Crime and punishment

What are the most common crimes in your town / city?

Have you or someone you know ever been the victim of a crime?

What would you do to reduce crime?

Have you or someone you know ever been on a jury?

Which of these do you enjoy?
  a reading detective novels **b** watching TV crime series

10 Advertising

Talk about…

■ an advert (or TV commercial) you love
■ an advert which really irritates you
■ a brand that has a memorable logo or slogan
■ an advert which made you buy something

1 Split crossword

An information gap activity

SS define words / phrases to help their partner complete a crossword. Copy one sheet per pair and cut into **A** and **B**.

VOCABULARY	Personality, illness, treatment

- Put SS in pairs, ideally face to face, and give out the sheets. **Make sure SS can't see each other's sheets.** Explain that **A** and **B** have the same crossword but with different words missing. They have to describe / define words to each other to complete their crosswords.
- Give SS a minute to read their instructions. If SS don't know what a word means, they can look it up in Vocabulary Banks **Personality** and **Illness and Treatment** and the glossaries with the text in Lesson 1A.
- SS take turns to ask each other for their missing words, e.g. *What's 1 across?* Their partner must define / describe the word until the other student is able to write it in his / her crossword. SS should help each other with clues if necessary.
- When SS have finished, they should compare their crosswords to make sure they have the same words and have spelt them correctly.

2 Revision race

A pairwork vocabulary race

SS read a series of clues and write the words. Copy one sheet per student or pair of students.

VOCABULARY	Clothes, air travel, adverbs

- Put SS in pairs and give out the sheets. Set a time limit. Tell SS that they have to write as many words as they can within the time limit. The pair who complete all the words correctly first are the winners.

1	stereotype	11	boarding pass / card
2	Pole	12	take off
3	loose	13	aisle
4	backpack / rucksack	14	airlines
5	fur	15	lately
6	patterned	16	nearly
7	matches	17	hardly
8	get undressed	18	fortunately
9	suede	19	especially
10	customs	20	even

3 Describing game

A card game

SS define words / phrases for other SS to guess. Copy and cut up one set of cards per pair or small group.

VOCABULARY	Crime and punishment, weather, phrases with *take*

- Put SS in pairs or small groups. Give each group a set of cards face down or in an envelope.
- Demonstrate the activity by choosing a different word from one of the three Vocabulary Banks, and describing it to the class until someone says the word, e.g. *It's a noun. It's a person who steals things from other people's houses = burglar.* **Highlight that SS are not allowed to use the word on the card in their definition.**
- SS play the game, taking turns to take a card and describe the word or phrase. The person who is describing mustn't let his / her partner see what's on the card. Tell SS to wait until the person has finished his / her description before trying to guess the word.

Extra idea You could get SS to play this in groups as a competitive game. The person who correctly guesses the word first keeps the card. The player with the most cards at the end is the winner.

Non-cut alternative Put SS in pairs. Copy one sheet per pair and cut it down the middle. SS take turns to describe the words to their partner until he / she guesses the word.

4 Split crossword

An information gap activity

See instructions for **File 1 Split crossword**.

VOCABULARY	Feelings, verbs often confused, the body

5 Revision race

A pairwork vocabulary race

See instructions for **File 2 revision race**.

VOCABULARY	Music, sleep vocabulary, the media

1	conductor	11	jet-lagged
2	lyrics	12	nightmare
3	choir	13	blankets
4	saxophonist	14	headlines
5	catchy	15	freelance
6	tune	16	biased
7	keyboard	17	review
8	snore	18	cartoon
9	yawn	19	regret
10	pillow	20	refuse

6 Alphabet race

A pairwork vocabulary race

SS read a series of clues and write the words. Copy one sheet per student or pair of students.

> **VOCABULARY**   Word pairs, city, science

- Put SS in pairs and give out the sheets. Set a time limit. Tell SS that they have to write as many words as they can within the time limit. Each word begins with a different letter of the alphabet. The pair who complete all the words correctly first are the winners.

> **Astronaut, Beggars, Cycle lanes, Dawn, Entertainment, Football stadiums, Get around, Homeless, Invented, Jam, King, Luggage, Memorable, Neighbourhood, Overcrowding, Pedestrian, Quiet, Rank, Slums, Theory, Ups, Volunteers, Weather, X-rays, York, Zoo.**

7 Describing game

A card game

See instructions for **File 3 Describing game**.

> **VOCABULARY**   *-ed* / *-ing* adjectives, business and advertising, words with prefixes

Revision

A pairwork card game

SS define words / phrases for their partner to guess. Copy and cut up one set of cards per pair.

> **VOCABULARY**   Revision from Files 1–7

- Give each pair a set of cards face down. Demonstrate by taking a card, telling SS what the word group is and defining the first word for the class to guess.
- SS continue in pairs, picking a card, saying the topic and describing the words and expressions on it for the other student to guess. **Remind SS that they mustn't use the word itself in the definition.** They should try to take no longer than two minutes per card.

Non-cut alternative   Put SS in pairs. Copy one sheet per pair and cut it down the middle. Give A and B each half, and continue as above.

A **ⓐ** Look at your crossword and make sure you know the meaning of all the words you have.

ⓑ Now ask **B** to define a word for you. Ask e.g. *What's 1 down? What's 4 across?* Write the word in.

ⓒ Now **B** will ask you to define a word.

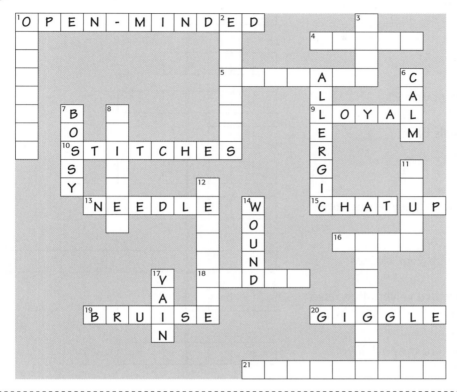

B **ⓐ** Look at your crossword and make sure you know the meaning of all the words you have.

ⓑ **A** will ask you to define a word.

ⓒ Now ask **A** to define a word for you. Ask e.g. *What's 1 across? What's 10 across?* Write the word in.

1 A fixed idea or image that people have of a type of person or thing.

2 Another way of saying a Polish person is a _____ .

3 The opposite of *tight*.

4 A bag which is carried on your back.

5 Humans have skin. Animals have _____ .

6 The opposite of *plain*.

7 Your bag _____ your shoes. They're the same colour.

8 A verb which means *take off your clothes*.

9 Soft leather with a surface like velvet often used to make jackets or shoes.

10 The place at an airport where they ask if you have anything to declare.

11 You need your _____ _____ before you can get on a plane.

12 A phrasal verb which is the opposite of *land*.

13 When you check in you can ask for a window or _____ seat.

14 easyJet was one of the first low-cost _____ .

15 A synonym for *recently*.

16 I _____ missed the bus today, but luckily I just caught it.

17 He's hurt his leg badly. He can _____ walk.

18 A synonym for *luckily*.

19 I like all summer fruits, _____ strawberries.

20 My neighbour is very unfriendly. He doesn't _____ say hello to me.

New English File Teacher's Book Upper-intermediate
Photocopiable © Oxford University Press 2008

a burglar

a judge

a vandal

a hurricane

a jury

shoplifting

scorching

a storm

a blizzard

a flood

to kidnap

a slippery road

a fine

a pickpocket

lightning

a drought

to sweat

sunburnt

to shiver

to take a risk

to take care of

to take it easy

foggy

below zero

4 Vocabulary **Split crossword**

A **a** Look at your crossword and make sure you know the meaning of all the words you have.

b Now ask **B** to define a word for you. Ask e.g. *What's 2 down? What's 19 across?* Write the word in.

c Now **B** will ask you to define a word.

B **a** Look at your crossword and make sure you know the meaning of all the words you have.

b **A** will ask you to define a word.

c Now ask **A** to define a word for you. Ask e.g. *What's 4 down? What's 7 across?* Write the word in.

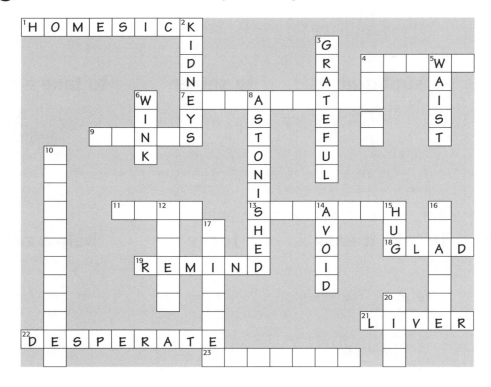

1 The person who directs an orchestra.

2 The words of a song.

3 My friend belongs to a _____. They sing together once a week.

4 The name of the person who plays a saxophone.

5 That song is really _____. I keep singing it to myself!

6 The 'music' of a song.

7 An electronic instrument like a piano.

8 To make a loud noise through your nose or mouth when you're asleep.

9 When you open your mouth wide because you're tired or very bored.

10 The thing you put your head on when you lie down in bed.

11 When you feel tired after flying to another time zone you are _____-_____.

12 A bad dream.

13 Put these on your bed to keep you warm at night.

14 The titles of newspaper stories are called _____.

15 She's a _____ journalist. She works for herself.

16 When a newspaper story isn't objective it's _____.

17 I think we should read a _____ of the film before we go and see it.

18 A small humorous drawing in a newspaper.

19 The verb that means you are sorry you did something.

20 It's a verb which means to say *no* when you don't want to do something.

New English File Teacher's Book Upper-intermediate
Photocopiable © Oxford University Press 2008

A

Neil Armstrong was
a very famous
_____.

B

People who ask for
money in the street.
_____

C

It's easy to ride a bike in
Amsterdam because there are
so many _____
_____.

D

The time of day when
the sun rises.
_____

E

The cinema and the
theatre are different forms
of _____.

F

Wembley and Old Trafford
are famous ones.
_____
_____

G

A phrasal verb meaning
to move from place to place
in a city. _____
_____

H

They live and sleep
in the street.
_____ people

I

The phone was
_____ by Alexander
Graham Bell.

J

When there are long queues
of cars in the rush hour, there
is a traffic _____.

K

Edward VIII was the only
British _____ who
abdicated.

L

Another word
for *baggage*.
_____

M

That holiday will always
be _____. I'll never
forget it.

N

The area where
you live is your
_____.

O

The problem in a city
when too many people live
there. _____

P

You can't drive here!
It's a _____ area.

Q

Another way of
saying *silence* is peace
and _____.

R

The place where
you can get a
taxi. _____

S

A poor area where the
houses are in a very bad
condition.
_____

T

Einstein is famous for
his _____ of
relativity.

U

They have their
_____ and downs but
they're happily married.

V

We need five people
to be _____ for
the experiment.

W

I hope the _____ is
going to be good tomorrow.
We're planning a picnic.

X

_____ wouldn't exist
without the discovery of
radiation.

Y

New _____ is
sometimes called the city
of skyscrapers.

Z

Most big cities have one.
You can see wild animals
there. _____

offended	**stressful**	**scary**	**embarrassed**
annoying	**a trolley**	**to import**	**to manufacture**
to make a profit	**a firm**	**a colleague**	**the owner**
a logo	**junk mail**	**the staff**	**an advert**
to do market research	**to queue**	**a refund**	**to misspell**
overpaid	**multinational**	**an autograph**	**subtitles**

The media

a newsreader	a presenter
the front page	an advertisement
censored	a critic

Towns and cities

harbour	the outskirts
homeless people	run down (adj)
a district	vibrant

Business and advertising

an employee	to do market research
a profit	a branch
a multinational	to set up a company

Personality

impulsive	easy-going
vain	conscientious
cheerful	bad-tempered

Illness and treatment

swollen	a blister
food poisoning	flu
to bleed	a specialist

Clothes

scruffy	patterned
silk	trendy
loose	to dress up

Crime and punishment

to burgle	blackmail
a witness	jury
to bribe	hijacking

Weather

a drought	smog
changeable	to pour with rain
a heatwave	damp

Feelings

thrilled	shocked
devastated	down in the dumps
relieved	over the moon

The body

an ankle	to shake hands
hips	to stare
to wave	to put your foot in it

Music

a lead singer	catchy
a soloist	drums
monotonous	out-of-tune

Sleep

yawn	insomnia
snore	jet-lagged
oversleep	blanket

SONG ACTIVITY INSTRUCTIONS

1 B You gotta be 1.5 CD1 Track 6

Listening for adjectives, predicting rhyming words

LANGUAGE	adjectives

- Give each student a sheet and focus on **a**. Tell SS to listen to the chorus, and write a–h next to the adjectives in the list before they write them into the lyrics. They will hear the chorus three times. Highlight that two of the adjectives are not needed.

- Play the song once. Check answers and get SS to write the adjectives into the song.

> **a** bad **b** bold **c** wiser **d** hard **e** tough
> **f** stronger **g** cool **h** calm

- Now focus on the task in **b**. Give SS a few minutes in pairs to try to guess some of the missing words. Stress that the example *sky* is numbered three because the third gapped word rhymes with it. Elicit ideas, but don't tell SS if they are right or wrong at this stage. Play the song and replay sections as necessary. Check answers.

> **1** holds **2** fears **3** cry **4** read **5** view
> **6** to **7** face

- Focus on **c**. Point out that sometimes SS may need to write two phrases. Play the song again while SS read the lyrics and think about the meaning. Check answers.

> **2** lovers they may cause you tears
> **3** Don't be ashamed to cry
> **4** Herald what your mother said; Read the books your father read
> **5** Some may have more cash than you
> **6** Others take a different view
> **7** time asks no questions; leaving you behind if you can't stand the pace

- You may want to play the song again for SS to sing along.
- Finally, tell SS to read **Song facts**.

2 A Englishman in New York 2.4 CD1 Track 29

Listening for extra words and sentence rhythm

LANGUAGE	sentence rhythm

- Give each student a sheet and focus on **a**. Give SS a few minutes to read through the lyrics. Then play the song once or twice as necessary. Check answers.

> **1** much **8** ✓ **19** ✓
> **2** only **13** the **20** is
> **3** ✓ **14** ✓ **21** you
> **4** just **15** still **22** ✓
> **5** the **16** may **23** but
> **6** ✓ **17** and **24** (the second)
> **7** that **18** ✓ *will*

- Now focus on **b**, and get SS to do it in pairs. Check answers.

> **1** accent (*line 3*) **2** cane (*line 6*) **3** alien (*line 9*)
> **4** manners (*line 13*) **5** ignorance (*line 15*) **6** no matter what (*line 16*) **7** modesty (*line 17*) **8** candle (*line 20*)
> **9** combat gear (*line 21*) **10** confront (*line 23*)

- Get SS to read the **Song facts**.
- Focus on **c** and elicit opinions. It may help if you elicit the meanings of *alien* (the legal term for a person who is not a citizen of a country in which they live and work / a person from another planet). Accept any possible interpretations of the phrase.

> *A possible interpretation is that although the singer is living in the country legally, he feels like he is from another planet – perhaps because he finds the country and its culture very strange.*

- You may want to play the song again for SS to sing along.
- Finally, tell SS to read **Song facts**.

3 B It's raining men 3.7 CD2 Track 13

Predicting rhyming words

LANGUAGE	rhyming words

- Give each student a sheet and focus on **a**. Give SS a few minutes to read the lyrics and guess what the missing words are. Elicit some ideas and tell them whether the word they guess is possible, but don't tell them if it's the right one at this stage.

Extra support You could go through the bold numbered words and elicit how they are pronounced, to help SS to guess the missing words.

- Now focus on **b**. Play the song once or twice if necessary. Check answers.

> **1** go **2** ten **3** wet **4** mean **5** tough
> **6** do **7** guy **8** begin **9** bed

- Focus on **c**. Play the song again and then give SS time to complete the glossary. Help with any other vocabulary problems. Check answers.

> **1** humidity **2** barometer **3** sources **4** specimen
> **5** lean **6** tough **7** take on **8** rip off

- You may want to play the song again for SS to sing along.
- Finally, tell SS to read **Song facts**.

4 A I will survive 4.9 CD2 Track 34

Correcting phrases

LANGUAGE	Mixed vocabulary

- Give each student a sheet and focus on **a**. Go through the phrases in **bold** and explain that SS have to listen and decide if these phrases are right (what the singer sings) or wrong (different). The first time they listen, SS just have to put a tick or a cross in column **A**. They shouldn't try to correct the phrases at this stage.

- Check answers (i.e. if the phrases are right or wrong), but don't tell SS what the right words are.

- Now play the song again and this time SS have to try to correct the wrong phrases. As the song is quite fast, pause after every wrong line, to give SS time to write the correct phrase.

- Let SS compare with a partner. Replay the song if necessary and then check answers, going through the song line by line.

1 ✗ I was petrified	15 ✓		
2 ✗ by my side	16 ✓		
3 ✗ so many	17 ✗ how to love		
4 ✓	18 ✓		
5 ✗ get along	19 ✓		
6 ✓	20 ✗ mend the pieces		
7 ✗ walked in	21 ✓		
8 ✗ that sad look	22 ✗ feeling sorry for		
9 ✓	23 ✓		
10 ✓	24 ✗ somebody new		
11 ✓	25 ✗ still in love		
12 be back	26 ✓		
13 ✗ walk out	27 ✗ to be free		
14 ✗ not welcome	28 ✓		

- If there's time, get SS to read the lyrics in pairs with the glossary. Help with any other vocabulary problems which arise.
- You may want to play the song again for SS to sing along.
- Finally, tell SS to read **Song facts**.

5 B I don't want to miss a thing 5.12 CD3 Track 20
Missing verbs

LANGUAGE	verbs collocations, verb with two meanings

- Give each student a sheet and focus on **a**. Give SS a few minutes to read the lyrics, using the glossary, and to guess what the missing verbs are. Elicit some ideas and tell them whether their guesses are possible, but don't tell them if it's the missing verb at this stage.
- Now focus on **b**. Play the song once or twice if necessary. Check answers.

1 stay	2 smile	3 spend	4 close	5 fall	6 miss
7 dream	8 beating	9 seeing	10 thank	11 hold	
12 feel					

- Focus on **c** and elicit / explain the difference between *stay (in bed)* = continue to be (in bed) and *stay (in a hotel)* = be somewhere as a visitor. Give SS, in pairs, time to find the other six verbs. Check answers.

2 hold	3 beat	4 miss	5 spend	6 see	7 fall

- You may want to play the song again for SS to sing along.
- Finally, tell SS to read **Song facts**.

6 A Space oddity 6.4 CD3 Track 35
Words to do with 'space'

LANGUAGE	words to do with space: countdown, spaceship, etc.

- Give each student a sheet and focus on **a** and the words in the list. Elicit the meaning of the words from SS, e.g. *capsule* = the part of a spaceship in which people travel, *circuit* = the complete path (of wires and equipment) along which an electric current flows, *countdown* = the moment before take off when they count backwards from 10 to zero, *ignition* = the electrical system of a vehicle.
- Give SS time, in pairs, to read the lyrics and try to guess where some of the missing words might go. Highlight that they won't be able to complete most of the song until they listen to it.

- Now focus on **b**. Play the song once or twice if necessary. Check answers.

1 helmet	7 stars	13 floating
2 countdown	8 world	14 moon
3 engine	9 Planet	15 Planet
4 ignition	10 earth	16 earth
5 capsule	11 spaceship	
6 floating	12 circuit	

- Focus on **c** and give SS time to answer the questions orally in pairs. Check answers.

1 10, 9, 8, etc. (countdown)
2 Major Tom is the astronaut in the spaceship. Ground Control are the workers (e.g. scientists, technicians etc.) who are guiding the spaceship (e.g. working at NASA).
3 a You've been a success.
  b You're now a celebrity so the papers will want to know all about your life.
4 He is referring to his spaceship, which probably seems very small and fragile out in space. A 'tin can' usually means a metal container for food or drink.
5 Mission Control lose contact with the spaceship, so Major Tom is left floating in space.

Extra support Do the questions in **c** as open class questions.

- You may want to play the song again for SS to sing along.
- Finally, tell SS to read **Song facts**.

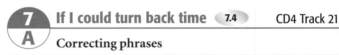

7 A If I could turn back time 7.4 CD4 Track 21
Correcting phrases

LANGUAGE	Mixed vocabulary

- Give each student a sheet and focus on **a**. Go through the phrases in **bold** and explain that SS have to listen and decide if these words are right (what the singer sings) or wrong (different from what the singer sings). The first time they listen, SS just have to put a tick or a cross in column **A**. They shouldn't try to correct the phrases at this stage.
- Check answers (i.e. if the phrases are right or wrong), but don't tell SS what the right words are.
- Now play the song again and this time SS have to try to correct the wrong phrases. Point out that the phrase she sings means more or less the same as the bold phrase in the lyrics.
- Let SS compare with a partner and then check answers, going through the song line by line.

1 ✗ find a way	12 ✗ give them all to you
2 ✓	13 ✓
3 ✗ you'd (would) stay	14 ✗ you used to do
4 ✓	15 ✓
5 ✗ said the things I said	16 ✓
6 ✓	17 ✗ I didn't care
7 ✓	18 ✗ then and there
8 ✗ I didn't really mean	19 ✗ I was sorry
9 ✗ to see you go	20 ✓
10 ✓	21 ✓
11 ✓	

- If there's time, get SS to read the lyrics in pairs with the glossary. Help with any other vocabulary problems which arise.
- You may want to play the song again for SS to sing along.
- Finally, tell SS to read **Song facts**.

a Listen to the song and fill the gaps a–h in the chorus with adjectives from the box. There are two adjectives you don't need.

calm	tough	bad	stronger	kind	bold	cool
hard	loyal	wiser				

You gotta be

Listen as your day [1]**unfolds**,
Challenge what the future [1]**h**_____
Try and keep your head up to the [3]**sky**

Lovers they may cause you [2]**tears**
Go ahead release your [2]**f**_____
Stand up and be counted
Don't be ashamed to [3]**c**_____
You gotta be

CHORUS

You gotta be [a] _____
You gotta be [b] _____
You gotta be [c] _____
You gotta be [d] _____
You gotta be [e] _____
You gotta be [f] _____
You gotta be [g] _____
You gotta be [h] _____
You gotta stay together
All I know, all I know
Love will save the day

Herald what your mother [4]**said**
Read the books your father [4]**r**_____
Try to solve the puzzles in your own sweet time
Some may have more cash than [5]**you**
Others take a different [5]**v**_____
My oh my

CHORUS

Time asks no questions, it goes on without [6]**you**
Leaving you behind if you can't stand the [7]**pace**
The world keeps on spinning, can't stop it if you tried [6]**t**_____
The best part is danger staring you in the [7]**f**_____

Remember listen as your day unfolds, etc.

b Look at the gaps 1–7 in the verses. Each gapped word rhymes with the **bold** word that has the same number. Try to guess the missing words. Then listen again and complete them.

c Listen again and read the lyrics. Use the glossary to help you. The song gives advice on how to live. Match the pieces of advice 1–7 to the correct phrase(s) in the song.

1 Don't let problems get you down
   Try and keep your head up

2 Be prepared to suffer because of relationships
   _____

3 Don't worry about showing your emotions
   _____

4 Learn from your parents
   _____
   _____

5 Don't be envious of people who are richer than you
   _____

6 Not everybody will agree with you
   _____

7 Don't waste time or you will miss opportunities
   _____
   _____

Glossary

you gotta be = you've got to be / you have to be

unfold = open out

challenge what the future holds = don't accept your fate, make your own future

release = let go

be ashamed = feel bad about

herald = say in public that something is good or important

can't stand the pace = can't go fast enough

spin = go round

stare = look at somebody / something for a long time

Song facts

This song was first recorded by Des'ree, one of the UK's most successful pop / soul singers of the 1990s. Her other big hits were *Life* and *What's your sign?*

a Listen to each line of the song carefully. If you hear an extra word, cross it out. If the line is correct, tick (✓) it. The chorus has <u>not</u> been changed.

Englishman in New York

1 I don't take much coffee, I take tea my dear

2 I like my toast done only on one side

3 And you can hear it in my accent when I talk

4 I'm just an Englishman in New York

5 See me walking down the Fifth Avenue

6 A walking cane here at my side

7 I take it everywhere that I walk

8 I'm an Englishman in New York

CHORUS

9 I'm an alien I'm a legal alien

10 I'm an Englishman in New York

11 I'm an alien I'm a legal alien

12 I'm an Englishman in New York

13 If 'Manners maketh the man' as someone said

14 He's our hero of the day

15 It takes a man to suffer ignorance and still smile

16 Be yourself, no matter what they may say

CHORUS

17 Modesty and propriety can lead to notoriety

18 You could end up as the only one

19 Gentleness, sobriety are rare in this society

20 At night a candle's brighter than the sun is

21 Takes more than combat gear to make you a man

22 Takes more than a licence for a gun

23 Confront your enemies but avoid them when you can

24 A gentleman will walk but will never run

If 'Manners maketh the man'…, etc.

CHORUS

b Which word or phrase in the song means…?

1 the way you pronounce the words of a language

2 a wooden stick to help you walk

3 a person who is not a citizen of the country in which they live / a being from another planet

4 'rules' of good, polite behaviour

5 'not knowing anything' (noun)

6 'it doesn't matter what' (phrase)

7 the opposite of *vanity*

8 something which burns to give you light

9 clothes a soldier wears

10 to face something – not run away from it

c Why do you think the singer describes himself as 'a legal alien'?

Glossary

it takes a man = you need to be a man
sobriety = not being drunk
notoriety = fame for being bad in some way
maketh = old-fashioned form of *makes*

Song facts

Sting was inspired to write this song by the highly eccentric British author and actor Quentin Crisp, who lived in New York for many years. Sting dedicated the song to Crisp.

a Look at gaps 1–8 in the lyrics. Each gapped word rhymes with the word in **bold** that has the same number. With a partner, try to guess the missing words.

b Listen and check.

c Listen to the song again and read the lyrics. Complete the glossary.

It's raining men

(Hi, we're your weather girls and have we got news for you!)

Humidity is rising – barometer's getting ¹**low**
According to all sources, the street's the place to ¹_____
'Cause tonight for the first time
At just about half past ²_____
For the first time in history
It's gonna start raining ²**men**.

It's raining men! Hallelujah! – It's raining men! Amen!

I'm gonna go out, I'm gonna let myself ³**get**
Absolutely soaking ³_____!
It's raining men! Hallelujah!
It's raining men! Every specimen!
Tall, blond, dark, and ⁴**lean**
⁵Rough and ⁵_____ and strong and ⁴_____

God bless Mother Nature, she's a single woman ⁶**too**
She took on the heavens and she did what she had to ⁶_____
She taught every angel to rearrange the ⁷**sky**
So that each and every woman could find her perfect ⁷_____

It's raining men! Hallelujah! It's raining men! Amen!
(Go get yourselves wet girls, I know you want to)

I feel stormy weather
Moving ⁸**in**, about to ⁸_____
Hear the thunder
Don't you lose your ⁹**head**
Rip off the roof and stay in ⁹_____

It's raining men! Hallelujah! – It's raining men! Amen!

Glossary

¹_____	= noun from *humid*
²_____	= an instrument for measuring air pressure which shows when the weather will change
³_____	= the people, books, etc. that you get information from
⁴_____	= a single example of something, especially an animal or plant
⁵_____	= slim
⁶_____	= not gentle; violent
⁷_____ (PV)	= to play against somebody / something, e.g. in a game / competition
⁸_____ (PV)	= take off violently

Song facts

This song was originally recorded by The Weather Girls. It was later re-recorded by Geri Halliwell, the ex-Spice Girl, and her version was used on the soundtrack of the film Bridget Jones' Diary. The song became a number one hit.

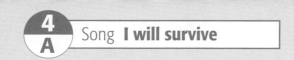
a Listen to the song. Are the phrases in **bold** right or wrong? Put a tick (✓) or a cross (✗) in column **A**.

b Listen again and correct the wrong phrases in column **B**.

I will survive

	A	B
At first I was afraid, **I was terrified**	1	
Kept thinking I could never live without you **at my side**	2	
But then I spent **such lonely** nights	3	
Thinking how **you did me wrong**	4	
And I grew strong and I learned how **to get on**	5	
So you're back **from outer space**	6	
I just **came in** to find you here	7	
with **that mad look** upon your face	8	
I **should have changed** that stupid lock	9	
I should have made you **leave your key**	10	
If I'd known for just **one second**	11	
You'd **come back** to bother me	12	

CHORUS

	A	B
Go on now go, **go out** the door	13	
Just turn around now, 'cos you're **not wanted** anymore	14	
Weren't you the one who **tried to hurt me** with goodbye?	15	
Did you think I'd crumble? Did you think I'd **lay down and die**?	16	
Oh no, not I, I will survive		
For as long as I know **who to love** I know I'll feel alive	17	
I've got all my life to live and I've got **all my love** to give	18	
And I'll survive, I will survive, hey, hey		
It took all the strength I had not to **fall apart**,	19	
Though I tried hard to **find the pieces** of my broken heart	20	
And I spent oh **so many nights**	21	
Just **feeling angry with** myself	22	
I used to cry. But now I hold my head up high	23	
And you see me, **someone new**	24	
I'm not that chained up little person **who's in love** with you	25	
And so you **felt like** dropping in	26	
And just expect me **to serve tea**	27	
Well now I'm saving all my loving for someone **who's loving me**	28	

CHORUS

Glossary

crumble = to break or make something break into very small pieces
chained up = tied up in chains, unable to move
drop in = visit somebody without letting them know in advance

Song facts

I will survive was first recorded by Gloria Gaynor and it won her a Grammy award for 'Best disco recording'. Though originally about moving on after a bad relationship, over the years the song has taken on meaning for people who have overcome almost any difficult situation, and it is statistically the song most often performed in karaoke.

a Look at gaps 1–12 in this song. They are all missing verbs. In pairs, try to think of one or two possibilities for each gap and write them in the column.

I don't want to miss a thing

	POSSIBLE VERBS
I could ____ awake just to hear you breathing	1 _____
Watch you ____ while you are sleeping	2 _____
While you're far away and dreaming	
I could ____ my life in this sweet surrender	3 _____
I could stay lost in this moment forever	
Where a moment spent with you is a moment I treasure	

CHORUS

Don't want to ____ my eyes	4 _____
I don't want to ____ asleep	5 _____
'Cause I'd ____ you baby	6 _____
And I don't want to miss a thing	
'Cause even when I ____ of you	7 _____
The sweetest dream will never do	
I'd still miss you baby	
And I don't want to miss a thing	

Lying close to you feeling your heart ____ing	8 _____
And I'm wondering what you're dreaming	
Wondering if it's me you're ____ing	9 _____
Then I kiss your eyes	
And ____ God we're together	10 _____
I just want to stay with you in this moment forever	
Forever and ever	

CHORUS

I don't want to miss one smile
I don't want to miss one kiss
I just want to be with you
Right here with you, just like this

I just want to ____ you close	11 _____
____ your heart so close to mine	12 _____

And just stay here in this moment
For all the rest of time

CHORUS

b Listen and fill the gaps with the correct verb.

c Many of the verbs in the song have more than one meaning. Write a verb for each pair of phrases.

1 *Stay* in bed
        in a hotel

2 _____ someone's hand
        a meeting

3 _____ your opponent
        loudly (a drum, heart)

4 _____ a train
        a person who's not there

5 _____ money
        time doing something

6 _____ a friend
_____ the sights in a city

7 _____ asleep
_____ in love
        down
        off your bike

Glossary

surrender (n) = abandon
treasure (vb) = value
close (adj) = near
wonder (vb) = ask yourself

Song facts

This song was probably the biggest hit of the American rock band Aerosmith. The song was featured in the film *Armageddon*, which starred Liv Tyler – the daughter of Aerosmith's lead singer Steven Tyler.

a Read the song lyrics and try to guess where some of the 'space' words go.

capsule	circuit /'sɜːkɪt/	countdown	earth (×2)	
engine	floating (×2)	helmet	ignition	moon
planet (×2)	spaceship	stars	world	

Space oddity

Ground Control to Major Tom, Ground Control to Major Tom:

Take your protein pills and put your ¹ _____ on

Ground Control to Major Tom, commencing ² _____,

³ _____'s on

Check ⁴ _____, and may God's love be with you

This is Ground Control to Major Tom, you've really made the grade

And the papers want to know whose shirts you wear

Now it's time to leave the ⁵ _____ if you dare

This is Major Tom to Ground Control, I'm stepping through the door

And I'm ⁶ _____ in the most peculiar way

And the ⁷ _____ look very different today

For here am I sitting in a tin can, far above the ⁸ _____

⁹ _____ ¹⁰ _____ is blue and there's nothing I can do

Though I'm past one hundred thousand miles, I'm feeling very still

And I think my ¹¹ _____ knows which way to go

Tell my wife I love her very much – she knows

Ground Control to Major Tom

Your ¹² _____'s dead, there's something wrong

Can you hear me, Major Tom?

Can you hear me, Major Tom?

Can you hear me, Major Tom?

Can you…

Here am I ¹³ _____ round my tin can, far above the ¹⁴ _____

¹⁵ _____ ¹⁶ _____ is blue and there's nothing I can do

b Listen and complete the song.

c Listen again and read the lyrics. In pairs, answer the questions.

1 What do you hear when Ground Control says 'Commencing countdown…'?

2 Who are Major Tom and Ground Control?

3 What does Ground Control mean by…?
   a 'You've really made the grade'
   b 'the papers want to know whose shirts you wear'

4 What does Major Tom mean by 'a tin can'?

5 What happens at the end of the song?

Song facts

David Bowie wrote this song in 1969 after seeing the Stanley Kubrick film *2001 – A Space Odyssey* and it was used by the BBC during their coverage of the 1969 moon landing. Major Tom, however, is not based on a real person. In a later song, *Ashes to ashes*, Major Tom appears again and sends a message from space saying, 'I'm happy, hope you're happy too'.

a Listen to the song. Are the phrases in **bold** right or wrong? Put a tick (✓) or a cross (✗) in column **A**. Listen again and correct the wrong phrases in column **B**.

b Listen to the song again and read the lyrics with the glossary. What does the singer wish she had/hadn't done and what does she wish she could do?

If I could turn back time

	A	B
If I could turn back time		
If I could **know where to go**	1	
I'd take back those words that have **hurt you**	2	
And **you wouldn't go**	3	
I don't know why I did **the things I did**	4	
I don't know why **I told you what I did**	5	
Pride's **like a knife** it can cut deep inside	6	
Words are like weapons, **they wound** **sometimes**.	7	
I didn't want to hurt you,	8	
I didn't want **you to leave**,	9	
I know I **made you cry**, but baby	10	
CHORUS (If I could turn back time…)		
If I could **reach the stars**	11	
I'd give them **to you as a present**	12	
Then **you'd love me**, love me	13	
Like **you did before**	14	
If I could turn back time		
My world was shattered, I was **torn apart**	15	
Like someone took a knife and **drove it deep** in my heart	16	
You walked out that door, I swore that **it** **didn't matter**,	17	
But I lost everything darling **at that moment**	18	
Too strong to tell you **I regretted it**	19	
Too proud to tell you I was wrong	20	
I know that **I was blind**, and darling…	21	

CHORUS (If I could turn back time…, If I could reach the stars…)

Glossary

wound /wuːnd/ = hurt
shattered = past participle of *shatter* = break into small pieces
torn apart = past participle of *tear apart* = pull so that it breaks
swore = past tense of *swear* = promised

Song facts

If I could turn back time was made famous by the American singer Cher on her best-selling album Heart of Stone. The video for this song was filmed on board the American warship USS *Missouri*.

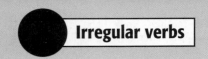

Irregular verbs

Infinitive	Past simple	Past participle
be	was / were	been
beat	beat	beaten
become	became	become
begin	began	begun
bend	bent	bent
bet	bet	bet
bite	bit	bitten
blow	blew	blown
break	broke	broken
bring	brought	brought
broadcast	broadcast	broadcast
build	built	built
burn	burned / burnt	burned / burnt
burst	burst	burst
buy	bought	bought
can	could	
catch	caught	caught
choose	chose	chosen
cling	clung	clung
come	came	come
cost	cost	cost
cut	cut	cut
deal	dealt /delt/	dealt
dig	dug	dug
do	did	done
draw	drew	drawn
dream	dreamed / dreamt	dreamed / dreamt
drink	drank	drunk
drive	drove	driven
eat	ate	eaten
fall	fell	fallen
feed	fed	fed
feel	felt	felt
fight	fought	fought
find	found	found
fly	flew	flown
forbid	forbade	forbidden
forget	forgot	forgotten
forgive	forgave	forgiven
freeze	froze	frozen
get	got	got
give	gave	given
go	went	gone
grow	grew	grown
hang	hung	hung
have	had	had
hear	heard	heard
hide	hid	hidden
hit	hit	hit
hold	held	held
hurt	hurt	hurt
keep	kept	kept
kneel	knelt	knelt
know	knew	known
lay	laid	laid
lead	led	led

Infinitive	Past simple	Past participle
learn	learned / learnt	learned / learnt
leave	left	left
lend	lent	lent
let	let	let
lie	lay	lain
light	lit	lit
lose	lost	lost
make	made	made
mean	meant	meant
meet	met	met
pay	paid	paid
put	put	put
read	read /red/	read /red/
ride	rode	ridden
ring	rang	rung
rise	rose	risen
run	ran	run
say	said	said
see	saw	seen
sell	sold	sold
send	sent	sent
set	set	set
shake	shook	shaken
shine	shone	shone
shoot	shot	shot
show	showed	shown
shrink	shrank	shrunk
shut	shut	shut
sing	sang	sung
sink	sank	sunk
sit	sat	sat
sleep	slept	slept
smell	smelled / smelt	smelled / smelt
speak	spoke	spoken
spend	spent	spent
spill	spilled / spilt	spilled / spilt
spoil	spoiled / spoilt	spoiled / spoilt
spread	spread	spread
stand	stood	stood
steal	stole	stolen
stick	stuck	stuck
sting	stung	stung
swear	swore	sworn
swim	swam	swum
take	took	taken
teach	taught	taught
tear	tore	torn
tell	told	told
think	thought	thought
throw	threw	thrown
understand	understood	understood
wake	woke	woken
wear	wore	worn
win	won	won
write	wrote	written